THE JEWS OF FRA

THE JEWS OF FRANCE

A HISTORY FROM ANTIQUITY TO THE PRESENT

Esther Benbassa

Translated by M. B. DeBevoise

PRINCETON UNIVERSITY PRESS   PRINCETON AND OXFORD

Copyright © 1999 by Princeton University Press
Published by Princeton University Press, 41 William Street,
Princeton, New Jersey 08540
In the United Kingdom: Princeton University Press,
3 Market Place, Woodstock, Oxfordshire OX20 1SY
All Rights Reserved

Second printing, and first paperback printing, 2001
Paperback ISBN 0-691-09014-9

The Library of Congress has cataloged the cloth edition of this book as follows

Benbassa, Esther.
[Histoire des juifs de France. English]
The Jews of France : a history from antiquity to
the present / Esther Benbassa ; translated by M. B. DeBevoise.
p. cm.
Includes bibliographical references and index.
ISBN 0-691-05984-5 (cloth : alk. paper)
1. Jews—France—History.   2. France—Ethnic relations.   I. Title.
DS135.F8B3613   1999
944'.004924—dc21   99-17461

British Library Cataloging-in-Publication Data is available

Cet ouvrage publié dans le cadre du programme d'aide à la publication
bénéficie du soutien du Ministère des Affaires Etrangères, du
Service Culturel de L'Ambassade de France représenté aux Etats Unis,
et du Ministère français chargé de la Culture–Centre national du livre.

This work, published as part of the program of aid for publication,
received support from the French Ministry of Foreign Affairs, the
Cultural Service of the French Embassy in the United States,
and the French Ministry of Culture–National Center for the Book.

This book has been composed in Janson

Originally published as *Histoire des Juifs de France*,
© Éditions du Seuil, 1997.

Printed on acid-free paper. ∞

www.pup.princeton.edu

Printed in the United States of America

3   5   7   9   10   8   6   4   2

TO THE MEMORY OF

Annie Kriegel

A JEW OF FRANCE

Contents

IN TRANSLITERATING Hebrew terms and personal names, which display slight differences between English and French, I have nonetheless followed the author in preferring familiar forms to technically more accurate but less common renderings. Thus, for example, *takkanot* is used rather than *taqqanot*, and likewise Solomon ben Isaac instead of Shelomoh Yitsḥaqi, Samuel ben Meir rather than Shemu'el ben Me'ir, and so on. The extensive diacritical apparatus of transliterated Hebrew has been kept to a minimum here as well. In order to disambiguate the letters *chēth* and *hē*, the conventional underdotted "h" (ḥ) is used to indicate the former (usually pronounced as a voiceless velar fricative, like the final consonant in "Bach"), and "h" (pronounced as in English) to indicate the latter. The letter *āleph* is indicated in medial position by the usual single quote (') and *ʿayin* by the inverted form of this mark (ʿ).

A strict and comprehensive system of Hebrew-English transcription may be found in the new *Oxford Dictionary of the Jewish Religion* edited by R. J. Zwi Werblowsky and Geoffrey Wigoder, which I have consulted (although not always obeyed) with regard to questions of orthography and, occasionally, substantive points. Here and there as a courtesy to the English-speaking reader I have added a note, or slightly qualified the French text, in order to explain certain terms more fully. A considerable amount of fresh material has been incorporated by the author in the final chapter of the present edition, as well as in the Chronology, with a view to updating the account of contemporary events. Throughout the text, figures calculated to hundredths of a percent in the original edition are rounded off, at times resulting in sums greater than 100 percent; readers interested in more precise approximations may locate them in the relevant sources given in the notes. Finally, English glosses of the many movements and organizations cited by their French names in the text are provided in the index.

Note to the French Edition

THE PRESENT WORK would not have been possible without the patience, critical sense, and friendship of its first readers, Valérie Hannin, Aron Rodrigue, and Jean-Christophe Attias, who have my warmest thanks. Their comments and suggestions have been invaluable to me. I am also grateful to my colleagues for having responded so generously to my various requests for information.

I have indicated dates of birth and death for the majority of Jewish figures mentioned in the text; similarly, foreign terms, concepts, and particular aspects of Jewish civilization are explained in the notes as they occur. I have not thought it appropriate, however, to supply comparable details regarding figures and facts familiar to the reader.

Preface

THE HISTORY of the Jews of France is an integral part of the history of the Jews as a people. Prior to 1789, the Jews of France played a central role in Jewish history as a particular incarnation of the multisecular existence of a people in diaspora, deprived of territory.[1] They have continued to do so since then, by introducing into this history an essential rupture, pregnant with "messianic" hopes, and a new departure, legally consecrated by emancipation and its corollary, citizenship, that represent the inclusion of the excluded. From that moment onward, France represented liberty—the Rights of Man—and stood as a model both in the imagination of its Jewish citizens and in that of Jews elsewhere, not only in Europe, but throughout the Near East. And while emancipation occurred only gradually in other countries, and not at all in some, in their minds France never fell from the pedestal that it had come to occupy in the concert of nations.

This book is intended chiefly as a synthesis. It draws upon classic works as well as the most recent and most innovative research. I have not written it, however, simply to add another stone to an edifice slowly and patiently constructed by my predecessors. The abundance of existing works on the Jews of France, and the diversity of the viewpoints found in them, are proof of the lively interest they have aroused in an era of heightened historical consciousness, when the descendants of the new Jewish citizens of the Revolution began to treasure their history and to inquire into the origins of their present place in French society; and also of the interest they have aroused outside France. Some of the most daring works on the Jews of France have been produced by scholars living in other lands.

As a specialist on the Jews of southeastern Europe and the Near East, I find myself confronted regularly with a reality that cannot be ignored: France—its history and the history of its Jews—has profoundly affected the contemporary history of Jewish peoples living far outside its borders. By providing a model that is both validated and validating, it has shaped the self-perception of these peoples no less than the course of their individual and collective histories, which in their turn are almost organically linked to France—that coveted "elsewhere."

Indeed, the Jewish leadership of France, proud of its achievements, convinced of the superiority of a country so generous to its Jews, and filled with gratitude toward it, labored to bring about the Frenchification of fellow Jews in the East. It tried to impose upon them, from above, a voluntarist style of westernization, with its own pattern of emancipation, and to give them a French-style education nourished by dreams of France. The results of such a policy were not perhaps, in the medium term, equal to the hopes of French Jewish leaders, owing as much to local circumstances as to resistance on the part of the groups concerned. Nonetheless, if only by its language and culture, France was unmistakably present at every level of daily experience. Emerging nations, in the Balkans as in the Near East, turned to the model of the French nation-state and ended up adopting it. In one way or another, Frenchness became an integral part of the plural identity of these Jews. The Dreyfus affair produced sadness and disen- chantment from one end of the Balkans to the other; but France, whether it was a source of disappointment or of admiration, did not cease to exer- cise a real fascination upon the Jews of these regions.

Mindful of the vicissitudes to which the French paradigm exported to the Jewish East has been subject, my purpose in writing the present work has been to reexamine this paradigm at close range, in the very place where it was actually devised. In this sense, the synthesis proposed here also rep- resents a personal undertaking—an attempt to grasp the mechanisms by which this symbolism has functioned, looking backward and forward in time. I needed first to immerse myself in the history of France and, in particular, in the experience of its Jews, in order to be able to deconstruct and reconstruct it, and then gradually to adopt the perspective of new re- search on certain less well known aspects of these histories. Others may find such an experiment in *dépaysement* to be of value as well. In approach- ing the history of the Jews of France from other horizons, as I have tried to do, they may be able to integrate it in a comparative way as part of a larger whole.

Like the rest of Jewish history, the history of the Jews of France poses right away a problem of periodization. Must one accept the familiar pe- riodization of the history of France? Or is there a distinct chronology in- herent in the history of the Jews, despite their great differences from one country to another, a chronology peculiar to a people so long deprived of state structures? Are expulsions, catastrophes, and pogroms the only events that mark off the stages of Jewish history? The latter assumption is all the more doubtful in the case of the history of the Jews of France as expulsions chiefly concerned the kingdom of France. Jews led an almost peaceful exis- tence on the periphery of the kingdom during the medieval and early mod- ern period, and developed a flourishing cultural life; even within the king- dom, they enjoyed moments of glory and respite from persecution. It therefore is not a question of writing a maudlin history, covering over a singularly diverse historical reality with a pessimistic vision reinforced by the trauma of the Shoah.[2]

Nonetheless, the present synthesis, which is addressed to both the spe- cialist and the general reader, cannot ignore historical detail, even if this is not its primary concern. Problems of periodization, structure, and presentation can only be surmounted by taking into account the ways in which the history of the Jews of France interacted with the history of the country as a whole, not omitting local developments. Under the Ancien Régime, in fact, the history of the Jews was a regional history, and it continued to be one for a certain time following their emancipation. By the mid-nineteenth century, however, this history had assumed an unmistakably national character. Since then, the history of the Jews of France has been inseparable from that of the nation.

The problems posed by periodization, inherent in the work of every historian of the Jews, are compounded by other difficulties specific to the Jewish experience in France. It should not come as a surprise that the works of certain authors are riddled with ideological prejudices, the product of their times and passions. The present-day historian may feel that these writers placed too much emphasis on the antiquity of the Jewish presence in France in attempting to justify this presence and legitimate the rights of Jews, and likewise placed too much emphasis on their condition of servitude in attempting to magnify the achievements of the Revolution. Another difficulty arises from the widespread assumption of assimilation during the modern period. The frequent insistence on the assimilation of French Jews surely owes something to the belief on the part of ideologues and Zionist historiographers that life in diaspora leads ineluctably to the erasure of Jewish identity. The most recent research shows, however, that for the majority of French Jews assimilation was not a reality. It was by no means indispensable for entering public life and assuming the most important responsibilities, even if there was certainly no shortage of obstacles. The institutions of an integrationist Jacobin nation-state, by relegating religious practice to the private sphere, exempted Jews from having to buy "their ticket for admission to society," as Heine put it—unlike in Germany and Austria, for example, where the price of such a ticket was conversion. In these countries the social integration of Jews had *preceded* their legal emancipation, creating a whole series of social and individual frustrations. Most German and Austrian Jews found that many doors remained closed to them, and this at the very moment when they felt themselves to be, as a matter of fact if not of law, an integral part of the nation.

Here we encounter one of the essential aspects of what made the French Jewish experience unique in Europe. It helped to fashion the discourse of French Jews about themselves and about the nation, their perception of themselves as Jews and as citizens, and their judgment of the country that had given them access to citizenship. With each breach of the contract between the nation and its Jewish citizens, whether during the Dreyfus affair, the surges of anti-Semitism that followed, or under the Vichy regime, their disappointment was commensurate with the illusions and hopes they had entertained.

What was mistaken for assimilation in fact masked the creation of new networks of solidarity and sociability that came to be substituted for the old terms of Jewish existence in France. Where integration and acculturation occurred, it was common to speak of assimilation, though these realities in no way implied an abdication of personal identity on the part of Jews, but rather an eclectic process of recomposition—a new way of declaring themselves Jewish and French, sometimes more French than Jewish. In the era of emancipation, Jews in western Europe were led to develop a variety of ways of being Jewish, regarding themselves in the light of the various social and professional circles in which they now moved, now that they were no longer confined to the sole sphere that until then had been viable—their community.

The history of the Jews of France can be understood only in terms of this defining plurality. Under the Ancien Régime, Jewish groups differed from each other according to their place of regional settlement. At first the line of division ran between north and south—between Jews who came under Rhenish influence and excelled in biblical and talmudic exegesis, and Jews who lived near Spain and the Mediterranean and drew inspiration from the secular traditions of philosophy and learning that flourished there. This axis then shifted: the southwest, fortified by the arrival of "new Christians" from the Iberian peninsula, now found itself opposed to the northeast. The differences between these regions naturally affected the perception that non-Jews had of Jews and the perception that Jews had of themselves, with the result that the Jews of the southwest, by exploiting these differences, came to be emancipated before those of the northeast.

Similarly, in the nineteenth and twentieth centuries, the relationship of native-born Jews with the surrounding society and with their own Jewishness was very different than that of immigrant Jews, even if the second generation of immigrants wound up always embracing the native Franco-Jewish model. It is necessary also to distinguish between immigrants from eastern Europe, immigrants from the Near East, and, later, immigrants from North Africa. Finally, looking back over the long term, it may be wondered whether French Jews today actually have anything in common with those of the Middle Ages who over the course of several centuries were expelled in stages from the kingdom of France.

The Jewish community of France, ceaselessly renewed and revitalized by the contributions of foreign immigrants, describes a complex trajectory at the juncture of French history and Jewish history. The words "assimilation," "integration," and "acculturation" thus have a number of different senses that vary with the expectations and commitments of the parties involved, as with historical, socioeconomic, and political circumstances. Keeping these things in mind, it becomes possible to understand the situation of the *israélite*, or French citizen of the Jewish faith; then the transition to French Jew; and finally, after the "imaginary Jew," the experience of living as a Jew in France. It needs to be asked how present-day Jews perceive themselves, and how they are perceived, now that to one degree or another these perceptions are influenced by the existence of the State of Israel.

Throughout this work, at least for the post-revolutionary period, which marks the transition to citizenship, I have for the most part avoided using the word "community," preferring the "Jewish collectivity," "Jewish groups," indeed "Jewry"—phrases that have the advantage of neutrality, even if they do not wholly convey the plurality that characterizes the historical experience of the Jews of France.[3] The traditional vocabulary, while rich in connotations, is not always in agreement with the facts. Is there now, as some maintain, a revival of the communal approach to Jewish affairs? Have state authorities reverted to a definition of Jews as a community at a moment when the general situation encourages such a view, when the behavior of certain fringes of the Jewish "community" appears to justify such a definition, and when certain Jewish institutions seem to lean in this direction? Has this movement of "recommunalization" been fed from both sides? How many Jews really subscribe to it? After all, as everyone knows, there is no organized Jewish lobby in France, nor any communal Jewish vote.[4]

It seems to me in any case illusory to postulate the existence in France of a Jewish population that shares a set of fixed beliefs, values, and symbols connected with the religious sphere and resistant to the wear of time and the stresses and strains of the environment. It makes little or no sense to speak of a perfectly autonomous French Judaism or of a compact French Jewishness that has endured over the long term or that exists today. At any moment of history that one may care to examine, the Jewish experience in France appears only as the outcome or renewal of a regular mixing of different populations from the north, the east, and the countries bordering the Mediterranean. No less than French identity itself, Jewish French identity has been constructed and reconstructed. This is particularly so in the case of migrations, both within the country and from the outside, some of which enjoyed the privilege of a relative antiquity. Of course, certain highly visible Jewish centers can still be found here and there in France today—self-consciously Orthodox Jewish communities or localized concentrations of Jews, as at Sarcelles, a suburb north of Paris. But these centers constitute a minority and, at the same time, exhibit differences among themselves. They are not sufficient to justify the communitarian thesis, which inevitably yields a reductive and differentialist view that is inadequate for comprehending the Jews of France in their entirety.

The present synthesis thus proposes to reexamine the history of Jewish populations in France over the long term, recognizing the unique characteristics they share in common as well as the differences between them. Symbiosis and containment, sealed alliances and broken contracts, the opposing voices of passionate debate—all these combine to weave the fabric of an account that must remain tentative, written in the expectation of fresh discoveries and reassessments that are as likely as they are welcome.[5]

THIS BOOK is both an overall synthesis of the history of the Jews of France from the period of Late Antiquity to the present and a reinterpretation of this history. Esther Benbassa has rendered a signal service to the general reader and the specialist by exploring all the themes that have marked the French Jewish experience with a fine eye for nuance and detail, and to have presented the most up-to-date, salient, and important findings of scholarship on this subject in one volume that is destined to remain a book of reference for a long time to come. The result of prodigious and rigorous work, this history of French Jewry is one of the best general histories of Jews in one country, and succeeds admirably in integrating the story within the larger contexts of French and Jewish histories in general.

Starting with the implantation of the Jews in Roman Gaul, tracing their fate through the making of the French kingdom and the vicissitudes of the tug of war between the monarch and the medieval church until the mass expulsions of the fourteenth century, the reentry of small numbers of New Christians in the Southwest and the falling under French rule of larger numbers through the acquisition of Alsace and Lorraine in the East, the history of the Jews in the premodern period is recounted here with great verve and acuity. Then comes the saga of modernity: emancipation, the onward march of social and political integration, the shifting demographic profiles with the emergence of Paris as the center of Jewish life, the developments in the Jewish participation in the realms of economy, society, culture and the arts, the mass migrations from Eastern Europe in the later nineteenth and twentieth centuries, the rise of modern anti-Semitism, the Dreyfus affair, deemancipation and persecution under Vichy and during the Shoah, and renewal after World War II with the reforging of new identities as a result of the preceding trauma and of the mass arrival of North African Jews. The picture is complete, thorough, drawn with a vivid brush.

But it is not only the rigor of the book, the exhaustiveness of the information that it presents and the bibliography that it draws upon that make its merit. Esther Benbassa also presents her own reinterpretation of the themes that are the fixtures of modern Jewish history such as assimilation, dejudaisation, integration, and acculturation. By stressing multiplicity and diversity and moving away from the image of a compact monolithic community, the author brings a sophisticated analysis that enriches the reader's understanding and grasp of a history that is all the more richer for having been recounted in all its complexity.

Aron Rodrique
Stanford University

THE JEWS OF FRANCE

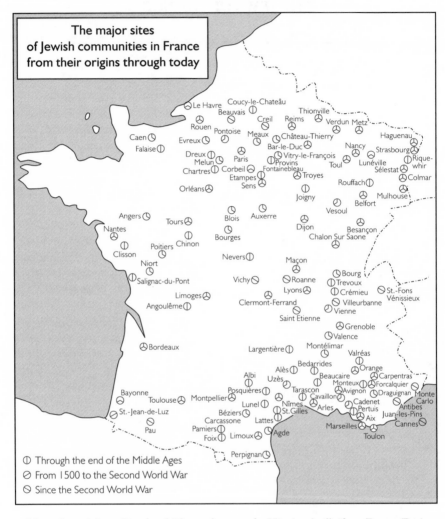

The major sites
of Jewish communities in France
from their origins through today

Le Havre Coucy-le-Chateâu
Beauvais
Rouen Creil Reims Thionville
Pontoise Meaux Verdun Metz
Caen Evreux Château-Thierry Haguenau
Falaise Bar-le-Duc Nancy Strasbourg
Dreux Paris Vitry-le-François Toul Lunéville Riquewihr
Melun Provins Sélestat
Chartres Corbeil Fontainebleau Rouffach Colmar
Etampes Troyes
Orléans Sens Joigny Belfort Mulhouse
Vesoul
Angers Blois Auxerre Dijon Besançon
Tours Bourges Chalon Sur Saone
Nantes Poitiers Chinon
Clisson Nevers Mâcon
Niort Bourg
Salignac-du-Pont Vichy Roanne Trevoux
Lyons Crémieu St.-Fons
Limoges Villeurbanne Vénissieux
Angoulême Clermont-Ferrand Vienne
Saint Étienne Grenoble
Valence
Bordeaux Largentière Montélimar Valréas
Bedarrides Orange
Alès Beaucaire Carpentras
Albi Uzès Monteux Forcalquier
Bayonne Posquières Tarascon Avignon Draguignan Monte
Toulouse Montpellier Cavaillon Cadenet Carlo
St.-Jean-de-Luz Lunel Nîmes Pertuis Antibes
Pau Béziers St.Gilles Arles Aix Juan-les-Pins
Carcassone Lattes Marseilles Cannes
Pamiers Toulon
Foix Limoux Agde
Perpignan

① Through the end of the Middle Ages
⊘ From 1500 to the Second World War
◒ Since the Second World War

Map adapted from Bernhard Blumenkranz, ed., *Histoire des Juifs en France* (Paris:
Privat, 1972), 7.

CHAPTER ONE

The Origins of the Jewish
Presence in Gaul

DUE TO THE absence of documents, it is difficult to attest the beginning of the Jewish presence in Gaul with certainty. The Bible makes no reference to this region. One does find in it the word *Tsarfat*, but this term designates the town of Zarephath (also called Sarepta) in Phoenicia, and only later came to be applied to France, as in Israeli Hebrew today.[1]

DURING THE ROMAN CONQUEST

Stretching from Antibes to Toulouse and, toward the north, as far as the vicinity of Lyons, the Midi found itself under Roman domination from 125–122 B.C.E. From the time of its conquest, in 58–51 B.C.E. by Julius Caesar, until its invasion by barbarians from the east and north in the fifth century, the history of inland Gaul was inseparable from that of Rome. The Jews who settled in Gaul did so as Roman citizens or protégés.

With the destruction of the Second Temple in 70 C.E. by the armies of Titus,[2] and then the last Jewish revolt against Rome, led in 132–135 by Simon Bar Kokhba, which ended with the destruction of Jerusalem under Hadrian, Gaul emerged as one of the new chosen lands for Jews who departed in forced exile or of their own will. The flow of emigration was directed mainly toward Rome, which sheltered Jewish communities living there in peace, and later reached the periphery of the Roman Empire. Julius Caesar had earlier granted the Jews a charter of liberty, confirmed by Augustus. The Jews' fidelity to these emperors was commensurate with their gratitude, which did not fail to arouse animosity toward them on the part of groups opposed to the regime. The suppression of Jewish revolts in Palestine had not called into question their status within the Roman Empire. The empire continued to tolerate different religions, in keeping with a realist policy by which the Romans, like other conquering peoples, obtained stability in exchange for respecting local religions. The old Roman religion itself was woven from a set of beliefs related to local gods along with others borrowed from the Greeks. This wave of Jewish emigration toward Rome is therefore unsurprising.

A number of legends surround the settlement of the Jews in Gaul. From the beginning of the Christian era, mention is made of certain Judean notables who were forced out of their native land by the Roman authorities. As a land of exile for condemned Roman politicians, Gaul must have also received Jews suffering the same fate. To claim, on the basis of this, that Jewish communities then existed in Gaul would nonetheless be risky. At difficult moments of their history on French soil, however, Jews have themselves asserted as much, hoping to counteract hostility by proclaiming the antiquity of their settlement. Here we encounter a recurrent theme in the history of the Jews, in France as in other countries, and one to which they regularly resorted when their situation became precarious.

In fact, it is not until the fourth century that written documents mention an actual Jewish presence in the region, confirmed in the centuries that followed. The Jews there did not all come from Palestine; many of them belonged to the diaspora, made up in part by populations converted to Judaism. The Christianization of the Roman Empire under Constantine the Great, with the recognition of Christianity as the official religion in 313, and the restrictions that gradually came to be imposed on the Jews, favored their emigration, particularly to Gaul, which was slower to become Christianized. Their numbers there, however, remained modest: there were only about thirty-five localities, situated for the most part along the Mediterranean littoral, such as Narbonne and Marseilles, but also in the active river valleys—commercial thoroughfares par excellence—and their environs, or in the crossroads of certain major routes such as those of Clermont-Ferrand and Poitiers.[3] The settlement of Jews along an axis following the valley of the Rhône and extending from that of the Saône to its juncture with the Rhine corresponds to the route taken by the Roman legions, which Jews followed as soldiers, tradesmen, or merchants in search of a better life and more favorable economic conditions. The Gauls considered them Romans.

The Jews living in Gaul benefited from certain rights and privileges deriving from their Roman citizenship, granted in 212 by Caracalla to all the inhabitants of the empire under the *constitutio Antoniniana*. These included freedom of worship, military service, and access to public office. Jews practiced trades that did not distinguish them from other Roman citizens, such as agriculture and wine-growing. Nor did they limit their activities to commerce alone. They dressed like the rest of the population, bore arms, and spoke the local language; even in the synagogue, Hebrew was not the only language used for rituals. Their ancestral names— biblical, Roman, and Gallo-Roman—did not differentiate them from other inhabitants. During this period relations between Jews and the surrounding society were relatively harmonious.

UNDER THE FRANKS

In the fifth century, Germanic barbarians invaded the western Roman Empire. Starting from the lower Rhine, the Franks, a loose confederation of small, more or less autonomous tribes, conquered the north of Gaul, some of their number advancing as far as the Meuse.

Gaul had resisted the Christianization of the Roman Empire for almost two centuries. Out of a concern for unity, Clovis, who had brought together under his authority many of the Frankish colonies established to the north of the Loire, converted to Christianity (probably in or about 498), and by virtue of this transformed himself into an ally and protector of the church. From then on, the church was able to establish its influence while helping the sovereign to combat the neighboring peoples and to enlarge his authority. The Christian faith thus came to unite the different elements of the kingdom, the former and the new masters of Gaul alike, even if manifest regional differences persisted, above all between the north and the south, which did not respond to evangelization in the same way. Nonetheless, the legal status of the Jews, inherited from the prebarbarian era, was not yet called into question. They continued to live in accordance with their traditional customs. The barbarian laws, drafted in Latin, were themselves largely influenced by Roman law.

Under the Franks, it is not until well after Clovis that one can speak of a radical separation between the Jews and the peoples newly won over to Christianity, which was yet unstructured on the level of dogma. Moreover, the rural population was still attached to paganism, while the Christian faith gained converts only among urban groups. This was true not only for Gaul but also for Germany. Jews during this period, lacking the Talmud,[4] adhered closely to the text of the Bible and to certain oral traditions. There existed a religious confusion between Judaism and Christianity, both with regard to prescriptions and to worship, a phenomenon that was not peculiar to Gaul. The manner in which people were won over to the new religion was still superficial, and there persisted a certain susceptibility to heresies such as Arianism, Donatism, and Manichaeanism, which reappeared with the barbarian migrations and for which the church, in this period of intense evangelization, held the Jews responsible.

THE CHURCH AND THE JEWS

By the fourth century, Christian theology had taken a clear position with regard to the Jews, who did not recognize the messianic character and divinity of Jesus. The state of inferiority in which they were to be kept was both punishment for their blindness and the sign of the authenticity of Christ's message. The church, from the time of its establishment in Rome, labored not only to curtail the privileges of the Jews but did its utmost to remove them gradually from social life, confining them to positions in which they could not exercise authority over Christians. They were thus disqualified from holding public office and owning Christian slaves. Over time this restrictive policy came to be extended to Gaul. The church set up council after council, while combating the religious confusion that persisted. There followed an open struggle against Judaism. It has long been maintained that the church's aim was to check active Jewish efforts at proselytizing—a claim that is challenged today. It is quite plausible that some pagans and Christians converted to Judaism in this climate of religious confusion; but we have no way of knowing how many did so or why.

The church forbade clerics from sitting down at table with Jews, and Jews from either going out in public during the tense period that lasted from Maundy Thursday through Easter Sunday or mixing with the Christian population. It prohibited exogamous marriages, which were relatively frequent, particularly under the Merovingians. The posts of tax collector and judge were closed to them. The fact that attempts were made to separate Christians and Jews is evidence of continuing relations between the two groups in Frankish society. At the same time, the fact that such restrictive measures were reiterated by councils between the sixth and seventh centuries suggests that the church had trouble applying them rigorously— trouble even making its voice heard. It undertook also to bring back errant lambs into the fold by conversion to Christianity, relying more on persuasion than coercion, as Pope Gregory the Great had recommended.

The pressure exerted by the church did not alter to any great degree the condition of the Jews in Gaul, despite the precariousness they imparted to it. Nor was the fate of these Jews at all comparable to that of their coreligionists in Visigothic Spain after the conversion to Catholicism of the sovereigns of that country, zealous neophytes who showed themselves to be especially harsh toward the Jews. Finally, in 613, the Visigothic king Sisebut obliged them to be baptized. In Septimania, a Gaulish enclave within the kingdom of the Visigoths, Jews were subjected to the same treatment.[5] Many sought refuge in more hospitable lands, notably in Provence. The Fourth Council of Toledo in 633 nullified Sisebut's measure ordering the forced conversion of the Jews and again advocated conversion by persuasion.

However, even if the situation in Gaul was less grave than in Spain, where Christianity was newly triumphant, the appearance of Islam and the ensuing Arab conquest led to a deterioration of the Jewish condition under the Merovingians in the seventh to eighth centuries. Once more, legend provides an apparent explanation. Under pressure from the Eastern emperor Heraclius, whose astrologers are supposed to have predicted the destruction of the Christian empire by a circumcised people, the Merovingian king Dagobert I demanded the conversion of the Jews in his kingdom, including those who had sought refuge from Spain. The alternative they were offered was to leave. There is nothing to prove that things occurred in this way. The fact remains, however, that from this time onward Gaul seems to have experienced a sharp decline in the number of Jews within its borders that lasted until the ninth century, except in areas close to Spain.

THE CAROLINGIAN "GOLDEN AGE"

The Muslim advance was checked in 732 at Poitiers by Charles Martel, the defender of Christianity against Islam. His son, Pepin the Short, founded the Carolingian dynasty in 751. The Pope went in person to France and, at the monastery of Saint-Denis, crowned Pepin king in 752. From this moment, the policy of the Carolingian sovereigns was marked by alliance with Rome and indulgence with regard to the Jews.

Expulsions were never total. It may therefore be supposed that the Jews did not wait for Charlemagne in order to settle in the lands of the Carolingian empire that he inaugurated in 800, but it was from this time that their numbers begin to grow under favorably peaceful circumstances.

The relations between the emperor and the Jews are surrounded by a certain number of legends spread by an entire narrative literature, notably the account from a Christian source known as the *Pseudo-Philomena*, composed by a monk in the thirteenth century, attributing to the Jews an essential role in the surrender of Narbonne.[6] This accusation was all the more serious since at a time when society depended on oaths and the sworn word, to betray one's masters was considered a crime. Thus the Jews were said to have traitorously delivered Narbonne to the future emperor—though it was, of course, his father who conquered the city in 759.

On this account, Charlemagne, after the taking of the city, divided it into three parts, one for the count, another for the bishop, and the third for the Jews, whose leader bore the title "king of the Jews." Reference to such a division is found in rabbinical texts of a historiographical nature, dating from the twelfth century, which probably inspired the Christian account. These sources thus erected Charlemagne into the protector of the Jews, typically attributing to the son what his father, Pepin the Short, had done on their behalf. This substitution, common in the *chansons de geste* that make up the Charlemagne cycle, helped to magnify his role.

Beyond their legendary character, whether in the matter of the king of the Jews (which may be connected once more with the myth of settlement, this time on Narbonnaise soil), or of the grant of a third of the city (which no doubt corresponds to a demand on the part of the community for confirmation of the status its members enjoyed under Muslim domination as "protected subjects"), such accounts attest to a significant Jewish presence in the city, a presence that had probably grown under its brief occupation by the Saracens (720–759).

TOWARD ROYAL ALLIANCE

Such accounts also reflect the good relations that existed between the first Carolingian kings and the Jews. This suggests many of them were attracted to the Carolingian empire, which, moreover, enjoyed a climate of peace. Very shortly one finds Jews at the royal court entrusted with diplomatic missions, such as the one carried out by Isaac the Jew on behalf of Charlemagne to the Abbassid Caliph Harun-al-Rashid in Baghdad. Polyglot, and having extensive connections throughout the Jewish communities of the Diaspora, they were in a position to provide indispensable contacts within the young empire. Charlemagne also needed them for economic reasons. The Jewish traders who then linked the West to the East were called Radanites—a term that may signify merchants and navigators from the region of the Rhône (possibly derived from the late Latin *Rhodanici*).

From the fifth century, following the example of the Byzantines (then known as "Syrians"), the Jews developed commercial activities on an international scale, operating by land and by sea. These two groups had the upper hand in Mediterranean commerce. After the defeat at Poitiers, this commerce passed in part under the domination of the Jews. They exported slaves, furs, and silk manufactures to Italy, Spain, and the Levant, and imported to Gaul spices, balsam, garum, dates, brocades, and precious metals. The crossroads of this luxury trade were located in the Meuse and at Narbonne. These traders could be found even in Paris, on the Île de la Cité, near the forecourt of Notre Dame today.

The trade in spices, owing to the contact it brought with the Orient, also contributed to the training of Jewish physicians. Around 825, Louis the Pious, son of Charlemagne, accorded Jewish merchants a number of privileges (such as exemption from certain tolls and other duties on the transport of merchandise as well as royal protection of their life and property), which suggests that these merchants played an important role in international commerce. Intermediaries between the court and the powers of other countries were recruited from the ranks of these merchants, whose clients also included high-placed ecclesiastics.

The usefulness of the Jews was not unconnected with the favored treatment they received. As in the Merovingian period, they continued to benefit from Roman law. They were not foreigners, but free men—albeit men whose liberty was circumscribed. They enjoyed the privilege of self-rule according to Jewish law and customs in exchange for a fee. They could own slaves, and import them from abroad, but in principle they did not have the right to sell them in other countries. They were permitted to employ free Christians, and this despite the opposition shown by the ecclesiastical authorities. In matters concerning them, Jews were judged in accordance with their own law. Their testimony was accepted in court, and, in place of the oath normally taken by the plaintiff and the accused, a special formula was devised—the *more judaico* oath—that made it unnecessary to invoke either the Trinity or the Gospels.[7] This formula had the additional advantage of shielding Jews, except in certain cases, from the judicial tests of ordeal by fire, boiling water, or flagellation—tests applied to non-Jewish subjects that were invoked in the name of the judgment of God and marked entirely by Christian religious elements. Charlemagne later endorsed an alternative form of ordeal in trials between Christians and Jews. Jews could bring suit against Christians; but in the event a Christian was required to present three witnesses, the Jewish plaintiff was required to present two, sometimes three times as many. Moreover, Jews were subjected to higher taxes than Christians.

Gradually, privileges and protection of individual Jews gave way to a desire for more complete control over their condition, and so for a more centralized form of administration. Some have seen in this the source of the appointment, probably by Charlemagne, of a *magister judeorum* (master of the Jews) charged with oversight of questions concerning them. We know very little about the prerogatives of this official. Louis the Pious displayed the same favorable attitude toward the Jews. Carolingian charters were largely influenced by feudalism and laid the foundations of a royal alliance between Jews and the central authority that, in the absence of legal statute, made them dependent, as a practical matter, on the good will of the sovereign. Such alliances—unilateral, fragile, varying according to economic powers and necessities, valid insofar as the Jews were useful, capable of being broken at any moment, when there was no longer any need of them—aroused against the Jews the enmity of those classes that were in conflict with the king or with the monarchy itself, and later with the feudal lords. The history of the Jews in European lands during the Middle Ages is also one of circumstantial alliances such as these, which determined the condition and, above all, the survival of the group.

ECCLESIASTICAL REACTION

The royal consideration shown toward the Jews provoked a hostile reaction on the part of the clergy. Agobard, archbishop of Lyons, expressed himself vehemently on this point and launched an anti-Jewish campaign.

Others followed his example. Louis the Pious, seeking unity for his empire, relied on court clerics and bishops such as Agobard. Strengthening the partnership with the church had the effect of aggravating the vulnerability of the Jewish population.

Following the grant of a privilege by the king to the Jews of Lyons, protecting them against the intolerance of the clergy, Agobard rose up in protest and composed four epistles. In the first, entitled "On the Insolence of the Jews," he denounced the benevolence of the *magister judeorum*, the physical abuse to which Jews submitted Christians, the privileges and honors from which they benefited at the hands of the court, the construction of new synagogues, the eloquence of their preachers by comparison with priests, the adjournment of market from Saturday until Sunday for religious reasons, and the theft of Christian children, subsequently sold as slaves. He sought to win over other bishops, and then the king himself, to his cause. On his death, he was succeeded as archbishop by Amulo, who continued his work, elaborating on the same themes with still greater vehemence, notably in an epistle of 846, "Against the Jews," in which he castigated their proselytizing. It must be said that the conversion to Judaism in 839 of Bodo, a deacon at the court of Louis the Pious, at the height of the anti-Jewish campaign, did nothing to relieve the tension.

The Councils of Meaux (845) and of Paris (846), in supporting Amulo by restrictive decrees, were barometers of the prevailing atmosphere in Carolingian society. Royal authority found itself weakened by the treaty of Verdun, which, in 843, carved up the empire into Western Francia, Middle Francia, and Eastern Francia (the latter becoming Germany). The Council of Toulouse, which met in 883 at a moment of wavering resolve on the part of the court, and therefore increasing Jewish vulnerability, ratified the restrictions of preceding councils and various public humiliations, such as the slap administered to a Jew at Easter by the Bishop of Toulouse on the steps of the cathedral, on the pretext that in the past the Jews had delivered the city to the Saracens (although it was known that Toulouse had never passed under Muslim domination).

Easter, by recalling the role that Jews played in the passion of Christ, charged relations between Jews and Christians with an intense animosity. In fact, the famous slap was administered to avenge the injury done by the Jews to Jesus. It was nonetheless customary to accuse them unjustly of a lack of loyalty. They were also held responsible for the Danish incursion at Bordeaux in 848. This ceremony, known as colaphization, was discontinued only in the twelfth century, on condition of payment by the Jewish community of Toulouse of a special tax to the clergy. These humiliations were repeated in other cities, such as Béziers, where, under the bishop's direction, Easter week turned into an anti-Jewish riot. Once again it would be necessary to wait until the twelfth century for such practices to come to an end, at which time the grateful Jews handed over to Bishop Guillaume, the architect of this result, a large sum of money, supplemented by an annual tax.

While the Carolingian royalty was weakening, retaliatory measures against the Jews multiplied, the church increasingly making its influence felt. In 876, the bishop of Sens expelled them, together with the nuns of the city, for reasons that remain unclear.[8] In a *diploma* of 898, Charles the Simple, a king devoid of authority, deprived the Jews of a part of their assets by assigning these, in the guise of royal alms, to the Church of Narbonne. Official communications of 899 and 922 subsequently confirmed these partial confiscations.[9] Of course these measures were not always strictly applied.

All these measures do not alter the fact that the Jews still enjoyed free status. They did not live at the margins of the dominant society; to the contrary, they participated fully in its life. Nor can their history be reduced to a series of persecutions. Rather than a kind of racial discrimination, it was more a question of theological anti-Judaism, directed against a religious group regarded as deicidal for its refusal to submit to the message of the Gospels and to recognize Jesus as the Messiah. For this reason the Jews were stripped of their initial status, to the benefit of the Christians, who were now the *Verus Israel* (or "true Israel"). The Jews were not inexorably damned, since by conversion, the sign of the second coming of the Redeemer, they could be saved. Though canonical law continued to uphold the principle of tolerance of the Jews, the ecclesiastical hierarchy, which often also enjoyed political power, did not always respect it. In the last analysis, however, the church did not aim at their destruction; to the contrary, the abiding existence of these loyal guardians of the Book, in which was printed the divine word, came to be seen as a genuine proof of Christian faith.

ECONOMY AND CULTURE

The Jews practiced a great variety of trades. At the beginning of the Carolingian period, because the church controlled substantial landholdings, they were not in a position to undertake farming on a large scale. Moreover, the prohibitions of various councils against Jewish ownership of Christian slaves gradually made working the land more difficult. They did, however, possess buildings, fields, orchards and vineyards, garden farms, and mills. They devoted themselves to agriculture and, in particular, wine-growing in the valleys of the Rhône, the Saône, and in the Paris region. Jewish wine production seems to have been still larger in the ninth century, to the point that it supplied foreign markets. Certain priests actually bought from Jews the wine that they used to celebrate the Eucharist. In the Middle Ages, vineyards and orchards could be planted near, or actually within, cities and subsequently required only tending. This allowed some proprietors, Jewish scholars among them, to pursue other activities.

A certain number of Jews managed the assets of bishops and abbots. Others were in the service of kings. They played an important role in East-West trade. They also practiced medicine. They were found, too, in trades such as the dying of fabric, and the tanning and currying of leather.

This picture is far removed from that of the Jew confined to commerce, particularly in money—a situation to which he was gradually reduced by virtue of political and economic circumstances, urbanization, and the increasingly numerous restrictions that came to weigh upon him.

The modest cultural boom that occurred under Charlemagne—sometimes called the "Carolingian renaissance"—seems to have had no counterpart in the Jewish world, except for certain inconsequential fits and starts. In any case, we have little information about it. The Jews were well integrated in the non-Jewish environment, which explains their use of Latin and ignorance of Hebrew, the language of the sacred Jewish texts. The centralized organization of Babylonian Judaism, with its academies and religious teachers, enabled it to serve as a beacon for the communities of the diaspora during this period. Oriental influence made itself felt on Frankish soil through the activity of Radanites who were in contact with the communities of the region, reaching its height in the twelfth and thirteenth centuries.

It was only toward the end of the tenth century, or the beginning of the eleventh century, that the Talmud arrived in France, and even then the Jews did not scrupulously observe its teachings. On the other hand, pre-kabbalistic texts seem to have been relatively well known. Contacts between the Orient and the Carolingian Empire led a doctor of law named Mahir to leave Babylonia and settle in Narbonne, where he founded a talmudic school that helped establish Jewish studies in France. It was not until the eleventh century, however, that there existed a real Jewish cultural life. Influences reached France also from Italy and Muslim Spain, where important Jewish cultural centers developed.

The Frankish period was therefore on the whole a peaceful one for the Jews, notwithstanding a certain amount of forced conversion and exile. Despite some variation, depending on the sovereign and the epoch, their condition of life and their occupations were not radically disrupted, still less as many decisions and restrictions were not rigorously enforced.

Nobles' Jews, Kings' Jews

IN LESS THAN a century, in the north of France, in Flanders, and in the western provinces, the dissolution of the Carolingian Empire led to a crumbling of authority and the emergence of large territorial principalities whose rulers, marquises, counts, and dukes refused to pay homage to the king, with certain provinces seceding. The power of the feudal lords, ecclesiastic and secular, was due to the size of their fiefs and the number of their clients. The first, weak Capetian kings, proprietors of a narrow domain composed of their personal holdings (Paris, Étampes, Orléans, Melun) and Carolingian heritages in the Aisne and Oise valleys, Compiègne, and Reims, were therefore helpless in the face of the great feudal lords. The shrinking of royal power under the last Carolingians and the first Capetians made the king himself a lord, even though he was crowned in his own domain. Under this system, the history of the Jews unfolded as regions and seigneuries dictated.

IN THE SEIGNEURIES

In the empire, where a higher authority prevailed, the Jews had been considered as being attached *ad cameram nostram* (to our chamber), which in general shielded them from the power of the seigneurs and princes. The growing partitioning of the region between the Rhine and the Loire into domains, each having its own organization, made the Jews henceforth the subjects of their lords. The question whether the Jew was a serf or not has drawn contradictory responses from historians.[1] In the absence of a central authority, their status varied from one lord to another. Status, in this context, is to be understood as referring to the types of taxation and exploitation suffered by Jews under the jurisdiction of different feudal lords. Bishops could also exercise suzerainty over Jews, and tax them as other lords did. This was the case in Arles, where royal donations from the ninth to the twelfth century had accorded the archbishop suzerainty over the Jews of the city. The king had done the same in giving control over the Jews of Saint-Denis and its environs to the abbey. These transfers of authority consisted in assignments of tax receipts rather than physical possessions.

Jews were also subject to ecclesiastical lords in Picardy and Champagne; sometimes they submitted to the authority of the secular vassals of these lords. In a city such as Narbonne, they came under the control of two suzerains, one lay, the viscount, and the other ecclesiastic, a bishop. The first, aware of the profits that he could realize from this community, did not hesitate to improve its lot by granting it in 1217 a charter of emancipation, on the model of the charters of settlement, by virtue of which the Jews disposed of a number of rights in exchange for payment. The bishop, for his part, even if briefly he gave in to the pressures of the church, ended up doing the same, fearing that the community would make common cause with the viscount, costing him a part of his income.

Whether they were ecclesiastics or laymen, suzerains were interested above all in the revenues that the Jews could bring them. Once again, it was the Jews' usefulness that was ultimately responsible for the protection that was granted them. Moreover, for a great part of the twelfth century, the taxation imposed on Jews had been neither arbitrary nor disproportionate by comparison with other revenue sources within a given domain. They still enjoyed mobility and could select the suzerain of their choice: many nobles guaranteed their property against the rapacity of the king's agents, and in this way resisted the encroachments of royal power. Indeed, Jews were spread out over an extensive geographic area.

Commerce in money held an important place in the activities of cities from the twelfth century. Among the transformations undergone by the West since 1000 was the development of a monetary economy. These transformations were associated with a demographic boom that led not only to a need for new land (major clearings took place during this period) but also for other activities, such as large-scale trade, requiring the more general use of money. Economic development, together with the incessant search for ready funds during a period of fluctuating domanial revenues, made the nobles dependent on cash income. Jews were in a position to meet their demands for liquidity, either through profits made from trade by those among them who practiced it or through recourse to credit. It should be noted that alongside Jewish lenders, whose role has been exaggerated, one finds other lenders, particularly from Cahors and Lombardy, who were very active in this line.[2] Nonetheless, even if extortion and acts of violence were not absent, the Jews' usefulness as financial intermediaries was the main source of the protection accorded them.

The eleventh and twelfth centuries saw the spiritual and cultural development of Jewish communities to the north of the Loire, particularly in Champagne, a region not dependent on the royal administration, which attests to the favorable conditions of life and work under the seigneurial regime. The gradual economic and cultural reconstruction of Jewish communities in the West from the Carolingian epoch onward began to have an influence upon Judaism as a whole in the twelfth century, leading to a shift of its center of gravity from East to West.

KINGS' JEWS

Throughout the twelfth and thirteenth centuries, marked by the reigns of Philip Augustus and Louis IX (Saint Louis), royal power asserted itself at the expense of seigneurial forces and particularisms. Though they attacked vassalic traditions, sovereigns appropriated to themselves the rights of the suzerain, relying on gold and diplomacy to break the barons' alliances and to foil their intrigues. This need for money sealed the fate of the Jews in the kingdom of France.

Philip Augustus, in deciding to expel the Jews from the kingdom, in 1182, was guided more by economic considerations than by pressures from the church. In fact, expulsion went against the teaching of the church fathers, councils, and popes who had advocated the protection of the Jews, not their disappearance or destruction; the salvation aimed for by the church in its redemptive work was to come from their conversion to Christianity.

Accordingly, during the persecutions that accompanied the crusades during the eleventh to thirteenth centuries, the church did not fail to intervene to put down popular outbursts of hatred in the name of humanitarian values and, above all, in the name of order. Initially, the crusades were directed against the Muslims, with a view to reconquering the Holy Land—this as part of a more general tendency to expansion in the wake of substantial demographic growth, under circumstances of religious turmoil reinforced by an extraordinary collective fervor. But to a certain degree the crusades also struck at the Jews, notably those of Rouen, though the events they experienced cannot be compared with the far more horrible ones suffered by the communities of the Rhine Valley. Jewish accounts of the persecutions accompanying the crusade of 1096 mention the protection offered by certain bishops. The church cannot in any case be held responsible for the massacres perpetrated against the Jews. This first crusade, moreover, seems not to constitute an important turning point in the history of the Jews of France.

During the second crusade, in 1146, the intervention of Saint Bernard, abbot of Clairvaux, slowed persecutions against the Jews; the memory of this is preserved in Jewish chronicles. The church suppressed the excesses it had provoked insofar as they posed a threat to the general order. The bull *Sicut Judeis*, a papal text of the twelfth century, guaranteeing the protection of the Jews, was reprinted throughout the Middle Ages and adapted to circumstances by various popes as the situation required.

Nonetheless, owing to their very inferiority, the Jews depended on princes who could make use of them as they pleased. And if their presence turned out to involve any danger, the sovereign could exercise his authority by expelling them. Was not the usury for which they were known, and which the church prohibited Christians from practicing, one of the famous perils menacing Christian society? Between the twelfth and the fifteenth centuries, many royal enactments and church canons ruled on the lending at interest practiced by the Jews, regulating the contracting and security of loans, and rates of interest. Moneylending gradually became the professional specialty of the Jews, since they were unable to engage in other trades, and ended up as the basis of the usefulness that justified their being retained, with the state indirectly supporting their activity. The condition of Jews in the Christian West was rooted in this ambiguity, which was a direct function of the circumstances in which the church and princes found themselves in relation to them.

In expelling his Jews, Philip Augustus aimed simply at taking possession of their property and putting the treasury back on its feet, while winning popular support for himself. The resulting revenues were not sufficient to cover the fiscal losses arising from their departure, however; and now that the exiles had gone back over to the side of the nobles, the income that France had formerly derived from the Jews now passed to the sovereign's rivals, who resided outside royal lands. In 1198, motivated still by economic need, Philip Augustus brought them back into the kingdom. He also concluded treaties with the nobles to ensure the return of the Jews they had received in their seigneuries while making them promise to extradite any Jews who might quit the royal possessions to choose domicile there. Between 1198 and 1231, eighteen such accords of nonretention were signed.[3] The Jews were also invited to swear allegiance, to sign undertakings, or to deposit sums of money demonstrating their willingness not to abandon domains under royal control.

Irrevocably tied to the domains of their masters, and deprived of freedom of movement, the condition of the Jews henceforth was nearer that of the serfs. Under Philip Augustus, by a ruling of 1218, the rate of credit legally allowable to be charged by the Jews was set at 43.3 percent per annum.[4] The king pursued his interventionist policy by subjecting their economic activities to registration and audit. Loan transactions were henceforth sealed by stamps issued by the kingdom. Both by virtue of his right to sell these stamps and by his right of inspection, the king became an economic partner of the Jews.

In 1223, Louis VIII decreed, with the agreement of twenty-five nobles of the kingdom of France, that none of them had the right to receive or to retain Jews from others. Rulings by Louis IX in 1230 and 1254 confirmed these arrangements and treated the Jew as though he were a serf (*tanquam proprium servum*).[5] During this period, moreover, serfs were not obligatorily tied to the land; they were subject to payment of fees to the nobles, as later the Jews would be as well. Though the Jews' personal freedom of

movement was not annulled, they were attached to the royal and seigneurial domains and exposed to the mercy and rapacity of the barons. Pointing
to the hardship that these circumstances entailed, Jewish leaders resisted
them in France as well as in the rest of Europe, and demanded perpetuation of the right, which formerly had been theirs, of living where they
wished—that is, of choosing their master.

In making law for the Jews of the entire kingdom, Saint Louis asserted
the growing authority of royal power, generally to the detriment of that of
the nobles, who found their position increasingly undermined. One also
sees taking shape during this period the desire to make the Jews, who were
a source of profit and taxable at the sovereign's pleasure, the king's Jews—a
pretension that, in the end, succeeded. Under Saint Louis, 43 percent of
the localities having a Jewish presence were centers of royal administration. As for Jewish communities as such, which is to say organized groups
of Jews, 84 percent of them were established in localities hosting an administrative seat.[6] This means that already by this time the lord on whose favor
the Jews depended was often the king. He had them regularly arrested, and
freed them only against ransom. He expelled them as he pleased from his
domains, and reduced their number in certain towns. Additionally, there
was the king's anti-Jewish policy, which, ultimately, argued in favor of his
canonization.

THE RELIGIOUS ZEAL OF SAINT LOUIS

The first measures of Louis IX against the Jews were decreed at the beginning of the regency of his mother, the pious Blanche of Castille. His
defenders maintain that they were dictated by purely religious considerations. It was always in this context, they hold, that he relentlessly combated lending at interest, though such lending had been legalized and regulated since the time of Philip Augustus. In this, then, he went against the
economic realities of the early thirteenth century. The subsequent adoption by the church of a similar attitude was proof of a hardening of policy.
In 1230, the treaty of Melun, which brought together the leading barons
of the kingdom, abolished the obligation to pay off the interest on debts
previously contracted with Jews; moreover, such debts were to be repaid in
three installments, the last one set to fall on All Saints' Day, 1233. The
barons were commanded to apply this ruling in their domains as though it
had the force of law. In 1234, Saint Louis annulled a third of the debts
owed to Jews. Lending at interest was later forbidden, in 1254, depriving
many Jews of all means of existence. At the same time, the barons, sene-
schals, and royal officers were ordered not to help Jews recover their debts.
Jews now found it impossible to reimburse their own debts to Christians

who acted as moneylenders to them, which led to the seizure of their personal property and land by the royal authorities, then to its confiscation. A good part of the revenues acquired in this way served to finance the crusade and religious institutions, with the blessing of the church.[7]

The prohibition of lending at interest had relatively serious consequences for Jewish communities, all the more as the Jews continued to be taxed as they had been in the past. If the king did not directly profit from the ruin of the Jews, he made use of it for political purposes, as much in his centralizing ambitions as in winning popular sympathy by releasing creditors from their debts. Prior initiatives relating to credit by Louis VIII, father of Saint Louis, in 1223, and Blanche of Castille, in 1227, had not been respected. Nonetheless, economic necessities taking precedence, Saint Louis's ruling of 1254 was in its turn circumvented in the royal domain by means of arrangements between Christians and Jews having shared economic interests, either through contracts established in the name of Christian associates or loans disguised as fictitious sales of assets. Commerce in money was economically indispensable, and Jews continued to occupy a relatively important place in it, even if the new circumstances weakened their position. The king, in obedience to his convictions, also undertook a vast campaign of conversion within the Jewish community, which now, owing to its impoverishment, was easy prey.

It was in this climate of religious enthusiasm that the king yielded to pontifical demands for the seizure of talmudic texts containing passages offensive to Christianity. He complied on 3 March 1240 and organized a disputation. In the past, such discussions gave evidence of the intellectual relationships that could develop between Christian and Jewish scholars. In a period of lessened tolerance, they worked clearly to the disadvantage of the Jews. Whereas until then disputations had concerned the interpretation of certain passages in the Bible, the one held in Paris in 1240 took aim at the Talmud and ended by condemning it. On 6 June 1242 (or 1244), in the Place de Grève, twenty-four cartloads of talmudic manuscripts were burned.[8] Article XXII of the ruling of December 1254 lent its support to the auto-da-fé, stipulating that the Talmud and other texts containing blasphemies be burned. It may have been at this time that the Talmud was expurgated of passages considered to be offensive to Christianity.

BETWEEN CHURCH AND TEMPORAL POWER

Between the twelfth and thirteenth centuries, a gradual attempt was made to impress upon the condition of the Jews certain characteristics associated with that of the serfs, without, however, actually turning them into serfs. It may be wondered whether the peculiar ambiguity of the Jew's position in society and its growing resemblance to a state of servitude, in particular, were not connected with his or her progressive exclusion. Disturbing symptoms, heralding the degradation of the Jewish condition, appeared to some degree everywhere in the West. To the accusations habitually hurled against the Jews a new one was now added, which henceforth punctuated their passage through the Christian world: the libel of ritual murder. With the approach of Passover, it was charged, they sacrificed a Christian adult or child and used the blood for ritual purposes. The first such accusation was made in 1144 at Norwich in England. Another accusation, made at Blois in 1171, resulted in the almost total destruction of the Jewish community there. It was followed by a third, at Pontoise in 1179. A bit later another accusation was brought against them: the desecration of the host. The most infamous instance occurred in Paris in 1291, under the reign of Philip IV (the Fair). Ideological anti-Judaism eventually ended up contaminating Christian society, markedly so from the thirteenth and fourteenth centuries.

Despite this climate of aggressive anti-Judaism, the Jews were not yet actually excluded, but they were hard hit by a whole series of restrictions. The obligation to wear a badge (*rouelle*) clearly distinguished them from the rest of the population. The Fourth Lateran Council—organized by the Pope following the launch of the crusade against the Albigenses (1209–29) to suppress heresy, though it did not spare the Jewish communities of the Midi—had ordered the wearing of a distinctive sign by the Jews in 1215. Saint Louis, by a ruling of 1269, enthusiastically applied the decision in France.

The crowning of kings sealed their alliance with the church and conferred upon the monarchy a divine character, bringing it popular approval as against the great vassals. The church worked together with French sovereigns to achieve the unity and supremacy they both coveted. "The French are one in the king," Saint Louis remarked, "as Christians are one in Christ." It is therefore not surprising that royal rulings concerning the Jews were marked by the influence of the church, nor that, as a consequence, secular powers carried out the prescripts emanating from it. And it was Saint Louis—canonized as Christian king, regal knight, crusader—whose anti-Jewish legislation reduced Jews to the condition of pariahs.

Royal policy was also imitated by certain nobles. Alphonse of Poitiers, brother of Saint Louis, whose domain in 1241 covered the Poitou, Saintonge, and Auvergne, and by 1249 the comté of Toulouse and the Comtat Venaissin as well, did not hesitate to follow the king's example. On 8 October 1268, he arrested the Jews in his domains and seized their property, including religious books. His nephew, Philip III (the Bold), renewed the order that required the wearing of a badge. Earlier, the Duke of Brittany had expelled his Jews with the king's approval on 20 April 1240, and in

1256 the Duke of Burgundy ransomed them in his turn. The reign of Saint Louis, and particularly his severe policy toward the Jews, served afterward as a model for his successors.

CONDITIONAL LIBERTY

The construction of the state gathered speed under Philip the Fair. His bureaucratic and centralized government, which extended to remote provinces, required substantial capital. The sovereign attempted to collect this through extraordinary taxes, confiscations of the property of Jews and Lombards, mandatory loans (such as those required of the Knights Templar), and other transfers of funds. Philip's pressing need for money caused him also to have recourse to various stratagems for extracting money from the Jews: forced gifts, ransoms, new taxes.

This period witnessed local expulsions, the concentration of Jews in towns and cities, and, from 1294, the establishment of special unenclosed neighborhoods. Under Saint Louis, the tendency to urbanization among the Jews was already clear: nearly 22 percent lived in villages, 38 percent in market towns, and 41 percent in cities.[9] With their consolidation in urban centers, which allowed Philip the Fair to better monitor his taxpayers and to prevent their flight to other baronies, Jewish landed estates that had been able to survive in the north, albeit with great difficulty, were now apt to disappear. The Jews sold their lands cheap. Their economic insecurity became more pronounced. They suffered from a lack of liquidity. Whereas before Jewish credit had grown with an expanding economy, the recession that was now visible on the horizon, at the end of the thirteenth century, signalled its end. And with that disappeared what had made the Jews useful.

In 1306 they were expelled, and their possessions confiscated. This expulsion was one of a series of similar measures befalling European Jewry— among them, expulsion from England and Gascony in 1290 by Edward I and, during the same period, various local expulsions in Germany and Italy. The expulsion in France affected a greater number of Jews (almost 50,000 persons) than that of 1182, given the increased extent of the kingdom, which now included Champagne, Normandy, and Languedoc.[10] Exiles found refuge in Lorraine, Alsace, the Rhine valley, even Poland and Hungary; in the duchy of Burgundy, the Dauphiné, Savoy, Provence, the Comtat Venaissin, and Spain. The anticipated revenues from the sale of Jewish assets were not sufficient to cover the losses occasioned by their departure, leaving a negative balance. The king then authorized a certain number of those who had been expelled to come back to recover their debts—and probably to share with royal officials the monies they collected.

Philip the Fair's successor, Louis X (the Quarrelsome), followed in the steps of his grandfather, Philip Augustus, in opening the way for the Jews' return in 1315. For the first time, this return was temporary, being valid for a period of twelve years. The king looked after them, indirectly authorizing commerce in money; their synagogues and cemeteries were given back to them, for a fee. The books of the law, with the exception of the Talmud, were restored to them. They could recover a third of the debts outstanding as of 1306, the remainder going to the king. Their privileges were renewed and protection granted them. Their situation did not, in fact, differ from that of the Lombards, Italian merchants who, following the example of the Jews, provided for the credit needs of private individuals and the royal treasury. But they were obliged to wear the *rouelle*. Thus they were indispensable, and so protected; but at the same time they were rejected, the objects of popular hatred. Many Jews left the country before the alotted time of their stay expired.

THE ERA OF CRISES

The late Middle Ages were marked by profound problems. Famines and epidemics were frequent. Populations were decimated. Everywhere in the West there were social, economic, political, and religious crises. Mystical movements grew up in various places and assumed exacerbated forms, as in the case of the Flagellants, a group of penitents who had a great popular impact. For such movements, often apocalyptic, Jews constituted an obstacle to the realization of messianic promises. The leaders of these movements stirred up the hatred of the poor against the Jews, who were accused of poisoning the wells and subsequently were massacred.

The specialization of the Jewish community in lending at interest, particularly in the north of France, and the increasingly insistent prohibition of this practice by Christians served to accentuate their differences—differences that originally had been for the most part religious in nature. The Jews now became a target for the particular fringe of society that constituted their clientele, especially in periods of famine and economic crisis, during which they were victims of popular hatred. It is enough to take a look at medieval plays to see that the Jew served as a foil, ranked alongside devils, executioners, and tyrants, opposed to saints and the pious. This negative image, conveyed by literature in the vernacular tongue, also shaped the perception of the Jew in the popular imagination. The Jewish community, degraded by the church and ostracized, came to be seen as vulnerable. Relations between Christians and Jews had not, of course, completely disappeared. They continued to exist, if only on the level of professional life, as well as in those largely Jewish neighborhoods, or ghettos, where Christians continued to live.

Utility and rejection together still determined the Jews' condition—a paradox that explains why their masters wished to keep them while at the same time attempting to dislocate their communities by expulsion, which, naturally, weakened the Jews, even when they were recalled. All of this took place against a background of sustained religious excitement favorable to rejection of the Jew as Other. Though not a serf, the Jew was different, and as such came under a statute that distinguished him from the rest of the population. He bore on his person the mark of this difference, the badge in France, a distinctive hat in Germany, a sign in the form of the Tablets of the Law in England.

In this period of insecurity, panic, and anxiety, the Other—ally of the devil, the enemy—was transformed into a scapegoat catalyzing fears of all kinds. The years 1320–21 witnessed the launch of a new paupers' crusade (there had been a similar one in 1250), composed mainly of shepherds, and so known as the "Shepherds' Crusade." It gave rise to persecutions and massacres of Jews in the Midi, then in Touraine and Berry, where they were accused, along with lepers, of poisoning the wells. Executions and confiscations of property followed. The king took advantage of the popular anger and imposed a heavy fine upon the Jews. He intended also to banish them from the kingdom, but this plan seems not to have come off.[11] The climate of insecurity that reigned was hardly conducive to their staying on, in any case, and until 1359 no organized community was to be found in France. In Upper Alsace, Jews suffered similar persecutions at the hands of poor peasants banded around a leader called "King Armleder." This movement displayed many similarities with that of the shepherds.

During the great epidemic known as the Black Plague in 1348–49, one of the gravest catastrophes Europe has known, Jews were accused of propagating the scourge and put to death in the few French localities where they were still able to reside. Even Pope Clement VI intervened in their favor, emphasizing the emptiness of the accusation and the fact that they themselves were victims of the disease. Whole communities were decimated in the Savoy and in Provence. In Alsace, Jews were burned at the stake.

ANOTHER RETURN

The pressing need for money of Charles of Normandy, then regent in the absence of Jean II (the Good), captured by the English, and in charge of collecting the ransom they had demanded for him, led to another recall. The Jews were once more authorized, in 1359, to reside in the kingdom for

a period limited to twenty years, again on condition of payment. This recall did not find many takers. Few were able to pay the substantial entry
fees—still fewer the heavy annual charges that were added on top of
these—and, in any case, the plague of 1348 and its aftermath had decimated the community of exiled Jews. Those who did return were concentrated mainly in the Île-de-France and in Champagne. On ascending
the throne in 1364, Charles of Normandy—now Charles V—extended the
deadline by six years; later, in 1374, in exchange for a large sum of money,
he added an additional ten years. The Jews were guaranteed a certain number of privileges related to the safety of their community. Henceforth, the
maximum annual rate of interest of loans was set at almost 87 percent.[12]

The royal intent to place Jewish affairs under centralized control now
became clear. A relative of the king was designated as "guardian general of
the Jews and registrar of their privileges" for the north of the kingdom, and
another for Occitania. This initiative was part of a more general tendency
to political, administrative, and judicial centralization that asserted itself
in the fourteenth century not only in France but indeed throughout the
West.

With the death of the king in 1380, his brother, Louis d'Anjou, then
regent, extended the Jews' stay until 1401. The expulsion decreed by
Charles VI in 1394, prior to the expiration of the deadline, affected only a
limited number of Jews, perhaps a few hundred, the Jewish community of
France having been much reduced by the vicissitudes it had experienced
throughout the century.[13] The edict of expulsion cited the complaints of
subjects overburdened by the weight of usury and mentioned certain
crimes committed by the Jews against the Christian faith. Some historians
have connected this decree with the disappearance of a recently converted
Jewish merchant in Paris named Denis Machaut.[14] The Jews were accused
of having attempted to bring him back to Judaism. This kind of incrimina-
tion is characteristic of the rhetoric of expulsion edicts, though generally it
is not possible to link such charges to specific facts.

Indeed, after the riots of 1380 and 1382, the Jews, robbed of the monies
owed them and otherwise bled dry, were no longer in a position to meet
their financial commitments to the king. Once again, they were no longer
useful. In the climate of religious intolerance that now reigned in the
West, there was no longer any place for them. The year 1391 was marked
in Spain by violent persecutions that constituted a turning point in the
history of the Jewish communities of that country, and led to a large number of conversions. In France, the madness of Charles VI, first manifested
in 1392 and followed by pilgrimages and processions orchestrated by the
queen, created an atmosphere of fervor in which the expulsion of the Jews
was seen as an act of purification. In the absence of national unity, the
kingdom, torn by its conflicts with England at the height of the Hundred

Years' War (1337–1453), now aspired to religious unity. A century later, in 1492, Spain set out on the same path by expelling its Jews.

Between the thirteenth and fifteenth centuries, the deterioration of the Jews' condition proceeded in parallel with the process of centralization, itself inseparable from the unification that was beginning to take hold in the lands of the crown. In France, the authority of the king nonetheless ran up against particularisms that intermittently produced regional revolts and some degree of provincial autonomy. Outside the royal domain, however, notwithstanding occasional flashes of hostility and the various restrictions imposed on them, Jews did not yet find themselves faced with such radical opposition. The Dauphiné remained outside the kingdom of France until 1349, permitting them to live there in relative tranquility. Even afterward, though they were banned from the kingdom, some Jews stayed in the Dauphiné until the expulsion of 17 September 1394 finally forced them out. In the Duchy of Burgundy, they suffered the same fate that had been decreed for them in the kingdom by the expulsion order of 1306. In the Comté of Burgundy, on the other hand, including the part administered by the king who had expelled them, their stay was not disturbed.[15]

NORTH/SOUTH

In the thirteenth century, a clear distinction emerges between the communities of the north and those of the south, which were subject to different forms of government. Gradually, however, the monarchy imposed on the south the regime that was in force in the north. The eastern provinces of Languedoc were directly attached to the French crown by the treaty of Paris in 1229 in the aftermath of the crusade against the Albigenses. The same occurred with the fiefs of the Count of Toulouse a bit later. In the Toulousain, government was confided during the transition period to Alphonse of Poitiers, who had no more respect for the Jews than his brother the king, Louis IX.

Nor was royal influence slow to make itself felt in the Languedoc. The city of Narbonne, a major center of Judaism located outside the royal domain in the Bas-Languedoc, received a great many Jews fleeing the possessions of the Crown, the royal seneschalsies of Toulouse, Carcassonne, and Nîmes, in the course of the thirteenth century. Rather than suffer the humiliating measures and exorbitant taxes of the royal domain, the king's Jews took the risk of seeking refuge in the more welcoming territory of the archbishop, viscount, and nobles.

As the centralizing efforts of the Crown intensified, the royal administration concerned itself with the lot of the nobles' Jews. Little by little, they came to be subjected to the laws of the kingdom, motivated by its old expansionism and, above all, a desire to recover the tax revenues of which it had been deprived by the exodus of the Jews. The nobles of Narbonne brought suit against the Crown to no real result, apart from partial concessions; but they showed little zeal in applying royal legislation. Despite the resistance of the nobles, the expulsion of 1306 affected the Jews of the region at a time when they were prospering, especially in viscountal Narbonne. Those expelled sought refuge in the states of the crown of Aragon, in Catalan lands and those controlled by the king of Majorca, and also in the comté of Roussillon and the barony of Montpellier. Until then, under the authority of the local nobles, they had benefited from tolerant legislation, which, still despite a certain number of restrictions, permitted them to integrate themselves socially and participate in almost all the professional categories of urban and rural life.[16]

In Provence, too, until the end of the fifteenth century, the Jews enjoyed relatively favorable conditions. Whereas, in the kingdom, a policy of Jewish exclusion was pursued under Saint Louis, the statutes of Marseilles enacted in 1257 made no juridical distinction between them and Christians, both coming under the category of "citizen" (*Civis Massilie*). And by the end of the fifteenth century, the legal condition of the Jews, despite a whole series of arrangements signaling their inferiority, was still not fundamentally different there than that of their fellow Christian citizens.[17] They were recognized to have the same status in Saint-Rémy-de-Provence in 1345, and in Tarascon in 1467.[18]

A relative peace reigned also in the Comtat Venaissin and in Avignon for the Jewish communities that had reestablished themselves there. These regions being papal possessions (from 1274 and 1348, respectively), expulsion was not the order of the day.

During the reign of the "good king René" d'Anjou, between 1434 and 1480, the Jews of Provence benefited from protection, dictated by royal decisions in domestic and foreign policy.[19] In this context, once again, the Jews' usefulness served the sovereign's purposes. Nonetheless, anti-Jewish disturbances were common throughout the fifteenth century, followed by movements of voluntary exodus.

Provence, which had formerly brought together flourishing Jewish communities, was annexed to the kingdom of France in 1481. The expulsion of the Jews was finally announced in 1498; the order was renewed in 1500 and 1501, and definitively took effect from the latter date. The Jewish populations of the kingdom proper subsequently disappeared, surviving only in a few localities.

CHAPTER THREE

Jewish Life in the Middle Ages

THE HISTORY OF THE Jews of France cannot be reduced to a series of expulsions. Nor can one speak in their case of a uniform history, but rather of a history that varies from one region to another, from one regime to another, with the gap between north and south becoming more pronounced from the thirteenth century. The great expulsions from the kingdom in the fourteenth century reinforced this regionalization. During this period, the Jews may be divided into two distinct groups: those of the *langue d'oïl*, in the center and the north of the kingdom, and those of the *langue d'oc*, with subdivisions even within the communities of the south, in the autonomous provinces of the kingdom. Their history is also one of communal organization, of an economic and cultural life that evolved with the vicissitudes experienced by Jews on French soil and again displayed particular regional characteristics.

In the thirteenth century, the Jewish population remained below 50,000. During the same period, in Paris, despite a growth due to immigration from Normandy and Champagne, their number did not reach 1,000.[1] In the counties of Provence, they were fewer than 10,000 (rising to 15,000 on the eve of the Black Plague in 1348).[2] Communities numbering between 500 and 1,000 persons were an exception; generally, they were smaller. Seventy percent of localities having no Jews were villages, whereas 77 percent of localities having a Jewish presence were market towns or cities.[3] Rural settlement existed, but the tendency was toward urbanization.

COMMUNAL SPACE

The organized community (*kahal*, in Hebrew) was, before everything else, an essentially urban phenomenon. It appeared in Europe in the tenth century and, three centuries later, supported a network of officers and institutions. Communal organization was required by the very status of the Jew in Christian and Islamic society. Having to be ruled and judged in accordance with rabbinic law, the *halakhah*, it was incumbent upon the Jews to gather together and form an entity endowed with its own institutions that could supply those services that were indispensable to the pursuit of Jewish life in conformity with tradition. The community took care of the individual from birth until death, as a member of the collectivity, assuring personal security and representation before various powers and creating a framework of institutional solidarity capable of meeting the needs of the most impoverished.

Rights and Duties

As such, the community was also a fiscal entity that raised the taxes owed to the sovereign or lord in proportion to the assets possessed by its members, the assessment being based on the declaration of individual members or on an estimate of the value of their assets—the rich paying for the indigent, good debtors for bad. Each person having an income was taxable, including widows and women owning property. In certain communities, talmudic scholars were exempt from paying tax. The question of the tax due to the authorities was a matter of major concern to community leaders. In addition to this tax there was the tithe (ma'aser) paid by the members of the community in order to finance its internal activities, in particular responsibility for the poor, and, if necessary, the regular tax. The Jewish community appears, then, to have been a sort of microcosm, relatively autonomous both within the larger society as a whole and in its relations with other communities. For ritual purposes, however, small communities depended on larger ones, which had the infrastructure needed to furnish the required services.

This regime of autonomy generally did not prevent different communities from maintaining close relations, nor their delegates from joining to take decisions by common agreement and in the mutual interest of their congregations. From the twelfth century, these synods multiplied without, however, leading to a structured and permanent form of intercommunal organization. In times of crisis, they made it possible for communities to act in concert. It sometimes happened, in periods of respite from persecution as well, that decisions taken by one community came eventually to be applied in others by virtue of their soundness, as was the case in the eleventh century with the prohibition of polygamy and of divorce without the wife's consent. Each community was responsible for payment of its taxes, but in the event of external pressure, at the level of the kingdom, province, or seigneury, several communities might form ad hoc associations (known as collectas) in order to facilitate the collection of monies owed.

The community granted or recognized the right of residence (ḥezkat ha-yishuv) in a given locality to a newcomer by the unanimous vote of its members. Originally intended to keep out those who might undermine communal discipline, this arrangement later served to exclude the shop-keeper or moneylender whose competition was feared. Criminal offenders were liable to excommunication in the locality (*ḥerem ha-yishuv*).

Administration

The community was led by the seven *boni homines* of the city, called *shiv'ah tovei ha-'ir*. These notables carried out the combined duties of politician, judge, arbitrator, and paymaster. Over time, dynasties of notables devoted to communal service emerged. In principle, the *parnass*, who was in charge of financial administration, was responsible for relations with the public authorities. In the Midi, Jewish administrators held the title of consul, but in fact they were only the delegates of the city's non-Jewish consuls.

The general assembly of members having the right to vote was the principal authority of the community, whose leaders were chosen in free elections by this assembly. External pressures were not inconsequential despite the steps taken to avoid them. Gradually, alongside the senior administrators of the community and the guardians of its customs, men of letters achieved prominence. Foremost among these men was the rabbi, who established himself as a spiritual leader and who at the beginning of the thirteenth century drew a salary without, however, having to renounce his business interests. The community also employed a cantor, a scribe, and, where rabbinical courts existed, magistrates' assistants. Communities long functioned as associations of persons subject to the same duties and taxes, but did not have responsibility for all religious activities.

Gathering Places

All the communities disposed of a synagogue, which was a place of prayer but, more than this, the seat of the community's activities—the place where Jews socialized. Some contained an oven for the preparation of unleavened bread (*matzah*) during Passover and were equipped with a ritual bath (*mikveh*), though this might be located elsewhere in the Jewish quarter. Religious study was conducted in the synagogue. The faithful had their own seats, which they purchased; almost nothing was provided for women, who in the best case gathered in a room or neighboring building that communicated with the synagogue by a window. Large communities possessed a hospice that served both as a hotel for visitors passing through and, if necessary, as a hospital. Some had their own meeting room, their own slaughterhouse, a communal oven, a marriage room. It fell to the commu-

nity to provide a Jewish funeral for all its dead. It possessed its own cemetery, outside the Jewish quarter and often outside the city, the administration of which was typically entrusted to a holy brotherhood, the *ḥevrah
kaddisha'*, whose members voluntarily saw to all arrangements relating to
death. Other fraternities devoted themselves to visiting the sick, providing
for dowries for indigent young ladies, and otherwise to charitable works,
religious study, and prayers. Each community had its own charity fund for
easing the plight of the poor, who were very numerous. Each also looked
after orphans and dealt with the ransoming of prisoners (*pidyon shevuyim*).

Education

In wealthy families, education was provided by preceptors. Communities
were gradually to assume responsibility for the education of poor children
of the male sex (girls having no official access to learning). For a long while
the two systems coexisted. Thus the *ḥeder* came into being as a place offering primary instruction to the children of the community. Pupils were
taught writing and reading in Hebrew characters—the characters used to
transcribe the vernacular language. There they also learned the rudiments
of arithmetic and geometry. Teaching was centered for the most part,
however, on reading of the Bible and its translation into the vernacular
language. A basic introduction was also provided to the Talmud, which
later would be at the heart of the higher, nonmandatory education dis-
pensed at the rabbi's home.

It was common for students in the course of their studies to attend various talmudic academies (*yeshivot*), in different countries, in order to receive
instruction from renowned teachers, notably in Champagne, Normandy,
the Île-de-France, and Narbonne. In certain schools, for example in Languedoc, scientific instruction was available, particularly in medicine and
astronomy, in addition to the traditional curriculum. In certain southern
communities, it was also possible to study secular philosophy.

Justice and Legislation

Within the community, Jews themselves administered justice in religious
matters, including matrimonial law, and had the upper hand in adjudicat-
ing civil disputes between co-religionists, at least insofar as such litigation
was authorized or tolerated. Criminal matters did not come within their
purview. The rabbinical court (*beit din*), which gradually established itself
as an institution, drew its authority not from the sovereignty of the law

but from the adherence of the members of the collectivity to a common discipline. Over time, the rabbi came to be primarily responsible for the administration of justice, a task in which he was assisted by other judges (*dayanim*).

Communities held on to this prerogative, as a measure of their autonomy, and long tried to prevent their members from bringing suit before a non-Jewish court. Many Jews, however, appeared before Christian civil courts, even ecclesiastic courts. Acts of excommunication were not enough to check this trend, which grew as the power of communities weakened, no longer having the means to defend themselves or to enforce the authority of rabbinical courts. The penalties imposed by these courts ranged from excommunication (*herem*) to corporal punishments.

Communities were ruled by informal sorts of constitutions composed of rulings (*takkanot*) handed down in the past. To these, others came to be added as a function of circumstances. Such rulings were no longer limited in the Middle Ages to rabbinical ordinances; they could now issue from a lay leader in the community or from a rabbi. The community itself was sovereign in the matter of accepting or rejecting proposed rulings. Moreover, these rulings were valid for a single community, and could not be imposed on others. In the main their influence was local, even if certain rulings were recognized, sometimes only after a few centuries, by other communities. Their application was limited in time, which meant that they were regularly renewed. They aimed at supplying a solution to a frequently recurring problem or to a crisis; at settling difficulties that arose in the internal functioning of the community or in its relations with the surrounding non-Jewish world. In some cases, an illustrious, apocryphal ancestry was attributed to a ruling in order to establish its authority.

Certain ordinances closely supervised family life and morality, as well as sexual behavior; others regulated the rights of tenants (*hazakah*), the assessment of taxes, and the rights of women; others concerned violent offenses, dress, lending at interest among Jews, and local commerce. These rulings covered all areas of religious as well as social life while at the same time protecting widows and orphans and outlawing games of chance played with cards or dice. In this way a sort of government came into being that allowed the community to function smoothly. Over time these arrangements came to be recorded in registers, thus constituting a sort of law. They were the expression of a communal life that was not without its share of abuses and permissiveness.

In addition to these rulings, and again as a function of circumstances, there were sumptuary laws that aimed at lessening the visibility of those Jews who were likely to arouse jealousy among their Christian neighbors while at the same time punishing a taste for conspicuous consumption. Thus it was forbidden to organize banquets, except on religious occasions;

the number of courses served was limited, as was the number of guests. The wearing of clothes and jewels was also regulated.

Over time a hierarchical society had grown up with its own notables, elected officials, men of letters, and rabbis, and endowed with an organization that was structured and effective owing to the consent and the discipline of its members. Within it unfolded the religious life of the community, concentrated around daily prayers, observance of the Sabbath (*Shabbat*), and festivals. Far from adhering to a single Orthodox model, it embraced a wide range of practices that varied between north and south.

It was only with the emancipation of the Jews after the French Revolution, and the granting of citizenship to them in 1790–91, that the autonomy of the community was abolished and an end put to forms of organization that had endured since the Middle Ages. Until then, Jews could not be imagined outside of their collectivity, owing to the impossibility of their finding a place in the surrounding society, unless through conversion to Christianity. Indeed, the most serious coercive measure that could be applied to a Jew was excommunication, which is to say banishment from the community.

Housing and Dress

Jewish life revolved around the synagogue, a place that served as an agora and provided certain structures required by the various needs of communal life. It is not surprising, then, that Jewish settlement should typically have been concentrated in a street or a neighborhood, where, nonetheless, Christians lived as well. The fact that so many consiliar rulings were aimed at separating Christians from Jews attests to the existence of interrelations of all kinds, as much in daily life and cultural activities as in the professional sphere.

The Jewish quarter or the Jewish street, which was found in the north as well as in the Midi, was situated in the center of the city, near the castle or the cathedral, in order that its residents might enjoy the protection of the established authorities. The closed ghetto was still far in the future. Here it was a question of streets or neighborhoods having a high density of Jewish residents. The internal necessities of the community and, increasingly, the discrimination practiced toward them led Jews to band together, without their dwellings being completely cut off from those of Christians, at least until the fourteenth century. This was the case, for example, in Paris, where the Jews tended more and more to live in houses grouped around a common courtyard, such as the "Cour de la Juiverie" located just off the Place de la Bastille on the present-day boulevard bearing the same name, or the "Cour Robert," now the rue du Renard.[4]

If housing sometimes suggested a separation, or at least a grouping together, clothing, by contrast, did not distinguish Jews from other residents—hence the need to impose upon them the wearing of the *rouelle*, or badge. The same was true with regard to their daily language.

Trades

In the early part of the Middle Ages, Jews practiced trades similar to those of their Christian neighbors. It was only later that they came to be restricted to a smaller number of occupations.

Heading the list of these activities was lending at interest, frequently regulated by kings depending on the situation. In the thirteenth century, not only did Jewish lenders make loans at interest; they also handled commercial transactions. In general, their clients were Christians, since lending at interest among Jews was prohibited by rabbinical rulings, even if these were not always respected. Rural residents predominated among this clientele, with artisans making up almost half of the total. The amounts of capital loaned were seldom large. When the liquid assets of Jewish lenders were insufficient to meet the incessant demands placed upon them, they availed themselves of the services of Christian lenders who were richer still—the Lombards. By and large, the role of the Jews in the banking profession in the Middle Ages was limited. Jewish credit, and the worthy purpose it served, began to disappear in the second half of the thirteenth century. In the meantime, lending at interest did not prevent Jews from practicing other trades. It also constituted a secondary occupation for Jewish physicians.

In the north as well as in the south, medicine was a profession in which the Jews excelled. In the south and southeast, the number of Jewish physicians was large. These practitioners did not reserve their talents for Jewish patients alone; in some cities, in fact, they served as municipal physicians. Medieval science in France also owed to Jewish physicians its acquaintance with a certain number of Arabic medical and pharmacological works, of which they were the translators.

In the south, Jews continued still at the end of the thirteenth century to occupy a place in all areas of economic life. Their activities were not limited, as in the north, to moneylending, medicine, and petty artisanry serving the specific needs of communities. In Languedoc they devoted themselves to the grain trade and the tilling of the soil; they held land and houses in fief; they worked as commercial representatives. Nonetheless, at the beginning of the thirteenth century, public service in the region was closed to them; Jewish bailiffs were no longer appointed.

In Marseilles, Jewish men and women alike earned their livelihood as brokers and auctioneers. Jews were also found in maritime commerce, and in the coral industry, both as traders and artisans, where they enjoyed a monopoly. In Arles, they were involved in the manufacture of soap.

The various campaigns waged against the Jews, the increasingly heavy taxes imposed upon them, and the economic crises and epidemics to which they were vulnerable ended up impoverishing Jewish communities in the south, which until then had been highly prosperous, just as they had the communities of the north.

CULTURAL SPACE

The cultural influence of Jewish communities on French soil likewise requires a regional approach, a distinction again being made between the north and the south. Preeminence went back and forth between the two regions, depending on the period. In the eleventh century, the first flowering of Jewish culture in France, the north dominated; a century later it had fallen into decline, to the advantage of Paris and the south.

The Beginnings

The ninth century witnessed the development of scholarship, above all in Narbonne, which maintained close ties with the academies of Babylonia, the center of Jewish culture. Biblical studies achieved prominence in the south. There, in the mid-eleventh century, the school of Narbonne was led by Moses the Preacher (Mosheh ha-Darshan), whose teaching is known to us through his successors.

Nonetheless, it was the schools of the Rhineland and Champagne, devoted to talmudic studies, that shaped Jewish learning during this period. In the second half of the tenth century, an important talmudic school was founded at Mainz. The most illustrious student of this institution was a native of Metz, Gershom ben Judah (more usually Gershom of Mainz, 960?–1030), known as the Light of Exile (*Me'or ha-Golah*). Considered the highest authority in Europe, the master of the Talmud, which had been introduced only recently to the continent, he trained many disciples who later spread his teaching through France, Italy, and Germany. His place in history is due mainly to the rulings (*takkanot*) attributed to him, which were to leave a lasting mark on the life of Jewish communities: prohibition of polygamy, and of desertion of the home by husbands for longer than eighteen months; the need for a wife to give her consent to divorce; the determination of the duties of community members toward its institutions.

Also in the middle of the eleventh century, at Limoges in central France, Joseph Bonfils (Tov Elem) introduced to the West the legal writings of the masters (*ge'onim*) of the Babylonian academies. Indeed, a whole legislative tradition came into being, evidence of a desire to structure communities as autonomous social bodies.

Rashi

With Solomon ben Isaac, better known as Rashi (1039/1040–1104/1105), the northern talmudic school reached its height. Born at Troyes, in Champagne, during the reign of Henri I and trained at the great academies of the day, he returned to his native city in order to devote himself to teaching.

In this period, the established Jewish communities in the county of Champagne enjoyed a genuine prosperity arising chiefly from its political and economic importance. The region's fairs probably contributed to the demographic, economic, and institutional development of the Jews of Champagne, who worked in a variety of businesses, trading in clothing, precious stones, silk, gold, and silver. In rural areas, they lived off their vineyards and gardens. Rashi himself, in fact, was a winegrower. At the same time a flourishing cultural life was emerging under the influence of the Rhenish centers and, in particular, the teaching of Gershom of Mainz and his disciples, as well as of the masters of the talmudic academy of Narbonne, which left its mark on Rashi's work, testifying to the interaction between communities of the north and south.[5] It was at Troyes that Rashi was to produce a complete commentary on the Bible and the Babylonian Talmud.

His biblical commentaries were made up of short notes, or glosses, the object being to give the explicated term the sense that was most appropriate to its context. While relying on the exegetical heritage of his predecessors and drawing selectively on traditional sources, Rashi aimed above all at restoring the obvious meaning or "plain sense" (*peshat*) of the verse in question. In this regard he belonged to the same movement as the Christian exegetical school that had grown up in the eleventh century and that assigned primacy to the literal aspect of sacred texts. The decline of this tendency was soon to be witnessed, however, in the last quarter of the century, in both the Jewish and the Christian worlds.

Likewise, in his commentary on the Talmud, Rashi closely followed the text, explicating it in a clear and precise style. He confined his attention to the talmudic literature itself, without resorting to mystical, philosophical, or even allegorical interpretations. This amounted to an exegesis of the text by the text.

In both his biblical and his talmudic commentaries, Rashi used French words to explicate difficult Hebraic or Aramaic terms. His readers spoke French—more exactly, the Champagne dialect of the period, but this was very different from the French spoken today. These words, or *lo'azim*, transcribed in Hebrew characters and numbering about 3,500 in the commentary on the Talmud, 1,300 or so in the commentary on the Bible, refer to the daily life and technology of the time; as such, they belong to the archaeology of the French language.[6] Thus one finds, for exampler, *bovier* (peasant), *bersedor* (archer), *barde* (axe), *viz* (spiral staircase), *jafraite* (armoire), *faveler* (to chat), *menusier* (to cut into tiny pieces).[7]

Rashi's glosses are still today an integral part of the education of observant Jews; it is difficult to conceive of biblical or talmudic studies without making reference to them. The influence of Rashi and his school made itself felt in later centuries, and in the Christian world as well. The *Postillae Perpetuae* of the Franciscan Nicholas of Lyra (1270?–1349), standard commentaries on the Bible until the sixteenth century, transmitted Rashi's commentaries to Catholics (and, later, Protestants) and to the first modern translators of the Bible—further evidence of cultural transmission between the Jewish and Christian worlds in the Middle Ages.

Rashi's *responsa*,[8] responses to questions posed from 1070 onward by Jewish religious authorities regarding legal, ritual, or other questions concerning their communities that were compiled by his disciples from their notes, constitute a rich mine of information about Jewish life in the Champagne region.

The Tosafists, Disciples of Rashi

The school of talmudists founded by Rashi and his teaching was perpetuated by his grandsons and their disciples over several generations stretching from the twelfth to the fourteenth centuries, from the reign of Philip I to that of Philip the Fair. This prestigious line of scholars produced "supplements" (*tosafot*) to Rashi's commentaries, whence their name *ba'alei ha-tosafot*—literally "the Supplementers," or Tosafists. The origin of these additions is inseparable from the activity of the talmudic schools, where students' questions drew responses from their teachers and so gave rise to debates. They were thus recorded initially as independent notes of variable length, written on sheets of paper. Compilation of these notes with a view to publication was undertaken in the thirteenth century.

Most of these supplements were composed in the Middle Ages, but only a fraction of them figure in modern editions of the Talmud. In current versions one finds, on the same page, the text of the Talmud itself (*gemara'*) in the middle column; Rashi's commentary (*perush*) in the inside column; and the supplements (*tosafot*) in the outside column. The authors of the latter material studied the text of the Talmud with the purpose of restoring its supposedly perfect coherence, removing apparent contradictions between different passages treating the same question, comparing the probable meanings of the text with interpretations given by commentators (Rashi foremost among them), and subjecting these interpretations to criticism, checking talmudic sources and offering fresh insights from which they drew practical conclusions for daily life.

The *tosafot* constitute a collective work. The names of their authors have nonetheless not been forgotten. Among the most famous Tosafists, who number in the hundreds, four from the twelfth century may be mentioned: Rashi's two grandsons, Samuel ben Meir, or Rashbam (1085–1158), an outstanding and original biblical commentator, and Jacob ben Meir, known by the name of Rabbenu (Our Master) Tam (1100–1171); Tam's nephew and successor Rabbi Isaac, known by the acronym Ri the Elder (1120–95), and Samson of Sens (1150–1230).

It was also in the twelfth century that Simḥa ben Samuel of Vitry (d. before 1105) composed the first real liturgical compendium of the Jews of the north of Europe, the *Maḥzor de Vitry*. Then there were Judah Leon of Paris (1166–1224), leader of the school of Paris, whose period of glory in the thirteenth century coincided with the decline of Champagne as a religious center; his pupil Moses of Coucy (thirteenth century), author of the legal code entitled *Great Book of Precepts*; his other disciple, Yeḥiel ben Joseph of Paris (d. about 1265), who, after the death of his teacher, took over as head of the Parisian rabbinical center and also established a branch in the Holy Land, at Acre, the Grand Collège de Paris (*Midrash ha-gadol mi-Paris*); Eliezer ben Solomon of Touques (d. before 1291); and Perez ben Elie de Corbeil (d. about 1295), author of the *Little Book of Precepts*. These men, who were also winegrowers, animal breeders, and shopkeepers, ran schools in Champagne, Normandy, Lorraine, Burgundy, Île-de-France, and England. Their disciples spread the movement to Bohemia, Russia, and Germany.

The schools functioned thanks to the benevolence of wealthy teachers who welcomed students into their homes or to the philanthropy of private individuals. The activity of these scholars also included consultations (*responsa*), which reflected the preoccupations of the Jews of northern France: the composition of rabbinical treatises and codes of religious obligations; poetry and communal work; the redaction of rulings and the convocation of synods. The condemnation of the Talmud in 1240, following a religious disputation in which Tosafists had participated (the leader of the Tosafist school of Paris serving as the spokesman of Judaism), and then the burning of the Talmud in 1242 (or possibly 1244), delivered a fatal blow to the Paris school.[9]

The Provençal Exegetical School

Provence, which in the vocabulary of the Jews of the Middle Ages stretched from the Pyrenees to the Alps, distinguished itself more in science, philosophy, and the codification of laws and customs (*halakhah*), influenced as it was by ideas coming from Spain and the Mediterranean. At the same time it drew attention to itself by its talmudic schools, notably those of Narbonne, Lunel, Montpellier, and Arles. These schools and their students were to set the tone for the intellectual life of the Provençal communities as a group for a certain period.

The most famous of these talmudists was Abraham ben David of Posquières (1120–98), known by his acronym Rabad. His celebrity was connected chiefly with the polemic he brought against the *Mishneh Torah* of Moses Maimonides (1135–1204), also called *Yad Ḥazakah* (literally "Strong Hand"), a code of Jewish law finished in Egypt about 1185 that it was feared might supplant the Talmud. General in its treatment, written in a clear and precise style, taking care to bring out fundamental principles without citing sources, and with an interest in settling controversies and establishing norms, this compilation of the *halakhah* stood diametrically opposed to the exegetical school represented by Rabad. Rabad rejected the very principle of codification, defending an analytical approach based on the standard texts and the chronological classification of the laws that made his works rather dense and difficult to read. Another peculiarity of Maimonides' code consisted in the fact that it also reserved a place for philosophical and ethical reflections. The debate thus clearly opposed two schools: the traditional school of exegesis associated with the line of disciples descending from Rashi, on the one hand, and the philosophical school, on the other, which was soon to enjoy its moment of glory in the region.

Menaḥem ben Solomon ben Meir, called Meiri (1249?–1315?), one of the first modern commentators on the Talmud but also inclined toward philosophical speculation, was among the last heirs of the exegetical school. Also deserving of mention are authors of religious codes, such as Isaac ben Abba Mari (1120?–1190?) and his kinsman Abraham ben Nathan (1155?–1215?), called *Ha-Yarḥi* ("of Lunel").

Translation, Philosophy, Kabbalah, and Poetry in Provence

In an urban setting of relative calm and economic prosperity, Provence rapidly became the center for translation of Arabic texts into Hebrew. The arrival in the twelfth and thirteenth centuries of Arabic-speaking Jews fleeing the wars of Muslims and Christians in Spain led to an important influx of philosophical ideas as well.

The Kimḥi and Ibn Tibbon families distinguished themselves in the domain of translation. In the one, Joseph Kimḥi (1105–70) and his son David (1160?–1235), and, in the other, Judah ibn Tibbon (1120–90) and his son Samuel (1150–1230), translated the great classics of Judeo-Arabic thought from Arabic into Hebrew, including the works of Saadya Gaon (882–942), Ibn Gabirol (1020?–1057?), Judah Halevi (before 1075–1141), and Baḥya ibn Pakuda (second half of the eleventh century). Not simply translators in the modern and usual sense of the term, these scholars also performed the work of grammarians and lexicographers in order to create a philosophical vocabulary as well as concepts in a target language, Hebrew, that did not yet dispose of them. They also devoted themselves to the translation of Greek and Arabic scientific works, particularly in medicine. The texts of the physician, philosopher, and mystic Avicenna (980–1037) and, especially, of the philosopher Averroes (1126–98) were translated from Arabic into Hebrew. Spanish Jews trained in their homeland in Arabic astronomy brought it with them to Provence; some invented astronomical instruments, others translated works from Latin. Important cultural interactions may be noted among the Christian, Jewish, and Islamic worlds in which these writings circulated and exercised their influence upon all the thinkers of the period.

Samuel ibn Tibbon produced a translation of Maimonides' *Guide for the Perplexed* (1200) that appeared before the author's death, in 1204, and with his collaboration. This cornerstone of medieval Jewish thought, an attempt at reconciling the traditional tenets of the Jewish faith with the Greco-Arab philosophical heritage, henceforth available in Hebrew and therefore accessible to non-Arabic-speaking Jewish communities, was to find itself for at least two centuries at the center of heated intellectual disputes.

The first controversy broke out around 1230 and resumed again toward 1303. Similar passions were aroused in the Christian world at about the same time. In 1210, the council of the ecclesiastic province of Sens forbade the reading of the "natural books of Aristotle as well as their commentaries, whether in public or in private, on pain of excommunication," and in 1228 Pope Gregory IX warned theologians against "profane novelties." After several decades of administrative opposition, however, Aristotelianism triumphed by the end of the thirteenth century.[10] The church's reservations with regard to Aristotle were not unreminiscent of the fears aroused in certain Jewish intellectual circles by the success of Maimonidean thought.

The debate over Maimonides' work concerned the dangers of philosophical research for faith. It also served as a cover for fierce power struggles among supporters of the two camps. Opponents of Maimonides followed in the tradition of the northern masters, who in their hostility toward philosophy likewise condemned his work and attempted to prohibit or restrict the teaching of secular sciences. This fratricidal war lasted for many years, undergoing a dramatic series of ups and downs. It invited interference from Spanish rabbis in the affairs of the communities of southern France, which gave rise in turn to excommunications and counter-excommunications. In 1233, the *Guide for the Perplexed* and the *Sefer ha-Madda‘* (Book of Knowledge, the philosophical introduction to the *Mishneh Torah*) were publicly burned by the Dominicans at the request of the anti-Maimonideans, in Montpellier according to some, in Paris according to others. Maimonides appeared as a heretic in the tense climate of the time, when the church was attempting to check the spread of the Albigensian heresy in the region. None of this was enough, however, to prevent Maimonidean studies from being pursued in Provence.

Indeed, Provence was also the homeland of Levi ben Gershom, commonly known as Gersonides (1288–1344). Born in Bagnols and considered to be the greatest philosopher after Maimonides, his most famous work remains *The Wars of the Lord* (1329). At once a philosopher and theologian, commentator on Averroes and biblical exegete, talmudist, mathematician, and logician, he was also the inventor of an astronomical instrument. Two of his scientific works were translated into Latin in 1342 at the order of Pope Clement VI. Gersonides' daring and independent work was to exert a great influence, though his orthodoxy was regularly found suspect, as well as his faithfulness to the spirit of the Bible and of tradition. Additionally, the physician Moses of Narbonne (1300–1362), a man of encyclopedic learning, was to comment on the Arabs Al-Ghazzali (1058–1111), Ibn Tofayl (d. 1185), and Averroes, and above all on Maimonides' *Guide for the Perplexed*, whose philosophical teachings he interpreted in a resolutely Averroist sense.

Provence, land of philosophy, was also a land of mysticism. It is there that the *Sefer ha-Bahir* (Book of Brightness), the first document of theosophic kabbalism, was compiled on the basis of oriental sources between 1150 and 1200. Languedoc furnished the first great figures of a tradition that was destined to grow and prosper, and eventually eclipse the philosophical movement: Abraham ben Isaac, president of the rabbinical court of Narbonne (d. 1180), and especially Isaac the Blind (1160?–1235)— grandson of Abraham ben Isaac and son of the previously mentioned Abraham ben David of Posquières—who developed a contemplative mysticism. Born in Provence and along the coast of Languedoc, the kabbalah was rapidly transplanted to Catalonia, which maintained close political and cultural ties with these regions. It was ultimately in Spain that, in the thirteenth century, there appeared a text that later was to acquire canonical status in kabbalist circles: the *Sefer ha-Zohar* (Book of Splendor), attributed to Moses of Leon (1240?–1305) and his school.

Poetry did not remain in the background in a region as rich in intellectual production as Provence, and poets attempted to rival their Spanish counterparts. Joseph ben Ḥanan Ezobi (thirteenth century), a native of Orange; Abraham Bederzi (1230?–1300?), *Ha-Badrashi* ("of Béziers") and his son Yedaya Bedersi (1270–1340), known as *Ha-Penini* ("The beaded one") and the author of *Beḥinat Olam* (Examination of the World), a book of moral maxims that enjoyed a considerable success; and the troubador Isaac Ha-Gorni (thirteenth century) were the principal representatives of this tradition of liturgical and secular poetry.

CHAPTER FOUR

The Jews of the South

THE SUCCESSIVE EXPULSIONS from the kingdom, and then from those areas that subsequently came under its sovereignty, in principle closed the doors of France to the Jews. In the sixteenth century, they were encountered in small numbers only in a few areas, typically in the south and east, under certain regimes and particular conditions. Their fate remained tied to circumstances and whatever usefulness they might offer. The long Middle Ages, which for the Jews lasted until the final decades of the Ancien Régime, was no longer marked by the same pace of cultural development as in preceding centuries. By virtue of this, the late medieval period represents a break in the history of the Jews of France. Their communities, save the one in the southwest, were exhausted. Confined to a small number of areas, inward-looking, and relatively cut off from the rest of the diaspora, they no longer had enough strength left to sustain the remarkable cultural ferment they had known since the eleventh century. What is more, they were to remain isolated from the Renaissance in Europe.

THE COMTAT VENAISSIN AND AVIGNON

At the beginning of the sixteenth century, the last vestiges of the Jewish presence in Provence, and therefore within the boundaries of the kingdom of France, were henceforth concentrated in two localities coming under papal authority: the Comtat Venaissin, definitively restored to the Holy See in 1274, and Avignon, which it acquired in 1348. In fact, at the end of the Middle Ages and then during the Renaissance, Jews found sure refuge only in the papal states, whether in Italy or in France, while elsewhere in Europe they were persecuted or simply expelled. Jewish presence in the region is attested since the twelfth century. During this period, they were the only non-Catholics authorized to stay in the Comtat Venaissin and Avignon and to practice their faith.

How did it happen that in the sixteenth century—a century marked by a hardening of Rome's position toward the Jews, in the aftermath of the Counter Reformation—the Jews should have been tolerated in papal possessions? A series of pontifical bulls, among them the famous *Cum nimis absurdum* of Paul IV in 1555, worsened their condition and restricted their economic activities. Indeed, the history of the Jews of Avignon and of the Comtat exhibits an ambivalent tension between the protection accorded them by the church, on the one hand, and, as a consequence of the anti-Judaism it professed, their rejection by the church on the other. This situation was to continue until their emancipation by the Revolution.

On the Jewish Condition

Commonly referred to as "the Pope's Jews," though in fact this term can only legitimately be applied to them from the thirteenth century on, the Jews of the communities of Avignon and the Comtat enjoyed a reputation in the Jewish world that was related neither to their numerical importance nor to their cultural influence. One of the reasons for this fame is their almost uninterrupted stay in these localities, lasting from the twelfth century until the present day.

Expulsion from the kingdom of France of 1306, and then from Provence in 1501, brought many Jews. As was customary in the Midi, they were considered "citizens."[1] Their affairs were adjudicated by Christian courts, and their contracts drawn up by Christian notaries. This did not prevent segregation, since from the time of the Lateran Council of 1215 they were required by the statutes of the city and of the republic of Avignon to wear a distinctive sign, in the shape of a wheel (*roue*) in the case of the men—hence the name *rouelle* for the male badge—and, in the case of married women, a particular sort of headgear. Close relations between Christians and Jews were also prohibited, especially after the twelfth century. There also existed Jewish streets, though they did not yet constitute closed compounds. Their trades did not distinguish them from the rest of the population, even if these were preponderantly associated with commerce.

In the fourteenth and fifteenth centuries, Christian-Jewish relations seem still to have been relatively harmonious, at least by comparison with the state of affairs in the north of France, and even if they were not entirely untouched by violence.

In the fifteenth century, the economic decline of the Comtat opened the way to popular movements that affected the Jews, as was also the case during the same period in the Dauphiné, in the principality of Orange, and in Provence. Accompanying this decline was a deterioration in their living conditions. During the same period, however, and despite the papal ban, the Jewish population experienced significant growth with the arrival of immigrants from the Dauphiné and Provence, and later of a certain number of exiles from Spain.

A brief issued by Clement VII in 1524 replaced the *rouelle* by a yellow hat or cap, which was perceived as a stigma, subjecting the person who wore it to mockery; it was worn by the Jews until the Revolution, though not without many compromises in the meantime.[2] The bull *Cum nimis absurdum* renewed the obligation to wear this distinctive sign and forbade Jews from owning land outside the neighborhoods reserved for them, as well as from engaging in professions other than moneylending and trade in used clothes and bric-a-brac, thus gradually reducing the Jewish community to the status of pariahs. Medicine, which they had practiced with success in preceding centuries, was also closed to them, as well as tenant farming and papal tax collection. It took time for these measures to be strictly applied; once applied, they were regularly renewed.

The Jewish population of the papal states probably did not exceed 2,500–3,000 at any time in its history. In 1569–70, at the demand of the *États du Comtat*, the Jews were to have been expelled. The plan was not carried out, but a good many of the Jews of Avignon and the Comtat left for other destinations, and the many small communities in the papal states disappeared. Some Jewish resettlement occurred later.

From the second half of the fifteenth century, the Jews had been confined in a designated district known as a *carriero*, from the Provençal word for street (*carrière* in modern French). In order both to assure their security and to keep them apart from Christians, in the cities and major market towns, this street or *carrière* was eventually closed off at each end by a gate, prefiguring the future ghetto. This nonetheless did not prevent a dispersed pattern of dwelling from developing in the villages. In 1624, the separation of Jews and Christians became clearer, with the Jews being relegated to four cities (*arba' kehillot*)[3]—Avignon, Carpentras, Cavaillon, and Isle-sur-la-Sorgue—known as the four *carrières* or, in Hebrew, the *messillot*.

The *carrières* were closed at night by guarded gates through which it was forbidden to pass. Jews were consigned to cramped quarters, several families to a house, and forced to submit at regular intervals to sermons meant to convince them eventually of their error and so lead them to break with Judaism. The holy books of the community were subject to censorship, and sometimes seized. Each *carrière* was nonetheless authorized to have a synagogue, called the *Eschole françoise* (French School) because it was also a place of study.

The situation in which the Pope's Jews found themselves by the second half of the sixteenth century—a poor, demeaned, ghettoized group isolated from the surrounding society—corresponded to the wishes of the authorities. During this same period, their numbers rose to 700–800 in Carpentras, to 200–300 in Avignon and Isle-sur-la-Sorgue, and to a hundred or so in Cavaillon.

In the eighteenth century, however, their condition improved under the influence of favorable economic circumstances. The Jews of the *carrières* extended their commercial activities to other regions, broadening the range of these activities as well. They now devoted themselves also to horsetrading, buying and selling both saddle horses and draft horses, and entered into the trade of silk and silk goods, offering very competitive prices. Many of them grew wealthy in a short period of time, as attested by the increasing size of the dowries given to their daughters, rising from an average of 590 pounds in the last quarter of the seventeenth century to 730 pounds for the years 1700–1709, to 1,650 pounds from 1730–39, then to 6,787 pounds between 1760 and 1769, and finally reaching more than 9,000 pounds on the eve of the Revolution—sums that are comparable to those with which the great aristocratic families endowed their daughters.

Moneylending also took a new turn. Not only the amounts loaned but also the borrowers changed. The clients were no longer peasants or artisans in financial difficulty but merchants, members of the clergy, even nobles. This period was one that saw many usurers and petty dealers in used clothes becoming bankers and merchants. Moreover, not being able to invest their profits in real estate or noble titles, Jews held sizable liquid reserves, and inevitably were led to accumulate more and more wealth. New synagogues were built in each of the *carrières* in place of the old, crumbling edifices—a renovation to which Cavaillon and Carpentras bear witness still today.

The discrepancy between the condition that society assigned to Jews and their social advancement is plain. The regulations that kept them in a state of inferiority were far from being abolished; to the contrary, the forty-four articles of the text published by the Holy Office in Rome in 1751 precisely enumerated all the bans weighing upon them. Those who became rich were still obliged to reside in the cramped, unhealthy, and overpopulated *carrières*, together with their poor brethren, whose demands upon them could only become more and more insistent.

In 1781, the regulations of the Holy Office were reissued with a new article concerning the closing of the gates of the *carrière*, which henceforth had to be done jointly with a Christian porter. Jews no longer had the right to keep the keys to the quarter as before. This amounted to imprisoning them each night in their ghetto. The hardening of papal policy triggered a movement to emigrate on the part of those who, on account of their business, were already in the habit of leaving the *carrières* for a part of each year. Notwithstanding the risks involved, they began to settle in France and later to send for their families.

By 1788–99, the *carrières* had already lost between a fifth and a fourth of their inhabitants—a trend that was to become more pronounced with the Revolution and the troubles that followed locally between 1791 and 1793.[4] The Jews of Avignon, like the Spanish and Portuguese Jews, became full-fledged citizens in 1790, as did the Jews of the Comtat when the papal states were finally united with France in September 1791.

Internal Organization

The *carrières* decided their own statutes, called *mishpatim* or, more commonly, *escamot*, a deformation of the Hebrew *haskamah*, meaning "approbation." They were written in Hebrew and translated into Provençal in order to be submitted finally for approval to the papal administration, which ratified them on payment of a fee, and on the condition that they did not contain anything that might be harmful to it or to Christianity. In principle, these "constitutions" were to be revised or reissued every ten years: their redaction fell to "article makers," experts appointed by the community council. To hold office it was still necessary to possess a certain capital. Those who were eligible were classified as a function of their income into three categories, called *mains* or *grases*.

The council, the supreme authority of the community, was composed of twelve members, which is to say four for each *main*, drawn by lot—a summer magistrate, a winter magistrate, a magistrate of manifests (these three being replaced later by *trésoriers de la taille*, or collectors of tallage, the tax paid by feudal tenants to their lords), and a counselor—who were responsible for the affairs of the community, the nomination of officials, and finances. A preponderant role was reserved for the first magistrate coming from the first *main*, the wealthiest of the twelve members.

In periods of crisis an assembly of all the family heads, or "general parliament," was convened. Several differences may be noted between the organizational model typical of Avignon, just described, and that of the Comtat. Isle-sur-la-Sorgue and Cavaillon formed a single administrative unit. The council chose from among its outgoing members or other eligible persons those who were to have responsibility for tasks of collective interest, which could not be refused: three *bailons du luminaire*, probably in charge of the lighting and maintenance of the synagogue; magistrates of studies, in charge of instruction; magistrates of alms, managing charitable institutions; three magistrates of the Jerusalem collection box, entrusted with the collection and handling of funds intended for the communities of the Holy Land. In addition to these posts there was another, filled by two auditors whose selection by the assembly was not subject to the law of the three *mains*. These auditors were charged with examining the accounts of outgoing treasury officials.

The revenues of the community came from gifts and offerings, and from regular contributions paid annually or on a weekly basis by the heads of family in each *carrière*, again in accordance with the system of *mains*. Additionally, there were various levies and fixed payments found in all the organized communities. The Jews were also subjected by papal authorities to various taxes and fees, some annual, some occasional, that except in a few cases were not higher than those paid by Christians; to these, however, were added various gifts, customary charges, and miscellaneous levies that placed a strain upon communal budgets. Responsibility for collecting such fees fell to the internal administration of the *carrières*. If one compares, for example, the 180 pounds levied in 1789 by the vice-legate of Avignon with the 2,400 pounds devoted that same year to the needs of foreign indigents taken in by the community (i.e., not counting the native poor), it may be seen how much more heavily internal expenses weighed.[5]

Alongside all these charges, voluntarily paid, the *carrières* retained a number of salaried employees in their service, foremost among them the community rabbi, and sometimes a teacher, cantor, and ritual slaughterer of animals as well. Here, however, the rabbi occupied a less privileged place than in the communities of the East.

The *carrières*, largely unchanged since the Middle Ages, functioned as many other Jewish communities did during the period and enforced the same coercive measures against those who broke their laws. Their autonomy was more limited than that of the Ashkenazic communities to the extent that they did not dispose of their own courts, authorized to judge in accordance with Jewish law. Apart from marriages and divorces, in which the Christian authorities also had a right of review and appeal, offenses and complaints concerning Jews were tried before Christian courts in accordance with the laws currently in force. In general, an attempt was made to resolve differences among Jews amicably, within the community, each *carrière* having Jewish deputies who acted as arbitrators in minor civil matters. Sometimes the community itself, through its magistrates, called upon Christian courts to decide certain cases involving its members, such as nonpayment of assessed tallage. Taxpayers might occasionally turn to these same courts as well, believing themselves to have been injured by the behavior of their leaders. Communities did their best to keep internal conflicts from leaking out. They sometimes resorted to excommunication, as a way of making their members see reason, but not without first having obtained the permission of the local Christian authorities—yet another indication of how fragile their autonomy actually was.

By the seventeenth century, rabbinical learning had already undergone a certain decline. Carpentras's rabbi during this period was brought in from Holland. Nor was Jewish scholarship being pursued at a high level at the time of the Revolution. Earlier in the eighteenth century, visiting emissaries from the Holy Land had drawn attention to signs of laxity among the Pope's Jews in religious matters. This phenomenon needs to be seen in its proper context, however, and understood in terms of the constraints under which they were obliged to operate. Their comparative lack of religiosity accounts in part for their experience immediately following emancipation.[6]

All of these communities had their own form of religious practice, the *rite comtadin*, which exhibited important Provençal influences in the various customs relating to marriage, childbirth, and the other cycles of Jewish life. Up until the Revolution, they preserved certain practices already abandoned by Jews elsewhere in Europe. This was true in the case of marriage, where sometimes several years passed between a couple's engagement (*erusin*) and the actual wedding itself. Prior to the wedding, a promise to marry was pledged by an oath sworn on the Pentateuch and the Ten Commandments, or else on the notary's cloak. It might be accompanied by a notarized dowry contract, in addition to the traditional deed of marriage (*ketubbah*). Local customs left their mark even on the formalities of marriage.[7] The average age upon marrying was 24 years for women and 26 years for men in Carpentras in the eighteenth century—younger than in non-Jewish urban areas, where only 64 percent of women and 47 percent of men married before the age of twenty-four. On the eve of the Revolution, the gap had narrowed: young Jewish men and women now married at an older age, thus bringing their matrimonial behavior more into line with that of Catholics and Protestants, evidence of the development undergone by Jewish communities during the same period.[8]

The Pope's Jews were distinguished from other groups of Jews not only in the domain of marriage, but also in their manner of pronouncing Hebrew and in the physical plan of their synagogues. These differences, which, among other things, contributed to the special character of the communities of Avignon and the Comtat, could not help but complicate their relations with other Jewish communities, all the more as communities elsewhere remained impervious to influences from the non-Jewish environment, such as adoption of Roman law with regard to the emancipation of children, dowries, and inheritance. If only by virtue of this openness, the Pope's Jews did not experience great difficulty integrating themselves when the Revolution enabled them to become full-fledged citizens.

NEW CHRISTIANS AND JEWS: SPANISH AND PORTUGUESE IN FRANCE

Throughout the Middle Ages, whether under Moslem or, later, Christian domination, Spain was the cradle of flourishing Jewish communities. Their situation deteriorated considerably with the persecutions of 1391, which began in Seville and spread throughout Christian Spain, giving rise to massacres as well as to conversions to Christianity. Before long, the "New Christians" (or *Conversos*) created by such conversions had become a problem for the country. These former Jews, who by their apostasy were able to escape the many social and economic restrictions weighing upon the community into which they had been born, could henceforth join in the various walks of life that until then had been closed to them, without, however, finding themselves really accepted by the old Christians. For want of political unity, unsuccessfully sought through the marriage of Ferdinand II of Aragon and Isabella of Castille in 1469, Christian Spain aimed at religious unity. New Christians, accused of heresy, posed an obstacle to this ambition. The Inquisition began its work in 1481 at Seville. In 1492, to put an end to their influence upon the New Christians, the Crown expelled the Jews from Spain.

These Sephardic Jews spread throughout Europe, North Africa, and the Levant. Some were conditionally admitted to Portugal, where they were forcibly converted in 1497. In this country they formed a close-knit group that, until the establishment of the Inquisition there in 1547, continued to practice a certain form of Judaism that departed more and more from traditional Jewish norms. This new practice came to assume the form of a crypto-Judaism transmitted secretly by individuals and families.

The establishment of the Inquisition in Portugal prompted those who could to leave the country. Unification of Spain and Portugal between 1580 and 1640, by opening the border between the two lands, allowed the departure of all those who suffered increasingly burdensome restrictions and who feared persecution—mainly New Christians (not only Spanish *Conversos* but also, and especially, Portuguese converts), who headed for southwest France. For those fleeing the harsh repression of the Inquisition by land, France, lying immediately adjacent to the Iberian peninsula, was an obligatory stopover.

The Exceptional Status of Guyenne

Officially, the kingdom of France had no longer provided a home for Jews since 1394. These new exiles could therefore no longer settle there as Jews. In June 1472, and then in February 1474, however, Louis XI promulgated two edicts aimed at encouraging immigration to Bordeaux, impoverished and depopulated by the Hundred Years' War. Thus all foreigners (excepting the English, who had occupied the city between 1152 and 1293 and again from 1303 to 1453) were at liberty to live in Bordeaux, exempt from the right of escheat by which the assets of non-naturalized aliens reverted to the French crown after their death. They enjoyed, moreover, the right to sell their wares without having to obtain letters of naturalization. Spanish and Portuguese merchants, profiting from the dynamic trade that had developed between the Iberian peninsula and Bordeaux, took up residence in this city for commercial reasons. Joining them were a number of New Christians, even if the chief motive for their departure was not initially a desire to return to Judaism. In the centuries that followed, the deteriorating atmosphere in Portugal and Spain swelled the ranks of crypto-Jewish immigrants from the peninsula.

These newcomers were long known as "Portuguese merchants." The majority of the first fugitives settled in Saint-Jean-de-Luz—later supplanted in the seventeenth century by Saint-Esprit-lès-Bayonne (a suburb of Bayonne),[9] located just on the edge of French territory, which became a crossroads of the Jewish faith for crypto-Jews from the peninsula who desired to enter into contact with the religion of their ancestors. They were found in the hinterlands as well, in Labastide-Clairence and Bidache in the Pyrenees, and in Dax and Peyrehorade in the Landes; and also in Biarritz, Marseilles, Lyons, Nantes, Rouen, and in the French colonies of America, particularly Martinique. The Portuguese community of Paris was linked in part with that of Rouen.

In 1550, despite the rumors of crypto-Judaism that hung over them, "the merchants and other Portuguese called New Christians" obtained letters patent from Henri II assuring them recognition and protection, freedom of personal movement and of commerce, and the right to purchase real estate without having to pay fees. Once again their economic utility was responsible for the tolerance shown toward them. Between 1550 and 1656 a series of eight acts—ignoring two others that ran counter to them—authorized the Portuguese to elect domicile in the kingdom with the same status as native-born persons (*régnicoles*).

The perception of these Portuguese by officials and in the texts promulgated by authorities from 1550 until the Revolution proved to be ambiguous. At first, they were tolerated as New Christians and not as Jews; however, in letters patent issued in 1723 and 1776, they were designated as Jews. Many officials nonetheless continued until the Revolution to refer to them as New Christians. It was only after a long process that these New Christians were recognized, or at least tolerated, as Jews.

At the beginning of the seventeenth century, a few gestures were made in the direction of expulsion. On 23 April 1615, Louis XIII demanded that all Jews, disguised or not, leave France the following month. It is clear that the Jewishness of these New Christians was a mystery to no one. The parliament of Bordeaux blocked application of this measure, going against even the wishes of the city's merchants. The same year, in order to better protect them, the New Christians were authorized to inhabit Bordeaux in exchange for payment of a fee. Two hundred sixty persons took advantage of the privilege of acquiring naturalized status, which gave them the right to open retail stores.

In 1656, confirming the privileges accorded by the letters patent of 1550 and 1574, Louis XIV limited residence for the New Christians to the province of Guyenne, whereas previous texts had opened the entire kingdom to them. In reality, the New Christians during this period enjoyed a privileged situation because they lived as good Catholics, baptized their children, married, and buried their dead in the Christian manner, without giving the least sign of any Jewish tendencies whatsoever. They nonetheless ended up gradually being considered Jews.

On 20 November 1684, ninety-three poor Jewish families were required to leave the country, again within a month's time. In his desire to achieve religious unity in a state whose parts were not yet consolidated, Louis XIV planned the expulsion of the country's non-Catholics. The revocation of the Edict of Nantes on 17 October 1685 brought about the emigration of thousands of Huguenots and the conversion to Catholicism of those who remained behind. During the economic crises that followed, one after another, the threat of expulsion came to weigh upon the New Christians as well.

Circumstances played their part, however, and a decision was taken in favor of taxing the Portuguese, who had demonstrated their economic usefulness, instead of expelling them. A tax not stipulated in the letters patent was levied upon them on 9 February 1700. In this particular case, they were treated in effect as Jews and not as New Christians. They no longer enjoyed the status of New Christians since the new tax contravened the privileges of the letters patent, which had made *régnicoles* of them. They remained in this precarious situation—neither New Christians nor, officially, Jews—until 1722.

That same year, the intendants of Bordeaux and Auch were required to draw up a list of Jews and their assets. This property was ordered to be seized and handed over to the king. So long as these Jews had been considered New Christians, they were free from all manner of confiscatory taxation; henceforth they were treated like the Jews of Alsace, Metz, and Lorraine, who enjoyed a number of rights in exchange for payment of heavy taxes.

The consequences of the revocation of the Edict of Nantes, the economic utility of the Jews, and, moreover, their ability to pay substantial sums of money to the government led Louis XV in June 1723 to promulgate, at Meudon, letters patent renewing the privileges of the preceding letters, still restricted to the province of Guyenne, while recognizing the New Christians as Jews by means of a formula—quite unusual for a Catholic kingdom—that referred to "the Jews of the said *généralités* [treasury subdivisions], known and established in our kingdom as Portuguese, or else New Christians." The price paid for these letters was 100,000 pounds. Though attempts were made to obstruct enforcement of this "statute," it was nonetheless maintained in force, and explains the peculiar condition of the Jews of Guyenne under the Ancien Régime.[10]

The parliament of Bordeaux, the jurats, and the royal intendants were unsparing in their efforts to convince Louis XIV and Louis XV to let the city's Jews stay in France. Without really constituting a major economic force, the Jews of Bordeaux saw how to profit from the commercial development of the city while contributing to it as well. Disposing of sizable liquid assets and considerable personal property, unlike their Christian counterparts, the Portuguese fueled the expansion of banking and credit. This was also due to the funds they were in a position to obtain from the Sephardim[11] of England, Amsterdam, and the Iberian peninsula at a time when lack of liquidity was a major problem for the French economy.

Jewishness Openly Avowed

In reality, the New Christians did not wait for the letters patent of 1723 to declare their Jewishness. In Labastide-Clairence, for example, they ceased notifying the local priest of their births, marriages, and baptisms in 1659. Moreover, the same year, a personal name was engraved on a gravestone in its Hebrew pronunciation. A similar thing occurred at Bidache. At Saint-Esprit-lès-Bayonne, between 1622 and 1633, the number of baptized Portuguese children was low; nonetheless it rose in 1634, and then underwent a contraction in the 1640s. An upturn was again noted around 1646, a dip in 1650–51, and once more an increase in 1652 and 1656. In 1663, unregistered births issuing from mixed marriages were fairly numerous. Toward 1660, growth is observed in the Jewish population, with the number of baptisms falling between 1665 and 1667.[12]

In 1654, the parish priest of Saint-Esprit served as a front man for the purchase of a cemetery for the Portuguese community, which was to allow its members to practice Jewish mortuary rites. At first, the names of the deceased buried in the Portuguese cemetery appeared in the registers of Christian burials. From 1668, this was no longer the case at all. The creation of a fraternal society for burials and related matters followed the opening of the cemetery and laid the basis for future community organization. In the year prior to the purchase of the cemetery, there had been a decline in the number of baptisms. This is explained by the desire of the Portuguese to declare themselves collectively as Jews, after many last-minute hesitations and attempts at concealment. The Portuguese of Saint-Esprit avowed their Jewishness sooner than those of Bordeaux, who, by too openly revealing themselves, risked losing the privileges offered by bourgeois status.[13]

In Bordeaux, they ceased having their children baptized between 1690 and 1700, and around 1711 their marriages were no longer blessed by the church. Nonetheless, burials were still performed in a Christian cemetery, and this until 1724–25. In 1699, the Portuguese created a charitable society (*Sedaka*), provided with a treasurer and syndic and responsible for looking after poor Sephardim. This society extended its activities to other sectors and was soon identified with the Portuguese community—indeed, with a form of communal organization. By the 1670s, the community of Saint-Esprit was already a functioning entity. Before even being officially recognized as Jews, its members were thus equipped with a well-established form of social organization, capable of monitoring and supervising the activities of the community.

The letters patent of 1776 did not even mention the neo-Christianity of the Portuguese. Their situation was therefore unique in European and French experience: Jews hindered by hardly any incapacity, subjects enjoying virtually all rights, including the right to purchase land and the freedom to choose their residential neighborhood without having to wear any distinctive badge.

How are we to explain the fact that, at the height of the movement toward integration, these Portuguese displayed their Jewish identity? If they decided to do so while they were in the process of laying the basis for communal organization, it is because they felt more secure in this regard. Their motivations were not religious in nature. During the waves of emigration of the seventeenth century, those who wished to live their Judaism fully headed instead to London, Hamburg, or Amsterdam. For Jews in the eighteenth century, which sounded the death knell for the centralized absolutism of the seventeenth, setting themselves up as a corporate body in France offered more advantages and guaranteed a security and a stability that letters patent no longer provided.

Nor ought one neglect the fact that the corporations of Bordeaux, being placed under the patronage of a saint, combined religious and commercial dimensions. They exercised a monopoly in their respective sectors and had the right to limit the number of their members. The Portuguese, in order to form a corporation in their turn that would serve to coordinate individual commercial and financial interests while preserving the unity of the group's members, had to give the appearance of being an organized body.

As a group, which was constantly increasing in number owing to successive waves of immigration, they also felt the need for the structure and discipline that an organized community brought, while providing specific services as well. The Inquisition did not hold sway in France; hiding one's Jewish identity was not essential. Their return to Judaism came about, then, over the long term.

On the Usefulness of the Portuguese

The New Christians were tolerated for mercenary reasons. For the same reasons, they were tolerated as Jews—as a way of officially recognizing a de facto state of affairs—after the issuance of the letters patent of 1717 regulating colonial commerce. Thanks to their family networks and their contacts in Europe and the Orient, the Sephardim were in a position to play a significant role in this trade.

Until then, they had devoted themselves mainly to local small- and medium-sized commerce and to the meager trade between Bordeaux and Spain. A few wealthy merchants invested in the leather and silk industries. A certain number practiced medicine. It certainly cannot be claimed that they were key figures in the economic renaissance of Bordeaux. Nonetheless, as brokers and merchants, some of them occupied important positions.

The Gradis family illustrates the use of such networks for purposes of trade. It established commercial relations with the Jews of London and Amsterdam to extend its activities to French islands in the Caribbean such as Martinique and Santo Domingo, exporting wines, liqueurs, salted beef, and flour and importing sugar and indigo. It also founded the Société du Canada, supplying the colony of Quebec, chartering and arming ships on behalf of the French king during the Seven Years' War (1756–63). Other great families—Lopès-Dubec, Raba, Furtado—likewise profited from their contacts and networks, playing an important role in banking, trade in wines and colonial products, import-export, and marine insurance.

In 1751, 30 percent of Bordeaux Jews were in banking and large-scale commerce; 47 percent in medium- and small-scale trade; 8 percent in the service sector; 11 percent in small business, craft industries, and so on; 5 percent were landlords, independently wealthy, or else retired. The commercial sector remained dominant. Overall, the members of the Portuguese community were bourgeois who enjoyed incomes at least above the required minimum, though there were a sizable number of poor as well who had come with the last waves of immigration. In 1751, forty-one women were counted in the census as engaging in a professional activity, among them a banker and a merchant, most devoting themselves to petty textile trades, a few others being employed as domestic servants.[14]

For their part, the Portuguese of Saint-Esprit engaged in local trade, manufacturing soap, chocolate, and snuff; some traded internationally, buying wool in Spain and sugar in Portugal, shipping these commodities to ports on the English Channel and the North Sea and bringing back to Spain what this country needed. Saint-Esprit was home also to a community of poor people supported by the charity of a few wealthy families.

In the eighteenth century, the Jewish population of Bordeaux varied between 1,500 and 2,000 persons, representing about 2 percent of the total population, with a large concentration in the neighborhood of the Place d'Aquitaine (now the Place de la Victoire), the well-off building townhouses and lavish residences for themselves in the smartest districts of the city and in adjacent localities. The population of Saint-Esprit declined from 3,500 persons to 2,500 on the eve of the Revolution. Though a minority in Bordeaux, the Jews made up sometimes a third, even a majority, of the population of Saint-Esprit-lès-Bayonne.[15] This faubourg cannot be considered to have really been a ghetto. If Jews were not allowed to live in the city of Bayonne itself, they nonetheless were not forbidden to live in the surrounding countryside and villages.

Community, Spiritual Life, and Society

The affairs of the Portuguese community were managed according to a hierarchical system. The electorate was divided into four categories: elders, incumbent and outgoing members of the council of the *Sedaka*, or charity fund; taxpayers; the assisted poor; and, finally, the unassisted poor, who were deprived of all power of decision. The administration of the nation did not much differ from that found in other communities of the period. Power was concentrated in the hands of the *parnassim*, whose responsibilities consisted in supervising taxation, the poor, and the practice of religion. A whole series of institutions peculiar to Jewish community life (*Hevrot* or *Hermandades*, religious fraternities), including ones devoted to education, carried out the balance of the activities of the *Sedaka*, whose regulations were ratified by the king on 14 December 1760. At Saint-Esprit, the *Hevra*, a mortuary fraternity, saw to the laying out of bodies and arranged for burial of the deceased; another frary, devoted to the sick and poor, brought food to the needy in their homes; the charity *Malbish 'Arumim* (literally, "Clothe the Naked") supplied them with clothes; and a fraternity for orphaned female children provided for the dowries of indigent young girls.[16]

To the leaders of the community fell the distribution and collection of the various taxes due the city and the king, the two most important being the head tax and the *vingtième* (a five percent levy on revenue). Added to this were internal payments for the support of communal institutions and assistance to the poor. Throughout the eighteenth century, the community had to deal with a host of problems: the growing number of poor persons needing to be cared for; the arrival of non-Sephardic Jews, especially from Avignon, and later the *Tudesques* (or Ashkenazim) and a few

Italian Jews; and the increasingly strong reluctance of the rich to assume communal obligations.

During this period, the Jewish *nation* of Bordeaux[17] was a sort of republic responsible for its members, a kind of omnipresent political body. In 1760, it appointed an official agent in Paris, Jacob Rodrigues-Pereira (1715–80), charged with acting as an intermediary between Saint-Esprit and Bordeaux, on the one hand, and the court, on the other. Official recognition of the nation led it to seek guarantees from the king's council for its institutions and its power. It submitted regulatory proposals to the council, which approved and authorized them from 1760 to 1763. The *parnassim* thus used royal authority to impose their own.

Before achieving this independence, the *nation* was long dependent on its omnipotent counterpart in Amsterdam, which supplied relief for the poor, intervened in diplomatic matters, and provided trained lay and clerical staff as well as religious and secular books. This situation of dependence was characteristic of the Portuguese crypto-Jewish period in France. The official recognition of the *nation* later restored a certain measure of equality between the French and Amsterdam Jewish communities, which favored frequent contacts in many fields.

In the first half of the seventeenth century, the religious practice of Portuguese observing Jewish customs in France was still bookish, being drawn from manuals and owing nothing to oral teaching or to imitation; women, who also had access to books, were not excluded. Afterward, the entry of rabbis into these crypto-Jewish communities signalled the end of the regime of books and autodidactic learning, and with it the favorable situation reserved for women under such circumstances.

Signs of profound religiosity or spirituality within the Portuguese *nation* are few. Nonreligious leaders usually had more influence than rabbis, who were called *Hakhamim* (wise men). This does not rule out the possibility that certain Sephardim may individually have been very attached to their religion. The fact that these New Christians were cut off from mainstream Judaism for a long period of time may provide a rough explanation for the practice on their part, and on that of their descendants, of a Judaism in harmony with the rationalism of the Enlightenment, characterized by a rejection of the Talmud and *midrash*[18] and reliance instead on the Bible.

In the eighteenth century, one finds seven synagogues (*esnogas*) in Bordeaux; thirteen in Saint-Esprit, a Jewish city within a city, in effect, with its own schools, ritual baths, and communal institutions marking off the Jewish area; one in Peyrehorade, one in Bidache, and one in Labastide-Clairence. Their operation was supported by private individuals. The majority of them had no particular architectural style and were housed in private buildings, rather more like oratories than actual synagogues. In their wills, the Portuguese asked to be buried in "the cemetery of the Portuguese Nation" or "the cemetery of the other Portuguese of [their] nation," and later "the cemetery of the Jewish Nation." In the southwest of France today there remain eight Portuguese cemeteries, not counting those of Paris and Marseilles.[19]

What relatively few intellectual documents the nation produced were in the Spanish language, with the exception of the odd writing in Hebrew. Its scholars even included a woman, Sara Oxeda, from Saint-Esprit. The *nation* long remained faithful to Portuguese, and then to Spanish, while nonetheless maintaining an ambivalent relationship with the peninsula at first, torn between rejection and attraction; over time it created for itself its own Jewish contexts in which references to the Iberian past gradually faded. The proximity of Spain prevented the development of a special Jewish language, unlike what occurred in the case of exiles from the peninsula who settled in the Balkans and in certain cities of Morocco, where their Spanish came to be sprinkled with Hebrew words and words borrowed from local languages.

Instruction in the schools did away with corporal punishments. Among the subjects taught were French and arithmetic, with Bible verses being translated into Spanish. This openness on the part of the Sephardim to the outside world explains why their teaching was later taken as a model by the advocates of the Jewish Enlightenment (*Haskalah*) in the second half of the eighteenth century.

That the Jewish *nation* was not cut off from its environment is indicated by many other things as well. The average age at which young Jewish women in Saint-Esprit first married in the eighteenth century was twenty-four, and less than twenty-seven for about half of the young Jewish men; though lower than the corresponding ages for Christians, the difference between them was not considerable and continued to narrow, which testifies to a progressive integration with the surrounding society. The gap in marriage age between Christian men and women was two to three years; among the Jews it was three to six years. Here one notices a continuity with Iberian tradition.

Between 1752 and 1787, the number of children per family was roughly four among the Jews of Saint-Esprit, whereas in the Christian parish of Bilhères d'Ossau it was close to six. Fertility seems therefore to have been lower than among Christians; births occurred during the first years of marriage, becoming less frequent afterward. Large families were rare. The Jewish family pattern of Saint-Esprit resembled that found elsewhere in Europe in the eighteenth century.[20]

In Bordeaux, the average marriage age for Jews, male and female together, was twenty-three years for the period 1777–92, and twenty-six years for the period 1793–1820. In 1751, the number of surviving children per couple was 2.7—or 3.4 if childless couples are excluded, which agrees with the modern rate. The mortality rate among Bordeaux Jews was also low in the middle of the eighteenth century (19 per 1,000), that of the general population of France under the Ancien Régime being reckoned at between 28 and 38 per 1,000; it was therefore nearer the rate for the present-day French population (12 per 1,000). This may be explained by a combination of adequate sanitary conditions and economic affluence, together with provision by the community of medical assistance for the indigent sick and relief for the needy during times of famine.

The proportion of endogamous marriages among the Portuguese—proud of their ethnic heritage and, owing to their numbers, able to choose their spouses—rose to 85 percent in the years 1775–92. Exclusion was directed mainly against other Jewish groups, such as the Jews of Avignon. Moreover, marriage was almost always (84 percent of the time) within one's socioprofessional class.[21]

All these elements taken together, combined with the perception of the Portuguese by the surrounding society and its leaders, placed them in the first rank of Jews amenable to emancipation when the opportunity presented itself.

CHAPTER FIVE

The Jews of the East and of Paris

METZ AND LORRAINE

Resettlement

As the communities of New Christians who had fled Portugal were establishing themselves in the southwest, in the second half of the sixteenth century, an initially quite minor resettlement of Jews was occurring at the same time in Metz, after a long absence of more than three centuries.

This return coincided with the entry of French troops into the city in 1552, which established the authority of the king of France, Henri II, over the Three Bishoprics of Metz, Toul, and Verdun, united to France permanently in 1648; and subsequently with the establishment in Metz of a large garrison, numbering between 1,000 and 4,000 men, that needed to be maintained. At the end of the sixteenth century, however, religious wars having disrupted state administration and finances, provision of this garrison and payment of its soldiers posed a serious problem. Once more the Jews could be useful.

In 1567 the military authorities, who were to control municipal administration until 1633, granted permission for permanent residence to four families in exchange for payment of an entry fee and an annual charge, provided also that they respected certain conditions, among them the obligation every month to hear a sermon in church. By letters patent, Henri III confirmed their privileges.

In 1595, the twenty Jewish households then existing in Metz officially constituted themselves as a communal body, providing themselves with statutes drafted in Judeo-German (the western branch of Yiddish)[1] and transcribed into French. Their number continued to grow. In 1637, the community numbered eighty-five households, totalling perhaps 351 persons out of a population of 15,023, and this despite eight successive ordinances, promulgated between 1600 and 1630, that pretended to limit the admission of new residents but actually sanctioned their increase. Henri IV, Louis XIII, and Louis XIV, during their respective visits to the city in 1603, 1632, and 1657, confirmed the privileges of the Jews by letters patent. In 1717, the city was home to 480 Jewish households, roughly 1,900 persons out of a total urban population of 26,516.[2]

This growth is to be attributed to the constant flow of immigrants, for the most part natives of the German Rhineland, but also of the surrounding low country—Ennery, Morhange, Créhange, Augny, Vantoux—and of Alsace as well. In the last decades of the seventeenth century, with the Huguenot exodus that followed the revocation of the Edict of Nantes in 1685, which drained off the city's dynamic elements and emptied it of 17 percent of its population,[3] Jewish immigration received fresh impetus.

Why did the military authorities and the monarchy authorize the development of a Jewish community in Metz, something truly exceptional in the kingdom of France at the end of the seventeenth century? The departure of the Protestants and the need that may have been felt to replace them with Jews do not explain everything. Great demands were made of Metz, which housed one of the most important garrisons in the country, during the wars that continually raged in the kingdom during the last decades of the seventeenth century and at the beginning of the eighteenth. The Jews of Metz not only advanced soldiers' back pay; they also supplied the army with horses. In 1698, a year of bad harvest, they stocked the city and the region with wheat. They are remembered also for their contributions to the economic recovery of the city. Jewish financiers frequented the royal court from the middle of the seventeenth century, acquiring enough influence to intervene on behalf of their co-religionists, both in their own community and elsewhere in Europe. They were now in a position to act as genuine mediators (*shtadlanim*).

A similar immigration occurred in ducal Lorraine,[4] during its occupation by French troops from 1633 to 1661 and from 1670 to 1697. In 1636, a few Jewish families were authorized to settle in Nancy, but, owing to the hostility shown toward them, they were expelled in 1643. A similar experiment was attempted at Bar-le-Duc that likewise did not succeed. The dukes tried from time to time to attract bankers to the region, granting them rights of residence. In 1721, a list was published of seventy-three families authorized to stay in the duchy; the others were expelled. Their number rose to one hundred eighty in 1733. Four years later, these families met at Morhange to provide themselves with statutes, while remaining within the area of influence of Metz, the dominant community of the region.[5]

The joining of Lorraine to France in 1766—Lorraine now becoming a *généralité*, or treasury subdivision, having its seat at Nancy—reinforced this dependence. Letters patent issued by Louis XV the same year renewed the privileges of the Jews in ducal Lorraine. On the eve of the Revolution, there were five hundred families in the former duchy of Lorraine, ninety of them in Nancy, fifty of which had settled there without permission; in 1753, by contrast, only twelve households were recognized as having a legal right of residence in that city. Additional accommodations were

obtained privately, which helped raise the number of households authorized to live there.[6]

In Lunéville, where the majority of Jews were natives of Metz and the
surrounding area, there were some thirty families on the eve of the Revolution—perhaps one hundred fifty or two hundred persons out of a total
population of 12,378, or a proportion of 2 percent—as against only two
families in 1753.[7] In Metz, one finds five hundred eighty-five households
during the same period, or about 2,223 persons, by comparison with a
non-Jewish population (the garrison excluded) of 33,595. Jews thus accounted for only 6 percent of the city's total population, as opposed to 7
percent in 1717, with a growth rate of 17 percent between 1717 and 1790,
while that of the non-Jewish population (again excluding the garrison) was
36 percent. This weak rate of increase is explained by the growing restrictions on immigration, and by rising emigration, limited generally to Lorraine, to cities such as Lunéville, Nancy, Étain, Sarrelouis, and the village
of Metzervisse.[8]

Housing and Community

The Jews of Metz inhabited the parish of Saint-Ferroy, which numbered
400 Jews among its 993 inhabitants at the beginning of the seventeenth
century. By the middle of the eighteenth century, this parish was 90 percent Jewish, which made it a truly Jewish quarter. Living conditions were
relatively moderate, with a certain number of restrictions similar to those
then in force in ghettos elsewhere in Europe, such as the prohibition
against leaving the quarter on Sundays and holidays, and guarded en-
trances. This situation lasted until the Revolution. The ghetto was overpopulated, and as late as 1793 there were on average nearly fourteen persons per house. A little more than a third of the dwellings were home to
more than twenty persons. The sanitary conditions were hazardous.[9]

In Nancy, the Jewish notables lived comfortably in the new neighborhoods and main streets of the city. One finds roughly the same situation in
Lunéville. But in Nancy they constituted a small stratum of privileged persons, by contrast with the majority of Jews who lived under difficult circumstances, crammed in around the rue des Pénitents, now the Quartier
de l'Équitation. Nonetheless there was no real ghetto in either Nancy or
Lunéville, nor in the former ducal Lorraine as a whole, even if an edict of
11 June 1726 did institute something of the sort in localities where Jews
were permitted to live.

As in Germany and in Central Europe, the community of Metz enjoyed
an autonomy recognized by the Crown in matters of civil justice, finance,
and security. It even had the power to grant or refuse the *Ironiss* or "free-

dom of the city" (i.e., the right of residence) to those who requested it. It enjoyed a real independence by comparison with the communities of Alsace, the duchy of Lorraine, and the county of Créhange. For fiscal purposes it maintained important links with the small communities of the *Généralité de Metz*.

Communal organization differed little from that prevalent in other Ashkenazic communities during the same period. Internal administration rested with the syndics (*parnassim*)—an aristocracy of learning and money—and with the rabbis. As a small state within a state, the community issued regulations for supervising the life of its members. In the beginning, six rabbis directed the community. Later responsibility came to be divided between the head rabbi, who was in charge of spiritual life, and the syndics, who were in charge of administrative affairs in general, security, and the levying of taxes. Both rabbis and syndics, who varied in number between four and ten depending on the period, were elected by the community by a system of suffrage based on tax qualification (in Jewish communities in France typically consisting of three categories determined as a function of income). While the head rabbi was remunerated, the syndics were unpaid and their service obligatory; most were traders, cattle dealers, and bankers. Owing to the conditions of eligibility for communal service, the government of the community amounted in effect to a gerontocracy. The syndics made up the council of the community (*kahal*), which held executive power; they were assisted by other paid administrators and employees. Following the example of the Portuguese in the southwest, the community maintained a permanent agent in Paris.

In 1721, Duke Leopold ordered the constitution of a single community of the Jews of Lorraine, which ran counter to a custom that had been widespread in France through the Middle Ages and up until the Revolution: the independence of communities with respect to each other. This was the first time that non-Catholic worship had been tolerated in Lorraine. On the eve of the Revolution, an independent community was finally able to be created in Lunéville, now a French city, and in 1786 a monumental synagogue was opened there.

Various ordinary taxes and exceptional levies weighed upon the Jews of Metz. The heaviest charge was the Brancas tax, instituted in 1715 under the regency of the Duke of Orléans in order to provide two of his associates—one of them the Duke of Brancas—with an annual income. The community also needed revenue in order to take care of its own expenses. Taxes were imposed for this purpose on meat, wines, and liqueurs, on the sale of horses and on successions. Nonetheless, receipts did not cover even half the sum of expenditures, which drove the community to a policy of borrowing that in the end proved ruinous. This state of affairs was due in large part to the unwillingness of Jews in the surrounding countryside to pay a share of the Brancas tax, which therefore fell entirely upon the Jews of Metz, further worsening the community's financial condition.

In ducal Lorraine, the Jews were in principle obliged to pay municipal taxes or else a subscription whose interpretation provoked much dispute, and on top of which other fees were added that varied from city to city.

Jewish Society

Jewish life developed in conformity with the rules and practices prescribed by rabbinical law as well as by local custom. The *Shulḥan 'Arukh* (Prepared Table), written by the Sephardi Joseph Caro (1488–1575) and augmented by the glosses of the Ashkenazi Moses Isserles (1525/1530–72), constitutes the chief reference work on the subject. A specific rhythm therefore imposed itself as much on daily life as on the existence of individuals: Sabbath, feasts, fasts, rites marking the principal cycles of life, and so on.

The Jews were distinguished from surrounding society also by the distinctive signs prescribed by their own religion: the wearing of a beard and a hat by men. Forbidden to copy the clothing fashions of non-Jews, until the Revolution in Metz they dressed in a black coat with a ruff, or collar, called the Jewish coat. Women wore a black cape with a ruff, with their hair hidden by a wig or an ample shawl. In the first half of the seventeenth century, they were required to wear the *rouelle*, or badge, imposed by Christian society. In Metz, they were obliged to wear a yellow hat, which gradually disappeared from use. Over time some of the city's Jews came to adopt the clothes of non-Jews, such as the wig, to give up the beard, and to abandon themselves to luxury and ostentation, as many did in the eighteenth century. The Jewish religious authorities opposed this tendency by enacting regulations concerning male and female dress and morals. In the second half of the eighteenth century, few external signs separated Jews from Christians.

Language constituted another element of differentiation. The Jews spoke a Judeo-German idiom, essentially the western dialect of Yiddish, transcribed into Hebrew characters; Hebrew remained the language of prayer, study, and law. The learning of French made little headway. At the beginning of the eighteenth century, French began to enjoy a certain prestige in wealthy Jewish society; but it was necessary to wait until the end of the century for publications in the French language to appear, including patriotic prayers on the occasion of the death of Louis XV and expressions of thanksgiving for the deliverance of Marie-Antoinette. A few philosophical and polemical texts were translated. On the eve of the Revolution, there were not more than fifty Jews in Metz able to read French periodicals.[10] The necessary books for worship and instruction were imported from Amsterdam or Germany until 1764, when the first printing shop was founded in Metz.

As everywhere else, the Jews of Metz and Lorraine were subject to restrictions that prevented them from practicing certain professions. The former attracted notice in particular as suppliers of horses and meat to the army. Jews were also quite active in the grain trade. They were found in banking as well. At the beginning of the eighteenth century, they advanced considerable sums of money to state agencies, especially the military. In the second half of the century, Jews from other localities took over the business of supplying the military from the local Jews.

Regulated moneylending was practiced at all levels. Poorer Jews engaged in horsetrading on a small scale. They were also butchers, goldsmiths, and dealers in bric-a-brac and second-hand clothes, these latter two trades being the most common. Peddling occupied a special place among the Jewish trades in Metz; ordinary people bought and sold clandestinely all sorts of merchandise.

At the beginning of the eighteenth century, the activities engaged in by the Jews of ducal Lorraine show that they were in contact with the rural world, trading in grains and livestock and lending money on a very small scale. In 1789, two-thirds of the heads of Jewish families in Nancy were active in commerce and trade. A powerful group of traders operated on an international level as well. The heads of these families, who were also Court Jews (*Hofjuden*),[11] consolidated their financial successes through strategic marriages. The banker Samuel Lévy, Lyon Goudchaux, the Cerf-Berrs, and the Brisacs of Lunéville stand out among those who made great fortunes; but even they sometimes experienced setbacks.[12]

The communities of Lorraine displayed a clearly traditionalist attitude, if only on the level of morality. Sexual relations outside marriage were severely punished, though cases are known of Jewish servant girls having relations with valets or with young men of their acquaintance. Pregnancies out of wedlock were very rare, as was abandonment of infants. Games of chance, even billiards, were forbidden. Austerity seems to have prevailed. Contemporary observers attributed the higher life expectancy of the adult Jewish population of Metz to this discipline.

Young Jewish women married earlier than did their Christian counterparts. The average age of women on their first marriage was a bit less than twenty-three years in the last decades of the eighteenth century and between twenty-eight and twenty-nine for men, which contradicts the evidence of contemporary observers, who put it at thirteen to fourteen years for girls and fifteen to sixteen years for boys.[13] Thus the average age of first marriage for Jewish men was very close to that observed among Christians during the period. By contrast, the young Jewish women of Metz, particularly those from wealthy families, married on average two to four years sooner than either Lorraine women or French women in general; but this still put them far above the marriage age authorized—indeed advocated— by rabbinical literature.[14] Among widowers, 49 percent remarried, as against 20 percent of widows.

Between 1740 and 1789, the average number of childern per Jewish family in Metz was a little less than four, while in Christian parishes of the region it approached five. These figures clearly invalidate the traditionally accepted image of large Jewish families. In fact, the Jewish population was less prolific than the surrounding populations in Lorraine, even if Jewish women married earlier than Christian women, and this owing to contraception. Indeed, the Jewish religion permitted the limitation of births in certain cases. Breastfeeding, and the time it required, contributed to the spacing out of pregnancies. The conditions of life influenced fertility as well.

Infant and juvenile mortality followed regional and national trends. Contrary to the pattern in the Christian world, however, it did not improve in the last decades of the eighteenth century. As a result of all these factors, the Jewish community of Metz diminished in numbers at the same time that a demographic boom was taking place in the city. The myth of the soaring increase of the Jews therefore needs to be revised.[15]

On the eve of the Revolution, Lorraine numbered some 7,500 Jews in all, grouped together in large communities such as those of Metz, Nancy, and Thionville, and in surrounding small towns.

ALSACE

Jewish Geography

The Jewish presence in Alsace, a German land under the authority of the Holy Roman Empire until the middle of the seventeenth century, dates back to before the crusades.[16] It diminished considerably in 1348–49 during the Black Plague, which occasioned massacres and expulsions of Jews and led to the disappearance of large communities. These were partially reconstituted at the end of the fourteenth century and during the course of the fifteenth. The expulsions nonetheless drove them out of the principal cities of the region for good, triggering, on the one hand, migratory movements toward Switzerland and the Baden region, and, on the other, a retreat toward the villages under the authority of the diocese of Strasbourg and the prefecture of Haguenau, domain of the Hapsburgs, where thirty-five Jewish families lived at the end of the fifteenth century. The Jews of Alsace were dispersed among many different seigneuries, dependent on the good will of individual nobles and subject to conditions that varied according to where they settled, local settlements not counting more than two or three families in the sixteenth century. Thus the Jewish population at this time did not exceed one hundred or one hundred fifteen families in the best case, a figure that later declined at the end of the century as a consequence of further expulsions.

The Thirty Years' War (1618–48) marked both the transition to French sovereignty and the beginning of the growth of the Jewish population in Alsace. In this troubled period, regulations concerning them were not respected, particularly in Upper Alsace, which encouraged illegal settlement in some villages. By the Treaty of Westphalia in 1648, France inherited those lands said to be of "old dominion"—formerly belonging to the house of Austria in Upper Alsace and the prefecture of Haguenau in Lower Alsace; at first it followed the policy of the Hapsburgs in these territories, tolerating Jews under certain conditions. The relatively favorable attitude shown by Louis XIV and the lords of the lands now said to be of "new dominion" (the bishopric of Strasbourg, the county of Hanau-Lichtenberg, the villages of the *Noblesse Immédiate*) thus explains why during the seventeenth century their number varied between 2,600 and 3,000. Their usefulness as suppliers of the army, above all for the remounting of the cavalry and artillery, but also as a source of revenue for the nobles, who welcomed them fairly readily, once more worked in their favor. In order to settle in a seigneury they paid an entry fee, arbitrarily determined by its lord and variable from domain to domain.

Their presence was officially recognized in royal Alsace—that is, in the lands of "old dominion"—with the letters patent of 1657 and then the ordinance of 1674. By virtue of the latter, the Jews of royal Alsace paid a fee for royal protection (abolished in 1790), enjoyed the same privileges as those of Metz, and were henceforth exempted from the "body tax" (*péage corporel*). On the other hand, those who lived in the rest of the province, called "foreigners," were subject to this tax. The text of 1674 thus accorded the Jews a quasi-legal status. The royal body tax as well as the Strasbourg toll (paid to spend the day or night in the city) were abolished by an edict of January 1784.

At the beginning of the eighteenth century, Alsace included between 1,269 and 1,348 families, or somewhere between 6,500 and 6,800 persons. In the last decades of the century, the Jewish population of Alsace, legal and illegal both,[17] may be estimated at 22,500 individuals. A higher proportion of families (74 percent of the total) and of localities sheltering Jews (129 of 179) was found in Lower Alsace. The remaining families (26 percent) resided in Upper Alsace, spread out over fifty villages. Still being denied access to cities, the Jewish populace remained scattered over rural areas, by contrast with the situation that prevailed during the medieval period. On the eve of the Revolution, there were 1,150 towns and villages in Alsace, of which nine hundred belonged to nobles who exercised the right to welcome Jews as they pleased. Jews managed to settle in only 179 to 185 villages. Letters patent of 1784, withholding the entry fee from the nobles and reserving it solely to the king, had the effect of blocking new settlements until the emancipation of 1791. In the middle of the nineteenth century, there were only six more localities inhabited by Jews by comparison with 1784, evidence of a certain stability in the geography of settlement.[18]

The Government of the Jewish Nation

At the beginning of the sixteenth century, the Jews of Lower Alsace elected a representative, who bore the name *parnass* (*vorsteher*) or *manhig* (also *leiter* or chief). Josel of Rosheim (c. 1478–1554), a theologian and diplomat, quickly established himself as the official representative of the Jewries of Alsace and Germany. He intervened often at court on behalf of his co-religionists, particularly before the German emperor Charles V, who bestowed upon him the title of *Befelshaber Gemeiner unser Judenschafft in Heiligen Reiche* (Commander of Our Jewish Nation in the Holy Empire).[19] The role of his successor remained confined to Lower Alsace. After him, the Jews were no longer entitled to an official representative.

In 1681, the rabbinate of the Alsatian Jews was created using the community of Metz as an organizational model. The political and territorial divisions of Alsace prevented the appointment of a single rabbi as the head of this community, which, by the second half of the eighteenth century, came under the jurisdiction of six rabbinical districts, every nomination to the post of rabbi requiring confirmation by the competent authority. It is probable that rabbis were elected and the decision submitted for approval. These rabbis carried out the same duties as those of Metz and, in addition to their religious duties, had responsibility for civil suits brought among Jews, marriage contracts, and agreements governing succession and guardianship.[20]

Alongside the rabbis, from the middle of the seventeenth century in the diocese of Strasbourg, and at the end of the century in the counties of Ribeaupierre and Hanau-Lichtenberg, lands of the *Noblesse Immédiate*, one finds regional *préposés* or syndics appointed by the Alsatian dynasts and charged with jointly managing community affairs within the framework of the seigneury. Locally, there was also a syndic for each community or village, or for several villages together, either named by the regency or elected and responsible for looking after internal security and taxes. In the 1770s, certain regional syndics claimed the title of *préposé général* of the Jewish *nation*. Thus Herz Cerf-Berr (1726–94), supplier of the army and a man well connected in governmental circles, a sort of Court Jew, had himself awarded this title in 1775. In his capacity as syndic of all the Jews of Alsace, he worked to bring about the formal creation of a Jewish *nation* headed by syndics enjoying real authority. In the memorandum he addressed in 1779–80 to the king, he demanded for native Jews (though not for "foreigners") total freedom of commerce and settlement, and official recognition of the authority of their syndics.

An era of reforms was announced in Europe with the Edict of Tolerance (*Toleranzpatent*) promulgated in 1781–82 by Joseph II, ruler of the Holy Roman Empire.[21] Earlier, the affair of the "false receipts" that unfolded in the Sundgau in 1777–78 and the outburst of popular feeling that ensued— peasants had borrowed relatively large sums from Jews at a moment of economic crisis and, finding themselves unable to reimburse the loans, presented fraudulent receipts written in Hebrew characters—had placed at the center of debate the question of Jewish usury, unduly exaggerated in some respects, along with that of the precariousness of the Jewish condition in the region.

Letters patent of 1784, proclaiming a new status for the Jews, were a response to the petitions of Cerf-Berr, without truly satisfying them; nonetheless they signalled a willingness on the part of the monarchy to come to terms with the Jewish problem. The twenty-five articles composing these letters related to settlement, ordering the expulsion within three months of Jews without fixed or known address, or of Jews who failed to pay the fees due the king, nobles, and towns as well as the taxes owed the community for its costs. Foreign Jews were forbidden to stay longer than four and a half months. Supervision of marriage was strengthened, with permission to marry being made subject to royal approval in order to prevent the increase in the Jewish population that it was supposed would otherwise follow.

In the economic sphere, measures were taken to encourage the Jews to devote themselves to activities considered to be useful to the state, such as agriculture and industry. They were authorized to rent land, farms, and vineyards on the condition that they worked them themselves without employing Christian servants; to work mines, undertake public works, and set up factories, smithies, glassworks, and potteries. Banking and wholesale and retail commerce were open to them as well. The seriousness of the Jewish question in Alsace had to do above all with the problems caused locally by usury, the Jews being held responsible for the indebtedness of the peasants. By favoring the practice of other professions it was hoped that the number of moneylenders might be reduced. Moreover, contracts of borrowing and sale were regulated, and the use of Hebrew for such transactions forbidden. Jews were also prohibited from buying real estate, unless for housing.

With regard to internal organization, the *préposés généraux* were replaced by syndics charged with managing community affairs, and particularly with assuring order and the distribution of taxes. They were elected rather than appointed, but did not have the right to act as spokesmen for the Jews, which is to say as the recognized heads of the Jewish *nation* (the very opposite of what Cerf-Berr had wished for). It fell to them instead to execute royal decisions. The authority of the rabbis was confirmed. The oligarchy remained cumbersome, with quite substantial powers reserved to notables and rabbis.

At the level of civil registration, the novelty of the decree of 1784 resided in the fact that Jews were henceforth obliged to declare births, marriages, and deaths before their local magistrate. Jewish men or women who had been legitimately married and subsequently converted to the Christian faith were allowed to remarry with Catholics only in the event of their being widowed, with every marriage contravening this condition considered null, and any children issuing from such unions considered bastard.[22] A general census was planned in order to expel those who did not enjoy legal right of residence.[23]

These letters patent aroused enthusiasm neither among the detractors of the Jews, who found them too lenient, nor among the Jews themselves, who remained subject to numerous restrictions regarding settlement and commerce. Their situation did not undergo any significant change following the publication of this decree, though it granted them greater security. Cerf-Berr, in proposing reforms to the king four years earlier, had sought to obtain civil rights for the Jews. This was to be achieved only with the Revolution. The letters patent of 1784 represented only a timid advance.

Demography and Society

Articles VI and VII of these letters, in submitting marriage to official authorization, aimed at regulating unions and legitimate births out of concern that Jewish population growth, if unchecked, might make it dominant in the province. The usual view of the Jews as a worrisomely prolific population is shown to be false by the statistical record. The census of 1784 reveals that a family had on average five members. The age of fathers agreed with the average for the society of the period and, for women, the average age for first births was 24 years. Even if the average marriage age for women remained lower than that of the non-Jewish population, it was considerably higher than that reckoned by the local magistrates, who put it at 14 or 15. Statistics collected for fifteen localities yield a rate of nearly 3 children per Jewish family, and 2.6 children per Christian family. The slight superiority observed in fertility is far indeed from justifying alarmist predictions of soaring population increase among the Jews. Foreign Jews, whose inflow authorities did their utmost to regulate, were far less numerous than claimed. The fear that in certain localities Jews were more numerous than Christians was equally unfounded. A 1780 census of thirty-five localities under the authority of the directorate of the nobility of Lower Alsace records 2,187 Christian families resident there as against 709 Jewish families. Anti-Jewish preconceptions continued to prevail over the reality of facts and figures long afterward.[24]

Since they remained in rural areas, the Jews of Alsace did not know the ghettos or semi-ghettos that began to come into being in urban Europe in the sixteenth century. Communal life developed within the framework of traditional norms, as it typically did for Jews elsewhere prior to emancipation. The fact that they were scattered geographically contributed to the rise of communities bound by ties of solidarity that, in places where settlements were limited to only a few families, jointly held religious services. Dispersed settlement also forced observance of the precepts of Judaism in full and open view of the non-Jewish population. In principle, each Alsatian community had a synagogue, usually an oratory set up in a private house. By contrast, only the largest communities, and especially ones that had been long established in the region, had a cemetery. Jews sometimes had to travel long distances, paying toll fees in order to pass through certain cities, in order to bury their dead.

The Jewish communities of Alsace were an integral part of the Rhenish Judaism of the Alemannic area (*Ashkenaz*) from which most of their members originally came.[25] Subsequently they were joined by Jewish exiles from the kingdom of France. The blending of these two populations created a whole with a unique character, which united elements of both in its mixed rite, called western German, and also in its language, Judeo-Alsatian, a branch of Yiddish including Hebraic and Aramaic elements among its various other influences. Contact with the ancestral Alemannic area was maintained over the course of centuries with the arrival of immigrants from the Rhineland and central Germany, and later with the immigration of Jews from eastern Europe fleeing hardship and persecution.

Alsace, though it was an important Jewish homeland, did not stand out as a great intellectual center. The culture of the communities in the region was profoundly marked by rural influences both with regard to rites of marriage and of death. The trades practiced by Jews kept them in permanent association with Gentiles. As peddlers and cattle dealers, they traveled from village to village during the week, coming back home only on the eve of the Sabbath and setting off again once it was over. They also dealt in second-hand clothing, bric-a-brac, and scrap metal, further strengthening their contact with rural populations. Lending on credit, historically a thorny problem for the Jews of the region, likewise attracted a peasant clientele. Peasants' complaints that their constant indebtedness was due to the Jews inspired regular and forceful public protests. These denunciations seem nonetheless to have been clearly excessive, at least to judge from the Strasbourg Register of 1791, according to which the sums loaned by Jews represented only 14 percent of the total. On the eve of the Revolution, the Alsatian communities, numbering between 20,000 and 25,000 persons and confined mainly to rural areas, had only a small number of wealthy families whose fortunes came from banking, manufacturing, and military supply. In 1784, about 10 percent of the Jewish population of the region lived off charity.[26]

PARIS

The history of the Jews under the Ancien Régime is therefore above all a regional history. At the same time as these large groups in the East were in the process of reconstituting themselves after expulsion from the kingdom of France, one finds a concentration of lesser size developing in Paris. Theoretically, the capital remained closed to the Jews until 1789. Nonetheless, on the eve of the Revolution, some five or six hundred Jews lived there. In a city of about 800,000, they were virtually invisible.

At the beginning of the eighteenth century, despite the prohibitions then in force, a tiny community formed in Paris made up of Portuguese from Bordeaux and Saint-Esprit-lès-Bayonne, Jews from Avignon and the papal lands who were effectively Sephardic in religious practice, and "Germans," so called because of their rite, from the East. This last group, which by itself numbered about three hundred fifty individuals, included one hundred fifty Jews from Metz, Lorraine, and Alsace (the contingent from Metz making up the majority) and some two hundred "foreigners" from Germany, England, Poland, Hungary, and Holland.[27]

The Portuguese engaged in trade, chiefly of chocolates and silks, and appear to have been a prosperous group. They inhabited the present-day neighborhoods of Odéon and the Sorbonne. Their community was equipped with offices and stable institutions. The Jews from Avignon resided in the same part of the city and likewise engaged in commerce. The Germans, for their part, were found in the hardware trade, dealing also in second-hand clothing and jewelry. They lived in what are now the neighborhoods of Saint-Merri and Arts-et-Métiers.

Until 1787, the Jews of Paris were excluded from the corporations (Christian guilds holding a recognized monopoly in a manual trade), the arts, and mechanical professions, which feared unfair competition. They could sell their wares only in outdoor stalls. Most were humble merchants, vendors of small household articles, hawkers, and peddlers. One also finds some Jewish bankers and a few manufacturers. Intellectuals also lived in Paris, such as Israël-Bernard de Valabrègue (d. 1779), the Hebrew specialist at the royal library and the author of several works; Daniel de Fonseca (1672–1740), the illustrious physician; Jacob Rodrigues-Pereira, agent of the *nation* of Bordeaux and creator of a method of communication for deaf-mutes; and Zalkind Hourwitz (1740–1812), a Polish Jew and laureate of the 1788 competition of the Academy of Metz.

Apart from a few Portuguese who had received letters of naturalization from Louis XV, the Jews of Paris were dependent on the willingness of the police to issue them a passport or residence permit, in principle for a limited period. They lived in hotels or boarding houses. In 1770, the Portuguese opened their synagogue on the rue Saint-André-des-Arts, followed eight years later by the Germans on the rue Brisemiche and, the following year, the rue du Renard. They also had separate cemeteries. Dissension among the foreign nationals of the various Jewish groups was widespread as well. In short, there was no Jewish *nation* in Paris.

In addition to these rather sizable Jewish populations, one finds a few concentrations of Jews in parts of the south as well. The prohibitions against residence in Provence did not actually prevent a recognizably Jewish presence from developing toward the end of the Ancien Régime, as in other regions; the diaspora issuing from the papal states largely contributed to it. These Jews, mostly shopkeepers, traders, and artisans, formed modest communities of a few hundred individuals in Marseilles, Nice, Montpellier, Arles, Aix, and even in Lyons.

On the eve of the Revolution, despite the edict of expulsion of 1394, renewed in 1615 by Louis XIII, which theoretically prohibited Jews from residing in lands under royal authority, about 40,000 Jews lived in the kingdom, forming a group of *nations*. Though they were loosely united around a tradition that drew upon diverse rites, these *nations* remained divided as much by differences in their material condition as in their cultural life, with a clear line of demarcation separating them geographically. The Sephardic *nations* of the south remained distinct from the Ashkenazic *nations* of the east, and, within each of these regional populations, local communities sought to assert their own particular identity.

Thus the Portuguese community of Bordeaux refused to let in Jewish immigrants from Avignon, who, in 1754, managed finally to obtain letters patent constituting them as a separate *nation* in that city. The Jews of the east of France were considered foreigners by the Portuguese as well, and, on arriving in their community, found themselves promptly expelled. Nor did the Jews of Avignon and the Comtat Venaissin feel any closer to the Portuguese or to the eastern Jews. The German Jewish communities of Alsace, Metz and its environs, and the duchy of Lorraine displayed cultural

and linguistic similarities, whereas the Jewries of the Midi did not. Lorrainers and Alsatians nonetheless formed two distinct groups nourishing
divergent aspirations and enjoying different legal status, and exhibited no
signs of attachment either to the Jews of the Midi or to immigrants from
Germany, Poland, and Lithuania to their own region. Nor, finally, did
Jewish groups in the East possess any common form of communal organization that could bring them together. All these factors were to come into
play in the granting of civil rights to the Jews after the Revolution.

CHAPTER SIX

On the Way to Emancipation

How WERE JEWS perceived by non-Jews at the end of the Ancien Régime? Gentile feeling was no more uniform than the Jewish community in France itself, a socially and culturally diverse population. Perceptions depended on the region, how many Jews lived there, and their social visibility. Often they amounted to nothing more than a mythical picture constructed from prejudices. Depending on whether it was a nonobservant Jew from Bordeaux who was relatively well integrated in a city where certain eminent Jewish figures lived like the local burghers; a traditionalist Alsatian Jew settled in a rural area; or a Jew of the *carrières*, confined to his ghetto, subject to papal authority but attached to the kingdom by a variety of ties— the perception of Jews by non-Jews was liable to vary considerably, as did their treatment of Jews, which ranged from indifference to ignorance, from acceptance to rejection.

Jewish groups themselves looked upon each other in different ways. The eastern Jews denounced the half-heartedness of their co-religionists from the southwest in matters of religion, while the latter judged themselves more advanced in their customs and education. The southwestern Jews were convinced that they belonged to the aristocracy, if only because they were descended from the leading families of the tribe of Judah,[1] and rejected German and Polish Jews on account of their supposed backwardness.[2] The sociocultural barrier that separated the two groups was clearly emphasized in the memorandum drafted in 1788 by the Portuguese during the debate in Paris over what status should be granted Jews in France. The image that the Portuguese succeeded in giving of themselves as integrated Jews, which had a certain basis in fact, enabled them to obtain emancipation before their eastern brethren.

THE ENLIGHTENMENT AND THE JEWS

In Non-Jewish Circles

The multiform perception of the Jew found expression in the debates conducted in philosophical and reformist circles over the Jewish question.

The philosophers of the Enlightenment had in general few regular contacts with Jews—which made them receptive to certain widespread stereotypes. Their attitude sometimes betrayed a certain Manichaeanism: either Jews were liberal-minded, in which case dialogue was possible; or else they were theologically committed, resistant to any opening, prisoners of tradition and of a way of life that rendered them unassimilable. Jewish communities displayed greater diversity than this.

If the philosophers of the Enlightenment did not know exactly how to analyze the Jewish situation, it would be unreasonable to tax them indiscriminately with anti-Semitism. They did not all express themselves in the same way, and their arguments need to be situated in the context of the period, taking into account also their aspirations to rationality and the role that they assigned themselves of freeing the individual from the oppressive yoke of religion, regardless of faith.

Though unsympathetic to the Jews, Montesquieu urged tolerance toward them in writings such as the *Persian Letters* (1721); this did not, however, prevent him from showing animosity toward both the Talmud and the rabbis. In the *Spirit of the Laws* (1748), he attacked the Spanish and Portuguese Inquisitors, and went so far as to call for the creation of a Jewish city in the Basque country, at Saint-Jean-de-Luz or Ciboure.

Voltaire did not distinguish between a monk and a pious Jew, least of all an Ashkenazi—both symbols of a past whose vestiges the *philosophes* expected to sweep away. Anti-religious militantism could not help but make an issue of Judaism, the root of Christianity. For Voltaire, the Bible was no different than any other sacred text concealing "superstitions." Accordingly, it served to focus his criticism, no less than the people who drew their instruction from it. Anti-Jewish prejudices inherited from the past played a part in the formation of Voltaire's image of the Jew. Some thirty of the one hundred eighteen articles in his *Philosophical Dictionary* (1764) contain virulent attacks against the Jews.[3] In the article on "Jews" in *Questions on the Encyclopedia* (the sequel to the *Philosophical Dictionary*), in a passage that combines aggression with prejudice, they are characterized as ignorant and uncivilized. Even so, Voltaire conceded, they should not be burned at the stake.

Voltaire's reflections upon the Jews revealed genuine ambivalence. Indeed, certain Jewish reformers of his time shared some of his views. Diderot and d'Alembert's *Encyclopedia* (1751–72) contained criticisms of Judaism, such as the article "Messiah" written by a disciple of Voltaire, the Protestant minister Polier de Bottens—the better to combat Christianity—but it also contained articles exhibiting an open-mindedness on the Jewish question, such as "Usury" and "Judaism," written by Diderot himself, and "Jews," by his assistant, the Chevalier de Jaucourt.[4] In the antireligious pamphlets circulating at the time, Jews and Christians found themselves in the same boat, all of them equally mistreated.

The Marquis of Argens, also a man of the Enlightenment, famous in his time but forgotten today, whose writings were broadly disseminated, urged tolerance in his *Lettres juives* (1736–37) while opposing talmudic teaching and the rabbis. He showed a genuine fondness for enlightened rationalist Jews, and a marked preference for the Karaite form of Judaism,[5] which did not depend on the teachings of the Talmud.

Rousseau, for his part, allied himself with the tradition of tolerance of certain Calvinist circles, illustrated on the one hand by Pierre Bayle (1647–1706), though he was closer to Voltaire, and, on the other hand, by Jacques Basnage of Rouen (1653–1723), a philosemite. While rejecting Judaism and its doctrines in his battle against the church and against intolerance, Rousseau thus displayed sympathy toward the Jews. He also advocated the founding of schools and universities for them, even a Jewish state, considering the Jews as upholders of natural religion.

Generally speaking, philosophers who were unfavorably disposed toward Judaism and the Jewish people but nonetheless hostile to oppression and discrimination demanded that greater humanity be shown toward them, without, however, really respecting their uniqueness or their otherness.[6] The same was true, moreover, of reformers who defended the Jews, such as the abbé Henri-Baptiste Grégoire, who in his celebrated *Essai sur la régénération physique, morale et politique des Juifs* (Essay on the Physical, Moral, and Political Regeneration of the Jews [1788])[7] denounced their propensity to multiply and their degeneration, denigrated the Talmud, advocated the disappearance of the Yiddish language, and demanded that the power of the rabbis be circumscribed, hoping, ultimately, for their conversion. Malesherbes belonged to the same camp. The apostles of the Enlightenment were concerned with the "regeneration" of the Jews rather than their emancipation. But this was also the case with Jewish reformers themselves.

In Jewish Circles

In the eighteenth century, the idea of reforming the Jewish world had already taken root in Germany, where the Jewish Enlightenment (*Haskalah*) developed as an extension of the German *Aufklärung*. The role played by Moses Mendelssohn (1729–86) in establishing a dialogue between Jews and Christians was considerable. An autodidact, Mendelssohn came to Berlin from Dessau as a young man. His religious and philosophical writings were admired by Kant and unanimously praised by his peers. Indeed, Mendelssohn was regarded as the very model of the "civilized" Jew, immortalized in his friend Lessing's play "Nathan the Wise" (1779). Though attached to Judaism, he nonetheless worked to improve the condition of the Jews, and to this end called for Jewish openness to the non-Jewish world and its culture, which quite suited the philosophers of the Enlightenment.

The movement launched by Mendelssohn and his friends (known as *maskilim*, or "enlighteners") also had its partisans in France, such as Moses Ensheim of Metz (1750–1839), a thinker and man of science, and tutor to Mendelssohn's children. Another resident of Metz, Isaiah Berr Bing (1759–1805), translated Mendelssohn's *Phaedon* (1767) from German into French and Hebrew, versions that appeared in 1786 and 1787, respectively. In this work, Mendelssohn combated superstition in ceremonies and customs as going against the truth of religion. Berr Isaac Berr (1744–1828), the syndic of the Jews of Alsace and spokesman of the delegation sent by the eastern Jews to speak before the Constituent Assembly in 1789, joined the movement in his turn. His translation into French of the work on education by Naphtali Herz Wessely (1725–1805), a German Jew and man of the Enlightenment, was published in Paris in 1790 under the title *Instructions salutaires adressées aux communautés juives de l'Empire de Joseph II* (Useful Lessons Addressed to the Jewish Communities of the Empire of Joseph II). Jews in Metz and Nancy subscribed to the Judeo-German journal of the Enlightenment, *Ha-Me'assef* (The Gatherer), which appeared in the years 1783–97 and 1809–11. Moreover, the *préposé général* of the Alsatian Jews appealed to Mendelssohn himself to intervene on behalf of his constituents. Even so modest a penetration of the movement in France testifies to a relative openness and sensitivity to ideas current in other Jewish communities, particularly that of Berlin, where Jews to a large degree were members of the middle class and attuned to the culture and customs of the surrounding society.

In Bordeaux, French replaced Spanish as the language used in communal records. Jews participated in the intellectual and cultural life of the city, read the *philosophes*, entered into dialogue with Christians and associated with them, thus conforming to the Enlightenment ideal that men overcome their religious differences and communicate on the basis of a certain number of shared interests. Jewish society was plainly not static, for even in those communities that were most attached to tradition internal disagreements began to emerge and, with them, a growing susceptibility to external influences.

Toward Reform

The idea of reforming the Jews thus had taken hold in the minds of the leaders of Jewish groups, albeit to differing degrees. At a time when awareness of the Jewish question was on the rise, in France and elsewhere in Europe, such a project naturally suggested itself. The Alsatian Cerf-Berr financed the plea in favor of the Jews by the Protestant historian Christian Wilhelm von Dohm, *Ueber die buergerliche Verbesserung der Juden* (On the

Civil Improvement of the Jews), written at Mendelssohn's request, which appeared in Berlin in 1781 and was translated into French the following year by Jean Bernoulli under the title *De la réforme politique des Juifs* (On the Political Reform of the Jews).[8] Mirabeau adopted some of the ideas contained in this work and, in 1787, published a pamphlet in London entitled *Sur Moses Mendelssohn, sur la réforme politique des Juifs et en particulier sur la révolution tentée en leur faveur en 1753 dans la Grande-Bretagne* (On Moses Mendelssohn, the Political Reform of the Jews, and in particular the Revolution Attempted on their Behalf in 1753 in Great Britain).

In 1785, the Royal Society of Sciences and Arts of Metz chose as the subject of its competition for 1787 the following question: "Do means exist to make Jews more useful and happier in France?"

As this title indicates, the emancipation of the Jews was hardly contemplated. Nonetheless, the possibility had already begun to be discussed in enlightened circles in France of improving their "productivity"—the sine qua non of any regeneration. Thus the Jews' falling behind was emphasized, together with the need to help them catch up. The question set for the competition also betrayed a vague desire to reform the legal status of the Jews, to better their lot according to the humanitarian perspective championed in enlightened circles of the day—as though the contest's organizers expected positive replies. Such an attitude was not uncharacteristic of political and administrative developments under the Ancien Régime in its final years. It found expression also in the context of the anti-Jewish disturbances in Alsace that led to the abolition by Louis XVI of the body tax in 1784 and to the letters patent of that year. The founding of the Royal Society in Metz, the relative familiarity of its members with local Jews, and the image presented by the Jewish community there, whose leaders were open to modern ideas and who watched out for Jewish interests, help to account for the new thinking as well, apart from the influence of the ideas of Dohm and Mendelssohn.

In a new competition on the same subject held in 1788, none of the essays presented the year before having been judged worthy of recognition, the society's prize was shared among three laureates: the abbé Grégoire (*Essai sur la régénération physique, morale et politique des Juifs*), the Nancy lawyer Claude-Antoine Thiéry (*Dissertation sur cette question: "Est-il des moyens de rendre les Juifs plus utiles et plus heureux en France?"*), and Zalkind Hourwitz, a self-educated Polish Jew introduced to the Enlightenment in Berlin who was living at the time in wretched poverty in Paris, uncomfortable expressing himself in French. No other Jew of higher social standing with a better command of the language presented himself as a candidate in the competition. With the exception of Hourwitz's contribution (*Apologie des Juifs, en réponse à la question: "Est-il des moyens de rendre les Juifs plus heureux et plus utiles en France?"*),[9] the portrait of the Jews that emerges from these essays is not free from prejudice. Their physical and moral degradation is emphasized, and the amelioration of their lot advocated, without any real practical remedies being proposed.[10] Hourwitz, for his part, replied to the society's question as follows: "Cease making them unhappy and useless, by granting them, or rather giving back to them, the right of Citizen of which you have deprived them against all divine and human law, and against your own interest, as a man crippled in one of his limbs. Voltaire is right to say, we are very well informed how to do evil, but not well enough how to do good."[11] He undertook a vigorous defense of the Jews, and of their "extraordinary" qualities, while refuting the argument that they must cease to be Jewish if they wished to become citizens.[12]

The attitude toward the Jews in governing circles evolved as well. If France wished to gradually enter the modern world, it had to establish a uniform political-administrative system applicable to everyone within its borders. Centralization proceeded through the abolition of states within a state and the elimination of privileges in favor of law. Even if it was impossible to contemplate ending discrimination toward the Jews altogether in a state that was still strongly Christian, one nonetheless detects a desire for equal treatment. Socioeconomic change also required the condition of the Jews to be reformed.

After the royal edict of November 1787 granting civil status to Protestants (and, for this purpose, the right to keep a separate register of births, marriages, and deaths), Malesherbes, to whom the edict owed much, was charged by the king in the spring of 1788 to study the situation of the Jews. Earlier he had taken an interest in the subject in his *Second Mémoire sur le mariage des protestants* (1786). He now drew up a questionnaire, sent it to officials whose *généralités* included Jews, informed himself about their situation in the different regions of France, received delegations and reports, compiled documents, and consulted with jurists, all in an informal manner. No doubt his intention was to prepare a memorandum on the Jews, on the model of the one he had written on the Protestants. He has even been credited with organizing the committee that has gone down in history as the "Malesherbes Commission," but which in fact never existed.[13] The Portuguese, in their *Mémoire pour la nation juive portuguaise* sent to Malesherbes on 15 June 1788 in response to the questions he had asked of their syndics, sought continuation and confirmation of the privileges granted them between 1550 and 1776 as well as of their traditional autonomy, freedom to settle in the place of their choice, and admission of their children to public schools and universities for the study of medicine. What they insisted upon most of all, however, was that they not be included in a law applying to all the Jews of France.

For their part, the Jews of the East, in another memorandum entitled *Réflexions sur l'enregistrement de l'édit des non-Catholiques au parlement de*

Metz, et projet pour rendre les Juifs plus utiles et plus heureux en France (Reflections on the Registration of the Edict concerning non-Catholics in the Parliament of Metz, and [the] Plan to Make the Jews More Useful and Happier in France)—an unsigned and undated document, but one nonetheless attributed to them—not only depicted their situation in dark terms but also demanded civil status for themselves, a regular and more democratic form of communal organization, and the right to acquire real estate, to work the land, and to take up the profession of their choice without having to renounce their institutions, their way of life, their customary law, or their traditional practices.

Nonetheless, the reports and memorandums presented to Malesherbes by non-Jewish observers, including Protestants, were not all favorable to the Jews—far from it. One should have thought that the memories of persons who had themselves been persecuted in the past would have been longer and that they would have shown compassion toward the Jews. But not at all.

Malesherbes did not have time to compose his *Mémoire sur la situation présente des affaires*, being occupied from July 1788 by other obligations and especially in preparing a report on "the present state of the Nation." With his disgrace and forced retirement a short time afterward, the matter was dropped. There has been much speculation about Malesherbes's intentions with regard to Jewish reform, and opinion remains divided. Certain Christian authors and monarchists have maintained that credit for the granting of civil rights to the Jews is due chiefly to him and Louis XVI, the Revolution having only followed their lead. Jewish historians have rallied to this thesis, though with qualifications and not for the same reasons. Republican historians, by contrast, have emphasized Malesherbes's coolness toward reform as a man of the Ancien Régime, and the historian Arthur Hertzberg has gone so far as to characterize him as a "conversionist" (i.e., an advocate of measures that would loosen Jewish ties to the community and lead ultimately to their conversion to the Christian faith).[14]

A POLICY OF EMANCIPATION?

The Estates General

Henceforth debate was in the hands of the Estates General, which were to bring about the fall of the Ancien Régime. The Jewish question came up in two forms. First, the *cahiers de doléances*, compilations of local grievances drawn up during the elections to the Estates General convened by Louis XVI on 5 July 1788 as a basis for examining the most pressing problems of the populace, testified among other things to the popular hostility toward the Jews, above all in the eastern provinces. The winter of 1788–89 was particularly harsh, and economic crisis was rife. The Jews were not a major source of concern; their neighbors mentioned them only incidentally. Three hundred seven *cahiers de doléances* called attention to the Jewish problem, in six provinces (*généralités*) and in thirty-three districts (*bailliages*).[15] Complaint centered chiefly on their unfair commercial practices and on usury. The solutions proposed ranged from expulsion to more rigorous enforcement of existing regulations; an intermediate position called for reform of commercial credit and lending against surety. Reading these books of grievances, it becomes clear that some advocated liberal measures toward the Jews while others inclined toward greater severity. The nobility was typically less severe than the clergy, with shifting positions occupied by the Third Estate.

The Jewish problem was posed in still another way when it was a question of their qualification to redact *cahiers de doléances* or to take their place in primary and provincial assemblies. The electoral law defined voters as men at least twenty-five years of age, French by birth or naturalization, domiciled and listed on the tax rolls, which did not in principle exclude Jews. Despite a certain initial reluctance, the Portuguese and Avignonese Jews of Bordeaux and Saint-Esprit-lès-Bayonne did actually take part in elections, but those of Alsace and Lorraine were barred from participating. The latter finally succeeded in obtaining authorization to confer and to send delegates to Paris in order to present their grievances, but in the form of a memorandum (*mémoire*) rather than a book (*cahier*).

It is striking to observe that the concern of Jews at this time was not with political rights. In fact, the representatives of the eastern Jews reiterated their demand for the maintenance and enlargement of their old privileges, seeking equality with respect to taxation, freedom to trade and to settle where they pleased, unfettered access to schools, and the elimination of abuses. The Alsatians also wanted a relaxation of the arrangements created by the letters patent of 1784. The Jews of the east of France aspired to preserve their communal organization, insisting on freedom of worship (particularly the Lorrainers) and permission to build synagogues as they needed. Neither the Sephardim nor the Ashkenazim wished to reexamine their particularism—and this at a moment when society under the Ancien Régime was in the process of coming apart. They asked only that they be allowed to live in peace.[16]

The Beginnings of the Revolution

The National Constituent Assembly was proclaimed on 9 July 1789; on 14 July the Bastille was taken, symbol of the fall of the Ancien Régime; feudal privileges and rights were abolished on 4 August; and on 26 August the Declaration of the Rights of Man and the Citizen (inspired by the American Declaration of Independence in 1776) was adopted. The grievances of the Jews were written out in the same month of August, emphasizing the gap that existed between their world and the rest of French society. At the same moment, riots broke out in Alsace. Once more the Jews were held responsible for the peasants' misery. They fled by the hundreds to Mulhouse and Basel.

It was against this troubled background that the Parisian Jews, nearer the nerve center of events and now ready to renounce their privileges and particular forms of organization, wrote to the assembly on 26 August to demand citizenship. On 31 August, the deputies of the eastern Jews, taking note of the divisions within the Ashkenazic bloc, revised their position and demanded civil and political rights in their turn while proposing that the autonomy of their communities be maintained. The Portuguese expressed no opinion, fearing they would be included in a measure that might lead to the loss of their own privileges, indeed of the community autonomy they wished to preserve. It may be that they preferred to negotiate separately; but perhaps they thought that they had already won their case.

Disturbances continued in Alsace with the return of fugitive Jews. On 14 October, the delegation of the eastern Jews was admitted to the bar of the Constituent; nothing came of this. Debate resumed two months later. The Ashkenazic deputies feared that adoption of the motion for reform would worsen the situation. The motion was tabled, on 24 December, by a vote of 408 to 403 after a stormy debate in which Barnave, Mirabeau, and Robespierre pleaded in favor of the Jews.[17] It was during this debate that Clermont-Tonnerre declared that "everything must be refused to the Jews as a Nation in the sense of a corporate body and everything granted to the Jews as individuals. . . . They must make up neither a political body nor an order within the State; they must individually be citizens."[18] Was this simply for the sake of rhetorical effect? Opinion remained divided. On the same day, however, the Protestants obtained their civil and political rights. Following this failure, Jewish deputies redoubled their efforts.

In January 1790, the Portuguese Jews, pointing to the length of their residence in France, their privileges, and their harmonious integration in society, once again demanded citizenship for themselves. There followed a stormy debate in which Talleyrand ardently defended their cause. Finally they obtained satisfaction on 28 January, by a vote of 374 to 224: "The National Assembly decrees that all the Jews known in France as Portuguese, Spanish, [and] Avignonese Jews will continue to enjoy the rights that they have enjoyed until now, and that are recognized on their behalf by letters patent; and in consequence, they will enjoy the rights of active citizens upon meeting the conditions required by the decrees of the Assembly."[19] The Avignonese Jews mentioned were likewise from Bordeaux. They had profited from their joint—but not always friendly—residence in that city with the Sephardim, finally obtaining recognition as a separate *nation*, as noted earlier, in 1754. The assembly's vote only served to ratify a de facto situation. A number of Bordeaux Jews had also joined the army during the Revolution, and many were members of the National Guard. The fact that, for the revolutionaries, they represented the very model of "emancipatable" Jews explains the priority accorded them.

The question of the Jews of the Comtat and the Ashkenazim remained unresolved. The revolutionary "patriots" of Avignon voted later the same year to join France and the decrees adopted by the Constituent Assembly in Paris were applied to them, including the one relating to the emancipation of Spanish, Portuguese, and Avignonese Jews in France in spite of the fact that it had been adopted prior to the unification vote. The Jews of the Comtat, for their part, decided to remain faithful to the Pope, while adhering to the French constitution and to the principles of the Declaration of the Rights of Man: nothing about their situation changed. It was not until the official proclamation by the assembly of the incorporation of Avignon and the Comtat with France the following year, on 14 September 1791, that all the Jews of the former papal states were to enjoy the right of citizenship.

The Parisian Jews, though they were receptive to the fashionable ideas of the day and served in the National Guard in large numbers, were turned away despite the intervention of the Paris Commune on their behalf. The status of the Jews of the eastern provinces underwent no change; during this time their adversaries, alarmed by the decree of 28 January 1790, excited the populace against them. The press flew into a rage as well, unleashing a violent anti-Jewish campaign. The Jews of Metz nonetheless managed to have the Brancas tax abolished in July 1790. It was only when the Constituent Assembly was on the verge of finishing its work, on 27 September 1791, and then by an almost unanimous vote, that all the Jews of France became citizens on the condition that they renounce their communal status. Surely it would have been difficult for the assembly to split up without having decided a question that touched so closely upon the rights of man.

Indeed, the emancipation of the Jews was the logical consequence of the Declaration of the Rights of Man—the outcome of a whole series of measures taken in the last decades of the Ancien Régime, following in a direct line of descent from the idea of tolerance, which continued to gain ground throughout the eighteenth century, and from the concepts of egalitarianism and individualism. Now citizens, the Jews of France were thus the first to be emancipated in Europe. The Revolution itself thus appears as the conclusion of a long evolution begun earlier under the Ancien Régime.

Having emancipated the Jews, and anxious to circumvent the opposition that the measure was likely to arouse among their adversaries, the assembly ordered that the debts owed them be submitted for review by the district *directoires*, which were charged with determining whether certain debtors deserved to be released from their obligations. Many such debts were never repaid. In the event, emancipation meant easy terms for Christian debtors and the cancellation of numerous debts. The methods of the Ancien Régime had not entirely disappeared.

The emancipation of the Jews had been negotiated by their leaders under circumstances that made it necessary. Ultimately, they were carried along by a movement that in many respects overtook them. No great changes in their way of living were noticeable at first. At the most, one sees a trend toward urbanization following upon the open access to cities, notably in Alsace. The majority of eastern Jews aspired only to a peaceful life; with the exception of a few wealthy families, the fact that they were eligible to vote and hold office was of very little concern to them. By contrast, the Comtat Venaissin lost a large number of Jews to emigration in the space of twenty years. Considering Jewish communities as a whole, one finds that their reactions to emancipation were quite varied.

CHAPTER SEVEN

New Perspectives

THE INTEGRATION AND ACCULTURATION of the Jews in France was the result of a long process of adjustment to new conditions and preparation for joining the society that henceforth welcomed them. Jewish "regenerators" appropriated the discourse of those who promoted emancipation in representing integration and acculturation as the sole path to becoming *Français-israélites*—French citizens of the Jewish faith. But resistance on the part of the receiving society was not altogether absent. In the nineteenth century this came to take the form of anti-Semitism under circumstances favorable to its continued development that revealed how fragile Jewish integration still was at this time.

Today it is frequently asked whether emancipation, through the disappearance of community autonomy to which it gave rise, was not fundamentally responsible for the gradual "dejudaization" of the Jews of France. What is perhaps not fully taken into account is the almost inevitable character of this disappearance. The new state, being based on law, could hardly tolerate privileged groups in its midst without contradicting Jacobin principles.

Moreover, recent work has shown that this supposed dejudaization (which would more accurately be called secularization) did not everywhere follow the same rhythm, and that widespread assimilation, in the sense of an effacement of Jewish identity, did not actually occur. Throughout the nineteenth century, if Judaism as a religion lost its appeal for many Jews, it nonetheless remained the theoretical frame of reference for all discussions of Jewish identity. Nor did emancipation at all weaken feelings of group identity and solidarity among the Jews of France.

In Germany, citizenship came only *after* the integration of the Jews with the surrounding society: from a very early stage German Jews had done their utmost to erase any professional and religious differences, as well as differences in appearance, that might hinder them in forming closer relations with other segments of society. The Wissenschaft des Judentums (Science of Judaism)[1] was thus born together with the Reform movement[2] in the first decades of the nineteenth century in a context that, though it was non-emancipationist from the legal point of view, showed increasing signs of integration. The aim of such movements was to attach a positive value to Judaism as a culture and religion in the eyes of the surrounding society, which was reluctant to make Jews full-fledged citizens. These developments, in their turn, provoked a reaction in the form of movements calling for a return to tradition, with a Neo- or Modern Orthodoxy[3] taking root at the same time as well.

In France, the opposite situation came about: emancipation preceded integration. The process of "regeneration" that occupied French Jewish reformers for a good part of the nineteenth century involved mainly socio-economic issues and education, and worship only to a lesser extent. The ambitions of community leaders proved to be nearer those of the leaders of the Jewish Enlightenment, who advocated reforms that were neither radical nor likely to alienate Jews from their faith.

THE TERROR

The Terror, with its anti-religious policy directed against recalcitrant priests, did not spare the Jews either. In September 1793, Protestant and Catholic churches along with synagogues were closed and turned into Temples of Reason, clubs, or public stores. Observance of the Jewish Sabbath (*Shabbat*) as well as Sunday services were prohibited. Religious instruction was stopped, rabbis were suspended from their duties, and liturgical objects confiscated. Nonetheless, worship continued to be carried on secretly in private homes. Jewish notables also began to be harrassed because of their political sympathies, real or imagined, and their activities. Some Jews were guillotined on account of their ties with the Girondins and various factions; others were accused in Alsace of complicity with opponents of the Revolution who had sought refuge there.

Persecution was not systematic, but certain Jacobins were still motivated by prejudices of a Voltairean sort. This was not the case, on the other hand, with Robespierre and his circle. A few Jews were also found among the anti-religious militants in Paris and in the southwest. Everything considered, the Jews did not suffer from events more than others, except in the East, where anti-religious struggle turned into anti-Jewish unrest.

Thermidor—the overthrow of Robespierre—and the subsequent restoration of freedom of worship put an end to abuses. But Jewish communities were disorganized and destitute. What is more, they were forced to rebuild their ranks at a time when members' ties to them were becoming loosened. Individuals were not any better provided for. Their economic condition, especially in the East, remained fragile. Throughout the Directory and the Consulate and until the beginning of the Empire they practiced the same minor trades—pawnbroking, for example—that aroused hostility on the part of their neighbors.

UNDER NAPOLEON

From a legal point of view, the Napoleonic period constituted a step backward for the Jews. On the other hand, at the level of religious organization, it marked a step forward.

As a consequence of the Concordat of 1801 and the "Organic Articles" of 1802, Catholics and Protestants were reorganized and submitted to official regulation. This was not the case with adherents of the Jewish religion, which entered into a period of relative anarchy—the direct effect of emancipation itself in liberating individual Jews from religious, financial, and other obligations vis-à-vis their communities. The question of the status of the Jewish faith was put off till later, the delay being justified by the fact that the Jews made up more a people than a religion. It was the Jewish communities themselves that demanded regulation in order to deal with their difficulties. They even presented proposals of their own.

Napoleon ended up posing the problem, though in quite different terms. And to this matter he added another having to do with the suppression of usury and the complete assimilation of the Jews as French citizens. At the beginning of his career he did not seem to harbor anti-Jewish sentiments. He did not know much about the Jews, even if he remained captive to a certain number of anti-Jewish prejudices. Passing through Strasbourg on his return from Austerlitz, on 23–24 January 1806, he heard complaints brought against the Jews by the prefect and local notables. As always, the complaints concerned usury. He resolved to give serious consideration to the matter. In this he was not influenced solely by the accusations he had heard in Alsace; the same question had been brought before him earlier, in March-April 1805, with the submission by his justice minister of a report on Jewish usury to the Council of State. The council decided not to limit the rate of interest then in effect.

Following Napoleon's stopover in Strasbourg, Catholics and monarchists calling for a return to the old restrictions launched an anti-Jewish campaign in the press. Jews (and some liberals) responded to these attacks by emphasizing the progress made by Jews since emancipation. Their arguments made an impression upon the emperor. The justice minister had not given up, however. Returning to the charge, he no longer demanded that the rate of interest be regulated, as he had done in the past; he now called for measures uniquely affecting the Jews. With Napoleon's approval the dossier was sent to the Council of State, which at the time had real advisory powers, accompanied by a note that contained the following clauses: annulment of mortgages held by Jews, prohibition against taking out new mortgages for a period of ten years, submission of all those who did not own property to professional licensing (from 1 January 1807) and revocation of the citizenship rights of this same class. These arrangements were to be particularly applied to Jews who had come to France during the previous ten years from Poland and Germany.[4] The interior minister also presented a report to the council in which he recommended delaying, under certain conditions, legal proceedings brought against delinquent debtors of Jews in the departments of the Haut-Rhin and the Bas-Rhin. Under the influence of anti-Jewish writings and denunciations, then, Napoleon left it to his ministers to devise measures that were contrary to revolutionary principles of equality.

After stormy debate, however, the Council of State decided almost unanimously to sustain existing legislation with respect to disputes between debtors and creditors in the Haut- and Bas-Rhin, declining to resort to emergency measures in the matter of the Jews. This legalistic position, presented by the council to Napoleon in its session of 30 April 1806, provoked a further show of hostility toward the Jews, who found themselves reproached by the emperor for their misdeeds, their moral degradation, and their lack of patriotism: "The French government cannot look with indifference upon a debased, degraded nation, capable of every sort of low action, having exclusive possession of the two fine departments of Alsace; the Jews must be considered as a nation and not as a sect. It is a nation within the Nation. . . . The Jews are not in the same category as the Protestants and the Catholics; they must be judged in terms of political law and not in terms of civil law, since they are not citizens." Napoleon now ordered a decree containing restrictive measures to be prepared. Then, in a sudden reversal, during the session of 7 May, he decided against taking arbitrary steps and in favor of including the Jews in reforms. He accepted that "it would be weakness to hunt the Jews; it would be strength to correct them." For this purpose he called for an assembly of the Estates General of the Jews, consisting of fifty or sixty representatives who were to convene in a "general synagogue of the Jews" in Paris on 15 June.[5] He may have hoped that by doing this it would be possible to avoid a clash with the Council of State.

The Assembly of Notables

A decree published on 30 May 1806 granted a respite of one year to debtors of the eastern Jews and summoned to Paris an Assembly of Notables chosen by the prefects from among the most upright and enlightened of the Jews, religious and lay leaders alike. The measure aroused discontent and anxiety in Jewish circles, for it allowed the government to gather information as a preliminary step toward the abolishment of usury and regulation of worship that would help carry out the famous program of Jewish regeneration.

The assembly, composed at the outset of ninety-five notables representing all the departments in which there were Jewish communities, gathered in Paris on 26 July 1806; sixteen others, coming from Italy, joined the group in August. It thus numbered one hundred eleven members, who seldom debated all together.[6] These notables were not really informed about the purpose of their mission or about the debates of the Council of State that had gone before. A dozen questions were transmitted to the delegates. They were aimed at determining whether Jewish laws agreed with the provisions of the common law and how great an attachment Jews felt to the empire. These twelve questions bore upon polygamy, divorce, exogamous marriages, brotherhood between Christians and Jews, Jewish patriotism, the appointment of rabbis, their authority and the extent of their jurisdiction, professions forbidden by Jewish law, and usury.

The notables hastened to reply that "[our] religion orders that the law of the prince be regarded as the supreme law in civil and political matters,"[7] which amounted to recognizing the supremacy of French civil law. Polygamy had already been abolished in Europe in the Middle Ages. Both civil and religious divorce were considered essential. As for the awkward question of exogamous marriage, which Napoleon wished to encourage in order to assist the integration of Jews in Christian society, the assembly tried to get around it by responding that "rabbis would not be more disposed to bless the marriage of a Christian woman with a Jew or of a Jewish woman with a Christian than priests would [be ready to] consent to bless such unions." The delegates unanimously proclaimed the patriotism of the Jews and condemned usury as contrary to charity, though they did not condemn lending at interest for commercial purposes, either between Jews or between Jews and Christians; these rates were calculated in proportion to the risk incurred. They added that Jewish law did not forbid the exercise of any profession. As for rabbis, neither law nor custom governed either their jurisdiction—nonexistent since the Jews had become citizens—or their appointment, the terms of which were variable.

The questions posed were not innocent ones, and the atmosphere in which they were formulated was not altogether benevolent. The welcome given to the responses varied, depending on whether they were heard by Champagny, the interior minister, who was well disposed to the assembly, or by the imperial commissioners, who were rather suspicious. On the other hand, virtually no echo of the proceedings reached the public. The few repercussions that could be detected in the press were unfavorable. The Jewish delegates, for their part, remained on their guard, convinced of the underlying hostility of the proceedings.[8]

THE GRAND SANHEDRIN

Having acquainted himself with the replies of the assembly, Napoleon expressed the wish that the notables form a "Grand Sanhedrin," thus restoring a political-religious institution of ancient Israel that had not existed for fourteen centuries.[9] Why a Sanhedrin? Because since the days of this ancient "high court," no Jewish authority had been competent to lay down rules that could be applied to the whole of the Jewish world. The new Sanhedrin, composed as before of seventy-one members—two-thirds of them rabbis, to reinforce the authority of its decisions—were to give religious form to the replies furnished by the assembly. Napoleon thus entertained the illusion of Jewish autonomy, seeking to establish laws that would seem to follow from wishes expressed by the Jews themselves. But these wishes had been expressed only on account of what was now at stake as a result of the questions that had been put to them.

The Grand Sanhedrin met in February 1807, presided over by the Alsatian rabbi Joseph David Sinzheim (1745–1812). Having been appointed by a civil power, this court could not pretend to have the same authority as its ancient counterpart in the eyes of traditional Jews. The replies of the assembly and those of the Sanhedrin differed only in tone. Whereas the former had expressed opinions, the latter gave orders. The Sanhedrin proclaimed that Judaism countenanced religious arrangements and political arrangements, the former absolute and intemporal, the latter admitting of suspension. The decisions of the Sanhedrin were presented as deriving directly from Jewish law rather than from any need to submit to temporal power. A month after its first session, having fulfilled its task, the Sanhedrin was dissolved.

The Assembly of Notables was then charged with examining the plans for reform. Agreement was reached on the question of reorganizing religious administration, though not with regard to the questions of usury and exogamous marriage, on which the emperor wished to impose his views. On 6 April 1807, the assembly, like the Sanhedrin before it, was dissolved.

Three decrees were finally promulgated on 17 March 1808. The first two concerned administrative reorganization and the terms of application of the ruling approved by the Assembly of Notables in December 1806. The autonomous communities of the past were replaced by a central consistory and, for departments having at least 2,000 Jews, a system of local consistories. These boards were composed of rabbis and laymen nominated by local Jewish notables and confirmed by the state, which amounted to official recognition of the Jews as a distinct religious group. Contrary to its policy with regard to the clergy of other denominations, however, the state would not pay the salaries of rabbis. This new system brought together for the first time all the Jews of France in a single centralized organization—something communities throughout the country, destabilized by emancipation and its aftermath, needed. At the same time, it played a useful role assisting the state in maintaining order within these communities. In its main features, however, the new dispensation did not differ greatly from the regime to which other faiths were subject.

The third decree, later known as the "infamous decree," was of a different nature and, in adopting some of the discriminatory practices of the Ancien Régime, subjected the Jews to a system of legalized inequality that was to remain in force for ten years. On the one hand, it ordered the reconsideration of debts owed to Jewish lenders and provided in certain cases for the reduction, indeed cancellation, of such debts upon judicial review; on the other hand, looking to the future, it required Jewish merchants to carry a license issued annually by the prefect, the granting of which would be conditional on the favorable opinion of the municipal councils and consistories. As for conscription, Jews could no longer hire replacements; this law was, however, relaxed in 1812. Immigration to Alsace was prohibited. Owing to exemptions granted Jews in certain other departments, only those of Alsace and Lorraine were affected by the provisions of the decree. In the last analysis it worked only to marginalize the Jews of France and of the kingdom of Italy, lately conquered by Napoleon's armies, by preventing their integration.

Another decree dated 20 July 1808 required Jews to register their patronymics and personal names with the local records office. The point of this was to oblige them to bear permanent names, which until then had not always been the case. At the same time they were forbidden from taking patronymics from the Bible or adopting local place-names.

THE CONSISTORIES

In 1808, the central consistory was set up on the model of the administrative organization instituted for Protestants with the establishment of Catholicism as the official religion. Next came seven departmental consistories, at the beginning of 1809, not counting those of the Jewish communities of the Rhineland and Italy, whose number varied depending on the pace of imperial conquest.

Over time a hierarchical and centralized organization took shape, becoming an integral part of Jewish life in France. The duties initially assigned to the consistories included administration of Jewish affairs, "regeneration" through education, increased productivity through apprenticeship in useful (specialized) trades, "moral" and social improvement and the maintenance of social order. Thus religious responsibilities were combined with secular ones as well. At the initiative of the consistories themselves, their authority was gradually expanded to include protection of Jewish personal and political interests, exclusive control of all Jewish institutions, and training of rabbis.

The central consistory in Paris, which stood at the summit of the consistorial hierarchy, was statutorily constituted of three rabbis and two lay members who were nominated by the government and subsequently elected. Through the Ministry of Religions it represented the Jews before the government. Then there came the local consistories, covering one or more departments—sometimes more than a hundred communities in all. They governed the affairs of these communities and were answerable in turn to the central consistory.

By statute, the consistories were initially composed of one or two rabbis and three lay members, elected by twenty-five notables named by the government from among the most reputable and wealthiest Jews in each consistorial district. The same persons were often reelected; they belonged to dynasties that had made their fortunes since the Revolution, descendants of the Cerf-Berr and Ratisbonne families, and later, most prominently, the Rothschilds. In general these figures were not observant Jews, but they were not assimilated, either. Typically they were businessmen. It was only toward the middle of the nineteenth century that a few academics and members of the liberal professions began to be elected. It may be wondered how far these consistories were representative of the Jewish masses. The oligarchic regime meant that the consistorial system rapidly ended up becoming conservative from the social and political point of view. Its constituents, not feeling themselves fully represented, showed less and less enthusiasm for paying the religion tax, instituted in 1811, which led as a result to significant financial difficulties.

It was only with the promulgation of a law favorable to minorities in 1831, under the July Monarchy, that the question was partly settled. Henceforth ministers of the Jewish faith, like those of the Christian denominations, drew salaries from the public treasury. During this period and under the Second Empire, moreover, Catholicism ceased to be the state religion, becoming instead the religion of the majority of the French population.

The central consistory created specifically Jewish institutions whose activities were concentrated in three areas: charitable works, administration of religious affairs, and supervision of youth through the creation of primary schools for poor children and of vocational schools. Pursuant to a decree of 1829, the Central Rabbinical School of Metz was founded the following year with a view to replacing the old talmudic academies (*yeshivot*) that had been closed during the Terror. Orphanages, childrens' homes, and a Jewish hospital (the Hôpital Rothschild, opened in Paris in

1852) completed this network of wholly Jewish institutions, modeled on those of other faiths at a time when the clergy insisted on their prerogatives in the domains of charity and religion.

Several amendments between 1819 and 1844 strengthened the consistorial system. The ordinance of 1844, signed by Louis Philippe and subsequently modified, was elevated into a sort of charter of Judaism, remaining in force until the separation of church and state in 1905.

The consistory, with broad powers that verged on despotism, was dominated by the lay element that chose rabbis and grand rabbis. The aim was to entrust the conduct of affairs to reputable liberal figures who would have preeminence over the ministers of the faith. The grand rabbi of the central consistory would later occupy a privileged place of authority that made him in some sense the equivalent in the Jewish faith of a Catholic archbishop. Those who held the office were on the whole considered progressive.

INTERNAL DIVISIONS

The revolution of 1848 and the short-lived triumph of egalitarian feeling led to the reestablishment of universal suffrage. In so doing it revived a longstanding debate within the Jewish collectivity between liberals on the one side and the Orthodox on the other, the latter being dominant among the poorer classes and excluded from the consistories owing to the system of tax qualification. The Orthodox enjoyed the support of the Jewish population in the East, particularly in Alsace, which resisted cultural uniformity and remained attached to tradition. Moreover, the Orthodox constituted the core of the opposition to the reformist tendencies of the leaders of the central consistory, forcing them to adopt a more moderate line. The government offered universal suffrage in the hope tempers would cool. This encouraged some Orthodox to enter into the consistories, again particularly in Alsace. But the liberals continued to dominate, above all among the consistorial authorities in the capital. Debate resumed in the aftermath of the coup d'état of 2 December 1851. In order to protect their supremacy, the liberals called for repeal of the decree of December 1849 conferring the right to vote on all Jews twenty-five years of age or more and sought to modernize the religion.

L'Israélite français—a moderate journal founded by Élie (Halfon) Halévy (1760–1826), a German Jew by birth, man of the Enlightenment, and father of the composer Jacques Halévy—appeared briefly in 1817–18, advocating the gallicization of worship and its adaptation to new conditions. Shortly afterward the question of reform was starkly posed by Olry Terquem (1782–1865), librarian of the Bibliothèque de l'Arsenal in Paris, whose writings appeared under the pseudonym "Tsarphati" (the Hebrew word for French). The appearance, beginning in 1821, of his *Lettres tsarphatiques françaises ou Lettres d'un israélite français à ses coreligionnaires* (French Sephardic Letters or Letters from a French Israelite to His Coreligionists), first in the form of pamphlets, then in articles published in the Metz newspaper *Courrier de la Moselle*, marked the beginnings of the liberal movement in France.[10] Terquem's argument consisted in saying that, though religion was immutable, the nature of worship could nonetheless be modified. He and other extreme liberals, whose influence faded in the 1840s, called for the *Shabbat* to be moved to Sunday, the use of the French language in worship services, the replacement of circumcision by a symbolic ceremony, abolition of certain practices judged to be unacceptable, and reexamination of the role of women, for example. By pulling down the barriers that kept Jews out of French society they hoped to bring them into closer contact with it. The question they asked themselves, and the question that other less radical liberals asked themselves as well, was how the Jewish religion could be made meaningful in the nineteenth century for Jews who were integrated in French society but who nonetheless felt alienated from Judaism.

Another pole of liberal thought, more moderate and by far the most important, was constituted by the creation in 1840 of the journal *Les Archives israélites* by Samuel Cahen (1796–1861), like Olry Terquem a native of Metz. In 1844, Simon Bloch (1810–97), secretary of the central consistory, founded *L'Univers israélite*, the mouthpiece of Orthodoxy. French Judaism was not reducible to these two tendencies, however. There were also those who described themselves as indifferent—a majority in bourgeois circles—as well as a small group of assimilated Jews, likewise coming from the wealthy fringes of Jewish society.

In 1856, a consistorial conference of rabbis decided to undertake reform of the service by abridging prayers considered too long, introducing a sermon in French, authorizing organ music (under certain conditions), and adopting the walking-out dress worn by Catholic priests for rabbis in the synagogues. It was also agreed to transfer the Rabbinical School of Metz to Paris, where from 1859 it was known as a "seminary," the *Séminaire Israélite de France*. Marriage and burial ceremonies were standardized, and the section reserved for women in the synagogues was enlarged. The liberals had gained part of what they wanted. There remained the question of balloting procedure in consistorial elections, which had undergone various modifications. Universal suffrage was definitively instituted only in 1880. These amendments, despite the introduction of some elements taken from the practice of Christian worship, proved quite moderate and did not lead to a genuine movement for reform as in liberal Jewish circles in Germany.

The consistories tried to achieve a certain unity by making very limited concessions to various factions in the hope of bringing back into the fold those Jews who were deserting their customary places of worship in ever greater numbers but who nonetheless had not renounced their Jewish identity. This mounting disaffection did not prevent the construction of great synagogues (now called, in the ideological terminology of the day, "temples"). Having become integrated in French society, Jews thus no longer feared displaying their identity in public. The first Jewish community to erect such a temple was that of Bordeaux, the longest integrated of the Jewish communities in France. Constructed in 1812, the building's facade was placed along the line of the street, something seldom done until then. In Alsace, synagogues were not visible from the outside until the 1840s. From 1790 to 1914, two hundred fifty synagogues were built. The accelerated integration of the Jews during the Second Empire was accompanied by a certain frenzy in construction, which subsided toward the end of the century and especially in the first decade of the twentieth century. The new immigrants from eastern Europe, still traditional in their ways, preferred oratories to monumental synagogal architecture, which reflected a desire for recognition on the part of native-born Jews who had contributed to the cost of their construction. In the twentieth century, up until the eve of the Holocaust, the style of synagogal architecture tended to simplicity—a simplicity associated with domestic architecture and dictated as much by social and political circumstances as by the redefinition of the synagogue itself, which was no longer solely a place of worship.[11]

The consistories were tangible proof of the renaissance of the Jews as a religious group and, moreover, furnished a guarantee of the patriotism of citizens of the Jewish faith. They served as a model for the institutions of other Jewish groups outside of France.

IN A SECULAR STATE

The separation of church and state in 1905 was a harsh blow to the monopoly of the consistories, founded on a fragile consensus. They were thus deprived of the political and financial support of the government. In response, religious associations were created that subsequently joined together to form the Union des Associations Cultuelles Israélites de France et d'Algérie. The term "consistory" was retained, now designating only the administrative council of each religious association. Responsibility for Jewish affairs at the local level now fell to these councils. Alsace-Lorraine, restored to France only after the Great War, was not subject to the same regime. Religious affairs in these provinces continued to be administered by the departmental consistories under the financial supervision of the state, which also paid the salaries of the rabbis.

Institutional activities diversified in the wake of these upheavals, accompanied by a religious pluralism whose development had been slowed by the ubiquitous presence of the consistories but not wholly arrested; attempts at reestablishing community autonomy, if only through the foundation of Orthodox communities, had already been made in the nineteenth century. In 1907, the Union Libérale Israélite de Tendance Réformée was legally recognized as a religious organization and the same year opened a synagogue in Paris, in the rue Copernic, that henceforth was attended by the Jewish elite. For their part, the Jewish immigrants who poured into France during the last decades of the nineteenth century, largely working class and still unused to their new environment, resisted the authority of the consistories. Taking advantage of the new system, they founded congregations that better responded to their actual aspirations and allowed them to choose their rabbis without obtaining consistorial approval.

The secularization of the state further deepened disaffection with the consistories. The consistory in Paris now counted among its members only 5.5 percent of the Jews living in the capital.[12] Despite the ensuing financial difficulties, the central consistory managed to maintain in operation its four primary schools, its vocational and professional schools, and its *université populaire* (providing instruction aimed at the immigrant working-class population) while continuing to carry on its charitable work. Even if it had lost a good many of its powers, the central consistory continued to represent French Judaism as a faith before the public authorities.

Entry into French Society

THE INTEGRATION AND ADVANCEMENT of the Jews did not come about at once under the influence of emancipating legislation. Some time was yet needed to absorb the repercussions of the past and to adjust to the new order of things under changing circumstances. Once more it is difficult to speak of uniform progress; there were steps both forward and back. The First Empire, with its exceptional measures, constituted a ten-year period of stagnation. The Bourbon Restoration, by not renewing the infamous decree on its expiration in 1818, lifted the last restrictions weighing upon the Jews. Under the July Monarchy, the ministers of the Jewish faith were remunerated by the public treasury, pursuant to the law of 8 February 1831, which represented an advance in the recognition of the Jews as a religious group. Under the same regime, thanks to the efforts of the future justice minister Adolphe Crémieux (1796–1880), the judicial procedure *more judaico*—by which Jews summoned to appear in court were required to take an oath on the Bible, in accordance with the ceremonial practice of an earlier time—was abrogated in 1846. The Second Republic, and above all the Second Empire, proved to be an auspicious period for the Jews, for it was then that integration began to become a reality. It is true that its rhythm was not identical for all Jewish populations in the country, whose local histories varied, any more than it was for different social classes within these populations. Additionally, there were differences in large cities, such as Paris, between groups of immigrants from other parts of France and Jews who had long been resident there.

Beginning with the last decades of the nineteenth century, moreover, the presence of new immigrants—especially those from eastern Europe—made complete integration more difficult to achieve. Immigrants continued to arrive until the eve of the Second World War. Their experiences were not all the same. Gallicized Jews who came from the Levant adapted more easily to their new homeland than others. Throughout the Third Republic, the gap widened between French-born Jews, for whom integration was no longer an issue, and the new immigrants from eastern Europe. This was due not only to the fact that these immigrants had only recently arrived but also to their differing strategies as groups in French society. The question of integration thus did not cease to matter within French Jewry; and it would continue to matter still after the Second World War, with the arrival of Jews from North Africa in the aftermath of decolonization. This time the situation was different, since a large number of the new arrivals were already French speakers and citizens. The question of integration is nonetheless inherent in the very nature of the French nation-state, which recognizes no category of ethnic community, preferring to consign nonindigenous elements to the melting pot of a single and indivisible French nation—an imposed model whose success depends in large part on the reactions of the people it aims at integrating, which vary as a function of their own backgrounds and expectations.

A SPECTACULAR INTEGRATION

The Jews of the Southwest

The integration of the Jews of the southwest (2,100 in Bordeaux and 1,100 in Saint-Esprit-lès-Bayonne in 1808) was not yet complete by the mid-nineteenth century, particularly among the middle and poorer classes. Despite their relative integration with the surrounding society, it would be an exaggeration to speak of assimilation in the sense of unreserved identification with the French model.

The demography of Bordeaux Jews at the beginning of the nineteenth century is that of an urban group that entered the modern age without giving up its attachment to the values of enlightened Judaism peculiar to the former Portuguese *nation*. In Bordeaux, between 1793 and 1820, there were only thirty-six mixed marriages (between Jews and non-Jews) out of a total of three hundred and ninety marriages. The high point was reached in 1794, the year of the Terror, with eight cases—a sign of the liberated morals of the Revolution. Generally speaking, exogamous marriage was a marginal phenomenon, with fewer than three cases in most years. Typically it involved a Jewish man and a non-Jewish woman; this sort of union, which caused the husband's status to drop somewhat in the eyes of both the Jewish and the Christian communities, usually amounted to regularizing a prior relationship.

Business relations between Jews and non-Jews were frequent, but rarely led to true association. A close look at the socioprofessional pattern of Jewish occupations in Bordeaux reveals that neither the Revolution nor emancipation brought about any profound change. In commerce and banking, such changes as there were followed the general trend in France as a whole and, in particular, that of Bordeaux during the revolutionary and Napoleonic periods. Commerce remained a dominant activity among Jews. Very few chose new occupations, as the advocates of emancipation had urged. The choice of trades from one generation to another was relatively stable and showed limited mobility.

At the beginning of the nineteenth century in Bordeaux, 88 percent of future spouses lived in the same neighborhood, with 88 percent belonging to the same socioprofessional milieu. This level of endogamy is a sign of the cohesion of the Jewish population, particularly among the Portuguese of the city, in the face of a regular flow of immigrants from the east and southeast. Though subject to no restrictions with respect to place of residence, they still continued at the beginning of the nineteenth century to inhabit a single neighborhood. Succeeding generations soon quit this "voluntary ghetto" and scattered throughout the city.

With a moderate birth rate (in 1808 the rate was 2.6 per couple; 3.1 if childless couples are not counted) and a relatively low mortality rate (20 per 1,000), the Jews of Bordeaux exhibited a pattern of family behavior that hardly distinguished them from the rest of the city's population.[1]

In the last decade of the nineteenth century, the Bordeaux and Bayonne/Saint-Esprit regions numbered 2,411 and 890 Jewish residents of long standing with solid economic interests, respectively. Only a few small towns, such as Bidache, Peyrehorade, and Labastide-Clairence had lost their Jewish population.[2] Even so, the area no longer attracted Jews; the poles of attraction were henceforth Paris and, secondarily, Marseilles and Lyons.

Throughout the nineteenth century, the Jews of Bordeaux participated in the political life of their city through their notables, who held various administrative posts. They appeared in a number of roles on the national stage as well. In cultural life, the writer Catulle Mendès (1841–1909) and the dramatist Georges de Porto-Riche (1849–1930) were among the best known. Bordeaux Jews also made their mark in journalism, with Eugénie Foa (née Rodrigues-Henriques, 1796–1850), Moïse Polydor Millaud (1813–71)—founder of the *Petit Journal*, among other papers—and Jules Mirès, who was also a banker; these last two, Millaud and Mirès, born in Bordeaux, came from Avignonese families. As historians, pedagogues (such as David Lévi-Alvarès [b. 1794], who devoted himself to the advancement of women's education), and musicians, they generally made their careers in Paris; their work rarely showed signs of Jewish inspiration. In the field of business, the names of two brothers stand out, Émile-Jacob (1800–1875) and Isaac (1806–80) Pereire, followers of Saint-Simon, as well as that of Olinde Rodrigues (1795–1851), the financier of Saint-Simonism.

The Jews of the Southeast

For their part, the Jews of the southeast emigrated very early to the cities of the Midi, and also to Lyons and Paris. In 1808, the number of Jews from the old *carrières* stood at 360 in Carpentras, 130 in Avignon, 49 in Cavaillon, and 22 in Isle-sur-la-Sorgue—out of a total Jewish population of 77,162 in sixty-five departments (including occupied territories); in 1815, this total fell to 46,663.[3] Under the Third Republic, the *carrières* of Cavaillon and Isle-sur-la-Sorgue disappeared. Their former inhabitants rapidly acclimated themselves to their new places of settlement, sometimes spectacularly so: neither by their language, nor their culture, nor their attitude to French society did they appear to be foreigners. As early as 1791–92 they had taken part in the political life of the cities where they now lived—in Nîmes, for example, where they supported the revolution in massive numbers. In general, however, this integration did not amount to total assimilation, eclipsing their Jewish identity, any more than it did for their fellow Jews in the southwest.

In 1870, Adolphe Crémieux—celebrated lawyer and statesman, future justice minister, French born and bred—arranged for French nationality to be granted to Algerian Jews by means of the decree that bears his name. Moreover, he worked actively in defense of Jewish causes. Other sons of Jewish families originally from the Comtat and Avignon made brilliant careers for themselves, particularly in the capital, as magistrates, journalists, writers, bankers, and politicians, among them Alfred Naquet (1834–1916), who sponsored the law establishing divorce in 1884. Later generations—notably including the composer Darius Milhaud (1892–1974) and René Cassin (1887–1976), winner of the Nobel Peace Prize in 1968—distinguished themselves in various fields as well.

FROM TRADITION TO INTEGRATION

Integration proceeded more slowly for Jews in the East, where communal customs and institutions persisted.

Between 1789 and 1861, French Jewry went from about 40,000 to 79,964, representing 0.2 percent of the total population—Jewish population as a proportion of the world population then being about 0.3 percent.[4] In the departments of the Bas-Rhin and the Haut-Rhin, and in Moselle, Meurthe, and Seine, this percentage ranged from 1.3 to 3.6 percent.[5] In 1808, 26,070 Jews inhabited Alsace and 10,896 Lorraine.[6] By 1861 these numbers had risen to 34,998 and 14,864, respectively, according to the general census, while the Jewish population in the country had increased by 71 percent between 1808 and 1861. In 1808, Alsace-Lorraine was home to about 79 percent of the Jewish population of France; by 1861 it contained only 63 percent, and five years later only 57 percent.[7]

In the middle of the century, Jewish groups in the East remained largely rural, and this despite a sizable shift of population to towns, above all on the part of Alsatians who had been forbidden to live in them under the Ancien Régime. They were generally concentrated in medium-sized towns and villages. In Lorraine, Jews lived for the most part in small communities. Jewish migration within France was not directly linked to industrialization, as was the case for the rest of the population. Mobility occurred in two stages: first, toward cities within the region, and then toward Paris and other major metropolitan areas.

Between 1820 and 1870, between a third and a half of the Jewish population of Alsace emigrated at least once, typically remaining in the region. Strasbourg, which numbered 1,476 Jews in 1808, had 2,820 in 1863— 3.4 percent of the city's total population, making it the second largest Jewish community after Paris. By the middle of the century, 72 percent of the men and 75 percent of the women in the city had been born outside Strasbourg.[8] The annexation of Alsace-Lorraine by Germany in 1871 increased emigration to France; the urban middle classes, more familiar with France (as much for economic reasons as from patriotic feeling), headed mainly for Paris and the Paris region, as did their non-Jewish compatriots. The rural populace looked instead toward the United States and Latin America, a movement already begun on a small scale during the period of crisis between 1846 and 1855. The census of 1872 revealed that 34 percent of the Jews in Paris were born in Alsace-Lorraine.

In 1871–72, 11 percent of the region's total population (all religions taken together) chose French citizenship. About 6,000 Jews did so during this period, and almost 12,000 between the years 1871 and 1914.[9] At the time of annexation, Alsace-Lorraine counted 40,938 Jews, amounting to almost 3 percent of the total population. In 1910, there were only 30,483 (a bit less than 2 percent of the total population), with nearly a quarter of this number having come from Germany owing to industrial development in the region. Not only emigration but also the decline in the birthrate contributed to the demographic decline.

In the first decades of the nineteenth century, only 25 percent of French Jewry lived in towns and cities. Its real urbanization occurred only between 1841 and 1860: by the latter date, half the Jewish population was urbanized. But, in 1871, only 22 percent of the Jews in Alsace lived in towns having more than 10,000 inhabitants. It was not until 1910, when Alsace-Lorraine was part of the German Reich, that the threshold of 45 percent was reached.[10] This evolution gradually signalled the demise of the ancient Jewish *nation* in the region and opened the way to a process of acculturation and embourgeoisement that was already becoming a reality, if only on the socioeconomic level.

At the very beginning of the nineteenth century, the average marrying age of young Jewish women in Alsace was about twenty-three years. Between 1820 and 1860 it went from under twenty-seven to over twenty-eight years. Their husbands were two or three years older at the time of marriage. Under the Second Empire, Jews married at an older age than

Christian couples in Alsace. The size of families in Alsace did not change considerably during the first half of the nineteenth century. According to the census of 1808, Jewish women in Alsace-Lorraine between the ages of forty-one and forty-five had on average 3.8 children living at home. If one considers couples in general for the same period, without limitation as to age, the average is 3.4. In 1846, it was 2.8 in Strasbourg and 2.9 in the countryside.[11] This tendency increased under the German occupation. The fertility of the Jews was less than that of the rest of the population. In 1896, it amounted to 19 births per 1,000 in Strasbourg, whereas it was 31 per 1,000 for the inhabitants of the city as a whole. In 1905, these figures were 18 and 28 per 1,000, respectively. The low proportion of Jewish marriages also explains such a low birthrate. This drop turns out to have been more significant in the cities of the region, a consequence of embourgeoisement since the middle class had a higher proportion of Jews than non-Jews in Alsace-Lorraine, and particularly Strasbourg. The rate of Jewish (planned) fertility corresponded to that for the non-Jewish bourgeoisie of Strasbourg. In 1910, in the two wealthy districts of the city, Place de la République and Université, the respective birthrates were 18.6 and 20.6 per 1,000; the rate among Jews living there was 21.3 per 1,000. Among the non-Jewish working classes, it was 40 per 1,000.[12]

Entry into the surrounding society offered Jews new economic opportunities without actually bringing about a radical change in their socioprofessional circumstances. At first, traditional Jewish trades persisted. Commerce proved to be the dominant occupation in Jewish circles in the East. Thus peddling gradually gave way to petty commerce. In the first half of the nineteenth century, trade in cattle and horses increased and even expanded geographically with migration. The liberal professions gained ground as time went on, but to a lesser degree than in Paris. Artisanal activity grew as well, albeit unequally, thanks to the efforts of the consistories and of certain societies encouraging apprenticeship in "useful" trades. In 1853, 51 percent of the Jews of Metz could be classed as artisans-workers, as against 5 percent in the Bas-Rhin and 2 percent in Strasbourg in 1843.[13] In the period between 1820 and 1862, in towns and villages having fewer than 2,000 inhabitants, 85 percent of spouses were in commerce at the time of their marriage; this rate was 61 percent in towns of more than 50,000.[14] In 1907, 58 percent of the working Jewish population in Alsace devoted itself to commerce, rural areas included.[15]

Notwithstanding a certain tendency toward embourgeoisement—the number of households in Strasbourg employing domestic staff went from 32 percent in 1846 to 50 percent in 1866—economic conditions continued to be precarious for many. In 1856–57, still 13 percent of Jews in the Bas-Rhin were indigent, as against 8 percent among Catholics and 5 percent among Protestants.

Alsace long remained a reservoir of cultural and spiritual inspiration for Jews, impeding the religious and ideological reforms that the central consistory hoped to put into practice in Paris. This circumstance obliged the consistory to adopt a more moderate line, all the more as the majority of rabbis in France were recruited from traditional milieus in Alsace—a pattern that would continue until the beginning of the twentieth century. The Jews of the east of France were not therefore denied opportunities for acculturation and integration, which in the 1840s owed much to the expanding network of Jewish schools in the region. Though French was enthusiastically taught in these schools, Judeo-Alsatian nonetheless did not disappear, surviving until the end of the nineteenth century.

In the countryside, a comfortable command of the French language still remained the privilege of an elite in the 1850s. Literacy in Hebrew declined during the same period without, however, being replaced by literacy in French. This was particularly true among women. Considering village marriages performed between 1820 and 1830, only 9 percent of the mothers of brides and 12 percent of the brides were literate. Between 1840 and 1850, the share of illiteracy fell to 36 percent for the mothers of brides and 11 percent for their daughters.

In Strasbourg, during the 1820s, when signing in other than Latin characters was prohibited, 11 percent of both the fathers of bridegrooms and grooms themselves were unable to affix their signatures to the register. In rural Alsace, on the other hand, fewer than 1 percent of fathers of grooms and only 2 percent of their sons found themselves in this situation since they were still allowed to sign in Hebraic characters. The illiteracy observed involved only the French language. By the 1850s, 95 percent of the grooms and 77 percent of the brides in villages of the Bas-Rhin were capable of signing in Latin characters; in Strasbourg, the proportion was 100 percent for grooms and 93 percent for brides, and in Colmar 100 percent for both. The teaching and promotion of French among the masses, and the efforts made in this direction by Jewish elites, who showed greater zeal in the matter than their Christian counterparts, had thus led to tangible results.

The choice of personal names is also telling with respect to the will to integrate. Looking at native Alsatians in the years 1770–80, one finds that 76 percent bore Jewish first names; in 1830, 69 percent. It was only during the 1850s that a more sizable shift occurred in favor of the adoption of French first names. In Strasbourg, in this decade, only 20 percent of Jewish men bore Judeo-Alsatian or traditional first names; among women, such names had begun to be less common from the beginning of the century.[16]

Despite these developments, the established settlement of Alsatian Jewry in a conservative rural environment tempered the erosion of religious identity and worked, on the whole, to preserve ties of ethnic solidarity.

PARIS: THE NERVE CENTER

Demographic Growth

Emancipation was accompanied by growth in the number of Jews living in Paris, which between 1789 and 1808 went from about 500–600 to 2,733 or 2,908, depending on whether the official census or the census of the central consistory is consulted.[17] From the latter date, conditions were right for Jewish integration in Parisian society to get underway; indeed, the capital provided an unparalleled stage for Jewish talent in all its variety, causing Jews everywhere in France to look to Paris. Between 1808 and 1831, the number of Jews in Paris almost tripled (rising to 8,684); then quadrupled between 1851 and 1891 (reaching 40,000).[18] By 1852, the Jewish population of Paris was the twelfth largest in the world, after cities such as Warsaw, Istanbul, and Salonika.

The population of Paris in the 1870s remained behind Warsaw, Istanbul, and Vienna, but, as the capital of the first country to emancipate its Jews, Paris became a major center of attraction for both French and foreign Jewry after the 1840s with the East-West shift in Jewish population. This trend accelerated in the 1880s, marked by pogroms in Russia and large waves of emigration. Paris was the last European capital before the crossing of the Atlantic toward the Americas.

In 1811, Paris had 6 percent of the Jews in France, 11 percent in 1841, 17 percent in 1845, 20 percent in 1853, and 26 percent in 1861. By this latter date, less than 5 percent of the total French population lived in the capital. At the end of the nineteenth century, Paris was home to slightly more than half of the Jews of France owing to substantial migratory movements from the annexed provinces of Alsace and Lorraine: Jews now represented 2 percent of the Parisian population; in 1808, this figure was 0.2 percent.

The arrival of Jews from the East was essential to the formation of the Parisian community. In fact, the Jewish population of Paris increased in the same proportion as that of Alsace-Lorraine decreased. In 1808, 79 percent of French Jews lived in Alsace-Lorraine and 6 percent in Paris; in 1861, these figures were 57 percent and 26 percent, respectively. Already in 1809, out of 2,908 Parisian Jews, only 1,324 were born in Paris, compared with a thousand or so natives of Alsace-Lorraine, whose numbers would only continue to grow throughout the nineteenth century. Emigration from Metz began fairly early and at first dominated the flow from the East. The bilingualism of Metz Jews encouraged this movement, and was the very basis of their rapid integration. In 1872, 48 percent of Jewish men in Paris and 36 percent of Jewish women were natives of Alsace-Lorraine. Other provinces also supplied their share of immigrants.[19] Foreign immigration, until the 1880s, converged on Paris, issuing for the most part from the German lands that formerly were joined together under Napoleonic rule in the Confederation of the Rhine.

Paris—city of myth, city of hope—did not attract only those who wished to improve their economic situation, but also political refugees, intellectuals, young people, and business elites from the rest of Europe. In 1872, 80 percent of Parisian Jews were born in France; between 1905 and 1907, this proportion was 54 percent. By this latter date, Jews born in Paris and Jews born in eastern Europe together made up two-thirds of Parisian Jewry. Nonetheless, the demographic evolution of the Jewish population of Paris roughly followed that of the Parisian population as a whole.

Birth of the Jewish Bourgeoisie

A new Jewish bourgeoisie developed in Paris whose influence obscured the fact that it constituted a minority within the city's Jewish population. Eventually it became the target of anti-Semites, who claimed that all Jews were rich. In 1809, its members accounted for 12 percent of the Jewish population of the capital as a whole, 7 percent belonging to the commercial bourgeoisie, with 3 percent in the liberal professions and 2 percent in various trades. Thirty years later, the proportion had risen to 17 percent, 10 percent coming from business, 3 percent from the professions, and 3 percent from trade.[20] Sixteen families belonged to the *haute bourgeoisie d'affaires*: Fould, Oppenheim, Furtado, Goudchaux, d'Eichtal, Rodrigues, Stern, Worms de Romilly, Laurent-Meyer, Dupont, Javal, Halphen, and Allegri, with the addition of Pereire, Millaud, and Maas under the July Monarchy and the Second Empire. The 1860s also saw the arrival in Paris of a certain number of Jewish aristocrats, such as the Camondos of Istanbul and the Genoese baron Léonino, swelling the ranks of their predecessors—financial magnates such as barons Rothschild, Koenigswarter, d'Almeida, and Menasce, and count Cahen d'Anvers, descendants of the court Jews of the eighteenth century.

Some (the Pereire brothers, for example) became ardent promoters of economic progress in the wake of Saint-Simonism, urging the creation of banks and railroads. This Jewish elite was already established at the beginning of the century, and a large part of the Jewish fortunes of the Second Empire had been amassed abroad earlier. Very often only successes are mentioned; but it was during this time that the fortunes of the Pereires and of Jules Mirès collapsed.

The substantial presence of Jews in financial circles was a reality. In 1872, there were ninety-five Jewish bankers. In 1865, 45 or 50 of the 300 leading financiers were Jewish; in 1892, of 440 heads of financial institutions, some 90 to 100 were Jews, not counting those who sat on the *conseils d'administration* of banks.[21] Finance having always been a Jewish occupation, it was inevitable that they would find themselves in the forefront of the profession once the principal barriers to their advancement had been removed. All the elements were in place, then, for the myth of Jewish banking to be born—a favorite theme of anti-Semites, though these bankers represented only a tiny part of Jewish society. Under the July Monarchy, given that communal suffrage was based on tax qualification, they were the only Jews to enjoy the right to vote. Thus in 1845 there were only 965 consistorial electors representing 1 percent of the Jewish population, proof that the vast majority was still of quite modest means.[22]

In the middle of the century, the Jews conformed to the tendencies of the surrounding society, and the level of wealth of bourgeois Jews approached that of their non-Jewish Parisian counterparts. If there was a difference, it lay in the composition of fortunes. Investment by Jews in real estate was lower for reasons related to their status in earlier times, the memory of which caused them to prefer commercial occupations. In 1851, there were almost six times more non-Jews in the landlord-rentier class than Jews in Paris. It was only in 1872 that they began to form a sizable group, a sign of adaptation to socioeconomic circumstances in the capital.[23]

The way of life followed by bourgeois Jews hardly differed from that of their non-Jewish counterparts, another sign of their social integration in the first half of the nineteenth century. A country house on the outskirts of Paris, household staff (often Jewish), jewels, silverware, paintings, mahogany or rosewood furniture for the very rich, wine collections, membership in various societies and clubs (such as the Ancien Cercle, the Cercle de la rue de Gramont, the Cercle du Commerce, or, more unusually, the Cercle Agricole and the Jockey Club for the Jewish banking elite)—these were some of the distinctive marks of their social group, in keeping with the bourgeois Parisian model.

Like the rest of the bourgeoisie, one married within one's social class—in this case, with other Jews. The Rothschilds, for example, entered into consanguinous marriages between cousins; with regard to legal control of conjugal property, they chose joint ownership rather than the Jewish custom of matrimonial division.

Women such as Mme. Arman de Caillavet (née Lippman, 1844–1910), born into a Jewish banking family in Austria and later a convert to Christianity who had a lasting relationship with Anatole France; Geneviève Straus (1849–1926), daughter of the composer Jacques Halévy, wife of Georges Bizet and muse to Marcel Proust, one of the most dazzling women of her time; and others now forgotten, such as Clara Bischoffsheim, a banker's daughter and wife of the celebrated banker Meyer Cahen d'Anvers, and Henrietta Goldschmidt, the wife of Achille Fould—all held salons where the elite of both Jewish and non-Jewish society met.

Under the Second Empire, one notes a higher rate of embourgeoisement among Jews than for Parisian society as a whole, especially at the level of the commercial middle class. The pyramid of wealth still remained close to that found in non-Jewish circles, but with the difference that the base of the pyramid was larger since the Jews were more numerous in the *moyenne bourgeoisie* and less numerous in the upper middle class. They entered sectors of the economy in which they had long experience—fashion, luxury goods, trade in livestock (in the East), finance, and shopkeeping; already under the July Monarchy they had begun to accumulate wealth, and they continued to do so under the Second Empire. They were twice as numerous in the liberal professions as non-Jewish bourgeois Parisians, with some brilliant successes. Even if Jews were generally better represented than non-Jews in the middle class in Paris, this proportion remained lower than 2 percent.[24] Jewish embourgeoisement increased only in the last decades of the century.

Social advancement in Paris was accompanied by a movement away from the old sixth and seventh arrondissements—now the third and fourth, respectively—where Jews made up 82 percent of the population; in the seventh arrondissement (today's fourth) they made up 65 percent, mostly working class and poor.[25] After 1860, the neighborhoods inhabited by the Jewish bourgeoisie were (in order of precedence) the ninth, second, tenth, third, first, eighth, fourth, and eleventh arrondissements. With only a few exceptions, then, the Jewish bourgeoisie settled in those arrondissements where there was still a Jewish neighborhood life and where the commercial and artisanal activity of the city took place, which distinguished them from other bourgeois Parisians. With the arrival of foreign Jews, who invaded the third and fourth arrondissements, they regrouped in the ninth, tenth, and eleventh. It was only toward the end of the century that they deserted the traditionally Jewish districts in favor of the *beaux quartiers*—the fifth, sixth, seventh, eighth, and sixteenth arrondissements.

SOCIOECONOMIC PROFILE

In Paris

In the first decade of the century, 55 percent of Parisian Jews were found in petty commerce (as traders of bric-a-brac, peddlers, and hawkers), 28 percent in "useful" trades, and 16 percent engaged in various "other" pursuits. There were no Jewish factory workers. Toward the end of the century there was a fall in the number of peddlers and a rise in the number engaged in useful trades (which included women as well). The industrial revolution contributed to the disappearance of the old Jewish trades under the July Monarchy and the Second Empire. In the first half of the nineteenth century, the number of Jews belonging to the working class diminished by 4 percent while the size of these classes as a proportion of the Parisian population remained stable. They thus seemed to be drawing even with their fellow citizens in the capital.

Nonetheless, more than one Jew in five (about 2,000 persons) still lived in the middle of the nineteenth century in a state of total destitution; they received assistance from the Comité de Bienfaisance Juif and from neighborhood welfare offices. This situation was due to a lack of professional specialization, itself the result of the still very oppressive weight of tradition. The persistence of poverty was greater in Paris than in the provinces.

Four percent of working class Jews, as we have mentioned, experienced a rise in social standing at the end of the First Empire and during the Restoration, moving up to the lower middle class. Indeed there were some spectacular cases of social advancement. This mobility in both the Jewish and non-Jewish worlds chiefly involved those who had left the provinces to go to Paris.

The working masses as a whole continued to live a wretched existence; wives and children contributed to household incomes. Rates of sickness and mortality were particularly high. Their social behavior and linguistic differences left them still more isolated from their neighbors, who continued to consider them as foreigners, though this gap would begin to narrow in the 1840s. At about this time, all social classes save the poor experienced an improvement in their economic conditions.[26] The census of 1851 showed that now only 14 percent of Jews belonged to the working classes, as against 22 percent of non-Jewish Parisians. During the same period, 20 percent of Jews in Paris lived in extreme poverty.[27] Each wave of immigration brought with it paupers who were obliged to practice unskilled trades. Among the first generation of immigrants, artisans and small shopkeepers were found as well.

In 1872, the Jews of Paris were relatively well off: only 10 percent of the population (compared with 45 percent in 1809) worked at jobs requiring no special training, peddlers making up the bulk of this category. During this period, more Alsatians earned their livelihood as peddlers than other Jews, being less privileged than native Parisians; Jewish women also worked as peddlers. German-born immigrants and newcomers from the Mediterranean countries were more likely to belong to the wealthy classes, distinguishing themselves in commerce and the liberal professions. In 1872, 24 percent of men and 30 percent of women in the workforce were engaged in artisanal crafts and industry, and 32 percent of men and 21 percent of women in commerce. Increasingly, Jews were salaried employees, though still relatively few served as government officials (17 percent of men and 5 percent of women). Only 8 percent of men and 2 percent of women practiced the liberal professions.

In the 1870s, a good many Jews began to make their way into the middle class. Between 1867 and 1907, the number of untrained workers grew continually smaller while the number of those in the professional and educated classes (physicians and lawyers, artists, senior executives, industrialists, and students) grew larger.

As artisans, Jews remained confined to manufacturing and traditional crafts—textile processing, leatherworking, cabinetmaking, and the like. Between 1867 and 1887, one artisan in two was Jewish; by the beginning of the twentieth century, only one in three. Jews were also found in bookmaking and bookselling, in watchmaking and jewelry, but few in emerging new industries. In short, the traditional artisanal trades endured. Jewish wage-earners worked chiefly in the service sector, but also as company workers in commerce and industry.

The massive arrival of Jews from eastern Europe in the 1880s contributed to the formation of a Jewish proletariat made up almost exclusively of immigrants. Except in Alsace, commerce was no longer the predominant socioprofessional category of French Jews.[28]

The soaring rate of urbanization blurred socioeconomic and cultural divisions between various Jewish groups, giving rise to a Franco-Judaic model to which newcomers to cities in France tended to adhere. Jews coming from rural areas, fewer and fewer in number, remained disadvantaged by comparison with urban Jewish populations. Differences were yet perceptible between city dwellers born in the capital and immigrants from elsewhere in the country and between French Jews and immigrants from abroad, with variations depending on the country of origin and the particular wave of immigration; but these differences tended to disappear within the space of a generation.

Between the end of the nineteenth and the beginning of the twentieth century, three groups within Parisian Jewry can be distinguished: immigrants from eastern Europe, at the bottom of the social ladder; at the top, native Parisians (among whom poverty continued to recede); and, in the middle, the Alsatians. Within each of these groups, dividing lines between rich and poor were very clear; also between immigrants and native-born in the case of the Alsatians and eastern Europeans. They did not inhabit the same neighborhoods, they did not marry into groups other than their own, their way of life was not the same, and the inequalities between them persisted over time. These differences did not really fade away until the interwar period, at which point new gaps began to appear as fresh waves of immigrants poured into France.

Within the immigrant communities there also existed distinctions of a socioeconomic nature. In Paris, those who came from Mediterranean countries were mostly well off until 1895–97; the ones who came afterward were mostly poor. The same was also true for immigration originating in Germany. As for Jews from eastern Europe, each new wave swelled the workforce, with the poor—who at almost all times made up half of the influx—taking the place of those who had benefited from a rise in social status.

The Case of Marseilles

In the last decades of the nineteenth century, the Jewish populations of the southwest and of the Midi were stable; new groups formed in the north, in the Lyons region, and in the Franche-Comté. A considerable number of Jews were still found in the areas of Lorraine that remained French. During this period, four provincial cities had more than 1,000 Jews: Marseilles (whose Jewish community was the second largest in France), Bordeaux, Nancy, and Lyons.

The figures collected for Marseilles in 1872 confirm the pattern of sociocultural development for Jews living in cities in the 1870s with, however, some peculiarities: this was a cosmopolitan city (foreigners accounted for 12 percent of the population) containing 2,662 Jews, of whom 80 percent were French and 20 percent foreign (Algerian Jews included).[29] Business and other professionals, shopkeepers, artisans, and company employees represented 75 percent of the Jewish working population. Only 6 percent of the workforce made their living by unskilled labor. Social advancement proceeded via commerce: 42 percent of those actively earning income were found in this sector. Marseillais Jews therefore belonged predominantly to the *moyenne bourgeoisie*.

One notes nonetheless a trend toward salaried status, which included 21 percent of those employed, generally in commerce. The textile and precision craftsmanship sector had 11 percent of the workforce. One also finds rentiers and landlords. In Marseilles, unlike in Paris, Jews were not yet very numerous in the liberal professions, which indicates a less rapid rate of integration than in the capital. Almost all of the Jews belonging to this sector were born in France and, in particular, in the southeast. This was also the case with those who went into the civil service. Jews were absent from the maritime trades as well as from those practiced by people in rural areas and the urban industrial proletariat.[30]

The first decades of the twentieth century witnessed a decline in the socioprofessional profile of the Jewish population of Marseilles, with the arrival of a sizable number of immigrants. The Jewish population stood at 8,500 or so in 1923 and between 12,000 and 13,000 in 1930. Of these foreign Jews, 85 percent were of Sephardic origin and only 15 percent Ashkenazic. Social advancement was subsequently considerable in Marseilles, in particular for those who were born in the city. The immigrants who settled there were of modest means, unlike in the last decades of the preceding century, when those arriving from Mediterranean cities and the Balkans (representing 17 percent of the Jewish population of the city in 1872) belonged to the wealthiest classes.[31]

The socioprofessional data collected from the Jewish communities in Paris and Marseilles (allowing for margins of error due to a reliance on limited samples) show that Jews in these cities integrated by practicing trades and professions that were already familiar to them and not by obeying the wishes of emancipationists who hoped that regeneration would come about by working the land and acquiring new skills. Periodic waves of immigration both inside the country and from abroad brought with them certain socioeconomic and sociocultural changes that were to alter the portrait of urban Jews in France sketched here. French Jewry was, and remained, heterogeneous in a way that makes it impossible to speak of a unique model of integration applicable to its members as a whole.

DEMOGRAPHY

Marriage

Economic integration was accompanied by sociocultural integration. The behavior of French Jews with respect to marriage provides a measure of their integration within French society, immigrants accounting for the majority of variation observed. In 1872, the marriage rate was almost the same among Jews and non-Jews; in the Seine department it was 102 per 10,000 for the former (who numbered 21,767) and 105 for the latter. Between 1877 and 1891, the marriage rate of the 3,000 or so Jews of Marseilles (amounting to less than 1 percent of the population) was 4 per 1,000, and so lower than that of their non-Jewish neighbors, which was 7.5 per 1,000. On the eve of the Second World War, the rate was still lower.

Cases of early marriage were quite rare. The typical age for Jewish women, in the last decades of the nineteenth century, was between twenty-one and twenty-five years, and for men between twenty-six and thirty years. In 1905, the typical marriage in Paris among the non-Jewish populace varied between twenty-five and thirty years for 43 percent of the men, and between twenty and twenty-five for 38 percent of the women. Marriage occurred in working class neighborhoods at a younger age than in bourgeois neighborhoods. In the former, both husband and wife generally worked; in the latter, the husband generally chose a younger wife with a substantial dowry, taking it upon himself to provide for the support of the household—tendencies that mirrored those in French society as a whole.

In Marseilles, 81 percent of Jewish women married between 20 and 29, the average age being 23 in the late nineteenth and early twentieth century; while for this same period the average marrying age of non-Jewish women in Marseilles was 26. Two-thirds of Jewish men married between the ages of 25 and 34, the average age being 30, while for non-Jewish males that age was 31. The tendency of men to marry at a later age is characteristic of the urban society of the time. On the eve of the Second World war, the average age of marriage for Jewish women was 24 years and for men 26 years (the available data, of course, cover only those married in a religious ceremony).

Geographic homogamy was common in marriages among both French Jews and foreign Jews. The 1872 census indicates that it was still more pronounced among the latter: 81 percent of the marriages celebrated in Paris between foreigners involved natives of the same country. In the Jewish bourgeoisie, Parisians married Parisians; marriages between provincials and Parisians occurred in less wealthy milieus. From 1872 to 1907, again in Paris, marriages between French Jews began to decline while marriages both between French and foreign Jews and between foreign Jews were on the rise—revealing, in the latter case, a tendency on the part of first-generation immigrants to keep to themselves.

In Marseilles, between the wars, immigrants from eastern Europe remained reluctant to marry outside their community. The proportion of marriages between French Jews and foreign Jews was only 36 percent, and that of marriages between foreign partners 47 percent. Jews from the Maghreb and the Levant were more open to this sort of union.[32]

Births

The Jewish birthrate was low while exhibiting some variation with respect to social background and geographic origin. Working-class families in Paris tended to be large. In the professional classes, on the other hand, the number of children was limited to one or two, which suggests that couples practiced birth control; the incidence of infant mortality was lower than among the working classes as well. Similarly, birth rates among the non-Jewish bourgeoisie during the same period were low. On the other hand, the proportion of Jewish couples having more than two children was higher when one of the spouses was foreign by birth. In the case of the French Jews of Paris, the proportion of large families was clearly higher among those from the provinces and particularly among the Alsatians, still attached to tradition and, for this reason, opposed to planned births. The birth rate for the Jewish population of the Seine Department in 1872 was lower than that for non-Jews: under 29 per 1,000 as against over 30 per 1,000.

In the Midi, in 1841, the number of children per Jewish family was 1.9 percent in Vaucluse, 1.7 in Rhône, and 1.4 in Bouches-de-Rhône. In Marseilles, in the last decades of the nineteenth century, the data on birth-rates for the upper classes are comparable to those for Paris. Salaried employees, shopkeepers, and artisans had between two and four children; religious ministers, on the other hand, fathered larger families. And again, considering Jewish men born in France, those from Alsace-Lorraine and the south had larger families; natives of Marseilles, on the other hand, had fewer children. Among foreign immigrant groups of Jews, those from the Levant, the Maghreb, and Italy had families of more than three children.

Toward the end of the century the Parisian Jewish family became "nuclear," heralding the modern family. The old expanded family remained more common among native Parisians (8 percent) than among newcomers (5 percent), but immigration did not favor the continuation of this pattern.

During the same period, in Marseilles, the model of the expanded family was represented by 21 percent of Jewish households; 19 percent of large families were French and 26 percent Levantine. In the following decades, the average rate was 23 percent of all Jewish households, with 24 percent of large families being from Marseilles and the south, and 23 percent from abroad (these latter households were composed of Jews from the Maghreb and the Levant who carried on a tradition imported from their native lands).[33]

Mortality

Between 1855 and 1859, the mortality rate of Jews in France was 18 per 1,000; for the rest of the population, it was 24 per 1,000. In 1872, the mortality rate for Jews in Paris was 21 per 1,000 and for non-Jewish Parisians 23 per 1,000. Here too one finds a diminishing gap between the two groups.[34] Within the Jewish population, mirroring the pattern for French society as a whole, there was a close correlation between socioeconomic status and the chances of survival. The fall in infant mortality, the improvement of sanitary conditions, and advances in medicine prolonged life expectancy among the well-off and the *moyenne bourgeoisie*, in particular among Jewish families long established in France. The poor, on the other hand, died in hospitals or hospices, with more than three-quarters of them being buried at no cost to their families.

In the years 1885–87, more than a third of Parisian Jews lived past the age of sixty, while in 1901 only 13 percent of the French population reached that age.[35] This discrepancy is explained by the relatively comfortable socioeconomic circumstances of the capital's Jewish population.

CHAPTER NINE

Advancement and Identity

ADVANCEMENT THROUGH EDUCATION

Education very quickly became inseparable from the advancement of the Jew in French society. Study had always occupied an essential place in Jewish life. The changed circumstances of the nineteenth century brought with them a new hurdle to be cleared—secularization. Jewish leaders very early took an interest in this aspect of the question. The first modern Jewish school for boys (particularly from the poorer classes) was opened in Paris in 1819 and the first school for girls in 1822. These leaders, who were themselves a direct product of the program of regeneration that they wished to apply to their fellow Jews, also emphasized professional instruction, providing training for trades considered to be useful. During the Second Empire, there were twenty-nine Jewish primary schools in Paris, and one secondary school in the Marais (the present-day fourth arrondissement).[1] At the same time, the Société Israélite des Amis du Travail was approved in 1825 by the Interior Ministry. It proposed to assist impoverished parents in placing their male children in workshops through subsidy grants. Female children got their turn with the founding in 1843 of the Société pour l'Établissement des Jeunes Filles Israélites. The Société de Patronage des Ouvriers et des Artisans Juifs made available loans of longer or shorter term that were likewise aimed at promoting employment. In the provinces, comparable efforts were made on behalf of education and productivity that helped put Jews ahead of the French population as a whole in these regards. Also set up in 1825, in Strasbourg, were the Société d'Encouragement au Travail parmi les Jeunes Israélites Indigents du Bas-Rhin and the Société pour l'Encouragement des Arts et Métiers parmi les Israélites de Metz. In Marseilles, the Société d'Encouragement aux Arts et Métiers parmi les Israélites à Marseille was founded in 1849, and five years later the Société des Arts et Métiers pour les Jeunes Filles Israélites à Marseille.

Between 1820 and 1830, Jewish children went mainly to Jewish schools owing to the fact that their parents remained attached to tradition. After this time, and especially under the Second Empire, the tendency among the middle and upper bourgeoisie was no longer to send children to these institutions. Education was still not free (the free and obligatory primary school championed by Jules Ferry dates only from 1881–82), which explains why Jewish schools were increasingly reserved for poor children. Regional variations may also be observed depending on whether one looks at rural areas such as Alsace, where Jewish groups had their own schools, or cities, where schooling increasingly took place in non-Jewish settings. Toward the 1870s, in Paris, one Jewish child in three did not go to a Jewish school. As for religious instruction, opportunities for Jewish children to receive it outside of family and synagogue were more rare.

Twenty-three percent of French conscripts during this period were illiterate; among their Jewish counterparts, however, the incidence of illiteracy was very low. Illiteracy (or what was considered to be illiteracy) was less frequent among Jews born in France than among those who were born abroad. In Paris, in the 1870s, 12 percent of women and 8 percent of men aged twenty years or older were illiterate. In 1885, only 0.5 percent of men and 1.2 percent of women signed their marriage licence with a cross or declared that they were unable to write their names. In 1905–07, only 2 percent of Jewish conscripts born in France had not completed their primary schooling as opposed to 14 percent of the recruits born abroad and 5 percent of those born in Alsace-Lorraine. The proportion of literacy among women was a bit lower than among men, particularly in the case of those from eastern Europe (though some women had been taught to read and write in Yiddish). In 1885–87, 9 percent of Jewish conscripts, and 13 percent in 1905–07, had been educated beyond the primary level, going on to lycée or university, which in general were attended by a narrow elite.[2] Gradually the Jews also gained entry to the *grandes écoles*, beginning with the Polytechnique in the First Empire, which opened the way to successful careers.

Social advancement was manifested not only by the entry of the second generation of Jews after emancipation into the liberal professions. They also distinguished themselves in the arts, literature, journalism, scientific research, the academy and the civil service, and republican political life—to a degree out of all proportion to the Jewish population's size in relation to French society as a whole.

IN THE ARTS AND LITERATURE

In music and the theater, less conventional and less conformist than other fields, Jews were welcomed very early. Music, in particular, is a universal language that transcends geographic, cultural, and religious differences—thus the brilliant careers of French Jews such as Jacques Halévy (1799–1862), son of a German immigrant and the author, among other works, of the opera *La Juive* (1835); Isaac Strauss (1806–88), born into a Jewish family in Strasbourg and later the *chef de bals* of the imperial court during the Second Empire; Charles-Valentin Alcan (1813–88), also the son of a German immigrant; Édouard Colonne (1838–1910), from Bordeaux; Émile Waldteufel (1837–1915), an Alsatian; and of foreign Jews such as Giacomo Meyerbeer (1791–1864), a German by birth; Henri Herz (1803–88), an Austrian; and Jacques Offenbach (1819–80), also a native German. Some of these musician-composers occupied posts in the service of prestigious institutions that brought them into contact with high government officials. There were other less famous figures as well. Success in the musical field in France did not depend on conversion, as it did elsewhere in Europe. Even if their work was not always inspired by Jewish themes, the majority remained attached in different ways to the Jewish community and did not wholly reject its traditions.

In the theater, Jews won attention both on the stage and as authors of serious and comic plays. Actresses such as Rachel (1821–58), Rosine Bloch (1827–1912), and Sarah Bernhardt (1844–1923), a convert to Christianity, brought down the house.

The belles-lettres were less open to welcoming Jewish writers, who long had to settle for writing light operas and comedies. With Marcel Schwob (1867–1905), Bernard Lazare (1865–1903), Julien Benda (1867–1956), and Léon Blum (1872–1950), as well as other gifted writers who came right after them, the Jews made a discreet entrance into what until then was a private domain of the national heritage.

The same was true of painting and sculpture, but here because these arts were foreign to the Jewish world due to prohibitions concerning figurative representation. This did not prevent the Jewish elite from devoting itself very early to patronage and the collection of works of art and to promoting the avant-garde, a predilection shared by Jewish art dealers. The Rothschilds, David-Weills, Camondos, and others took their place among the dynasties of collectors. Above all, they donated their splendid collections to French museums. The impressionists were adopted almost at once by Jewish collectors, who effectively launched their careers at a moment when they were denigrated by conventional opinion in artistic circles.

Jews also succeeded in journalism as newspaper proprietors during the July Monarchy but also, and especially, under the Second Empire. This tendency was confirmed under the Third Republic with Arthur Meyer (1844–1924), one of the rare Jewish converts to Christianity of the period, who headed *Le Gaulois*; Eugène Meyer, owner of *La Lanterne*; Camille Dreyfus (1849–1915), *La Nation*; Abraham Dreyfus (1847–1926), *Gil Blas*; and the Gambettist Joseph Reinach (1856–1921), *La République*. Bernard Lazare wrote for anarchist papers. The Natanson brothers founded *La Revue blanche* in 1889, which opened its pages to writers who would later achieve literary fame, such as Barrès and Proust, and also to Lazare and Blum.

Nor were Jews absent from the world of bookselling and publishing. The brothers Michel (1821–75) and Calmann (1819–91) Lévy founded one of the largest bookselling firms in France in 1848. They also laid the basis for modern publishing, bringing some of the century's greatest writers before the French public from 1856 on.

IN THE ACADEMY AND STATE ADMINISTRATION

Jews occupied important academic posts as well—at the Sorbonne, the Collège de France, the École Normale Supérieure, the Polytechnique, and particularly the École Pratique des Hautes Études, but also in provincial universities. During the July Monarchy, Jewish orientalists distinguished themselves in the academic world: first among the pioneers was the Silesian Salomon Munk (1803–64), holder of the chair in Hebrew and Aramaic at the Collège de France, followed by Joseph Derenbourg (1811–95), a German by birth, his son Hartwig Derenbourg (1844–1908), Jules Oppert (1825–1905), also of German extraction, Joseph Halévy (1827–1917), a native of Adrianople, the philologist and linguist Michel Bréal (1832–1915), professor at the Collège de France, James Darmesteter (1849–94), the Hellenist Salomon Reinach (1858–1932), and Sylvain Lévi (1863–1935), who also taught at the Collège de France. The careers of these academics—some of whom, in addition to their specialities, also contributed to Jewish studies—are of great interest in trying to understand certain facets of the Jewish experience in nineteenth century France, an age that witnessed the formation of family dynasties in the world of scholarship, among them the Reinach and the Darmesteter brothers, and the Derenbourgs, father and son.

In higher education, outside the oriental field, Jews distinguished themselves in philology, law, literature, and medicine. More exceptionally still for the period, Adolphe Franck (1809–93) occupied the chair of philosophy at the Collège de France. In 1895, of the two hundred sixty members of the Institut de France, seven were Jews.[3] The Third Republic only encouraged a movement that had already begun. The philosopher Henri Bergson (1859–1941) was elected in 1914 to the Académie Française: he was the first Jew to be so honored, a further sign of the definite acceptance of the Jews in France. While Jews made their way in the various established fields of science, some were also involved in founding the new social sciences. In this connection it suffices to mention Émile Durkheim (1858–1917), the father of modern sociology, and his nephew Marcel Mauss

(1873–1950). Though these scholars were Jewish by birth, and though their names, having gone down in history, are often cited to emphasize the successful integration of the Jews in the space of a few generations, their relations with Judaism were rather complicated.

Jews began also to enter the *corps d'État*, especially during the Second Empire, which favored the development of the administrative bodies on which its power rested. The secular Third Republic, with its avowed commitment to meritocracy, promoted Jews in the service of the state without their having to convert, as certain of their predecessors under the July Monarchy and the Second Empire had been obliged to do. During the Third Republic there were one hundred seventy-one Jewish prefects, *conseillers d'État*, generals, magistrates, deputies, and senators.[4] The state Jews found their place either in the legislature or in the upper levels of the civil service, some rising to high positions as ministers or *présidents de Conseil* with the revolution of 1848. Adolphe Crémieux and Michel Goudchaux (1797–1862) served respectively as justice minister and finance minister of the provisional government. This trend continued at the beginning of the Third Republic and then in the ones that followed. Anti-Semitic circles were to exploit the myths of "Jewish France" and, later, the "Jewish Republic," just as in the past they had denounced "Jewish banking."

Judaism, so far as it was considered only a religion, came within the private sphere. In the context of republican egalitarianism, and by virtue of the Jacobin tradition of the French nation-state, opposed to particularisms and combating them in the name of a rational universalism, the Jews—like all French citizens—had a priori the right to serve in any of the *corps d'État*. In principle, then, their religious attachment should not have prevented them from rising in the public sphere, establishing themselves as figures of consequence—indeed as decisionmakers, controlling their own destiny. In the framework defined by the novel category of citizenship, uniquely linked to the state, it was now possible for them to become state Jews. This was something completely new: in the past, powerful Jews contented themselves with being court Jews, at the mercy of their masters.

Even under the republic, however, certain sectors of state administration (such as the Quai d'Orsay or the army) resisted admitting Jews into their ranks or promoting them to the upper grades more than others did. And if, generally speaking, the Third Republic welcomed state Jews more readily, it cannot be claimed that their path of advancement was unhindered by anti-Semitic prejudices. Their careers met with discriminatory treatment on the part of the state, which considered them as members of a close-knit group and not as full-fledged citizens, devoted though they plainly were to public service. Their thorough-going adherence to the values of the republic made state Jews targets during the Dreyfus affair

(1894–1906), which nonetheless they managed to survive. Vichy later pushed this logic to its furthest extreme by excluding and utterly betraying these faithful and enthusiastic servants of the state.

On whichever side they stood politically, state Jews were frequently confronted with anti-Semitic insinuations and attacks, especially when they occupied posts of high responsibility in the state bureaucracy. Though the fact of being Jewish did not prevent them from attaining the highest offices of the secular republic; though for the majority of them their Jewishness implied no particular practice; and though they considered themselves to be Frenchmen before everything else, these servants of the state nonetheless continued to be perceived and attacked as Jews. They paid a heavy toll in the "Franco-French wars" that rocked contemporary political life in France. Whether Gambettist or socialist, they did not escape anti-Semitic caricature, which typically held them up to public opinion as foreigners, agents of cosmopolitan capital—revolutionaries without pity for any of the things that made up the French and Christian heritage. Nor would Léon Blum, Jules Moch (1893–1985), or Pierre Mendès France (1907–82) be spared later.

ALTERNATIVE PATHS

Saint-Simonism

The integration of the Jews occurred also by roundabout routes. Saint-Simonism, which became popular after the revolution of 1830, had served already during Saint-Simon's lifetime as an avenue of socialization for the young Jews who were welcomed into it. Just the same, their importance in Saint-Simonian circles must not be exaggerated, especially not in later years; nor can one go so far as to speak of a "Jewish movement." Nonetheless, in Saint-Simonism they did not have to fear segregation—not the least of its attractions for them—and the movement long influenced the thinking and action of its Jewish sympathizers.

Claude-Henri de Rouvroy, comte de Saint-Simon (1760–1825), advocated progress, believing in the future of science and the human race and presenting himself as the apostle of an optimistic industrialism in which the interests of industrialists and workers spontaneously harmonized with each other. In his famous article "Parabola," which appeared in the first issue of *L'Organisateur* in 1819, he laid down the primacy of economics over politics. Science and industry were to constitute the very foundation of the new order, in which an elite would assume responsibility for religious and political matters. Indeed, this bourgeois government had a duty to improve the lot of the poor.

The Saint-Simonians took a close interest in religion in general and in Christianity in particular. Saint-Simon intended to found a new religion, for which his posthumously published work *Le Nouveau Christianisme* (1825) served as a bible for his disciples. Also developed in this work were the presocialist themes on which the Saint-Simonian school relied after the master's death.

Certain Jews such as Eugène Rodrigues and Gustave d'Eichtal (1804–86) allied themselves with the movement for religious reasons; others, such as Léon Halévy (1802–83), Olinde Rodrigues (1795–1850), and the Pereire brothers were attracted by the socioeconomic dimensions of its doctrine. All of them saw themselves as standing at the advent of a new age having a single cult and dogma—a common, universal religion. The fusion of all religions was heralded as another form of messianism, one that had its origins among the Jews and their prophets but that went beyond them, since Judaism was decadent and a more vigorous religion was needed, without involving a break with the past.

This marginal movement paved the way for integration within the universalist religion revealed by Saint-Simonism: the Jew would no longer suffer discrimination owing to his faith and would naturally find his place as part of this unity. This symbiotic religious vision, untraumatic for Jewish identity, prefigured the secular option that took shape, though not without a messianic aspect of its own, under the Third Republic: Franco-Judaism. In the era of integration, Jews sought to stand solidly behind the society that welcomed them without wholly losing their distinctiveness as a people—and this within the framework of a new order realizing the fundamental aspirations of Judaism. Similarly, in central Europe, Jews joined the ranks of socialist movements in order to reestablish traditional religious values and, impelled by a sort of messianic dread of the modern world, to create an ideal society.

These young and, for the most part, bourgeois Jews discovered in the thought of Saint-Simon and his disciple Auguste Comte a synthetic, scientific, rational vision of the world elaborated on the basis of Judeo-Christian elements and, at the same time, the intensity of group life organized as a sort of "Commune"—a place of socialization par excellence. It is perhaps not surprising that this should have occurred during the Restoration, an extremely difficult period when both the universities, under the iron rule of the church, and public administration were still closed to them.

Olinde Rodrigues, a founder of the Saint-Simonian school and later one of its principal leaders, came from a family of Bordeaux financiers. Rodrigues became acquainted with Saint-Simon some time after the latter's attempt at suicide in 1823, staying with him until his death two years later while providing for his needs and financing publication of his three last works. For a time Léon Halévy served as the master's secretary. It was after Saint-Simon's death that Rodrigues, along with Prosper Enfantin, started a weekly (later monthly) journal to which Comte briefly contributed, *Le Producteur*, that helped develop the doctrine of positivism. It ceased publication in 1826. Rodrigues was interested above all in the social aspect of Saint-Simonian theory and in 1844 proposed establishing a workers' pension fund—an institution that came into being only with the law of 1912. With Gustav d'Eichtal, another Saint-Simonian of Jewish birth (later converted to Christianity), he also fought for the abolition of slavery. This was achieved in 1848.

If Saint-Simonism attempted in its early years, between 1825 and 1833, to set up a philosophy and a religion, later on it exalted the spirit of enterprise and promoted economic progress, the creation of railroads and banks and so on, above all during the Second Empire when its sympathizers had risen to occupy important posts in the political and economic fields. Well trained in financial activity by past experience, Jews found in a doctrine that advocated universal emancipation and conferred upon businesses and banks a quasi-religious dimension the means for realizing a new social dream, one that held out the promise of creating through work the conditions for happiness on earth—all of this in association with Christians. Thus Saint-Simonism, a movement of Christian inspiration, managed to reconcile morality and money, making bankers the new prophets and industrialists the priests of the state, and indirectly attached a positive value to the commercial vocation of the Jews. Breaking with the aims of emancipationists who hoped to "regenerate" them through trades thought useful, they took advantage of their long experience in the financial field rather than set out upon paths that were unknown to them. The state itself ended up recognizing their historical aptitude in the matter by appointing Michel Goudchaux as finance minister during the Second Republic and Achille Fould (1800–1867) during the Second Empire. The emerging Jewish bourgeoisie, even if it did not join the movement in great numbers, found itself legitimated by virtue of the very fact it had been asked to take part in the building of the new order. Its most enterprising representatives, who were also key figures in Saint-Simonism, set about this task. Among them were the Pereire brothers, who worked to expand credit and lower interest rates. They collaborated with the well-known economist Michel Chevalier on railroad projects and, in 1852, founded the Crédit Mobilier with the purpose of helping create commercial firms and industrial concerns, as well as the Compagnie Générale Maritime, which later became the Compagnie Générale Transatlantique.

Saint-Simonism served also as a tribune for certain Jews who stood outside official institutions and did not share their opinions. It allowed them to avoid breaking with their fellow Jews while not having to come before their representative bodies. Saint-Simonian Jews were later to found their own organizations, such as the Alliance Israélite Universelle in 1860.

Freemasonry

Freemasonry also figured among the paths, both alternative and complementary, that certain Jews took in their journey to integration. Unlike Saint-Simonism, however, it did not encourage the development of personal and professional solidarity.

Though the principle of universality buttressed masonic doctrine, it was not always consistently applied, and the history of the Jews' relations with freemasons is an ambivalent one characterized by both acceptance and rejection. Freemasonry allowed Jews to enter into contact with social circles to which they had previously been denied access, to say nothing of the prestige that such membership conferred. With the Revolution, in France as well as other countries conquered by the French armies, the barriers to the admission of Jews were lifted.

The Rothschilds were Scottish Rite Masons. The Scottish rite was renowned for the welcome that it extended to minority group members and for its tolerance, greater than that of the Grand Orient (the Grand Lodge of France). Jews represented only 1 percent of the upper grades of French masonry; in the lower ones, they were scarcely more numerous. In the Lodge of the Rosicrucian Knights of the 18th Degree, they made up less than 1 percent. These percentages do not take into account the importance of certain Jews in the ruling levels of masonry, such as Adolphe Crémieux, who toward the end of the 1860s became a grand master in the Scottish rite. Between 1830 and 1853, only 1 percent of the officers were of the Jewish faith, and this proportion declined during the Second Empire. In 1862, no Jews figured among the list of dignitaries.

Jews did not enter into freemasonry out of self-interest. Men such as Crémieux remained members even after they had become famous. If in certain cases it brought moral and financial support to those who had neither money nor connections, masonry was for the most part a tolerant society in which Jewish observance was not incompatible with their membership. Freemasonry, and in particular the Scottish rite, allowed Jews to reach positions of influence at the summit of the masonic hierarchy; some of them, who moreover were members of the consistory, waged an underground struggle for the improvement of the condition of the Jews in the world. In the second half of the nineteenth century, however, masonry did not attract bankers, wealthy merchants, or members of the bourgeoisie who had made their fortune in the army. At least some bourgeois Jews must have felt that their international family networks were the equal of whatever masonry could offer them.[5]

The myth of a Judeo-Masonic plot thus had no foundation in reality. It was inseparable from the battle waged against secular forces, thought to be spearheaded by the freemasons, with whom the Jews were linked. Additionally, there was the element of anti-Semitism—which gradually came to penetrate masonic circles themselves. The slogan "Jews and Freemasons" first began to be heard in France in the 1880s, and subsequently became the credo of the anti-Semites. The translation of the *Protocols of the Elders of Zion* into German in 1919, and then into French and English in 1920, helped crystallize an amalgam that betrayed a paranoid fear of possible world domination by this chimerical pair.

AND WOMEN

The integration of women and their social mobility did not follow the same pattern. Like the majority of French women of the upper bourgeoisie and middle class of the period, they were tied to the domestic world. It would be necessary to wait until the twentieth century for greater contact with the outside non-Jewish world, if only through a larger presence of women in the workforce or owing to the opportunities offered them for higher education. In the upper bourgeoisie, some women distinguished themselves by holding salons, but the majority contented themselves with good works within the confines of the Jewish community. It was nonetheless possible to venture beyond these boundaries. Some worked on behalf of charity—a privileged social occupation outside the household—in both the Jewish and non-Jewish worlds.

Womens' work (whether artisanal activity or household service) was the business of the lower classes, mostly unmarried women and childless widows being recruited into these settings. Foreigners were likewise overrepresented in the less qualified trades. Women who practiced liberal professions were very few, and among them foreigners were virtually absent. In 1872, in Paris, the share of working women born in the capital was 19 percent while that of women born abroad was 17 percent. Alsatian women who had recently arrived in Paris, and therefore were still less well off than others, worked in greater numbers (22 percent of Alsatian women were employed in the capital). Among Jewish women from eastern Europe or women having married a Jew from eastern Europe, the proportion working was 18 percent, whereas among German women it was 4 percent and among Sephardic women 6 percent, the latter two groups of immigrants being well-to-do. In Marseilles, during the same period, 51 percent of Jewish women practicing a trade were born in that city, 32 percent were born elsewhere in France, and 17 percent abroad.[6]

At the beginning of the twentieth century, there were more Jewish working women; as in French society as a whole, however, their socioprofessional circumstances were inferior to those of men. Studies of the integration of Jewish women in France are virtually nonexistent. Nonetheless, what little statistical data there is seems to justify the view that it occurred neither at the same pace nor in the same way as it did in the case of men, despite certain exceptions in the arts. A few famous actresses, certain journalists and writers such as Eugénie Foa and Amélie Pollonais (née Cohen, 1835–98), the sculptor Léonie Rodrigues-Henriques (1820–84), wife of the composer Jacques Halévy and sister of Eugénie Foa, and a small number of women from elite families could pride themselves on social success and integration. In any case, the unique sense of Jewish identity felt by Jewish women in general, and by those who broke down the barriers facing women, cannot be ignored.

INTEGRATION AND JEWISHNESS

Even if it did indeed run up against certain obstacles, Jewish integration in France was relatively rapid and harmonious, on account of which it has sometimes rather hastily been concluded that integration was accompanied by a loss of Jewish identity. To be sure, under the changed circumstances of the time, religious practice showed a clear decline. With emancipation and attainment of citizenship, Jews were no longer tied to the community—until then the only possible sphere of activity for most of them—nor were they required to submit to its religious obligations, themselves the foundation of the very notion of community. In principle, as citizens of a universalist France, they differed in no way from other Frenchmen and women, their religion being a private matter to which they were free to accommodate themselves as they pleased.

Attachment to Jewish tradition, when it was a matter of choice, no longer expressed itself in the same way. With their gradual move away from religious practice, the Jews of post-emancipation France were left to experience a secularized Judaism that for them did not at all mean abandoning their historical responsibility, contrary to what Theodor Herzl (1860–1904), the father of political Zionism, had claimed. If by assimilation is meant a renunciation of one's own identity and a desire to melt into the surrounding society, then it is clear that the majority of French Jews did not choose such a course.

There were few cases of conversion to Christianity in the nineteenth century, even if the fame of certain neophytes made it seem with time that there were many of them. Between 1808 and 1840, there were a hundred or so converted families; under the Second Empire, only a small part of the bourgeoisie defected from Judaism; by the end of the century, the number of those leaving the faith had increased.[7]

It is true that, as Geneviève Straus put it, French Jews were no longer religious enough to feel the need for another faith. Moreover, unlike the situation in Germany or in Austria, their Jewishness was not a hindrance to their advancement in the most varied walks of life. In a society that made a clear distinction between the public and private spheres, Jews could lead their lives as good French citizens without having to radically reject their origins and the Jewish tradition. Of course, the modes of expression of Jewish identity changed.

In Judaism, ethnic and religious elements are not in principle dissociable. What, then, did it mean for Jews who felt removed from religious practice to have an identity whose principal foundation was religion?

FROM JEW TO *ISRAÉLITE*

The particularism of French Jews was tolerated by the state only because its content was uniquely religious (or at least so it was believed). But was this in fact the case? The answer is far from simple. French Jews made common cause with Jews from other countries, welcomed into their country immigrants from abroad, inquired into their own history and accepted their historical responsibility as Jews. The ambiguous circumstance of belonging to a religion and belonging to a people did not disappear. The latter attachment sometimes weighed more heavily, for example after the Dreyfus affair, but always within the framework of a Franco-Judaism that emerged and assumed its full dimensions under the Third Republic. Now that the Jews identified their own interests with those of a republic to which they were grateful for having emancipated them, it was natural that they should enter into alliance with each other.

The loss of Alsace-Lorraine in 1871, the rise of anti-Semitism and its subsequent dissemination by the anti-republican extreme right, and the republican values of liberty, equality, and fraternity combined to confirm the Jews in their support for the government. For them, the Revolution had realized the grand ideals of justice and Jewish progress, the republic having continued its work in constructing a society founded on the values contained in Judaism. Jews could therefore feel at ease under such a regime. There was not only a community of interests between republican France and its Jews but also a common identity.

The orientalist James Darmesteter gave theoretical expression to this synthesis of progressive Jewish and French values. Already in the first generation of emancipation, voices such as those of Alexandre Weill (1811–99) and Joseph Salvador (1796–1873) were raised in favor of a more or less similar combination. Darmesteter was himself influenced by the ideas of Salvador. Franco-Judaism, in the formulation he gave it, brought about the transition from Jew to *israélite* and led to the apparent abandonment of the notion of the Jewish people—that is, of a collective culture and identity going beyond the framework of religious rites and beliefs—in favor of a boundless patriotism, which was to await its highest expression during the Great War.

The Jews of France were henceforth *français israélites*—French men and women of Jewish ancestry—and, accordingly, embraced patriotism as a way of repaying their debt to the republic. As members of the United Front (*Union sacrée*) that rallied all French citizens against the enemy in 1914, the Jews, following the example of their fellow citizens, became French. In this guise they gave their body and soul in the struggle to liberate Alsace-Lorraine and its oppressed peoples and to throw off the (anti-Semitic) yoke of the Reich. Allegiance to the ideals of Franco-Judaism made it possible to overlook the fratricidal character of a war that pitted French and German Jews against each other. On the French side some 40,000 Jews enlisted—among them 8,500 foreign volunteers, perhaps a quarter of the immigrant Jewish community—out of a population of 190,000, French Algeria included. The tribute paid was heavy: 7,500 dead,[8] 1,600 of them foreigners. Henceforth the *israélite* considered himself as an integral part of the history of France. The United Front nonetheless rapidly gave way to a resurgent and virulent anti-Semitism that, among other things, did not cease to downplay the role of French Jews during the Great War.

Integration vs. Assimilation

Zionists accused European Jews of having chosen a course—assimilation—that would lead ineluctably to the disappearance of the Jewish people. Historiography has seized upon this version of events and enshrined it as a truth. But when the matter is examined closely, it becomes apparent that the process of integration culminating in Franco-Judaism, long central to the way the Jews of France thought of themselves, did not involve a break with Judaism.

If one considers as evidence the giving of a biblical or Jewish personal name, clear differences can be observed between immigrant and indigenous groups, between native Parisians and immigrants from elsewhere in France, and also between different social strata. Immigrants from eastern Europe and Mediterranean countries, as well as working-class Jews, were more likely to have Jewish forenames. Looking at the census data of

1872 regarding the Jewish population as a whole, one notices that, though single Jewish personal names were less common than they had been, such names were now attached to a French personal name, which came first. The French name was used in dealings with French society and the Jewish name in the private sphere, in certificates of marriage, burial, and so on—a practice also found among state Jews during the Third Republic. On the other hand, the political elite bore Jewish personal names less frequently than senior civil servants. In any case, the majority of Jews kept their patronymic, the public sign of their membership in the Jewish community.

As for the proportion of exogamous marriages, this was only 14 percent among the Jewish Parisian bourgeoisie under the Second Empire; nor was the number any higher among well-known musicians during this period and during the Third Republic. In the commercial upper middle class, this kind of marriage was exceptional. In government and military circles, 95 percent of the members of the *préfecture*, 83 percent of the generals, 78 percent of the magistrates, and 73 percent of the deputies and senators of the Third Republic married within the Jewish community. Many state Jews were to go on following the same route up through the interwar period. Most had themselves buried in the presence of a rabbi, as did the celebrated Jewish composer-musicians of the nineteenth century. The fact that they were in the service of the state did not prohibit them from privately carrying on certain Jewish traditions—a telling illustration of how French Judaism actually worked. Complete integration did not mean total assimilation.[9]

The composer-musicians did not hesitate to give specifically Jewish titles to their works; certain themes of their compositions were evocative of Jewish life as well. Some served as Jewish community leaders. Jacques Halévy was active in the consistory. The same was true of a great many state Jews. Others such as Isaac Strauss, court musician to Napoleon III, collected Jewish liturgical objects. These public men, who in some sense constituted the elite of French Jewry, had a strong awareness of their Jewishness and did not at all deny their Jewish identity. Moreover, instances of conversion were very few among both musicians and state Jews. Nor did the latter shirk their historical responsibility as Jews, responding publicly to anti-Semitic intrigues not only before the Dreyfus affair but also during the interwar period.

Women and Their Identity

Little is known about the identity of Jewish women during this period of economic, social, and cultural ascendency in certain strata of French Jewry. Emancipation had changed the condition of women only in a legal sense:

women were still dependent on marriage and confined to the domestic sphere, where they were expected above all to be good wives and good mothers. In the most integrated families, these women were less removed than their husbands from tradition and religious practice. In the division of roles within the family, religion was the responsibility of the woman, who transmitted moral values with a view to strengthening the social order. It therefore fell to her to see to the child's moral and religious education, both in the upper bourgeoisie and in the middle class that imitated its habits. Indeed throughout the West at the end of the nineteenth and the beginning of the twentieth century it was generally the mother who per- petuated the Jewish sensibility within the household and transmitted Jew- ish identity and Jewish traditions to her children. Cases of conversion and exogamous marriage continued to be fewer among women than among men as well.

Women in the arts and the noted *salonnières* of the day did not fit this model, which to one degree or another held for most Jewish women in France during the period. The fact remains that even when they re- nounced their Jewishness or tried to hide it, such women were still consid- ered to be Jewish; talk about them was full of references to their back- ground, which made it difficult for them to construct a clear-cut identity for themselves. Their friendships—for example, that of Rachel, the great tragedienne, with the Jewish statesman Adolphe Crémieux—and the stands they took during the Dreyfus affair—such as that of Geneviève Straus (née Halévy), who defended the Dreyfusard cause against the ma- jority of her friends—show that even those women who were furthest re- moved from Judaism did not completely cut their ties with it.

MODERN SOLIDARITY

For many Jews, the connection with Judaism no longer took the form of synagogue-going or strict observance, but instead of a more modern type of solidarity: emancipated Jews now went to the aid of their brethren in Europe, Africa, and the Near East.

During the Conquest of Algeria

In 1830, France conquered Algeria, which had between 15,500 and 16,000 Jews or about a tenth of the country's urban population. The government appointed a "head of the Hebrew nation" and the emancipated Jews of France assumed the task of "regenerating" the Jews of Algeria after the French model. In 1842, the central consistory, with the help and recom- mendation of the War Ministry, sent a fact-finding mission led by Jacques-

Isaac Altaras (1786–1873), president of the Marseilles consistory, and Joseph Cohen (1817–99), a young lawyer from Aix-en-Provence. The findings of the Altaras-Cohen mission, summarized in its "Rapport sur l'état moral et politique des Israélites de l'Algérie et des moyens de l'améliorer" (Report on the Moral and Political State of the Jews of Algeria and on Ways to Improve It), were instructive. The Jews are characterized in the report as a useful element of French domination in Algeria, which made their integration in French culture and society—taken to be superior—a matter of urgent concern. In this respect the position of the authors was opposite that of the Governor General of Algeria, for whom the Jews constituted a danger to colonization. Additionally, they established a hierarchy among the various local populations, placing the Jews above the Moors and nomadic Arab peoples. With regard to the question of what progress the Jews could make, Altaras and Cohen took a rather optimistic view. The Jews' present position was explained by the pernicious effects of their environment; therefore "regeneration" was considered to fall within the realm of possibility. Recommendations for reform were made along these lines. The extreme poverty of the native Jewish population was also emphasized. Further reports, composed by other Jewish leaders, subsequently examined the question and proposed various measures, both administrative as well as social and cultural, aimed at integrating the Jews of Algeria.

The government, for its part, also appointed two commissions made up of Jewish notables to study the question, one in Algeria in 1840 and the other in Paris in 1843. An ordinance of 1845 provided for the creation of three consistories in Algiers, Oran, and Constantine that would be attached to an autonomous central consistory of Algeria. Finally, the Algerian Jews were provided with French-style organizations without anything having been decided with regard to their civil and political status. Adolphe Crémieux made several trips to Algeria and championed equal rights for its Jews, a cause he defended on entering the provisional government in 1848. It was only in 1870 that he succeeded in arranging for them to become French citizens, thanks to the decree bearing his name (which did not include the Jews of the southern territories). In the course of integration, between 1851 and 1900, the Jewish population of Algeria grew from 21,048 to 57,538, or 1 percent of the total population, not counting 1,423 Jews in the southern territories. The census of 1931 recorded their population as 102,013.[10]

The European population of Algeria, regardless of political preference, viewed the promotion of the country's Jews without great enthusiasm. From the promulgation of the *décret Crémieux* until the end of the nineteenth century, Jews were the target of local anti-Semitic attacks. The decree was abrogated in October 1940 by the Vichy government and reinstated by the Comité Française de Libération Nationale on 20 October 1943.

The Damascus Affair

The episode of the Damascus affair, which lay the groundwork for institutionalized Jewish solidarity, provides further evidence that the French Jewish elite did not regard Judaism only as a religion. In 1840, a Capuchin monk named Brother Thomas disappeared along with his servant. They were never found. At the instigation of the French consul, the crime was imputed to the Jews. Accusations of ritual murder had become more and more frequent in the Ottoman Empire during the period. But this affair was played out in the context of France's imperialistic ambitions in the Middle East under Louis Philippe. Jews were arrested and imprisoned; some were tortured. Their co-religionists in Europe, emancipated or in the process of being emancipated, could not help but react to the reappearance of this medieval calumny, still less since the head of the French government, Adolphe Thiers, supported by the Catholic press, endorsed the claim of ritual murder. A delegation composed of the British philanthropist Sir Moses Montefiore (1784–1885), his secretary, the orientalist Louis Loewe (1809–88), Adolphe Crémieux, at the time the vice president of the consistory in Paris, and the French orientalist Salomon Munk (1805–67) left for the Middle East. They obtained the release of prisoners and declarations attesting to the innocence of those who had been blamed. Montefiore managed also to extract from the Ottoman sultan a firman, or edict, acknowledging the emptiness of the accusation of ritual murder in the hope that such an admission would sway European public opinion in the matter.

This affair allowed the Jews of Europe to rediscover their co-religionists in the Near East, whom from now on they worked hard to emancipate and westernize after their own fashion through education. It also gave an important impetus to the development of the Jewish press, the modern and indispensable tool of communication. Thus, at the same time as similar journals were being established elsewhere in Europe, *Les Archives israélites* (1840–1935) and *L'Univers israélite* (1844–1940) appeared in France.

Creation of the Alliance Israélite Universelle

The Damascus affair and then in 1858 the Mortara affair, which involved the forced conversion to Catholicism of a Jewish child in Italy, led two years later to the creation of the Alliance Israélite Universelle, in 1860. Founded by the initiative of a handful of young people (some of them Saint-Simonians) outside the consistorial system, this organization aimed at defending the interests of Jews throughout the world. Beginning in 1862 it threw itself into an immense program of education with missionary zeal, accompanied by an emancipationist ideology and the ambition of remodeling other Jewish communities in the idealized image of modern Franco-Judaism. It opened hundreds of schools for boys and girls in North Africa and, in particular, the Middle East, offering elementary instruction in the French language and introducing the curricula of French schools, supplemented by the teaching of Jewish subjects.

The Alliance interceded regularly on behalf of Jews outside France who suffered persecution. It developed into a sizable organization, playing a role of the highest importance both in Jewish affairs under the republic in France and in the countries where it set up schools.

SCHOLARSHIP AND THE PERPETUATION OF TRADITION

Fearing that integration would lead to the disappearance of the Jewish people, some scholars began at once to write its history. At the same time they tried to give Jewish history a legitimacy it had formerly lacked; in traditional historiography, which approached the past from the perspective of nationality, the Jews as a people seemed almost by definition not to have a place. A postbiblical history that did not reduce Judaism to a religion thus filled a gap. The first of these histories, the *Résumé de l'histoire des Juifs modernes* (Summary of the History of the Modern Jews), was published in 1828 by Léon Halévy, the son of a German immigrant, brother of the composer Jacques, and a Saint-Simonian. Already in this work one finds the germ of what would later become Franco-Judaism. Halévy was followed by many others, including Élie-Aristide Astruc (1831–1905), Moïse Schwab (1839–1918), Isidore Loeb (1839–92), James Darmesteter, Léon Kahn (1851–1900), Théodore Reinach (1860–1928), as well as a number of regional historians.

Certain Jewish orientalists also devoted a part of their work to Jewish studies, especially during the Third Republic. There was no exact equivalent in France of the Wissenschaft des Judentums, which grew up among Jewish intellectuals in Germany from 1809. Subsequently the Verein für Kultur und Wissenschaft der Juden was founded in 1819 in Berlin by a group of young Jews trained in philology and philosophy in the German universities, which Heine joined in 1822. This movement, the founding father of which was Leopold Zunz (1794–1886), assigned itself the task of submitting the sacred texts of Judaism to the methods of modern critical research in order to free them from the influence of traditional exegesis. Judaism, which for these Jews was moribund as a religion, now became the object of detached study in the hope that nothing would be lost in the flood of secularization. It was also a way of opening up such study to other scholars and thus to remove it from the narrow circle of Jewish religious specialists by showing that Judaism was also a culture, a history, and a politics. To be sure, the Berlin association was dissolved very shortly thereafter, in 1824, but the current of thought it represented was closely tied to the Jewish Reform movement and lastingly influenced modern approaches to Jewish studies.

In France, those who harbored similar ambitions conducted such research for the most part in addition to their main work and not as qualified specialists in the field. Moreover, with the exception of Salomon Munk and Joseph Derenbourg, they did so in a private capacity. The position of Jews in French society, mirrored by that of Jewish scholars in the academy, did not in fact justify a specific—still less exclusive—investment in this area. In the academic world in which these scholars moved, the study of Judaism occupied a place comparable to that of Judaism itself in French society: for the most part it came within the private sphere of individual life. These scholars unquestionably cultivated a concern for objectivity and, like their German colleagues, managed in the eyes of their non-Jewish compatriots to confer scientific respectability upon the study of Judaism using a historical-critical approach. Nonetheless, whereas in Germany those who devoted themselves to such activity did so outside the university, where they remained unwelcome, in France there was not the same need for acceptance on the part of emancipated Jewish scholars, who were socially and professionally integrated, and so the study of Judaism remained a secondary pursuit. What is more, in France this branch of study could in certain cases actually have its own place in the university: thus Munk held a chair in Jewish studies, an exceptional situation in Europe and something possible only in France, a country where Judaism was nothing more than a religion and therefore, as an object of analysis, no less legitimate than any other religion.

To channel and sustain this impulse, the Société des Études Juives was created in 1880 together with the journal *Revue des études juives*, both of which still exist. Jewish scholarship developed in the years that followed through the contributions of scholars such as Israël Lévi (1856–1939), Théodore Reinach, Mayer Lambert (1863–1930), Maurice Liber (1884–1956), and others previously mentioned. Though such scholarship on the whole was scientific in spirit, it is nonetheless true that not all the work done in this area by French scholars met a high standard of methodological rigor. Some of it was devoted to manufacturing arguments in support of the ideology of Franco-Judaism.

The various attitudes we have examined in this chapter, ambivalent though they may sometimes seem, testify to the persistent place occupied by Judaism in the Jewish imagination. There was nonetheless no single way in which Jews identified with Judaism in the nineteenth and early twentieth century, any more than there was later. Their relationship to Judaism was complex and plural, involving men and women, immigrants and natives, immigrants from within France and immigrants from abroad. Jews did become integrated and acculturated; but for the most part they did not completely renounce their uniqueness. Emancipationists, in keeping with their universalistic conception of society, had advocated assimilation—the disappearance of Jewish particularism—as the essential condition of fully assumed French citizenship. Their hopes were to be disappointed.

It is clear that immigrants newly arrived in France from more traditional Jewish societies were slower in adopting the values of the French Jewish community, which, moreover, were not altogether the same for all its members. It must not be forgotten, however, that immigrants came from different regions and so had been subject to different cultural influences. These influences were to be decisive in shaping their behavior in their new homeland. It is a mistake to treat the immigration to France that began in the 1880s as wholly emanating from eastern Europe. A great many Jewish immigrants did come from there, but there were others who came from other places as well. And to believe that these newcomers were slow to absorb the Jewish and non-Jewish values of the West betrays a certain romanticism. Here once again not only geographic origin but also membership in different sociocultural groups played a nontrivial role in determining whether adherence to the values of traditional Jewish society was larger or smaller. Sooner or later, descendants of these various populations who were born on French soil came to adopt the norms shared by the Jews of France. But not every wave of immigration chose the same strategy with regard to the surrounding society, which was at once French and Jewish.

CHAPTER TEN

Breaches in Franco-Judaism

MARKED BY THE MASSIVE ARRIVAL of new immigrants, the birth of modern anti-Semitism, the Dreyfus affair, and the emergence of Zionism, the end of the nineteenth century destabilized the model of Franco-Judaism that until then had been inseparable from integration *à la française*.

IMMIGRATION

The assassination of Tsar Alexander II in 1881 and the pogroms that slaughtered the Jews in its wake, the restrictive measures adopted in Romania, then the Kishinev pogrom in 1903 and the crushing of the Russian Revolution of 1905 triggered very large waves of emigration. Of the 3.5 million Jews who left central and eastern Europe between 1880 and 1925, 2.65 million settled in the United States, 210,000 in England, 150,000 in Argentina, 112,000 in Canada, and 100,000 in France. In the last decades of the nineteenth century, the United States was considered by Jewish immigrants to be a sort of promised land—something that was not yet the case with France.

In Paris, prior to World War I, the immigrants numbered 30,000 to 40,000—nearly half of the total number of Jews in the capital, and in any case representing a major change in the composition of the Parisian Jewish community. Nonetheless, on the eve of the war, Jewish immigrants from eastern Europe represented only a fifth (17 percent) of the total number of immigrants in Paris. Until the 1920s, the Jewish migratory movement was transatlantic. France remained chiefly a stopover for Jewish migrants en route to the United States and Argentina. At this time, the noninterventionist policy of the western countries meant that border controls were not strict. Jewish immigrants were not, however, well regarded. They were considered revolutionary agitators and typically treated as anarchists.[1]

The development of modern anti-Semitism also dates from the 1880s. French Jews, now that they were on the verge of achieving integration for themselves, feared the arrival of Jews whose appearance reminded them of what they themselves had looked like before emancipation. Concerned that a concentration of Jewish immigrants whose customs seemed to belong to another time would arouse anti-Semitic feeling, they sought to direct this immigration toward other countries. During the same period a wave of xenophobia broke out in reaction to economic crisis and the subsequent rise in unemployment, also to uncertainty and worry in the face of modernization, which led to the foreigner being made a scapegoat. In reality, given their small numbers, Jewish immigrants represented no danger. The fact remained, however, that they were foreigners.

This immigration caused the non-Jewish world to discover the existence of a Jewish proletariat—even if most Jews did not work in factories—at a time when there was a great deal of talk in the non-Jewish press about Jewish banking, finance, and commerce. In fact, the newcomers were mainly skilled workers and artisans—typically leather craftsmen, hatters, furriers, woodworkers, cabinetmakers, jewelers, and clothing manufacturers. French-born Jews remained silent on the subject of these immigrants, from whom they were separated by linguistic, cultural, and economic barriers. These were Jews who spoke Yiddish, who were still attached to Jewish traditions, and who were poor; to them, the indigenous population seemed very un-Jewish. French Jews adopted a paternalistic attitude, hoping to make the new arrivals share their devotion to the culture and civilization of their new homeland—to make of them French men and women of the Jewish faith. The schools of the consistory and the lay school system of the republic succeeded in realizing this aim.

The years that followed Dreyfus's rehabilitation, from 1906 until the Great Depression in the 1930s, were a time of respite for immigrant Jews, happy to be able to "live like God in France" (*Lebn vi Got in Frankraykh*), as the Yiddish proverb put it. This climate encouraged their integration, which had to proceed on two fronts: integration with both the new host society and the French Jewish community. Immigrants did not ask themselves whether they were Jewish: naturally they were, without supposing this to be incompatible with either their attachment to France or their feelings of gratitude toward it. Each wave of immigration thus reawakened a sense of Jewishness within the increasingly secularized Jewish population of France.

The integration of these new immigrants was accompanied by social mobility, more often than not into the middle classes. Their children succeeded in the liberal professions, public administration, and the academy. In the case of certain sons of immigrants, such as André Citroën (1878–1935), who was born of Polish parents in Paris, the climb up the social ladder was spectacular.

In reaction against the rejection that they met with among French-born Jews, the newcomers created specifically immigrant organizations that would be capable of responding to their needs and help mitigate the indifference of French and French Jewish institutions. They founded their own periodicals (thirteen newspapers between 1906 and 1914); their own cultural organizations, including a Yiddish theater in 1907; their own mutual aid societies, including societies of fellow countrymen (*landsman-shaftn*), a kind of association for the defense of common interests; their own philanthropic societies, including the Asile Israélite de Paris; their own pedagogical organizations; their own oratories; their own nonconsistorial synagogue; and their own restaurants and kosher butcher shops.[2] The Fédération des Sociétés Juives de Paris, a group of twenty-two immigrant associations, was created in 1913. It signalled the desire for independence on the part of immigrant groups in relation to French-born Jews and their interest in managing their own affairs.

Additionally, they organized their own trade union movement on the eve of the First World War. The ideological currents that swept through the Jewish and non-Jewish worlds during the period were imported by immigrant groups, among them Bundists (members of the Bund),[3] anarchists, revolutionary socialists, and Zionists.

This period also saw the emergence of largely Jewish neighborhoods in Paris, such as the *Pletzl* (little square) in the Marais. The solidarity born of the immigrant experience in these neighborhoods went hand-in-hand with plurality in religious and political expression.[4]

Francophone Jews from the Levant—practitioners of the Sephardic rite—also made their way to Europe, especially after 1909, fleeing the obligatory military service instituted in the Ottoman Empire and later the Balkan wars of 1912–13. In 1911, they numbered 4,568 in the Seine department.[5] These descendants of the Jews expelled from the Iberian peninsula in the fifteenth century naturally looked to France, whose language and culture they had learned in the schools of the Alliance Israélite Universelle and in the French congregationist schools established in the Near East. Some North African Jews—particularly Algerians, French since the *décret Crémieux* of 1870—joined these groups of immigrants. The Levantine Jews (or *Orientaux* as they were usually called) were concentrated in the eleventh arrondissement, in the neighborhood bounded by the Place Voltaire, the rue Popincourt and the rue Sedaine, and adjacent streets.

Less numerous than the Jews of central and eastern Europe, who adhered to a different rite, they too built their own synagogues and created their own associations. In 1909 they founded the Association Cultuelle Orientale de Paris, responsible not only for supervising religious practice but also for bringing moral and material assistance to Ottoman Jews arriving in the capital. The integration of these immigrants was straightforward, for they already knew French before they arrived, and so they rapidly ceased to appear to be foreigners.

In the beginning of the twentieth century, many Jewish artists, painters, and sculptors settled in Paris: Louis Marcoussis (1883–1941) in 1903, Jules

Pascin (1885–1930) and Sonia Dalaunay (1885–1979) in 1905, and Amedeo Modigliani (1884–1920) in 1906. Jacques Lipchitz (1891–1973) and Ossip Zadkine (1890–1967) in 1909, Moïse Kisling (1891–1953), Marc Chagall (1887–1985), and Chaïm Soutine (1894–1943) in 1910, Chana Orloff (1888–1968) in 1911, Michel Kikoïne (1891–1968) in 1912, and Mané-Katz (1894–1962) in 1913 were followed after the war by many others, such as Jean Atlan (1913–60) and Marcel Janco (1895–1984). In the years preceding the Great War, La Ruche, a circle of artists whose studios were located in the Passage Dantzig in Montparnasse, offered shelter to Jewish artists such as Marek Schwartz (1892–1962), Joseph Tchaïkov (1888–1986), and Léon Krémègne (1890–1981), who tried to create a new Jewish art: their group was known as the Maḥmadim (The Precious Ones) after the title of the journal they had founded. In the years following the Dreyfus affair, Paris was the triumphant capital of art and liberty. Jewish immigrants participated in the great artistic movements that blossommed in the city and contributed to the renown of what was improperly called the School of Paris, also known in the 1920s as the Jewish School. The fact that during this same period there was a large number of Jewish art dealers and critics drew an anti-Semitic reaction at a time when nationalism and conservatism were rife.

Foreign-born Jews massively signed up as volunteers during the Great War: they numbered about 8,500, of whom 2,000 or so were to die in combat.[6] In a way, then, they had repaid their debt to the country that had welcomed them and demonstrated their patriotism to their fellow, French-born Jews.

ANTI-SEMITISM

The anti-Semitism that began to develop in France in the 1880s was a sort of composite result of the Christian anti-Judaism of right-wing and clerical circles, the Judeophobic anticapitalism of the socialists and working classes, and the elaboration of the pseudoscientific concept of race. This last concept, which derived from recent discoveries in biology and owed much to the success of positivism and Darwinism, led to a theory of racial inequality according to which the "Jewish race" was inferior to the "Aryan race."

An obscure journalist named Édouard Drumont united all these elements and brought them to the attention of the widest possible audience. Anti-Semitism gathered momentum in the context of the industrial revolution, under the pressure of urbanization and the upheavals it brought about in a country that was traditionally rural and Catholic. It fed on the worries aroused by the economic depression of the last quarter of the

century and the fears generated by unemployment, on the political crises
that shook the government, the secularization of society, the growth of the
workers' movement, anarchist scares, the triumph of science and new tech-
nologies—all this against the background of a singular mixture of nationalism and xenophobia in Europe and, in France, nervousness and anxiety.

Anti-Semitism had taken root earlier in central and eastern Europe with
the development of pan-Slavism and pan-Germanism before attracting a
following in France. In 1878, the first anti-Jewish party was founded in
Berlin by the Lutheran minister Adolf Stöcker and the journalist Wilhelm
Marr. Marr was the first to use the word "anti-Semitism," a term of con-
tempt expressing all the hatred and resentment felt by Germans discon-
tented with their lot in relation to the Jews, whom they regarded as infe-
riors. His example was imitated with enthusiasm in other countries.

It certainly cannot be said that France at the end of the nineteenth century was fundamentally anti-Semitic. Even so, French popular culture was
still influenced by Judeophobic cliches inherited from the past. Jews were
not yet seen, despite their integration and acculturation, as a full-fledged
citizens—even though governments had looked favorably upon them since
the reign of Louis Philippe. Christian and right-wing anti-Semitism persisted in a latent state. It manifested itself during the Damascus affair of
1840 and the Mortara affair of 1858 and reappeared whenever the church
felt itself threatened, as it had under the July Monarchy. During the Third
Republic it became virulent, beginning in 1879 with the reaction to the
secular reforms undertaken by the new government. Thus opened an era
of denunciations of Jewish conspiracy, a recurrent theme that was supposed to explain all the dysfunctions of society and politics and that soon
was to be inseparable from the twin theme of masonic conspiracy. The
Jew-Freemason tandem was long-lived, with the Jew being considered the
architect of revolution and anticlericalism, the persecutor of the clergy,
and the destroyer of Christian religion and civilization.

From the beginning of the century onward anti-Judaism in its modern
form produced a substantial literature: it grew in size under the Second
Empire with the appearance in 1869 of *Le Juif, le Judaïsme et la Judaïsation
des peuples chrétiens* (The Jew, Judaism, and the Judaization of the Christian
Peoples) by the aristocrat Henri Gougenot des Mousseaux, which was to
become the bible of anti-Semitism; aided by the press, it kept growing in
the years ahead with the appearance of newspapers such as *La Croix*, a daily
founded in 1883 that exploited the Jew-Freemason angle. Such publications had the effect of exacerbating the ambient anti-Semitic sensibility.

The left was susceptible to similar inclinations—not until the Dreyfus
affair would it renounce them once and for all. The industrial revolution and the subsequent emergence of the problem of the workers produced a new theme that supported left-wing anti-Semitism: anticapitalism.

The Jews as a whole were identified with the Rothschilds. Certain Saint-Simonian Jews had in fact been ardent promoters of the industrial revolution and of mechanized production. Socialists such as Charles Fourier and Pierre Joseph Proudhon denounced the consequences of this revolution as well as the train of injustices that followed in its wake, and advocated a return to the preindustrial stage.

Alphonse Toussenel, a disciple of Fourrier, stigmatized the reign of money in *Les Juifs, rois de l'époque: histoire de la féodalité financière* (The Jews, Kings of the Age: History of Financial Feudalism), a two-volume work published in 1845 by the Librairie de l'École Sociétaire. It was reissued in 1847 and subsequently in 1886 and 1888, a period that saw the rise of a venomous anti-Semitism. Toussenel's work inspired extremists such as Drumont as well as a conservative and rural anti-Semitism that later found its most perfect expression in the Action Française. Georges Duchêne, a close friend of Proudhon, also followed in Toussenel's footsteps. At the beginning of the Third Republic, the most important anti-Semitic writings came from the pens of socialists such as Albert Regnard, Gustave Tridon, and Auguste Chirac. While certain early socialists confused Jews and Jewish bankers with capitalism, others became anti-Semites owing to anti-religious convictions. The Rothschilds fueled the fantasies of anti-Semites on both the left and the right, together with the corollary dread of occult Jewish power.

Pseudoscientific anti-Semitism, with its hierarchies among races, idealized the Aryan while making the Jew—visibly afflicted by the physical signs of his inferiority—the negation of the Aryan. It found ardent defenders not only in Germany but also in France, notably in the person of Édouard Drumont, who succeeded in giving it a very large audience, drawing as he pleased upon a variety of authors including Hippolyte Taine and (though his thought was much more complex and nuanced) Ernest Renan. Maurice Barrès was to base his particular brand of anti-Semitism in turn on Drumont's popular pseudoscientific racism.

These various anti-Semitic tendencies fed on events from 1880 on and converged in a *fin de siècle* characterized by political, social, and economic transformations that destabilized French society. The crash in 1882 of the Union Générale, a Catholic bank created in 1878 by Paul-Eugène Bontoux, a former employee of the Rothschilds, was attributed to them, even though at trial Bontoux was found guilty of fraudulent dealings. The right and the Catholic press flew into a rage against the Jews. In fact, the Jews were only scapegoats and the crash only a pretext. It was followed by the eruption in 1892 of the Panama scandal, a case of corporate corruption extending over a five-year period (1888–93) in which several Jewish businessmen were implicated, ending in the ruin of thousands of small savers. From this point on, anti-Semitism was feverishly deployed in all its forms.

Anti-republicanism became merged with anti-Semitism, all the more since with the advent of anticlerical republicans the clergy and aristocratic elements had been removed from power. An all-out religious war between Catholicism and rationalism was at hand. The Jewish conspiracy served both as explanation and justification for the discontent in Catholic circles. Between 1882 and 1885, three attempts were made to start up anti-Semitic newspapers, two in Paris—*L'Anti-Juif* and *L'Antisémitique*—and one in Montdidier—*Le Péril social*—none of which lasted beyond the first few issues.[7]

Between the Union Générale crash and the Panama scandal, a genuine turning point occurred with the publication in 1886 by Marpon and Flammarion of Drumont's major work, *La France juive*. Issued in two volumes and totalling 1,200 pages, it crystallized all the new anti-Semitic tendencies. The work turned out to be a remarkable publishing success: the initial printing of 2,000 copies was bought up at once; within two months more than 70,000 copies had been sold and more than 100,000 by the end of the year. By 1887 the book was already in its one hundred forty-fifth printing. Dozens of reprints and run-on editions followed. By 1914, the number of printings exceeded two hundred. Given that each printing consisted of between 1,000 and 5,000 copies, the impact of such a work may readily be imagined.[8] The massive circulation of the book, which initially was published at the author's personal expense, is explained by the fact that the public was already disposed to be receptive to the arguments developed by the author, without any vigorous promotion having to be done on its behalf. The press, now freed from its shackles by the law of 1881 limiting journalistic criminal liability, did its part to contribute to the work's success, though this was slowed by the author's death in 1917 and the United Front (*Union sacrée*) of the war years. In the 1930s, however, its theses came to be adopted by the many newspapers and various other publications of the extreme right.

The anti-Semitism advocated by Drumont rallied the disunited Catholic and working class forces of the nation in combat against a republic that was seen as capitalist, Judaized, and—naturally—anti-Catholic. As it developed into an ideology and political program capable of explaining crises and absorbing discontent, it came to crystallize French national identity in opposition to the Jew, who was now perceived as a menace to the integrity of the nation. The extreme right was henceforth to exploit this line to the fullest.

In 1889, Drumont and Jacques Biez organized an anti-Semitic society that was dissolved a year later, however, for lack of support. In 1892, Drumont started his own newspaper, *La Libre Parole*, which publicly broke the Panama scandal. Notable for its highly anti-Semitic and polemical tone, its sales were weak despite an initial print-run of 200,000 copies.[9] The various Parisian and regional editions of *La Croix*, published by the Assumptionists, and of the *Pèlerin*, amounting to some 500,000 copies, and associations such as the Ligue Antisémitique, which claimed as many as 11,000 members in July 1898, helped bring about the boom in popularity of an anti-Semitic movement that had only to be fed by the press in order to explode during the Dreyfus affair.[10] For its part, the left did not yet condemn anti-Semitism during this period and remained susceptible to certain of its overarching themes.

THE AFFAIR

The Facts

Anti-Semitism was nonetheless far from being a violently hostile phenomenon in the mid-1890s when the Dreyfus affair erupted, in a nation that included some 130,000 Jews (60,000 of them in Algeria).[11] At the end of September 1894, army intelligence accused Captain Alfred Dreyfus (1859–1935), a French Jew and artillery officer attached to the general staff, of authorship of a letter—the famous *bordereau*—addressed to the military attaché of the German embassy in Paris. Dreyfus was arrested on 15 October, committed to Cherche-Midi prison, convicted of treason on 22 December 1894, and sentenced to deportation and imprisonment for life in a fortified compound. He protested his innocence. An appeal for review of the case was nonetheless rejected as unwarranted. Anti-Semitic passions broke loose during Dreyfus's public degradation on 5 January 1895—a ceremony that was to make a powerful impression on the future founder of Zionism, Theodor Herzl, who witnessed the scene as a correspondent for the Viennese newspaper *Neue Freie Presse*. Dreyfus was deported to Devil's Island, off Cayenne on the Guyanan coast.

At the outset the matter was considered to be an ordinary case of treason. Dreyfus's sentencing failed to arouse controversy. Then in 1896 the affair took a new turn. Army intelligence intercepted a telegram—the *petit bleu*—sent by the German embassy to a Major Esterhazy, who had been placed under close surveillance. The new chief of the intelligence section, Lieutenant Colonel Georges Picquart, discovered in the course of his inquiry suspicious contacts between Esterhazy and the embassy's military attaché. On reopening the secret dossier on Dreyfus, he became convinced that Esterhazy was the real author of the *bordereau* attributed to the Jewish officer. Suspecting a miscarriage of justice, he tried in vain to sway his superiors, who refused to reopen the case. Picquart was exiled to Tunisia.

Picquart's assistant, Major Hubert Henry, handed over to the deputy chief of the General Staff a document that was damning for Dreyfus—a document that Henry had, in fact, fabricated himself: the *faux Henry*.

Meanwhile the captain's brother, Mathieu Dreyfus (1857–1930), had furnished the journalist Bernard Lazare, a French Jew and anarchist sympathizer, with a series of documents in February 1895 that established Alfred's innocence. Lazare reported the results of his investigation in a pamphlet published on 6 November 1896 under the title *Une erreur judiciaire: La vérité sur l'affaire Dreyfus* (A Miscarriage of Justice: The Truth about the Dreyfus Affair). By this act, Lazare—an intellectual with a passion for justice—atoned for his earlier writings, which had a whiff of anti-Semitism about them, and so redeemed himself as a French citizen of the Jewish faith. As in the case of other Jewish intellectuals, the affair gave him the opportunity to change direction and commit himself to the struggle as a Jew—and later as a Jewish nationalist of a particular type—without, however, disavowing his anarchist convictions. His stance was far from characteristic of the attitude of his fellow Jews, who at first preferred to avoid stirring up trouble by denouncing the court's mistake, blindly trusting in the fairness of the French legal system.

France Divided

Evidence of a miscarriage of justice divided France into two camps, Dreyfusards and anti-Dreyfusards. There was also a third faction made up of what might be called "Dreyfusians"—those who wished to see an end put to the affair and hoped things would return to normal for the sake of social and political order, followed by the secularization and transformation of the political class.[12] Events took another dramatic turn when, the mistaken verdict having been exposed, military authorities continued to cover up the facts of the matter to protect the honor of the army, the ultimate guarantor of the country's security. The Dreyfusards sought to bring about the victim's rehabilitation and thereby to defend justice and the rights of man. The anti-Dreyfusards, citing reasons of state and the national interest, opposed any reconsideration of the case. Thus two political ideologies clashed: democracy, defended by the Dreyfusards, and authoritarian government, advocated by the anti-Dreyfusards, who had recruited a very mixed group of supporters including not only republicans but also Communards, anti-Semites, revolutionary syndicalists, and anarchists. The leading thinkers of this new nationalist and anti-Semitic right were Maurice Barrès and Charles Maurras. Catholics and the military bolstered their ranks while the opposing camp enlisted antimilitarist and anticlerical forces. The political struggles of the years prior to the affair found themselves perpetuated in this new confrontation. Over time the left detached itself from the nationalist values it had previously defended as part of the Jacobin tradition of patriotism—values that were subsequently to become those of the right. Early on, however, Dreyfus's conviction aroused indignation neither on the part of the socialists nor of the anarchists.

On 13 January 1898, Émile Zola published his open letter to the president of the republic in Clemenceau's newspaper, *L'Aurore*, under the title "J'accuse." Zola attacked the military hierarchy, denounced the reasons of state behind which it had sought to hide as well as the flagrant injustice of the case fabricated against Dreyfus, and proclaimed the captain's innocence. At the same time he criticized the shameful exploitation of anti-Semitic passions. Zola's letter provoked numerous demonstrations against its author, against the Jews, and on behalf of the army. Anti-Semitic violence also broke out in Algeria. Petitions calling for the case to be reopened circulated as well. The intellectual left was born. Zola's trial (7–23 February 1898) ended with a sentence of one year in prison and a fine. On 4 April the court of appeal annulled the verdict on a technicality. In the aftermath of this decision, on 4 June, the Ligue des Droits de l'Homme was founded; it stood firmly behind Dreyfus. At the same moment the anti-revisionist forces were mobilizing. On 31 December 1898 they created the Ligue de la Patrie Française; a year later, its membership stood at 500,000.[13] Large public demonstrations for and against reexamining the case were organized by the two leagues.

The anti-Dreyfus movement soon turned in the direction of nationalism, inseparable in this instance from anti-Semitism. Anti-intellectual, anti-individualistic, anti-Protestant, antiparliamentary, xenophobic, and militaristic, it looked to authoritarian nationalism to rescue the country from its decadence by rallying support for its institutions, chiefly the army and the church, in the context of a strong state resting on traditional values. The system of values its supporters hoped to reconstruct was based on order, authority, and country. Protestants, Jews, Freemasons, and foreigners posed a danger to the national community of ordinary decent folk—all those left behind by economic growth—who made up the bulk of the anti-Dreyfus forces. From the political point of view, Dreyfusism became merged with the defense of republican institutions and democratic values, clarifying the dividing line between left and right. From this point on, the left also had to stand in opposition to anti-Semitism, now the monopoly of the right.

On 8 August 1899, Dreyfus's second trial opened in Rennes. He was found "guilty of complicity with the enemy, with extenuating circumstances" and sentenced to ten years in prison. On 19 September, he was pardoned by President Émile Loubet, anxious to calm the passions aroused by the affair. But Dreyfus continued to ask for rehabilitation. Finally, on 12 July 1906, he was formally rehabilitated and reinstated in the army.

Dreyfus's brother and wife fought hard during these long years on his behalf with the unanimous support of the Dreyfusards. The affair, which so deeply divided France, was a relatively insignificant matter at the beginning. It ended up marking a turning point in the history of the country. But what did it mean for the Jews?

The Affair and Anti-Semitism

The Dreyfus affair surely cannot be treated simply as a Jewish question. Anti-Semitism nonetheless played an important role in the captain's being found guilty, even if several kinds of anti-Semitism were involved. But for a long time Jews refused to see this. The captain himself did not attribute his downfall to anti-Semitism, at least not to judge from his journal, *Cinq années de ma vie (1894–1899)*, which appeared in 1899. And those who took up positions alongside Dreyfus did not do so at the time in order to denounce anti-Semitism. It must not be forgotten, however, that already in 1892 Drumont's newspaper *La Libre Parole* had launched a campaign against Jewish officers in the French army, provoking duels and deaths. Upon Dreyfus's arrest, the anti-Semitic press accorded great importance to the identity of the accused. The captain's own brother wrote, "If Alfred were not a Jew, he would not have gone to Devil's Island."[14] Bernard Lazare likewise denounced the anti-Semitism underlying the sentencing and the refusal to review the case.

What is to be said, however, about the cautious attitude of the Jews toward the affair? First of all, it was probably less cautious than is usually supposed. In defending one of their own, neither French Jews nor their leaders wished at this point to risk putting in doubt their loyalty and their attachment to the country that had granted them emancipation. Hence the silence about the Jewishness of the accused for a certain time. Intellectuals and bourgeois Jews gradually came to take up Dreyfus's cause for various reasons. And at least among certain sections of French Jewry, the affair was to have lasting repercussions.

Anti-Semitism was used as a weapon by the anti-Dreyfusard camp, even if some anti-Semites individually declared themselves in favor of reopening the case; indeed it reached a new peak during the affair. The affair invested anti-Semitism with new functions and captured the attention of the general public, including the working classes, which were influenced by all sorts of anti-Jewish prejudices. Anti-Semitism thus came to achieve widespread popularity, and not only in cities in France. One of its most

striking manifestations was the erection of a monument to Major Henry—
the man who had earlier forged the evidence that was to damn Dreyfus—
following Henry's suicide in 1898. A subscription was also taken up among
anti-Dreyfusards to help his widow cover the costs of various legal actions
she had initiated. It must nonetheless be acknowledged that anti-Semitism
was not the principal motivation behind the Henry memorial—better seen
as an expression of the nationalism that took shape during the 1880s—and
that it was not the only tendency to feed the anti-Dreyfus movement.[15]

Between Dreyfus's rehabilitation and the end of the First World War,
anti-Semitism subsided somewhat. Even so, *La Libre Parole* continued to
appear. Action Française, a monarchist movement founded by Charles
Maurras during the affair in 1898, organized a league in 1905 and three
years later began publication of the anti-Dreyfusard and anti-Semitic daily
L'Action française. It also sponsored violent demonstrations. The anti-
Semitic press continued to broadcast the themes of Judeo-Masonic conspiracy, Jewish invasion, German Jewish espionage, and ritual murder
under the bylines of authors such as Léon Daudet and Albert Monniot.
Catholic circles remained susceptible to anti-Semitic propaganda as well.

In Algeria, the Esterhazy trial and the publication of Zola's "J'accuse"
triggered anti-Semitic unrest in January 1898. The year before, in Mos-
taganem, a clash broke out during a cycling race that led to the pillage of
the Jewish quarter by Moslems and Europeans. Max Régis, the new president of the Anti-Jewish League and the future mayor (elected in 1898) of
Algiers, sent his supporters into the city's Jewish neighborhood with cries
of "Long live the army! Down with the Jews!"; more than a hundred people were injured, and Jewish stores were looted. Bloody riots followed in
Algerian cities with Jews as their targets. Suppression of the violence was
halfhearted. The toll was heavy. This climate of unrest was to last for several years. Did the Dreyfus affair help give greater scope to an anti-Jewish
movement that already existed in embryonic form? The same Max Régis
had also started *L'Anti-Juif*, a newspaper inspired by Drumont's ideas with
a print-run of 20,000 copies—an exceptional figure at the time in this
country. Drumont himself was triumphantly elected, with Régis's support,
député in the second district of Algiers in 1898; three other candidates on
the same slate won elections in Algiers, Oran, and Constantine. Thus, four
of the six Algerian deputies in the Chamber of Deputies belonged to the
anti-Semitic camp. In Algeria, anti-Semitism came close to being a mass
movement.[16]

The First World War diluted anti-Semitism in the patriotic fervor of
the United Front advocated by Barrès. In the same spirit, Barrès consented
in 1917 to include the Jews among the various spiritual families of
France—*Les Diverses Familles spirituelles de la France*, the title of the book he
published that year.

ZIONISM

Zionism under the leadership of Theodor Herzl was primarily a diplomatic movement aimed at finding a solution to the question of Palestine (under Ottoman rule until 1917) in negotiation with the great powers. It needed therefore to take into account the interests of France, a ubiquitous presence in the Ottoman Empire, particularly from the commercial point of view; in addition, France was the custodian of the Ottoman debt and the protector of the holy places in Jerusalem. At first, however, political Zionism had a hard time gaining a foothold in France.

The Zionist Federation of France, founded in 1901, was notable for its recruitment of Jewish immigrants (especially intellectuals) from eastern Europe. On the eve of the First World War, it included eight associations in Paris, one in Nice, and two in Tunis. Apart from André Spire (1868–1966) and Bernard Lazare, who joined the movement for a brief time, Zionist leaders in France were foreign-born from the beginning: Alexandre Marmorek (1865–1923), who in 1899 started the newspaper *L'Écho sioniste* (1899–1905/1912–14, appearing between 1916 and 1921 under the title *Le Peuple juif*), Baruch Hagani (1885–1944), and Myriam Schah (1867–1956). French Jews—brought up to respect the ideals of the French Revolution, proud of their emancipation, concerned to present the image of a thoroughly integrated group, and obsessed with proving their patriotism in a country that was experiencing a rise in anti-Semitism—could greet the young movement founded in Basel in 1897 only with skepticism, indeed anxiety. Ultimately, it risked calling into question the very principles of universalism and patriotism that the French Jewish community stood for. Opposition to Zionism was not clear at all levels of French Jewish society, however, and a number of different positions emerged.

The old established Jews and their institutions, such as the consistory and the Alliance Israélite Universelle, long resisted Zionism. The Quai d'Orsay more often than not found support for its attitude toward Jewish nationalism in the anti-Zionism of the spokesmen of the French Jewish community and, in particular, of its two main institutions, which did little to encourage it to take an interest in a movement that it considered to be of minor importance. Yet the Cambon Declaration of 11 June 1917,[17] drafted by foreign ministry officials, came only shortly before the Balfour Declaration, and indeed precipitated it—without, however, leading to any concrete result. By contrast, the statement on 2 November 1917 by the British Foreign Secretary, Arthur James Balfour, that Great Britain looked favorably upon the establishment of a Jewish homeland in Palestine marked a major turning point in the history of Zionism.

The Balfour Declaration aroused little enthusiasm among native-born

French Jews and, in some, hostility. The Jews of France resisted Zionism, sometimes attacking it vigorously. In this connection the comments made in February 1919 by Sylvain Lévi, a distinguished scholar and member of the central committee of the Alliance Israélite Universelle representing all French citizens of the Jewish faith before the Council of Ten at the Paris Peace Conference, were typical. While recognizing the benign purpose of Zionism in seeking to colonize Palestine on behalf of the unfortunate Jewish masses, he insisted on the difficulty of the Zionist enterprise and, in calling attention to the political and economic pitfalls facing it, restated some of the objections voiced by western Jews. "It seems to me shocking to both reason and feeling," he added, "that scarcely have we gotten past the stage of waiting to obtain equality of rights, we should now demand privileges and exceptional circumstances for the Jews of Palestine. Every exception always ends up backfiring on the person who asks for it and who benefits from it."[18] The Zionist leader Chaim Weizmann (1874–1952) reacted angrily to this speech, going so far as to describe Lévi as a "traitor."

Palestine came under British administration in 1920. The British presence in Palestine was made official in 1922 by the mandate entrusted to it by the League of Nations, providing for the creation of a national homeland and the formation of representative institutions for the whole population with a view eventually to establishing self-rule. France thus lost out, though the Sykes-Picot Agreement of 1916 had granted it control of part of Palestine. Attempts at reconciliation were made in the 1920s, but it was not until the Second World War that the Quai d'Orsay grasped the full implications of the Zionist program.

The Zionists, for their part, displayed great coolness toward France. Moreover, this reserve was part of a francophobic tendency that was widespread in the Jewish world as a whole at the end of the nineteenth century and apparent in Herzl's thinking. The Dreyfus affair probably accounted for a large part of it. Herzl showed a clear liking for Germany, on the other hand, and even greater fondness for Great Britain. Despite intermittent episodes of rapprochement between France and the Zionists, this tendency was predominant in Zionist policy until the Second World War.

This missed encounter—missed on both sides—is primarily explained by ideological and cultural incompatibility. The mistrust was to last after the founding of the State of Israel in 1948; even though Israel showed some signs of flexibility toward France, France leaned more to a policy oriented toward the Arab world. Past disagreements thus continued to poison Franco-Israeli relations.

Curiously, however, Zionism in its early days met with a favorable response in anti-Semitic circles influenced by Drumont's ideas. They saw in it a solution to the Jewish problem in France, through massive emigration to Palestine.

Between the Wars

MIGRATION

In the interwar period, the scale of Jewish immigration from eastern Europe to France increased owing to the fact that the United States, in 1924, closed its borders—a move soon imitated by other countries in the Americas and by South Africa. France subsequently became the favored country for immigration, recording its highest influx ever in the 1920s; after 1924 it received about 200,000 foreigners per year, whereas the United States until that time had an annual inflow of only 170,000.[1] Among the Jewish arrivals were Russians fleeing the Revolution of 1917 as well as Poles, who accounted for the majority; but also Hungarians, Lithuanians, and Latvians in search of better economic opportunities, Romanians come to pursue their studies, and revolutionaries of all nationalities.

More than three quarters of the immigrants came from eastern Europe, with the remaining quarter coming mainly from the Balkans, for economic reasons. They came also in smaller numbers from Germany following Hitler's coming to power in 1933 (most of these German Jews were in transit to other countries); from the Saarland in 1935; from Austria, after the *Anschluss* in 1938; from Czechoslovakia in 1939, in the aftermath of the German conquest; and from North Africa.

Between 1906 and 1939, from 175,000 to 200,000 Jewish immigrants arrived in France, representing 15 percent of the total number of immigrants in the country, the majority of whom were natives of Spain, Italy, and Poland.[2] Exhausted by the Great War, France suffered from a serious labor shortage. The new immigrants therefore did not yet arouse the hostility that would befall those who came after them in the 1930s—a time of world economic crisis marked by Hitler's arrival in power in Germany and the flare-up of xenophobia and anti-Semitism in France. Some 70,000 immigrants from central and eastern Europe settled in Paris between 1920 and 1930, and, if to this number are added those who came before the war, one arrives at a figure of 90,000—three-fifths of the 150,000 Jews inhabiting the capital, now one of the largest Jewish centers in the world. About 15,000 Levantine and North African Jews also elected domicile there. Immigrant Jews were therefore more numerous in Paris than native-born Jews. Unlike the pre–World War I immigration, some of these latest newcomers headed toward the cities of the north, east, and south.[3]

Laws applying to foreigners nonetheless became increasingly restrictive during the 1930s, with immigrants considered to be undesirable being expelled or turned away at the border.

NEIGHBORHOODS AND TRADES

With this most recent influx, Paris saw a new zone of Jewish concentration develop alongside the *Pletzl*—the Belleville neighborhood, astride the eleventh, nineteenth, and twentieth arrondissements, which attracted a population of immigrant artisans and workers. Others settled in Montmartre and Clignancourt. Levantine Jews constituted 4–5 percent of the population of the administrative quarter of La Roquette in the 1920s and 1930s (the total number of Levantine Jews on French soil being estimated at about 35,000).[4] At the same time, French Jews moved to the posh precincts of the western part of the city, followed by some prewar immigrants who had made their fortune in the meantime.

This concentration in specific districts, though it helped strengthen the bonds among immigrants, worked only to reinforce the separation between immigrants and native-born Jews, if only geographically. The latter felt that, by huddling together, immigrants were apt to feed xenophobia; for the former, the move westward in the city by older residents betrayed a desire for assimilation, deliberately removing themselves from the vital centers of Jewish life.

The professional profile of the immigrant groups of the interwar period was not very different from that of prior waves, though now artisanal workers clearly predominated. In Paris, 75 percent of Jewish bankers were recruited from among the native population. Only 15–20 percent of the immigrant population chose to go into commerce and more than half of those who worked in this sector were peddlers and sellers of bric-a-brac, just getting by. Among the immigrant groups, 50 percent of Levantine Jews made their living from trade, a category that includes both wholesalers and ordinary employees.

Twenty percent of French Jews worked in industry as owners or managers of companies manufacturing textiles, jewelry, and precision tools. Among immigrant Jews, 60 percent worked in manufacturing or artisanal trades, 83 percent of these in the textile and clothing fields, working at home or in shops. Of 50,000 immigrants working in this sector, fewer than half were salaried and employed in shops; more than 10,000 worked at home as pieceworkers, quite simply because they had no chance of finding legal employment, which required that their papers be in order. They were also found in booming sectors such as metallurgy. Two percent of the Jewish working population was employed in the book industry in the 1930s; on the other hand, only 19 percent worked in manufacturing. At most five percent of French-born Jews were workers (in the preindustrial sense of the term) at this time. Eight percent of immigrants were in the liberal professions versus 25 percent of French Jews. Between 15 percent and 20 percent of immigrant Levantine Jews were workers, while 9 percent practiced in the liberal professions.[5]

This employment pattern was not specific to Paris, being found also in the provinces. It differed from that of other immigrants, who were fairly uniformly distributed throughout the various economic sectors, whereas the Jews—grouped together by neighborhood, looking to their relatives for help in finding work, often unskilled—were concentrated in a few fields. These were traditionally Jewish trades, chiefly clothing and leather goods but also, to a lesser degree, furniture, jewelry, and watchmaking. The workers in these trades were recent immigrants, the wholesalers of the products they made were older immigrants, and the retailers were French Jews, who themselves feared that this concentration in a restricted number of trades might rekindle anti-Semitism.

We have very little information on female employment. Women helped their fathers and husbands in crafts production, commerce, and manufacturing, juggling piecework, seasonal employment, and domestic jobs. Their presence in the service sector increased as well. In Marseilles during this period, the proportion of women older than fifteen years of age in the workforce was 23 percent, as against 82 percent of men in the same category. These women worked for the most part in household service and as salaried employees in the textile industry (as tailors, dressmakers, laundresses, milliners); some devoted themselves to commerce. In any case, their socioprofessional status was lower than that of men. Among women below the age of thirty, 20 percent were in the service sector and the artisanal trades. The share of women working was greatest for those between the ages of fifteen and nineteen (31 percent). Considering the main age brackets of the female working population, the fifteen to twenty-five age group had the highest proportion of active women (31 percent). In the thirty to sixty group, 22 percent still participated in economic activity, most often in an unskilled trade or as shopkeepers. After the age of sixty, only 12 percent were represented in the workforce, and then exclusively as members of household staff.

In Marseilles, not only did fewer Jewish women of French birth and fewer Jewish *Marseillaises* work than foreign Jewish women, who made up 78 percent of working Jewish women in that city, with French-born Jewish women accounting for 9 percent and Jewish women born in Marseilles for 13 percent; this was also the case by comparison with the general population. Geographic origin also determined professional orientation. Thus one finds French Jewish women employed in skilled artisanal trades (as dressmakers, for example) and in small-scale commerce, and foreign Jewish women working in salaried nonfactory positions (in small shops, for example). Even if more Jewish women were represented in the workforce than in the last decades of the nineteenth century, these were unmarried women for the most part; 79 percent of married women with families to take care of did not practice a trade. The woman's role as wife and mother remained primary during this period.[6]

CONCEPTION OF JUDAISM

Like their prewar predecessors, immigrants from eastern Europe during the interwar period held to a conception of Judaism that did not separate the secular from the religious, the individual from the community, the private sphere from the public sphere, or the fact of belonging to a people from belonging to a religion. In France, as earlier in their native country, the Jewish identity of these immigrants was not defined as a function of the opinion of the non-Jewish world. Indeed, in eastern Europe, the lives of a great majority of these men and women developed in isolation from the vicissitudes of the larger society. For them, the Jewish community remained central.

Of course, the immigrant Jewish population displayed great diversity. One finds Communists as well as Orthodox believers. Nonetheless, despite their very numerous differences, all were agreed on the necessity of preserving their *Yiddishkeit*—the cultural fabric of the *shtetl* or small Jewish village of eastern Europe, centered upon the usage of Yiddish, the language spoken by 80 percent of foreign-born Jews in Paris in the 1930s.[7] And if left-wing immigrants wished to retain only its progressive elements, they were at the same time fiercely opposed to assimilation.

Once settled in a new homeland, these immigrants mainly sought to regain their old way of life—with variations, naturally, that reflected their heterogeneity. Thus they created a great number of organizations, independent of the consistory, whose activities went well beyond the religious and philanthropic domains. They not only brought with them new behaviors and different conceptions of Judaism by comparison with the norms embraced by native Jews, in whom they inspired misgiving and, occasionally, hostility; they helped at the same time to reinvigorate the Jewish community in France, which was in danger of being absorbed by the surrounding society, if only on account of its numerical weakness.

Faced with an increasingly hostile environment, these immigrants had neither the time nor the chance to integrate themselves. Those of their children who were born on French soil nonetheless opted for integration on the standard model of Franco-Judaism—and this despite the fact that the memory of immigration was still very much a living thing for them.

The immigrants of the interwar period came to France without any hope of returning home. France, henceforth, was their country. About 50,000 Jews, taking advantage of a law passed in 1927 that granted them certain opportunities, became naturalized French citizens between then and 1940.[8]

Religion was an integral part of *Yiddishkeit*. In the 1930s, there were hundreds of small synagogues (*shuln*) in Paris where immigrants continued to worship according to the customs of their native land. On the eve of the Second World War, more than half of these immigrants belonged to *landsmanshaftn*—associations of fellow countrymen that functioned as mutual aid societies—of which there were some two hundred. The Fédération des Sociétés Juives de France, created in 1926, united between fifty and ninety such societies (depending on the period) with a total membership of some 20,000.[9] The organization drew most of its support from the middle class, which led the Communists to describe it as *petite-bourgeoise*. In the 1930s, it was headed by Zionist sympathizers. It organized cultural and educational activities while overseeing charitable works available to the immigrant community as a whole and not only to members of its constituent societies. It also had its own university, library, clubs, and *cercles*. Similarly, in 1934, left-wing immigrants created their own educational network, their own university, their own choir, and a Yiddish workers' theater; four years later the Union des Sociétés Juives de France (Farband), a Communist alliance, was formed.

The institutions created by the Jewish immigrant population during the interwar period also included a host of organizations that responded both to its cultural and socioeconomic needs. But the 1930s were also marked by the politicization of the Jews, even if a majority of the immigrants remained outside any political movement and continued to belong to the *landsmanshaftn* as in the past. One finds them in the Bund, the largest socialist movement among the immigrants, which in France had existed since 1900. The French branch was very close to its Polish counterpart, advocating world revolution and Jewish cultural autonomy; in France, it remained aloof from the socialist party (known officially as the Section Française de l'Internationale Ouvrière). Communism also played a large role in this group even though the number of Jews belonging to the Communist party was not high. They were found in the language sections—the Main-d'œuvre étrangère and later, from 1932, Main-d'œuvre immigré—created by the Confédération Générale du Travail Unitaire and the Communist party for the benefit of immigrants who did not understand French. Jewish immigrants were affiliated with the Yiddish subsection, which eventually permitted the consolidation of the workers' movement.

Paris in the 1930s was home to a large number of Zionist movements representing all political tendencies in the immigrant community, from the left to the right, as well as its religious wing. Though their influence varied, Zionists nonetheless managed to recruit a good part of their supporters from this community. The Communists characterized Zionism as "bourgeois nationalism" and opposed it in the name of universal revolution, which was supposed to settle the Jewish question. The Bundists, fierce defenders of cultural autonomy, were likewise hostile to the movement.

Yiddish cultural life also experienced a remarkable boom during this period. Between 1918 and 1919, immigrants founded one hundred thirty-three publications, some of which appeared regularly. The best known were *Parizer Haint* (The Parisian Today, 1926–39), anti-Communist and pro-Zionist; the Communist *Naïe Presse* (The New Press, 1934–39), which replaced *Arbeter Shtime* (The Voice of the Workers, 1923–29), the weekly *Emes* (Truth, 1930–32), and *Der Morgen* (Morning, 1933), which came out every three weeks. Together these daily newspapers sold between 15,000 and 18,000 copies, not counting various other apolitical, literary, and specialized papers and magazines.[10]

A certain number of cultural associations were also formed in Paris and in the provinces, many of them eventually coming under Communist control. Paris became an important Yiddish cultural center. Each of the immigrant political movements—the Communists, Bundists, Zionists, and others—had its own library, centers of instruction in Yiddish, public university, and cultural events. Each movement, whether traditionalist or revolutionary, sought to transmit to younger generations its own conception of the world and its own values.

Levantine Jews, who already knew French and were familiar with French culture through the education they had received in their native countries at the schools of the Alliance Israélite Universelle, integrated themselves more easily into the surrounding society, both French and Jewish, preferring to organize within the established framework of the consistory. The Association Cultuelle Orientale de Paris, founded in 1909, continued to function between the wars. The Levantines had their own synagogue, charity, and school, each affiliated with the consistory.

REVIVAL OF ANTI-SEMITISM

The outcome of the Dreyfus affair had restored the confidence of French-born Jews in the values of the republic and strengthened their belief in the uniqueness of their experience. The Great War and the United Front it inspired had granted a brief respite from anti-Semitic unrest, which picked up again after the war.

From 1919, the circulation in the West of the *Protocols of the Elders of Zion* was to provide grist for the mill of the anti-Semites. This forgery, concocted at the beginning of the century by the Tsarist police, revived the famous myth of a Jewish (and Masonic) conspiracy aiming at world domination. A whole literature developed around the *Protocols* in the 1930s, years that also saw the crumbling of the international order. In 1933, Nazism triumphed in Germany. The economic and political crises that shook France gave anti-Semitism a wider scope than it had known in the past. Xenophobia and anti-Semitism made a perfect couple. Foreign Jews became a favorite target—though in 1940 they represented less than 0.4 percent of the French population.[11] It was not long before Jews and foreign Jews found themselves lumped together.

Besides Action Française, founded during the Dreyfus affair and numbering some 60,000 members in 1934, antiliberal groups obsessed with the decline of France—such as Jeunesses Patriotes (started in 1924), the Ligue des Croix-de-Feu (1927) of Colonel François de la Rocque, Solidarité Française, and Francisme (both founded in 1933)—challenged the very foundations of the republican order.[12] They were dissolved in 1936. The Stavisky affair of 1933–34, a financial scandal named after its chief figure, a Russian Jew, which furnished the pretext for the riot of 6 February 1934; the anti-Semitic activism of the antiparliamentarian leagues just mentioned, which had a large popular following; the publication in 1934 of Hitler's *Mein Kampf* (in French); then the victory in 1936 of the Popular Front and the formation the same year of Léon Blum's government; and, finally, the assassination in November 1938 of Ernst von Rath, the secretary of the German embassy in Paris, by a Polish Jew who had recently entered France from Germany as an illegal immigrant—all these events, though they differed in nature and importance, helped fuel anti-Semitism. Nazism in Germany lent it further support.

Once again the old prewar themes were sounded: the Jewish revolution, the Judeo-Bolshevik alliance, the Jews as stateless invaders, as eternal, unassimilable foreigners, dangerous, evil, deicidal beings responsible for all the ills and all the disorders (especially economic) from which France suffered. The Popular Front, under Blum's leadership, stood to Jewify France; it aroused an implacable hatred. A large segment of public opinion was influenced by this fresh outburst of anti-Semitism, which fed on new elements furnished by circumstance and on the anxiety that flowed from it, especially with the growing threat of war in the aftermath of the Munich Agreement (recognizing Germany's annexation of the Sudetenland, formerly part of Czechoslovakia) in 1938.

The anti-Semitic press consisted of forty-seven newspapers and magazines in 1938, among them *Gringoire* (600,000 copies sold in 1936), *Candide* (465,000 copies in 1936), and *Je suis partout* (from 40,000 to 80,000 copies a week), to which Robert Brassilach and Lucien Rebatet contributed; they gave voice to an uncommonly virulent anti-Jewish hatred, taking their place alongside *L'Action française*, organ of the movement of the same name that had led the anti-Semitic pack since the beginning of the century and had a daily print-run of 72,000 copies in 1936. Leagues and political parties of the extreme right—the Parti Populaire Français and the Rassemblement Antijuif de France among others—were also working actively in the same direction. Writers such as Louis-Ferdinand Céline, Marcel Jouhandeau, Paul Morand, Jean Giraudoux (who called for the creation of a Ministry of Race in 1939), Pierre Drieu La Rochelle, Camille Mauclair, Maurice Bedel, and Maurice Constantin-Weyer (the latter two were winners of the Prix Goncourt in 1927 and 1928, respectively) sided with them. Others, such as Claude Roy, Kléber Haedens, Henri Massis, and Thierry Maulnier participated in anti-Semitic movements and wrote for anti-Semitic newspapers.[13] The Marchandeau decree of 21 April 1939 (which took its name from the justice minister of the period) provided for penalties for inciting racial hatred, but it came a bit late. The Communist party and the Confédération Générale des Travailleurs were also overcome by xenophobia, and the working class was riddled with it.

From 1933 on, voices were heard demanding loudly and clearly that entry into France be denied to Jews and German Jewish refugees, who were accused by some of being in a position to work as spies in the service of Germany in case of war, by others of actually trying to push France into war against Germany. In the same vein, there were calls for legislation that would make the Jews second-class citizens. The way was thus prepared for the first Statut des Juifs (Jewish law) enacted in October 1940.

Faced with the surge in anti-Semitism, the majority of progressives and moderates, along with many Christians, joined ranks with the Jews to fight against racism. Christian youth publications—among them *La Vie catholique* (with a print-run of 40,000), founded in large part to counteract the arguments of Action Française; the magazine *Esprit*, which despite a modest print-run of 4,000 copies enjoyed substantial prestige because of the persons who sat on its editorial board; the weekly publication of the Dominicans, *Sept* (between 50,000 and 60,000 copies in 1936); the social democratic daily *L'Aube*, started in 1932 (and printing 14,000 copies a day in 1939); the periodicals *La Jeune République*, *Le Monde Ouvrier* (organ of the Jeunesse Ouvrière Catholique), *Le Bulletin catholique international*, and *Le Bulletin catholique de la Question d'Israël* of the Fathers of Zion—helped spread the thinking of philosemitic Christians. Oscar de Férenzy's role in promoting philosemitic Catholic publishing needs also to be emphasized. His journal *La Juste Parole*, which began to appear in October 1936 and had 6,000 subscribers in 1939, led the battle until 1940. Of those books and pamphlets published in the 1930s in defense of the Jews, 36 percent appeared between 1933 and 1936, accompanied by an equivalent proportion of writings hostile to the Jews; 47 percent of pro-Jewish books published during the decade appeared between 1937 and 1939, matched again by an equivalent percentage of anti-Jewish texts. The Jewish press, which occupied an important place in this struggle, was represented by organs such as *L'Univers israélite, Paix et Droit, Samedi, Les Cahiers du Renouveau, Cahiers juifs, Le Volontaire juif, La Terre retrouvée*, and *Le Droit de vivre*.

Outside the press, campaigns in the name of solidarity were launched in various circles concerned with the Jewish question, notably socialist ones, aimed at battling Fascism within the framework of organizations such as the Ligue des Droits de l'Homme, the Comité Matteotti, and the Secours Rouge Communiste.[14]

REEXAMINING JUDAISM

While not abandoning Franco-Judaism, the official ideology of French Jews, a few intellectuals such as Bernard Lazare, André Spire, Henri Franck (1888–1912), and Jean-Richard Bloch (1884–1947) began to reexamine their personal identity in the wake of the Dreyfus affair and the crisis of Jacobin universalism that ensued. The rise of anti-republican nationalism, substituting for this universalism a particularist conception of nation and country in which the Jew no longer had a place, was decisive in the new interpretations of Jewish identity that were now being sketched.

The massive arrival since the beginning of the century and throughout the entire interwar period of Jewish immigrants who were still attached to Jewish culture and traditions, and who were acquainted with nationalist movements (particularly Zionism), prompted many young people and certain intellectuals to redefine their identity as Jews, which was plainly no longer founded solely on religion. The grand themes of Barrèsian nationalism allowed authors such as André Spire and Edmond Fleg (1874–1963)—whose influence on the interwar generation was not insignificant—to see themselves in terms of the continuity of Jewish history, to turn toward the past of the Jewish people in the hope of rediscovering their own land. These intellectuals reformulated their identity in cultural terms, in terms of belonging to a people, but still within the framework of the Franco-Judaism of their predecessors. Though they were receptive to Zionism, those who worked on its behalf did so without denying their loyalty and their love for France.

This crisis of identity affected only a minority. Nonetheless, in addition to the work of Spire, Fleg, and Bloch, as well as that of Albert Cohen (1895–1981) and Armand Lunel (1892–1977), all leading figures who were already present on the literary scene and who continued writing during the interwar years, this period generated a stream of Jewish literature in

French—another way of openly affirming Jewish identity. The constant waves of immigration, the pogroms in eastern Europe, and the rise of Zionism were not without their effect upon this new generation of authors, who came from a great many different countries. They posed fresh questions about assimilation, exogamous marriage, the integration of immigrants in French society, and the mission of the Jews in the world. Josué Jéhouda (1892–1966), Pierre Paraf (1893–1989), Lily Jean-Javal (1882–1958), Irène Némirovsky (1903–42), Pierre Créange (1902–43), and Benjamin Fondane (1898–1944) were among those belonging to this movement;[15] in the case of some, their work also opened upon other horizons having nothing to do with Judaism.

A remarkable outpouring of books, magazines, and cultural events testifies to the enormous debate about Judaism that took place during this period. The ferment of the 1920s developed outside the established institutions of the French Jewish community, whose leaders looked unfavorably upon this unreligious return to Judaism. Others, by contrast, took part in political and literary movements that were developing within French mainstream society—yet further evidence of the plurality of the Jewish community as a whole.

At the same time, given the prevailing climate of anti-Semitism, in which Jews were perceived as an unassimilable element even though they contributed to the renown of France in a range of fields—as intellectuals, artists, writers, filmmakers, journalists, economists, and scholars in the humanities and social sciences—some looked to conversion as a way out of the impasse. Among the converts were a great many recent immigrants. Of 769 Jews who converted to Catholicism in Paris between 1915 and 1934, 43 percent were born abroad.[16] Some who chose this path were intellectuals: Raïssa Oumançoff (1883–1960), a Russian by birth and wife of the philosopher Jacques Maritain, the writer Max Jacob (1876–1944), René Schwob (1895–1946), and two native Egyptians, Jean de Menasce (1902–73) and Georges Cattaui (1896–1974).

YOUTH MOVEMENTS

Jewish youth movements came into being after World War I along with a whole series of religious, political, social, and scouting organizations, which laid the basis for a Jewish politics that was foreign to the conception that French-born Jews had held until then of their Jewishness and of their place in French society. These new associations supplemented existing—but, under the changed circumstances of the day, inadequate—social and philanthropic activities. Not all the youth movements were politicized: thus one finds Chema Israël (Hear O Israel), consistorial in tendency, a group founded in 1919 that two years later had provincial chapters, though three-quarters of its 1,500 members in 1928 were in Paris; and Rouah Israël (Spirit of Israel), similarly aligned but more independent, which during the same period worked to spread religious spirit and Hebrew culture, the Zionist ideal, and a curiosity about Palestinian products. In 1924, the reformist Union Libérale Israélite founded the Jeunesse Libérale Israélite, which sought to contribute to the renewal of French Judaism in accordance with its own conception of religion, and which remained open to Zionist ideas without subscribing to them.[17]

Alongside these religious movements of education and propaganda, other groups aimed at combating indifference both toward Judaism and its doctrines and toward the Jewish past. Two that played an important role in the revitalization of Jewish life, while trying to bring together the different components of Jewish society through their communal and educational activities, were the Union Universelle de la Jeunesse Juive (UUJJ) and the scouting movement Éclaireurs Israélites de France (EIF). The UUJJ entered the French scene in 1923 with the move to France of its two founders, Charles Néhama and Jacques Matalon,[18] both natives of Salonica; the EIF was established in 1923 by Robert Gamzon (1906–61), known by his scout name, Castor.

The objective of all these organizations was primarily the survival of the Jews as a people. To this end some challenged the ideology of preceding generations in condemning assimilation, adopting a critical attitude toward Jewish institutions, proposing plural definitions of Jewish identity, and revising the terms of integration in French society, which with the exacerbation of anti-Semitism displayed an increasing reserve toward them.

The UUJJ opted for an apparent neutrality. It had been founded originally in order to win over Jewish youth to Zionism, in France and elsewhere. Though it did not openly declare itself to be Zionist, it undertook to help bring about a Jewish renaissance through instruction in Hebrew and the history of Israel while seeking to bring together Jewish youth in all countries and lending its support to the work being done in Palestine. It attracted figures such as Edmond Fleg and Aimé Pallière (1875–1949), a Christian, who became the leader of the movement, as well as leading Zionists. In 1928, it numbered about six hundred members in Paris and, in 1929, a thousand. With a few exceptions—Marseilles, for instance, where it opened up a chapter in 1928 under the name of the Union de la Jeunesse Juive de Marseille—it struggled to establish itself in the provinces.

The EIF wished, on the one hand, to lead young assimilated Jews back to Judaism and, on the other, to assist the integration of young immigrants by giving them access to French culture. The group enjoyed the approval of the consistory when it was founded, if only because of the social origins of its first scouts, who came from the upper Jewish bourgeoisie of Paris. Fleg had a great influence upon the organization, which had 1,200 scouts in Paris alone in the 1930s and a network of chapters in the eastern provinces of the country, the Midi, and in North Africa. With the rise of Nazism, the movement drew closer to Zionism and expanded its activities while continuing to strengthen the religious identity of its young members, both girls and boys.

In Marseilles, the first organizational attempt to bring about a renaissance—that is, a conception of Jewishness located between the religious and the ethno-cultural spheres—occurred at the very beginning of the century. In 1902, Jews from North Africa set out to establish an Association Amicale Hébraïque for the purpose of "studying the Hebrew language from a religious, literary, and philosophical point of view." One year later, an Algerian started the newspaper *Le Flambeau* (The Torch), which carried the subtitle *Annales politiques et littéraires des populations israélites du Midi de la France, de l'Algérie et de la Tunisie* (Political and Literary Annals of the Jewish Populations of the South of France, Algeria, and Tunisia); this paper still appeared in 1914, now under the name *Le Flambeau d'Israël*.

The organizational experiments of this movement continued in the 1920s and 1930s. Young Jews from Marseilles founded the Cercle Sinaï in 1921. The purpose of this society was to contribute to the cohesiveness of the Jewish community in Marseilles, the integration of young immigrants, and the strengthening of Jewish identity among the young. Women were permitted to join. Local branches of Parisian associations also attracted the city's Jewish youth.

Some of these movements deeply influenced young people during the interwar period. The most progressive among their members wished henceforth to serve France as Jews and not as citizens of the Jewish faith, thus delivering a blow to the emancipationist ideology of their predecessors. Such movements also helped reawaken a sense of Jewishness in the younger generation, preoccupied with the search for identity. Nonetheless, despite attempts at criticizing, redefining, and amending it, and despite the multiplicity of opinion, debate, and division among native-born Jews and immigrants, Franco-Judaism remained the primary frame of reference for French Jews throughout the interwar period.[19]

REPOSITIONING ZIONISM

If the youth movements were not hostile to Zionism, this was not the case with the two main official Jewish institutions, the consistory and the Alliance Israélite Universelle, which now changed tactics, going on the attack and abandoning their position of relative neutrality—a neutrality that consisted in the fact that, until this point, they had regarded Zionism as a utopia without a future.

A good many Jews, French-born and immigrant alike, were displeased with the hostile attitude shown by their institutions toward Zionism. Since the First World War, this movement had attracted sympathizers and members even among Jews born and bred in France. Thus, in 1917, on the initiative of André Spire, the Ligue des Amis du Sionisme was created, with the purpose of bringing together Jewish and non-Jewish intellectuals. Zionism nonetheless did not experience anything like real growth at this time. In 1919, the Fédération Sioniste de France contained thirteen associations and numbered some 2,700 members, half of whom lived in North Africa. It broke up in 1921, depriving the French Jewish community of a central organization capable of representing it at world Zionist conferences.

Zionist leaders sought to open up the movement to non-Jewish sympathizers in order to advance their cause in the eyes of public opinion and governments. To this end the Comité France-Palestine was founded in 1925 as the successor to the Ligue des Amis du Sionisme. This committee was made up of eminent political figures such as Raymond Poincaré, Aristide Briand, and Léon Blum, who had been associated with the Zionist cause since World War I.

Despite hostility on the part of the established institutions of French Jewry, certain notables joined immigrant leaders in serving on the council of the Jewish Agency for Palestine from 1929 onward.[20] They believed they could take part in the philanthropic work of the movement without associating themselves with its ideology, which considered the Jews to be a people in exile and lobbied for its resettlement in Palestine—a position incompatible with Franco-Judaism. Xenophobia and anti-Semitism, and the prospect that Jews might face a still worse fate in countries such as Germany, made even the fiercest opponents of Zionism aware that Palestine could usefully serve as a homeland for victims of persecution. From then on, the official position changed. Jews who feared that the least expression of support of Zionism might be interpreted as evidence of dual allegiance now had an excuse to commit themselves.

It is true that the number of Zionist activists in France, whether native-born or immigrant, did not exceed 10,000. Nonetheless, certain elements of Zionist ideology had a profound influence, particularly upon Jewish youth who needed to gain confidence in themselves and to take pride in their Jewishness as the condition of the Jews became more precarious during the course of the 1930s. In Alsace-Lorraine, Zionism in its cultural and religious aspects appealed to a large segment of public opinion and had its own ramified organization.

Zionism in France functioned by means of a whole series of associations of various ideological tendencies that offered young men and women alike a range of cultural activities. Women actively took part in defending the cause through their own associations as well, in the provinces and in Paris. Thus, in 1924, on the initiative of the lawyer Yvonne Netter, the Union des Femmes de France pour la Palestine was established, and became the French section of the Womens' International Zionist Organization, founded in 1920 in London. The 1930s saw the creation in Paris, under the aegis of the EIF, of the pro-Zionist society Kadimah, which brought together middle-class women.

Zionist organizations whose purpose was to collect funds for the purchase of land in Palestine and the restoration of a Jewish state, including Keren Kayemet le-Yisrael (founded in 1907) and Keren ha-Yesod (founded in 1920), set up branches in France in the 1920s.

Zionists made a point of meeting Jews wherever they were to be found, including the synagogue. They also tried to infiltrate Jewish institutions in France, hoping eventually to win them over to their cause. Zionism in France also had its own press—three in Paris, *L'Écho Sioniste* (1906–22), *La Nouvelle Aurore* (1922–26), and *La Terre retrouvée* (1928–39), and one in Strasbourg, *Le Juif* (1919–21), as well as journals published by its various associations, not to mention periodicals favorable to Zionism that, without officially belonging to the movement, were receptive to its ideas. In the immigrant world, the newspaper *Parizer Haint* openly defended the Zionist cause. At a minimum, Zionism between the wars played a role in the debates over identity that troubled French Jews and offered some of them a new ideological perspective.

More harmonious relations came to be established between the French Jewish establishment and the Zionists during the Second World War, now that they had to work together. But it was not until 1942, with the formation of the Organisation Sioniste de France, that an end was put at last to the movement's chronic disorganization in France.[21]

THE NAZI PERIL

The ways in which Jews in France conceived of their Jewishness also influenced their responses to the Nazi peril in the 1930s. The variety of these responses and the debates that accompanied them, among immigrants as well as among the native-born, once again testifies to the heterogeneity of the French Jewish collectivity.

French Jews, considering themselves French first and Jews second, did not feel any immediate obligations toward other Jews. To be sure, they set up a whole network of assistance for the newcomers. They feared that with the rise of anti-Semitism these immigrants, whose mode of life was markedly different from theirs and whose particularism was much insisted upon, risked giving ammunition to the anti-Semites—ammunition that was likely to be used against native-born Jews themselves. It was necessary therefore to move quickly to assure their integration. Even if natives and immigrants were not wholly separated from each other, contacts between the two groups took place primarily at the institutional level. Native Jews did their utmost to apply their own model of Jewishness to the immigrants, acting in a paternalistic manner and always through institutions they controlled; the great majority of these immigrants rejected the model, however, which was foreign to them and whose pernicious effects they denounced.

In the struggle against anti-Semitism, new differences further widened the already existing gap between the two groups. Instead of searching for ways to combat anti-Semitism, the consistorial authorities in Paris attributed it to the large number of unintegrated Jewish immigrants and to their political activities. In the aftermath of the wave of anti-Semitism arising from the Stavisky affair and the riot it triggered in February 1934, a small group of conservative Jews, upper middle class and for the most part assimilated, many of them having ties to the Union Libérale Israélite de Tendance Réformée, created the Union Patriotique des Français-Israélites under the direction of Edmond Bloch (1884–1975), a figure associated with the Parisian extreme right. In principle, this organization was to counter the activity of the Ligue Internationale Contre L'Antisémitisme (LICA), which was founded in 1928 by Bernard Lecache (1895–1968), the son of immigrants from eastern Europe, and which it accused of promoting social revolution rather than opposing anti-Semitism. Owing to its firm attitude in the struggle against anti-Semitism and to its vigorous political activity, LICA attracted both French and immigrant Jewish youth. By 1939, its membership—500 in 1928, 30,000 in 1936—had risen to 50,000; already by 1936, its organ Le Droit de vivre had achieved an average print-run of 35,000 copies.[22] The Union Patriotique, for its part, admitted no immigrants to its ranks, flaunted its patriotic ideals, which came before all else, and called for national unity. Its vocabulary was borrowed by groups such as the Croix-de-Feu. It nonetheless remained a marginal influence, never numbering more than 1,500 members.[23] It made a point of calling attention to Jewish participation in the First World War, in the tradition of the associations of former French Jewish and immigrant combatants that were formed during the 1920s. The patriotic enthusiasm of the Jews, as adoptive children of the nation, redoubled in response.

The consistory was careful to distance itself from the left. In 1932, during a religious service in memory of the soldiers of all faiths killed in action during the Great War, five hundred members of the Croix-de-Feu paraded inside the Synagogue de la Victoire. This ceremony was repeated in 1934 and 1935, again with the same participants, and once more in 1936 following Léon Blum's triumph, of which the consistory took a dim view. In addition to welcoming the Croix-de-Feu to these ceremonies, Rabbi Jacob Kaplan (1895–1994) addressed meetings of the group, warmly praising its activities and its leader. By supporting such organizations and advocating national unity, Jews imagined they were allying themselves with the defenders of the democratic and liberal ideals of France, which had emancipated them; but these organizations scorned them.

The consistory, official spokesman for the Jewish collectivity in France in the eyes of government authorities by virtue of the size of its following and its influence in Jewish circles, was far from representing French Jewry as a whole. In 1936, it finally broke with movements of the French right while continuing to maintain relations with the Union Patriotique.[24]

French Jews avoided mounting a specifically Jewish response either on the national or international level, reasoning that to reply to the attacks of the anti-Semites would play into their hands by making it seem as though French-born Jews were not an integral part of the French nation. They trusted the government to put an end to the turmoil. Nor were they pleased by the agitation in immigrant and youth circles. Indeed, anti-Semitism did not overly alarm French Jews—they underestimated it, thinking it would go away. As in the Dreyfus affair, they were convinced that a generous and wise republic would see to it that reason prevailed in the end. Despite their public statements, however, they did not in fact feel themselves to be full-fledged members of the nation. Once again they tried to demonstrate their loyalty while refraining from taking part in any action that might cast doubt upon it.

French Jews were also confronted with the problem of German and Polish refugees, who poured into France from Germany with Hitler's ascent to power. Their numbers only grew following *Kristallnacht* (Crystal Night) of 9–10 November 1938, in the course of which stores and apartments belonging to Jews were looted across Germany, heralding a time of increasingly discriminatory measures against them. Already by 1933 France had received more than 26,000 Jewish refugees.[25] The unification of the Saarland with the Reich, the annexation of Austria by Germany, and then the conquest of Czechoslovakia all added to the stream of Jews fleeing Nazi occupation. Support committees were established, later centralized by the consistorial authorities; even so, frictions persisted. Some 45 million francs were collected in donations between 1933 and 1940.[26] Along with efforts to provide material assistance, French Jews intervened on behalf of the immigrants with the authorities, proposing that they be redeployed as farm workers and artisans. Many of these immigrants belonged to the upper socioeconomic levels of Jewish society in central Europe, intellectuals and members of the liberal professions who were acculturated to their native lands in the same way as Jews born in France. Solidarity was stimulated by the fear that so great a number of refugees would bring the wrath of the anti-Semites upon the Jews as a whole, and so every effort was made to find a place for them. At the same time, an attempt was made to channel this immigration away from France. French Jews feared inconveniencing their fellow citizens and the authorities and, for this very reason, did not respond vigorously to an anti-Semitism that they believed had been imported from Germany.

In immigrant circles, the terms of a response were much more actively envisaged on both a national and international level. The fate facing Jews in Europe during this period concerned them greatly since, according to their conception of Judaism, all Jews belonged to a single people. Whereas French-born Jews thought that by avoiding concerted action altogether they would not expose themselves to anti-Semitic attacks, the immigrants inclined to a wholly different view, though one that admitted of variations. At the heart of their concern was the tragedy of the German Jews. Far from underestimating the Nazi threat, they tried on numerous occasions to organize large-scale protests in Paris, from as early as 1935; but each time their efforts were in vain, owing to the incessant divisions that reigned among the immigrant organizations.

In the face of these setbacks, they turned to the government for help, though they did not share the idealized vision of the republic that French-born Jews had. The immigrants expected energetic measures to be taken and placed much of their hope in the advent of the Popular Front. This turned out only to be a brief interlude, however, ending in 1937 with a return to the previous government's inertia in the matter. In 1937–38, after the failure of the Jewish Popular Front,[27] which coincided with the fall of the Popular Front, the Jews no longer expected anything of the French authorities. They chose instead to establish a strong communal organization uniting French and immigrant Jews in combat against anti-Semitism. Disagreements were nonetheless very numerous, as much on account of internal conflicts within each of the two groups as of struggles between natives and newcomers for control over operations. Until the eve of the war, the search for unity was to remain unsuccessful.

The Jewish subsection of the Communist party was dissolved in 1937. The party thus showed that it could not shelter a movement whose concerns were principally related to the Jewish question. The Jewish left subsequently opposed the Nazi-Soviet Pact of August 1939, there no longer being any compatibility between Jewish interests and those of the Communists.

French and immigrant Jews alike found themselves paralyzed, incapable of action, deeply isolated, liable to the worst fears. If the inertia and excessive patriotism of consistorial circles, disavowed by Jews themselves, had led to an impasse, the activism of immigrants and the young had also shown itself to be useless, having produced no tangible results. The Jewish community, so divided and so heterogeneous, thus confronted the war in the most profound despair—a despair that now was shared by everyone.

The Dark Years

THE WAR

In 1939, the number of Jews in metropolitan France was estimated at about 300,000 to 330,000. One year later, this figure had grown by 10 percent owing to the dislocations brought about by the war.[1] About 90,000 of them were French-born—Alsatians, Lorrainers, and the descendants of Jews originally from Portugal and the Comtat; the rest had come with various modern waves of immigration. Almost eight inhabitants out of a thousand in France were Jews (or nearly 0.8 percent of a total population of 43 million).[2] With the declaration of war, on 3 September 1939, they displayed the same patriotism they had shown during the Great War. In January 1940, the French army counted 60,000 Jews in its ranks, a mobilization rate of 20 percent as against 15 percent for the rest of the population. All parts of Jewish society were represented. Foreign Jews volunteered en masse, and 16,000 managed to enlist for the duration of the war despite the obstacles placed in their way by the authorities (the share of rejected candidates amounted to 20 percent). Many of them hoped in this way to obtain French citizenship. Some 4,500 of these immigrants served in irregular volunteer regiments and 5,000 in infantry regiments of the Foreign Legion, or almost a tenth of the 100,000 or so combatants who made up these corps; there were another 4,000 to 5,000 in the Polish army reconstituted in French territory and 1,300 in the Czechoslovak army. By the end of 1943, they numbered 40,000.

Combat losses were sizable. During the rout in 1940, Jewish soldiers and officers, like their non-Jewish French counterparts, were taken captive by the Germans. Between 10,000 and 15,000 passed the remainder of the war in prison camps. Other foreigners were interned in camps set up by the French government and in the Groupements de Travailleurs Étrangers (GTE).[3]

At the moment war was declared, the French authorities feared, curiously, that German and Austrian refugees—a good many of them antifascists—would take the side of the Nazis, whom, after all, they were fleeing. Suspected of espionage and rounded up in detention centers, these refugees were thought to make up a "Fifth Column." With the rout of June 1940, they were sent to internment camps in the south of France, where they suffered in agony from hunger, sickness, and cold. They had ended up being identified with their persecutors. Of these 18,000 to 20,000 internees, the majority were Jews.

Some 15,000 Jews fled their native lands of Alsace and Lorraine from September 1939, followed by 40,000 refugees from Belgium, Holland, and Luxembourg after the German offensive began in May 1940. With the annexation of Alsace-Lorraine by the Germans in July 1940, the remaining Jews in the region, numbering about 3,000, were expelled; they set out for the central and southern part of the country. In October 1940, the Germans expelled 6,504 Jews from the Palatinate and Baden, who were sent to a camp in Gurs in the Pyrénées Atlantiques.[4]

The French government quit Paris on 11 June 1940; the chief rabbi and the leaders of the central consistory and of the immigrant organizations did the same. The consistory, not being allowed to settle in Vichy, retreated to Lyons, where the Fédération des Sociétés Juives de France had gone earlier. The principal Jewish social organizations reestablished themselves in Marseilles.

In May-June 1940, France was invaded by the German army. An armistice was signed on 22 June 1940 by the government of Marshal Henri Pétain. France was divided into a zone occupied by the Germans, to the north of the Loire and including the Manche and Atlantique regions, and a zone to the south of the Loire constituting "Free France." On 10 July 1940, the chamber of deputies and the senate, meeting at Vichy in National Assembly, conferred full powers on Pétain and authorized him to draft a new constitution. The death knell of the Third Republic had sounded.

The geography of the French Jewish community shifted radically as well. Half of its population was now in the southern zone. Native Jews were more likely to have family or friends who could put them up; in any case, they had the means to go on paying for their needs in a new place of residence. For many local people in these areas, this was their first real contact with the Jews whom the press and radio vilified. One third of those who moved to the south went back to Paris. Before long they found it more and more difficult to move around. Nonetheless, in the southern zone (also called the "free" or unoccupied zone), Jews felt less threatened. Jewish refugees continued to pour in. The anti-Semitic press continued to raise an outcry against them. Instances of anti-Semitic graffiti multiplied. Windows and storefronts of Jewish businesses were damaged.

FROM CITIZEN TO PARIAH

In the northern zone, the Vichy government was represented among the occupying forces by a Délégation Générale du Gouvernement Français dans les Territoires Occupés. In the summer of 1940 there were many anti-Semitic demonstrations in Paris, though they did not attract large numbers of people. The Marchandeau decree of 1939, punishing defamation or injury in the press, was repealed on 27 August by the French government, which gave free reign to the most despicable writings and speeches in the newspapers and over the airwaves. Exclusion began to affect Jewish artists and journalists, who were no longer able to find employment. Collaborationist groups operated with great vigor. Ordinary life, with its daily ration of fresh restrictions, became difficult for Parisians. Kneejerk anti-Semitism gained ground, marching to the rhythm of accusations and denunciations.

The first discriminatory measures in the occupied zone were the work of the German authorities. Subsequently, the French authorities in Vichy and the occupation forces tried to outdo each other in finding ingenious ways to tighten the net around both French and foreign Jews, whether in the north or in the south.

On 27 September 1940, the Germans promulgated in the occupied zone an ordinance that opened with a definition of who counted as a Jew, expressed in religious terms: "Those who belong or have belonged to the Jewish religion or who have more than two Jewish grandparents are considered as Jews." Next, it forbade Jews who had left the occupied zone from returning. Those who came within the terms of the definition given in the ordinance were required to register by 20 October with the local *sous-préfet*. In Paris and its suburbs, 149,734 Jews went to register, of whom 86,664 were French and 65,070 foreigners; 7,737 Jewish businesses and 3,456 Jewish societies were registered in the occupied zone.[5] Those who avoided this obligation were few. Jewish shopkeepers also had until the end of October to place a notice in the window of their store identifying it as a Jewish business (*Jüdisches Geschäft*).

A week after the German ordinance, the Vichy government, acting on its own initiative and without German pressure, enacted a Statut des Juifs on 3 October 1940; the decree was then published in the *Journal officiel* of 18 October of the same year. Hoping to assert its sovereignty in both zones, Vichy promulgated its own legislation. This time Jewishness was defined with reference to racial criteria. Any person having three grandparents of the Jewish race or, in the event his or her spouse was Jewish, two grandparents of this race, was regarded as Jewish. The law drove Jews out of public office, journalism, cinema, theater, and radio. The Statut des Juifs was applicable in both zones, in the colonies, in the French protectorates of Tunisia and Morocco (since 1881 and 1912, respectively), in the mandated territories, and in Algeria. A law dated 7 October 1940 (and published the following day in the *Journal officiel*) abrogated the Crémieux decree of 24 October 1870, thus bringing about the collective denaturalization of the Jews of unoccupied Algeria. Discriminatory measures affecting the Jews of metropolitan France were also applied to those of North Africa.

A second Statut des Juifs was promulgated on 2 June 1941, inspired by Xavier Vallat, a notorious anti-Semite well before Vichy who some days previously had been appointed commissioner for Jewish questions, that linked the religious and racial criteria: "Anyone who belongs to the Jewish religion or who belonged to it on 25 June 1940 and who is descended from two grandparents of the Jewish race is considered Jewish." This law limited the access of Jews to positions in industry, commerce, and the liberal professions. Registration in metropolitan France and in the colonies was again imposed by the French authorities, this time on the same day the statute was promulgated. Since October 1940, in the northern zone, identity cards carried by Jews had described the bearer as a Jew, male or female (*Juif* or *Juive*). It was not until the occupation of the southern zone, after the landing of the Allies in North Africa on 8 November 1942, that the practice was introduced there, from mid-December 1942 on, with the exception of the region stretching from the eastern bank of the Rhône to the Italian border, occupied by the Italians until September 1943.

At the end of June 1940, a quota was applied to universities in Algeria that limited the number of Jewish students to 3 percent. Primary and secondary instruction was also affected by these restrictions, which fixed the percentage of Jewish students attending class at 14 percent, and later 7 percent. A quota was also imposed in Tunisia (14 percent) and in Morocco (10 percent). In the protectorates, the existence of a Jewish educational network administered by the Alliance Israélite Universelle made it easier to cope with this situation. A quota was also instituted in metropolitan France at the beginning of the new school year in 1941; in the universities, the proportion of Jewish students was limited to 3 percent.[6]

A law of 22 July 1940 created a commission to review naturalizations approved later than 10 August 1927; those who had been naturalized after this date found their French nationality withdrawn.

The law of 4 October 1940, likewise published in the 18 October issue of the *Journal officiel*, concerned "foreign nationals of the Jewish race" and their internment in special camps by the sole decision of the prefect of their place of residence. The southern zone thus witnessed a proliferation of camps that from November of the same year came under the direct administration of the French authorities (in Argelès, Rivesaltes, Les Milles, Recébédou, Noé, and elsewhere). Thousands of foreign Jews joined those who were already living there in appalling conditions—anti-Nazis, anti-fascists, Spanish republicans, and Jewish refugees from central Europe. At about this time there were twenty-six camps in the northern zone and fifteen in the southern zone. The number of Jewish internees now stood at 50,000, or about one-quarter of the roughly 200,000 Jews not possessing

French citizenship. More than 35,000 of these were detained in camps of the GTE, which rounded up foreign Jewish volunteers who had not been demobilized after the defeat and who were considered "surplus foreigners in the French economy." At the end of 1940, 70 percent of all those interned were Jewish. In February 1941, there were 40,000 Jews in the camps in the south, where they represented 75 percent of the camp population. In April 1942, owing to the release or reassignment of internees in the interval, the camps held only 17,000 persons, 11,000 of them (or 63 percent) Jews. When deportation was underway, they numbered 10,000. Of the 11,000 finally deported from the southern zone, more than 4,500 had been interned in the camps there, which were turned into deportation "reservoirs." In the occupied zone, in the camps at Beaune-la-Rolande, Pithiviers, Drancy, and Compiègne, there were 8,176 Jews at the end of 1941.

In North Africa, there were work camps as well as camps for interning foreigners after the armistice, notably Jews who had served in the Foreign Legion; foreign Jews from the free zone were also transferred there. Additionally, Algerian Jews who did not share the opinions of the Vichy government were interned in these camps. In occupied Tunisia, Jews suffered under the German yoke until 1943. In 1941, between 14,000 and 15,000 Jews were interned in North Africa; in 1942, only 7,500 were interned, and these were not deported.[7] The situation of the Jews in North Africa, home to more than 400,000 Jews according to the 1941 census (117,646 in Algeria, 89,360 in Tunisia, some 200,000 in Morocco) was not at all comparable to that of their co-religionists in metropolitan France, however.[8]

Between 8 October 1940 and 16 September 1941 alone, twenty-six laws, twenty-four decrees, and six orders concerning Jews were published in the *Journal officiel*. Jews were now second-class citizens. The Vichy authorities set an example for the Germans, who promulgated their own ordinances, which Vichy then adopted in their turn and applied in the free zone until November 1942. Jewish property was enthusiastically plundered in both zones in accordance with the policy of "Aryanization"—the transfer of Jewish goods and businesses to "Aryan" or non-Jewish officials—which was intended to eliminate all Jewish influence in the economy. Thus, in the summer of 1941, about 50 percent of the Jewish population found itself deprived of all means of subsistence.[9] Their isolation was aggravated by an ordinance of 13 August 1941 ordering confiscation of their wireless radio sets. An ordinance of 7 February 1942 regulated when they could go out in public and prohibited them from changing residence. The German ordinance of 29 May obliged them to wear the yellow star in the occupied zone, but Vichy balked at imposing it in the free zone. Few Jews wore the star.

In the space of two years, then, they had become pariahs, unable to support themselves, perplexed by the jumble of ordinances concerning them, living in fear of failing to comply with the law. The fate of the Jews

between 1940 and 1944 was linked to two pieces of legislation, one due to
the occupying authorities, the other to the Vichy government, which at
first had hoped to be able to reserve a measure of autonomy for itself by
taking anti-Jewish measures; in this it drew inspiration as much from the
native anti-Semitic tradition as from German and Italian anti-Jewish legislation. In 1940, Vichy was under no pressure to devise the Statut des Juifs
or to abrogate the Crémieux decree, which had been in force in Algeria
since 1870; yet it did so in early October, freely of its own will, to remind
people of its supremacy over all French territory. Indeed, the German ordinance of 27 September was on several points less restrictive. Vichy prepared itself for collaboration. The occupiers took advantage of its enthusiasm in order to go further. German pressure on Vichy intensified after the
Wannsee Conference of 20 January 1942 (so-called after the street where
the meeting was held in suburban Berlin), which settled the terms of the
"Final Solution"—the term used by the Nazis to refer to the extermination
of the Jews. The Jews were to be deported to extermination camps set up
in Poland. Marshal Pétain and Pierre Laval were consequently to participate in the implementation of the Final Solution in France itself.

THE ROUNDUPS

Already in 1941 three roundups took place. On 14 May, Polish, Czech, and
Austrian Jews were arrested in Paris. This was not yet a true roundup, for
they had been summoned for the purpose of checking their papers; 3,747
were sent to the camps of Pithiviers and Beaune-la-Rolande in the Loiret.

On 20 August 1941, the eleventh arrondissement of Paris was surrounded in the early morning hours. The French municipal police, armed
with lists drawn up on the basis of the prefecture's files, in collaboration
with the *Feldgendarmerie*, were ordered to arrest all "Jews of the male sex
between the ages of eighteen and fifty," with the exception of those who
held American passports. Three thousand persons were subsequently arrested, taken first to neighborhood police stations and then interned at
Drancy in dreadful conditions. In the next two days, arrests continued in
other arrondissements. A total of 4,232 Jews were rounded up in three
days. Further arrests were made sporadically for a few more weeks.

The Drancy camp was administered by French authorities but came
under the control of the Gestapo's department for Jewish affairs. On
12 December there was another roundup, conducted this time by the Germans: 734 Jews, mostly from wealthy backgrounds, prominent figures and
intellectuals, were arrested and transferred to the camp of Compiègne-
Royallieu. The end of 1941 saw the execution by the Germans of hostages accused of acts of resistance and sabotage; a certain number of these
were Jews.[10]

In Paris, anti-Semitic activity proceeded at a brisk pace. The Parti Populaire Français led by Jacques Doriot, and the collaborationist press—*Au Pilori, Les Nouveaux Temps, L'Appel, La Gerbe, Le Cri du peuple, L'Illustration, Je suis partout, Le Matin*—set to work in this direction with great energy. The film *Le Juif Süss* (The Jew Süss) enjoyed a broad audience after its initial release. Also in 1941 an institute for the study of Jewish questions was established in Paris, entirely funded by the Germans, to orchestrate anti-Semitic propaganda. In June of the same year, large anti-Semitic posters were put up on the walls of the subway and in the streets. In September, a show entitled *Le Juif et la France* (The Jew and France) opened at the Palais Berlitz in Paris, and attracted some 200,000 paying visitors before closing in January 1942. Synagogues were sacked. All this occurred in a climate of massive public indifference.[11]

Between December 1941 and July 1942 there was a momentary pause in the roundups. The Germans did not have enough trains to evacuate the Jews detained to the east. And yet the Nazi death machine was working at full capacity in the east of the Reich. At the Wannsee Conference of 20 January 1942 it was decided that France must supply 100,000 Jews of both sexes, between the ages of sixteen and forty, including 10 percent unfit for work, the deportation from France being intended to supply forced labor at the rate of three trainloads per week. Four days after this meeting, Theodor Dannecker, head of the Gestapo's department of Jewish affairs, limited his ambitions: 39,000 Jews were to be deported in three months by a series of three weekly trains.[12] The Germans needed the collaboration of the French police in order to carry out the roundups in the occupied zone and the free zone at the same time.

France gave into German pressures on the condition that French Jews were not affected. Laval proposed to add foreign children younger than sixteen to the convoys, again in exchange for the protection of French Jews. About 4,500 policemen were ordered to arrest some 27,300 stateless Jews, between the ages of two and fifty-five in the case of females, and between two and sixty in the case of males, on 16–17 July 1942. Indiscrete remarks by police chiefs, pamphlets, and rumors had been spread beforehand by Jewish organizations, warning against possible deportation. The men having left their homes the night before, most of those rounded up were women and children. The final tally of arrests was 13,152, a figure well below what had been expected. Single persons and married couples without children were sent to Drancy, families to the Vélodrome d'hiver in Paris. It is this latter detention center that is remembered, having given the short form of its name to the event, thereafter known as the "Vel' d'hiv roundup."

The 8,160 men, women, and children herded into the Vélodrome lived in the most complete destitution before being transferred in two stages, on

19 and 22 July, to the camps of the Loiret. The heartbreaking scenes witnessed by the local population did not fail to leave their mark. Arrests and roundups were also carried out in Bordeaux and in cities of the southern zone. The total amounted to some 11,500, 9,000 of whom were taken to the Rivesaltes camp and then to Drancy. Vichy had exceeded the demands of the Germans, who had set a figure of 10,000 for the southern zone. Other roundups also took place in Paris between July and August 1942.

The abolition of the southern zone on 11 November 1942 following its occupation by the Germans, with the exception of the departments lying to the east of the Rhône, extended the persecution to the whole of the country. From then on, neither French Jews nor stateless Jews nor foreign Jews were spared. The hunt for Jews was carried out systematically. The largest roundup in the former free zone began 22 January 1943 in Marseilles and continued through 27 January. Others followed. In the zone of Italian occupation in the southeast, until its invasion by the Germans in September 1943, Jews were less threatened; roundups then began during the night of 8–9 September, intensifying after the tenth. Between 10 and 14 September, 1,819 Jews, 1,000 of them from Nice, were arrested and sent to Drancy.[13]

In the year 1942 alone, 42,655 Jews were deported from France to Nazi camps; in 1943, the figure was 17,041; and in 1944, 16,025. Of these deportees, 6,012 were below the age of twelve, 13,104 between the ages of thirteen and twenty-nine, and 8,687 above the age of sixty. About 24,000 were Jews of French nationality. Some 26,300 were Polish Jews, 7,000 German Jews, 4,500 Russian Jews, 3,300 Romanian Jews, and 2,500 Austrian Jews. The total was 75,721. Only 2,500 survived the gas chambers and crematorium furnaces. The last train left on 17 August 1944. In the end, 23 percent of French Jews were deported. The percentage was 66 percent for Jews in Germany, 55 percent in Belgium, 50 percent in Hungary, and 16 percent in Italy. In Poland, out of a population of 3.4 million Jews, only 50,000 remained in 1945.[14]

The sufferings of those who were deported, during the various stages of the infernal transit that led to the death camps, have been told in numerous accounts. Those who avoided it lived in hiding, hunted; many lived in wretched poverty; others were executed by the Milice (the paramilitary organization that collaborated with the Nazis) or shot as members of the resistance.

The anti-Jewish legislation independently passed by Vichy and its collaboration with the Germans followed from the logic of exclusion inherent in its doctrine of national revolution, from a political program that called for such collaboration, and from a tradition of anti-Semitism *à la française* that was rooted in society and, to a still greater degree, in the extreme right—of which the Vichy government was the expression and result.

PUBLIC OPINION

How did it happen that the Jews of France were relatively less subject to deportation than those of the majority of European countries? The policy of the Vichy government itself evolved, of course, and the enthusiasm of the first months turned into reluctance with regard to some of the demands of the occupier, especially toward 1943, in the face of growing awareness of the Jewish question after the roundups of the previous year on the part of the public and the clergy, who increasingly identified Vichy with the Germans. But it was certainly not Vichy that saved three-quarters of the Jews of France.

Owing to the indifference and apathy of a populace more concerned with providing for its everyday needs, and to the silence of both its spiritual leaders and the nascent underground press, there was little chance at first of offsetting the influence of either the official press, which explained in detail the reasons for the policy being carried out by the government, or the wholly unscrupulous collaborationist press—all this in the context of general support for Marshal Pétain. But things gradually changed: the wearing of the yellow star, then the arrests and deportations that gave rise to such wrenching scenes, led the French to take notice of the situation and to adopt a more detached view with regard to the regime. The anti-Jewish measures of the Germans and of Vichy had aroused doubts in people's minds. The churches, particularly the Protestant church, took a stand. Despite the Vatican's failure to respond, high Catholic dignitaries openly denounced the persecutions; these denunciations were followed by rescue missions and assistance. The underground press of the resistance, in its turn, began to attack the roundups. Acts of solidarity—not only by Jews—on behalf of the occupier's victims multiplied, and networks of resistance developed.

It was in this clandestine sphere, outside the reach of government, that Jewish and non-Jewish rescue groups were able to operate. Indeed, Vichy's success in carrying out its policy depended on how society reacted to it; that is, on the relation between government and public opinion. This explains, among other things, the survival of a great number of Jews, despite the atmosphere of anti-Semitism and the denunciations to which it gave rise.

Other factors also favored the Jews. The occupation by the Italians, between November 1942 and September 1943, of the eastern bank of the Rhône allowed Jews to take refuge there, thus buying time for themselves. The heterogeneity of French Jewry, which included foreigners, naturalized citizens, and citizens of neutral countries (such as Turkish Jews), as well as the division of France into two zones, splintered the efforts of the

Germans. During this period public opinion evolved, the resistance grew in strength, the government showed itself less accommodating in the matter of Jewish persecution, and Jews began to understand that they had to hide while Jewish and non-Jewish rescue networks were being organized.

Some Jews managed to emigrate; others succeeded in crossing the border into Spain, which had remained open under the pressure of the Allies, who hoped to be able to exploit it for their own purposes. Many Jews, especially foreign Jews, melted into the anonymity of the resistance. Some survived thanks to the solidarity shown by non-Jews, to material assistance from Jewish organizations, to the black market, to false papers, to personal networks of contacts in the case of French Jews, and, in the case of foreign Jews, who were highly politicized and whose integration had occurred as a group, to collective networks.

The diversity of attitudes shown by Jews in the face of persecution is only a reflection of the heterogeneity of the French Jewish community and of the plurality of its connections and its identities. The majority of Jews registered with the authorities in the two zones out of a desire to comply with the law. No directive had been issued by Jewish organizations, which were caught up like the rest of the population in the panic surrounding the fall of France. The concerns of Jews from October 1940 on did not differ from those of the population at large, preoccupied with the daily search for subsistence. But the promulgation of laws marginalizing the Jews meant that day-to-day survival would become still more precarious.

During the same period, the various Jewish organizations in both the southern and the northern zone were divided by important ideological differences. In addition to those that already existed, others emerged. The Comité de Secours (usually referred to by its address, the rue Amelot in Paris) was very active, particularly on behalf of foreign Jews. Founded during the German occupation of the capital, it operated up until the liberation, providing money, setting up food kitchens, issuing false papers, securing hiding places, arranging passage to the southern zone, and sheltering children whose parents had been arrested. All these organizations had a common objective: coming to the aid of their fellow Jews.

THE UGIF

The German strategy consisted in reorganizing these associations in order to have greater control over them. On the order of Theodor Dannecker, in January 1941, the Comité de Coordination des Œuvres de Bienfaisance du Grand-Paris was set up in the northern zone. In the southern zone a Commission Centrale des Œuvres d'Assistance was created. The Nazis wished to create a Jewish Council (*Judenrat*) as they had in the occupied countries in the east. By the law of 29 November 1941, Vichy lay the groundwork for the Union Générale des Israélites de France (UGIF), intended to represent the Jews before the public authorities in matters of planning, assistance, and social and professional reclassification. All existing associations were dissolved, save cultural associations, and their assets came under the administration of the UGIF. All French and foreign Jews were required to belong to it. In the northern zone, the UGIF was an aggregate of seven organizations and allowed the Comité Amelot to function autonomously. In the southern zone, it had a federal structure.

The UGIF arouses debate still today.[15] It was vigorously criticized at the time by the Communists, who accused it of complicity with the enemy, and by immigrant Jews, who regarded it as a creation of French Jews looking to defend their own interests. In the days immediately following liberation in the summer of 1944, passions became exacerbated further.

In fact, the leaders of the UGIF agreed to carry out the role assigned to it in order not to compromise assistance to the Jews at a tragic moment of their existence. They did not, however, subscribe either to German aims or to those of the national revolution advocated by Vichy. By maneuvering between the two governments, the leaders of the UGIF tried to save whomever they could. They shielded Jewish associations, whether members or not, so that these groups could continue to act according to their own methods; and they paid for their commitment to the UGIF with their lives and those of their families.

Contrary to what certain of its detractors claimed, the UGIF was not a hotbed of Gestapo intrigue. It operated canteens, provided aid for thousands of Jews, and organized rescue missions. Some of its officials distinguished themselves by acts of bravery; others distinguished themselves rather less. The UGIF has rightly been reproached for a lack of vigilance not only in failing to prevent roundups from being made in its offices, but also for having brought two hundred Jewish children previously hidden in "Aryan" households in the countryside to its houses in Paris, where they were then found and deported by the Gestapo. Moreover, with the capture of its files and addresses, the UGIF inadvertently became a trap for the very Jews it meant to help.

Should it therefore have ceased operations after the summer of 1943 when it became clear that there was no longer any room for maneuver? From the beginning, the UGIF had privileged the social at the expense of the political, basing itself on a legal contract that tied its leaders to Vichy. It continued to work in this way even though the option was no longer viable.

Organizations that were not part of the UGIF pursued their own activities in parallel with it. The central consistory created its own commission for charitable and social assistance. Jews continued to worship throughout the war.

THE RESISTANCE

The Jews of France, French and foreign alike, participated from 1940 on in various resistance movements—Jewish and non-Jewish, in France and in London—displaying a number of different ideological tendencies; armed and unarmed, they operated underground in overlapping networks.

In response to General Charles de Gaulle's appeal of 18 June 1940, many Jews went to London to enlist in the Free French Forces, prompting de Gaulle's remark that at the beginning his entourage consisted only "of fishermen from the Île de Sein and Israelites."[16]

Jewish resistance encompassed a variety of nationalities (French and foreign) and political tendencies (Communism, Zionism, and others), and tried not only to assure the safety of the Jews but also to take its place as part of the larger *Résistance* so that the rights of Jews might ultimately be restored.

The Œuvre de Secours à l'Enfance and the Service d'Évacuation et de Regroupement des Enfants, as well as the Éclaireurs Israélites de France (EIF), hid children in "Aryan" families with the help of Christian organizations and arranged their safe passage to Spain and Switzerland, helping in this way to save a great many of them. In the end, 26 percent of adults over the age of seventeen suffered deportation as against 13 percent of children.[17]

Specifically Jewish resistance was organized among the Jewish immigrant proletariat in the Main-d'œuvre immigré (which during the war recruited more and more non-Communists—in 1943, only a third belonged to the party); also through Stekols, a wholly Jewish group, and Popa, a mixed group; and through paramilitary organizations such as the Valmy group, which belonged to the Francs-Tireurs et Partisans. Jewish Communists also published tracts, bulletins, and newspapers supporting the activity of these groups and calling upon the Jewish population to resist.

In 1943, the Jewish Communists regrouped within the Union des Juifs pour la Résistance et l'Entraide. While remaining loyal to the party and continuing to carry out its objectives, they fought also to prevent the destruction of the Jews. The course of events showed that the priorities of the party did not coincide with those of the Jews.

The Jewish Army was created in 1941 in the southern zone by a group of young Zionists. At the beginning, it was entirely oriented toward emigration to Palestine. It recruited widely within the ranks of the EIF. In 1944 it became the Organisation Juive de Combat, which allowed it to adapt more effectively to the circumstances of underground French politics and to fit into the framework of the resistance. Its motto was "Resist wherever you are." The Jewish Army established transit routes into Spain, rescued children, took action against informers in Nice, organized underground networks (*maquis*), and gave financial and military support to other underground units, such as the one set up by the EIF, and collaborated locally with various resistance groups.

Despite the tensions between French Jews and foreign Jews, despite the political differences between them and the tragic fate that awaited them, large numbers of men and women committed themselves in support of the resistance, managing even to establish a Jewish resistance.

All these things in combination enabled the Jews of France in large part to escape extermination. There remained the question that was to go on troubling many after the war: were there two Frances—Vichy France, on the one hand, and, on the other, Republican France, innocent of the crimes of collaboration? This question quite recently received a reply from the president of the republic, Jacques Chirac, on 16 July 1995, the fifty-third anniversary of the Vel' d'hiv roundup. Chirac insisted on the joint responsibility of France and of the state, refusing to endorse the distinction between two Frances that had endured since the end of the war—and so at last coming to terms with this dark episode in the history of the French nation. "France," he said, "birthplace of the Enlightenment and of the Rights of Man, land of welcome and of refuge—France on that day [16 July 1942] did something that cannot be undone. Breaking its word, it delivered those under its protection to their executioners." In the same speech Chirac went on to clearly state the necessity of "recognizing the wrongs of the past and the wrongs committed by the state. Unquestionably, mistakes were made; wrongs were done; the blame falls on all."[18]

Recovery

AT THE END OF 1944, France was almost entirely liberated from the German occupation. The French Jewish collectivity was exhausted. It numbered no more than between 180,000 and 200,000.[1] It had lost roughly a third of its members, owing to deportation and also to deaths in internment camps, combat, and execution. Very few showed an interest after the war of departing for the Americas or Palestine. Institutional, economic, and demographic recovery was urgent. The survivors had lived through the tragedy of the occupation; it now remained for them to find a normal life once again.

They believed that the end of the German occupation would be followed by a return to the situation prior to 1940, with the restitution of property and homes lost to "Aryanization." This was not to be the case. Work, lodging, funds to make a new beginning—all these had to be arranged. Jewish children dispersed in non-Jewish households had to be restored to their families. Survivors had to be reunited and reintegrated into society and the economy.

Jewish organizations were to play an essential role in the restructuring of the Jewish collectivity in France, but their work was handicapped by the fact that they too were scattered in the aftermath of the war. Old differences of opinion reasserted themselves alongside new cleavages born in the wartime underground. What is more, because these organizations had been deprived of their leaders, there was a lack of spiritual guidance. Places of worship had been damaged or completely destroyed. Entire communities, especially in the countryside, had disappeared.

The seeds of unification had nonetheless been planted in the underground. Partly this was due to the Conseil Représentatif des Juifs de France (CRIF). Founded in 1944, it brought together the various ideological elements of French Jewry in both its immigrant and native branches. Considering itself "solely qualified to be the spokesman of Judaism in France before the authorities and public opinion as well as before the Jewish organizations of other countries and before international authorities," it assigned itself the mission of bringing about the "creation of constitutional guarantees against any attack on the principles of equality of race and religion; recognition of the equality of Jews with their fellow citizens; [and] restitution of the civil, political, and economic rights and nationality of the Jews through repeal of all emergency laws." It also called for reparation of material and moral damages and supported the demands of the Jewish Agency and other organizations for annulment of the White Paper of 1939[2] and for freedom of Jewish immigration and colonization in Palestine, while at the same time working on behalf of understanding between Jews and Arabs in the region.[3] It constituted a united front in dealing with French authorities in the task of reconstruction. By favoring a political form of representation, the CRIF went beyond the limits of what had previously been considered acceptable by French Jews. The war and its tragic companion, the Holocaust, had prepared the way for this inevitable transition from Jewish Frenchman (*Français israélite*) to the French Jew (*Juif français*) of plural identity.

In the immediate postwar period the CRIF remained under the control of the consistory, which aspired to the leadership of organized French Jewry.[4] Divisions among immigrant Jews posed obstacles to the smooth functioning of the new organization as well, with the result that it was far from fulfilling the mission it had undertaken. In an attempt at revitalization, the CRIF modified its by-laws in the early 1950s to make it incumbent upon the organization to work on behalf of the Jewish people as well as in defense of other political causes not falling under its direct authority, which led to the alienation of Jewish Communists. There were also sharp disagreements over the formula to be adopted concerning the relationship of the CRIF to Israel. In the end it was decided to express support without, however, indicating whether this support was to take an active form. By 1954, however, ten years after its founding, passions had calmed down and the CRIF was able to act as the representative of a unified Judaism before French and international authorities, both in seeking aid for refugees and in combating the resurgence of Nazism and anti-Semitism. Additionally, in 1952, as a party to the Conference of Jewish Material Claims Against Germany, the CRIF signed the Luxembourg accords governing German reparations and closely monitored the course of negotiations regarding the indemnization of French nationals by the Federal Republic of Germany, which eventually occurred in two stages, in 1954 and then in 1960.

Following the war, the Comité Juif d'Action Sociale et de Reconstruction (COJASOR), created in 1945 as the social arm of the CRIF, provided vital assistance to foreigners and displaced persons with the financial support of the American Joint Distribution Committee (or the "Joint"),[5] which had itself been active during the occupation. In 1949, the Fonds Social Juif Unifié (FSJU) was founded as the central agency for the collection and distribution of funds coming mainly from the Joint during this period. The FSJU very quickly became transformed into a planning authority. In addition to its considerable social work, it undertook important cultural responsibilities, supervising instruction in schools at all levels, administering youth programs through a whole series of educational and recreational networks, helping reconstruct provincial communities, and providing support for various publications, notably among them a journal founded in 1950 that later became *L'Arche*. Afterward the FSJU applied itself to the task of integrating immigrants from North Africa and Egypt. It also created community centers that brought together religious, cultural, and social activities under the same roof. In the 1980s, it supported the founding of many Jewish schools. The activities of the FSJU are financed by private contributions. During the Arab-Israeli War of 1967,[6] it launched a special campaign, the Appel Juif Unifié, which provided both for its own needs and for assistance to the State of Israel.

After the Second World War, one of the essential tasks was to locate missing children and restore them to their parents or, in cases where children had been orphaned, seeing to their education. The Œuvre de Secours à l'Enfance, which through its various groups offered both liberal and religious curricula, the Commission Centrale de l'Enfance, an organ of the Communist Union des Juifs pour la Résistance et l'Entraide, and the Bund together provided for the instruction of thousands of children, each organization remaining faithful to its own ideological orientation. In 1947, they sponsored sixty or so children's homes that took in some 3,000 orphans and more than a thousand young survivors of the camps.[7] Jewish organizations also assisted youth in reestablishing contact with family members, both in France and abroad, defraying the cost of their housing and offering emotional support at a time of great distress.

Isaac Schneerson (1879–1969), an industrialist who emigrated from the Soviet Union to France in 1920 and subsequently devoted much of his life to social work, founded the Centre de Documentation Juive Contemporaine (CDJC) in Grenoble in 1943, in order to assure that the history of this dark period would be written and that its memory would be bequeathed to survivors and to future generations. The CDJC, which operated secretly during the occupation, was transferred to Paris in 1944. Its documentary collections were built up largely owing to the efforts of Léon Poliakov (1910–97), who managed to obtain the archives of the SS administration in France that had been used at the Nuremberg trial.[8] The CDJC became one of the archival depositories of this trial as well, to which other important collections were later added. It saw to it that the history of the genocide and persecution of the Jews of France was written. Research on this subject appeared in its journal, *Le Monde juif*, or in works that it published itself—forty-six volumes between 1945 and 1975—including several books by Poliakov that have since come to be acknowledged as classics.

At the beginning of the 1950s, again with the purpose of assuring the transmission of historical memory, Schneerson resolved that a Tomb of the Unknown Jewish Martyr be erected in Paris. In 1950, the cornerstone for this memorial was laid on the rue Geoffroy-l'Asnier, in the Marais, in a large ceremony attended by the highest officials of the French government. In 1956 the CDJC's headquarters was dedicated, containing in addition to its own archives a library, which today includes 40,000 volumes, picture collection, exhibition hall, and the memorial itself in which, the following year, an urn containing ashes from the extermination camps was placed beneath an eternal flame. This was, in fact, the first memorial to the Holocaust constructed anywhere in the world. In 1997, by order of the president of the republic, Jacques Chirac, a subsection of the National Archives was set up at the CDJC as official depository for the "Jewish files" discovered in the Ministry of Veterans' Affairs, which led to a round of stormy recriminations.

At the same time, following the war, institutions that had been in existence prior to 1939 carried on with their work. In the immigrant community, the Fédération des Sociétés Juives de France, which supported the creation of a Jewish state in Palestine, included 120 organizations in 1946. Children's charities, social and cultural associations, and fellow-countrymen societies fully assumed their responsibilities. During this period, Communist organizations enjoyed great prestige on account of the exploits of the Red Army against Nazi Germany and of Jewish Communist militants in the resistance. The favorable position adopted by the Soviet Union in the United Nations debate on the creation of the State of Israel further strengthened sympathy toward them.

Surviving concentration camp prisoners came home traumatized. Eyewitness accounts began to appear. But discussion of this unspeakable and unbearable experience was not yet possible. Silence prevailed. Some hoped to be able to reintegrate themselves by covering up their Jewish past, the source of so much suffering. They changed their patronymics, keeping those acquired underground; others converted in order to completely assimilate themselves with the surrounding society. Between 1947 and 1950 there were 2,150 changes of name. Because these changes also affected wives and children, they involved some 8,000–10,000 people out of a total Jewish population at the time estimated at roughly 200,000, or about 5 percent—a proportion that doubles if one takes into consideration as well those Jews who adopted gallicized patronymics on acquiring French citizenship. Officially approved changes of name between 1945 and 1957 were six times more numerous than those recorded between 1809 and 1939, and for the most part concerned patronymics of eastern European origin.[9] Exogamous and secular marriages also multiplied. Already before the war, religious observance had begun to subside. For many immigrants who had fought in the ranks of the resistance, integration in the France of the Revolution was accomplished through this glorious episode, which conferred upon them full rights of citizenship. Some, aligning themselves

with majority opinion, sought to go back to the old models of the France
that they had so loved. If Jews reacted in many different ways, their attachment to France remained wholly intact.

Traditional Judaism underwent a revival during the same period, especially among the young. Jews were called upon to deepen their knowledge
of Judaism. Meeting places meant to encourage such activity were established. The École des Cadres Gilbert Bloch at Orsay, where between 1946
and 1970 several hundred young Jews were to rediscover the sources of
their faith, contributed to the development of Jewish philosophical instruction under the direction of teachers such as Jacob Gordin (1896–
1947) and Léon Ashkénazi (1922–96), better known by his scout name,
Manitou. In the 1950s this school took part in the founding of the Centre
Universitaire d'Études Juives de Paris, a Jewish institution existing alongside the official university world that enjoyed a brief moment of glory in
the 1970s before entering into decline during the following decade. The
talmudic teaching of Emmanuel Levinas (1906–95), pursued until 1989
and directed to a cultivated French-speaking audience, participated in this
same movement of revival. On 24 May 1957 a small gathering of Jewish
intellectuals at Versailles marked the birth of the well-known Colloque des
Intellectuels Juifs de Langue Française within the institutional framework
of the World Jewish Congress. As of 1997, thirty-seven conferences had
been held, bringing together noted Jewish and non-Jewish figures to dis-
cuss a variety of subjects, accompanied by publication of the proceedings.
In the same spirit, new Jewish schools—such as the École Maïmonide and
the École Yabné in the Paris region and the École Akiba in Strasbourg—
were established, very different from the consistorial institutions of the
beginning of the century. Other Jewish schools resumed their activities.
Religious youth movements were founded. A Jewish press grew up in the
1950s as well with the reappearance of old newspapers and periodicals.
Yiddish-language publications, which were to fold for want of readers in
the 1990s, enjoyed a new life in this decade with *Naïe Press* (New Press) and
Unzer Wort (Our Word). The consistory published *Vendredi Soir* and the
Journal des Communautés, later renamed *Information juive* on the occasion
of its merger with the newspaper of this title published in Algiers until
1962. The Zionist tendency was represented by *La Terre retrouvée*, which
had existed before the war. *Évidences*, which first appeared in 1949, concerned itself more with questions of Jewish identity. The scholarly *Revue
des études juives*, published since 1880, enjoyed fresh popularity under the
direction of the orientalist Georges Vajda (1908–81). Additional publications gradually came to supplement an already diverse range of choices.
Broadcast began of a radio program, "Écoute Israël." Already existing Jewish libraries, such as that of the Alliance Israélite Universelle and the
Bund's Bibliothèque Medem, continued with their work while others were

created. Zionism was no longer opposed by the Jewish establishment. It benefited from a huge reservoir of sympathy in non-Jewish public opinion deriving from the sufferings of the Jews during the dark years. After the war almost everyone in the Jewish world was agreed about the necessity of a Jewish state in Palestine, even if certain marginal elements thought that it would serve mainly as a refuge for Jews from central and eastern Europe.

After the liberation, some who had collaborated in racial persecution were sentenced but a good many managed to escape judgment. The modifications to the Marchandeau decree made by the provisional government severely punished anti-Semitism. Nonetheless, as memories of the liberation receded, anti-Semitism reemerged in the press. The Ligue Internationale contre l'Antisémitisme (LICA) redoubled its efforts to battle against this scourge, in the Soviet bloc as well as in the West, denounced all forms of racism, and mobilized support against German rearmament. During the Algerian war it protested repressive methods and the recourse to terrorism. Its anticolonialist position notwithstanding, LICA devoted itself no less vigorously to defending Jews and remained committed to the State of Israel. In 1949, the Communist Mouvement National contre le Racisme (MNCR), secretly created during the war by the Jewish section of Main-d'oeuvre immigré, became the Mouvement contre le Racisme et l'Antisémitisme et pour le Paix (MRAP)—a movement born of the failed attempt to merge MNCR with LICA, inspired by Communist strategy and dedicated to fighting more for de-Nazification and peace. The Jewish question was later to trigger a rupture within the MRAP itself, with many Communist militants refusing to denounce Soviet anti-Semitism. The MRAP adhered to the official Soviet version of the Moscow trials as well as of the trials that were taking place in the popular democracies of the Eastern bloc. Its activities expanded to include the struggle against colonialism and against anti-immigrant, anti-Arab, and—in the United States— anti-black racism. In 1977, it resolved no longer to distinguish anti-Semitism and racism, becoming the Mouvement contre le Racisme et pour l'Amitié entre les Peuples.

Men of good will such as the historian Jules Isaac (1877–1963) tried to encourage closer contacts through the Amitié Judéo-Chrétienne, founded in 1948, followed a bit later by the creation of a short-lived quarterly publication of the same name. It reappeared in 1963 and from 1975 onward was published on a monthly basis under the title *Sens*. Provincial chapters were established in a number of cities. In 1967, the Catholic priest Roger Braun formed an association called Rencontres entre Chrétiens et Juifs, together with a quarterly journal of the same name, with a view to providing Judeo-Christian dialogue with a sound doctrinal basis. This proved to be a difficult task. The Finaly affair (1948–53) reminded Jews that anti-Judaism and anti-Semitism had not totally disappeared. Two Jewish boys from Grenoble whose parents had been deported were subsequently com-

mitted to the care of a Catholic guardian. After the war, the guardian refused to return the children to their aunts, arguing that they were now
Catholics. Trials followed, with public stands being taken by the church,
among other parties, putting the affair on the front page. In the end, the
Finaly brothers were returned to their original family, a result to which the
consistory and the *grand rabbinat* had largely contributed. The unfolding
of the affair reawakened still vivid memories within the decimated Jewish
population. The populism that developed in the 1950s around the Union
de Défense des Commerçants et Artisans, led by Pierre Poujade, which
won a significant share of the vote in the 1956 legislative elections;[10] the
Suez campaign in 1956–57;[11] and later the course of events in Algeria in
the 1960s, all these made fashionable once more a certain melange of xenophobia, anti-Semitism, and anti-Zionism that greatly disturbed Jews, who
now were hypersensitive to such displays of animosity.

Jules Isaac managed to obtain several audiences with Pope John XXIII
with a view to reexamining the foundations of Judeo-Christian relations.
But it was only in the mid-1960s that the church officially revised its teaching concerning the Jews, with the Second Vatican Council and the Declaration on the Relationship of the Church to Non-Christian religions (*Nostra Aetate*). Some thirty years later, on 30 September 1997, French bishops
published a "declaration of repentance" regarding the attitude of the
church toward the Vichy regime, read during a memorial ceremony at the
Drancy internment camp. On 16 March 1998, the Vatican issued a document entitled, "We Remember: A Reflection on the Holocaust." In it,
Pope John Paul II condemned "the erroneous and unjust interpretations of
the New Testament relating to the Jewish people and to their guilt." He
added that these errors "engendered feelings of hostility toward the Jews
and helped dull consciences, so that, when the wave of persecutions broke
over Europe . . . , alongside Christians who made every effort to save the
persecuted at risk to their [own] lives, the spiritual resistance of many was
not what humanity was entitled to expect on the part of Christ's disciples."
This statement nonetheless denied the existence of a direct causal relation
between the historical anti-Judaism of Christians and the anti-Semitism of
the Nazis, exposing it to criticism in Israel as well as in France. In particular, it was accused of unduly exculpating the church and especially Pope
Pius XII, who was careful during the Second World War not to speak out
against the tragedy that was taking place.

THE INFLUX OF NORTH AFRICAN JEWS

The arrival of North African Jews, who have played such an important role
in the construction of Jewish identity in France during the postwar period,
was preceded immediately after the war by the influx of persons displaced

by the gradual closing of refugee camps and of Jews fleeing countries in central and eastern Europe, now under Soviet control. The independence of Tunisia and Morocco in 1956, the Suez War the same year, and then, in 1961, the Bizerte affair, the imminent victory of the Front de Libération Nationale (FLN) in Algeria,[12] and this country's independence in 1962 soon triggered massive departures. The nature of Jewish engagement during the Algerian War reflected the composite character of the Jewish communities in these countries. Their organizations elected to take a cautious line, taking care not to commit themselves politically. Some Jews fought in the ranks of the FLN; others, in greater numbers, in the Organisation de l'Armée Secrète (OAS);[13] but the majority chose the path of prudent moderation.[14] Routes of emigration depended on whether or not one held French citizenship and on the degree of familiarity with French culture. During the period when the countries of North Africa achieved independence, there were 140,000 Jews of French nationality in Algeria, 105,000 Jews in Tunisia (of whom 71,000 were Tunisian citizens), and 225,000 Jews in Morocco (the majority of them Moroccan citizens). Between 1956 and 1967, about 235,000 North African Jews settled in France. Tunisian Jews were split, some going to France, some (60,000 between 1948 and 1963) to Israel; Moroccan Jews for the most part chose Israel (about 210,000 for the same period). As for Algerian Jews, the great majority went to France (with only about 12,000 going to Israel). Only 4,000 Jews still remained in Algeria after independence. In 1984, their numbers stood at about 200 in Algeria, 3,500 in Tunisia, and 13,000 in Morocco. For two or three generations beforehand, North African Jews had migrated in massive numbers from the countryside to cities and from small towns to large urban centers. Those who came to France were therefore already urbanized. Geographic mobility was accompanied by social mobility. On the eve of decolonization, 90 percent of the Jewish population of Tunisia and 60 percent of that of Morocco knew how to read and write in French, while in Algeria illiteracy among Jews had been eliminated well before the Second World War. Settlement in France was therefore in a sense the outcome of a process of gallicization begun in North Africa. The immigration of Jews from the Maghreb was not prompted by persecution but by uncertainty about the future.

The law of 26 December 1961 concerning the reception and resettlement of overseas French citizens was the fundamental legislative text shaping the attitude of the government toward repatriated Jews and non-Jews. Other decrees supplemented this law. Jews from Algeria, Tunisia, and Morocco were entitled to relocation benefits, employment assistance, integration in the French bureaucracy in the case of civil servants, and preferential treatment for public housing. It was only in 1962, with the signing of the Armistice of Évian, that these Jews began to enter France en masse and the government responded by setting up a ministry in charge of repatriation. Philanthropic societies of all denominations organized reception committees. Various Jewish institutions, whose leaders did not wish to repeat the mistakes of the past, set about the task of welcoming these Jews as well.

The Algerian repatriates did not have a high opinion of metropolitan France, however. Like other *pieds-noirs*, they felt bitterness toward France for having abandoned Algeria. They also learned that General Charles de Gaulle had for a time considered satisfying the requests of the FLN in the matter of the "Algerian" nationality of the country's Jews, thus going back on the right to French citizenship that had been granted them by the Crémieux decree of 1870. All this contributed to the deep hostility shown by the repatriates to de Gaulle in particular and to the Gaullist regime in general. This hostility was strengthened during the Six Day War by de Gaulle's attitude toward Israel, which many repatriates likened to the abandonment of Algeria to the Arabs, at a moment when Egyptian president Gamal Abdel Nasser and the Palestinian leader Ahmed Shukayri had announced the Arab determination to push the Israelis into the sea. The repatriates did not shrink from loudly expressing the anger they felt over French policy in the Middle East, breaking with the traditional reserve of French Jews in similar circumstances.[15]

The North African immigration led to the creation of many new communities and the recomposition and redistribution of old ones. The newcomers settled throughout France but particularly in the Paris region and in the Midi. In Paris, the traditional Jewish neighborhoods underwent a change of appearance. North African Jews repopulated the old Jewish immigrant quarters of Belleville and the Marais. They took up trades practiced in the past by Ashkenazic immigrants, in the clothing industry for example. Sentier, a right-bank neighborhood in Paris, is significant in this connection.

This immigration completely altered the profile of the Jewish collectivity of France. Earlier the native Jewry had been overwhelmed by immigrants from eastern Europe; now these immigrants were overwhelmed by Jews from the Maghreb. The newcomers assumed their place in the communal apparatus and breathed a new dynamism into the collectivity, infusing it with new values: a greater religiosity, a conception of Judaism that regarded it as something much more than a practice confined to the private sphere—as something that included every aspect of social life, and so stood apart from the confessional and integrated conception held by native Jews. In 1981 a Sephardi, René Samuel Sirat, was elected chief rabbi of France; his successor, Joseph Sitruk, elected in 1987 and reelected in 1994, is also a Sephardi.

On their arrival in France, repatriated Jews suffered from a lack of Jewish schools, synagogues, supervisory bodies, spiritual leaders, and shops supplying foods conforming to Jewish dietary laws. The consistory and the FSJU undertook new programs—"Chantiers du Consistoire"—aimed at providing the new arrivals with joint synagogue/community centers that would allow them to worship in their own way and to respond to their own needs; the first opened in 1962 in Villiers-le-Bel, followed in 1965 by another in Sarcelles. This time Jewish institutions did not attempt, as they had in the past, to impose their own model of integration, which had been put to a strenuous test by the war; to the contrary, despite their differences, they tried not to infringe upon what was unique about this multifaceted immigration.

The newcomers began to organize themselves in their turn, creating their own forms of associational life. They revitalized an aging Jewry, decimated by the war, by recreating a Jewish way of life that was to become increasingly visible to the rest of French society. Their numbers and the fact that they were dispersed throughout France strongly contributed to this visibility. Between 25 percent and 30 percent of the repatriates—about 40,000 persons—settled in Paris and the surrounding region; almost as many were found in the southeast, with about 30,000 in Marseilles and environs; another 10 percent to 15 percent in the southwest; about 10 percent in the Lyons area, including 15,000 in Lyons itself, with the remaining 10 percent to 15 percent distributed over dozens of localities elsewhere, in small towns and villages. They rapidly adapted to the French way of life while, in the case of the vast majority, clinging to their prior habits, if only ones relating to diet. Among young people, devotion to religious practice and tradition nonetheless exhibited a decline associated with socioeconomic integration.[16] They nonetheless recomposed their identity in new forms, very far removed from the Franco-Judaism of the prewar period—an identity that incorporated the State of Israel as well as the Holocaust while preserving an element of ethnic specificity.

The integration of North African Jews was distinguished from that of the Askenazic immigrants who preceded them by their geographic proximity and cultural ties to France. In the first place, they knew the French language—a decisive factor in the process of integration. The Jewish repatriates from North Africa were French citizens as well and therefore benefited, as other non-Jewish repatriates did, from the aid and support given them by the authorities. Moreover, those who were civil servants continued to perform the same duties that they had in their native countries, which was not a negligible consideration. The integration of these newcomers was remarkable in every respect. At the same time, influenced by their spirit and energy, official Judaism broke with its traditional policy of reserve and began to display a collective political and religious visibility in urban centers, with dozens of new restaurants, snack bars, butcher shops, and kosher sections in food stores.

The Suez campaign in 1956, and the deterioration of relations between Arabs and Jews in Egypt that followed from it, led the most gallicized elements of the Jewish community there to emigrate to France—about 10,000 in all, most of them arriving in a quite impoverished condition despite coming from wealthy backgrounds. Their assets had been confiscated, their businesses sold for derisory sums, their bank accounts frozen. The French authorities and the institutions of the organized Jewish community, aided by the Joint, came to their aid. Many of these refugees settled in suburbs of Paris such as Villiers-le-Bel, Sarcelles, Orly, and Créteil; others went to Provence. Owing to their relatively small numbers, their impact on the remaking of the community was limited.

THE NEW FACE OF FRENCH JEWRY

The choices available to urban Jews, their sense of ethnic belonging, their socioeconomic and religious background, the generational phenomenon, and the influence of new ideas all entered into play in reshaping the identity of the Jews of France from the 1960s on. The Six Day War of 1967 strengthened Jewish solidarity toward Israel, which was believed to face a new threat of genocide. The conflict also created a favorable tide of opinion in non-Jewish circles—whether out of admiration for the achievements of the young Jewish state or out of anti-Arab feeling, a legacy of the Algerian War—which had the ancillary effect of making French Jews feel they were now a legitimate and accepted part of French society. The war thus affected Jewish thinking in two important ways. The atmosphere of mutual sympathy between France and Israel to which it gave rise for a brief period was still to be found, though in a weaker form, during the demonstrations that followed the attack in the rue Copernic in Paris in 1980 and the desecration of Jewish graves in the Carpentras cemetery ten years later. At the same time, however, de Gaulle's public references to Israel as a warlike state and to the Jewish people as "sure of itself and domineering" rekindled fears of an anti-Semitic campaign of denigration.[17] The parties of the extreme left in turn condemned Israel, taking up the Palestinian cause.

Although the majority of Jews sided with Israel, a certain number of Jewish intellectuals and students on the extreme left supported the Palestinian resistance. The student unrest of May 1968 reinforced this stand, though they had very little influence within the Jewish communities of France. Nonetheless the massive presence of Jews in the events of May 1968, and the important role that they played in extreme left-wing organizations, cannot be allowed to go unremarked.[18] Of the twelve members of the political bureau of the Ligue Communiste Révolutionnaire, only one was a non-Jew; apart from Daniel Bensaïd, a North African Jew by birth,

ten were Jews from eastern Europe—leading Daniel Cohn-Bendit, the un-
disputed symbol of the student revolt in Europe, to remark that the national leaderships of the groups on the extreme left, despite their differences, could speak together in Yiddish.

In the nineteenth century, young Jews from the bourgeoisie, particularly in Germany, developed a taste for socialism, Marxism, and anarchism.
They thought that in the new socialist society there would no longer be a
Jewish question and that the restrictions placed upon Jews by the old society would disappear. Their minority status and experience of oppression
and injustice could only bring them together with others who were oppressed, no matter what their religion or nationality. Additionally, the real
or mythic values of their faith, now in the process of being destroyed,
would prompt them to seek greater justice and equality. In the twentieth
century, this tradition of engagement by Jewish European intellectuals on
the side of the underprivileged members of society came to be confirmed
and extended.

If this earlier generation of intellectuals did not act as Jews, neither did
those who were at the head of the student revolt in May 1968. They made
a clear distinction between their radicalism and their Jewishness. Though
they did not have a clear sense of the meaning and import of their faith,
they did not reject it; still less did they make a secret of the fact they were
Jewish. For some, such as Pierre Goldman, there was a direct link between
their Jewishness and their political commitment. Nor is the hostility
shown by some toward Israel and Jewish institutions to be seen as an expression of self-hatred. This had nothing to do with their motives for action. In the 1980s, in fact, some leaders of the movement—Alain Geismar,
for example—retracted violently anti-Israeli statements made earlier.

For the majority of these young people, though in different ways, Fascism along with the Holocaust and its repercussions were at the very heart
of their engagement. It should be kept in mind that the Jewishness of these
radicals cannot be reduced to their experience of genocide as the children
of survivors. They considered themselves "citizens of the world" and, accordingly, set off in search of a homeland in distant countries, from which
they returned without having found what they were looking for. In the
end, for many of them, the Holocaust was the sole remaining component
of their Jewish identity. Many wound up returning to a Jewishness they
may never have really abandoned—unlike their revolutionary forebears,
such as Karl Marx and Rosa Luxemburg, who distanced themselves from it
or displayed genuine hostility toward it. This return occurred slowly during the 1970s, then became more pronounced in the following decade,
manifesting itself in the ferment of Jewish culture during this period. A few
chose the path of religion. Thus, for example, Benny Lévy, known at the

time as Pierre Victor, one of the leaders of the Maoist movement of the proletarian left, became a rabbi and now lives in Jerusalem.

The budding young revolutionaries of May 1968 sought to find a place for themselves in a different world, a new and egalitarian world. They wished to escape the burden of Jewish existence without, however, wishing to break with their Jewishness. By becoming involved politically, they hoped to set themselves apart from their parents, who had not awakened to the fascist danger in time and who, in their view, had not fought hard enough to contain it. Their vigilance testified to a determination not to repeat their parents' mistakes. The denunciation of western imperialism and colonialism sprang from the same motivation: what happened during the dark years of the war must not be allowed to be repeated. For this reason they placed themselves on the side of those who suffered oppression by the West. There are many still today who have not abandoned the struggle, though now they pursue it in a different form. They are engaged in humanitarian combat—thus, for example, Bernard Kouchner, son of a Jewish father and, since 1997, secretary of state for health, who founded the organizations Médecins sans Frontières and Médecins du Monde; they participate in groups such as SOS-Racisme, working alongside Arabs; and, since 1996, they have been involved in challenging immigration laws, even where these do not directly or indirectly concern the Jews of France.

To return to the Six Day War, and de Gaulle's scathing remarks, these events constituted a turning point for many French Jews. In the years that followed they openly came to terms with their Jewishness and also, in the same way, with their relationship to Israel. North African Jews were largely responsible for the firm expression of unfailing support for the Hebrew state, unprecedented within the French Jewish collectivity. The "imaginary Jew" described by Alain Finkielkraut tended to become a memory. A marked sense of Jewish identity was also manifested by the desire to play a political role. In the decade following the Six Day War, the lawyer Henri Hajdenberg formed the Renouveau Juif, a movement aimed at creating an American-style Jewish lobby and putting together a Jewish vote. The idea eventually achieved a certain place in public opinion, though it had no justification in reality. Studies have contradicted the existence of any Jewish vote whatsoever in France: Jews cast their ballot just as the rest of the French people do, according to their own personal interests and not according to Jewish interests. The only consistent patterns in their voting are that they rarely endorse extreme positions, whether of the right or the left, and that more Jews tend to vote for the left than for the right. The absence of a Jewish vote does not mean that Jews do not have political influence, however. All parties take them into account in devising their strategies. In 1980, Hajdenberg drew 100,000 people to the Porte de Pantin in Paris for a "Twelve Hours for Israel" rally. The vicissitudes of recent years, particularly the war in Lebanon and the Intifada, have somewhat moderated unconditional support for Israel since then. Between 15 percent and 20 percent of French Jews now describe themselves as critical or hostile, not a negligible percentage.[19]

In the early 1970s, the memory of the Shoah—a term that, in preference to Holocaust, came into quite general use in France with the release in 1985 of Claude Lanzmann's film of the same name—reemerged as part of the search for meaning that engaged the French Jewish collectivity. It became a vital issue not only in the culture of the Jews of France but at the national level as well. This reawakening was not peculiar to France. It touched all the descendants of the survivors of the tragedy, and derived from the same impulse as the reexamination of the Vichy regime and the role of French anti-Semitism during the 1930s. The same impulse also inspired films such as Marcel Ophüls's *Le Chagrin et la Pitié* (The Sorrow and the Pity, 1971) and books such as Robert O. Paxton's *Vichy France: Old Guard and New Order, 1940–1944* (which appeared in French translation in 1973). The trials that took place over the years between 1973 and 1998 revived the memory: former SS captain Klaus Barbie, extradicted from Bolivia in 1983 and sentenced four years later; Paul Touvier, convicted in 1994 of having executed seven Jewish hostages in Rillieux during the war; Maurice Papon, former *secrétaire général* of the Gironde prefecture, sentenced to ten years in prison in 1998. There were also a number of celebrated cases in which charges were brought but which did not end up going to trial, such as that of Jean Legay, the agent in the occupied zone of René Bousquet, former *secrétaire général* of the Vichy Police and one of the organizers of the Vel' d'hiv roundup of 16–17 July 1942. Legay died in 1989 before being tried. Bousquet, a personal friend of President François Mitterand, was charged in 1991 but assassinated before being brought before a court. At the same time, commemorative ceremonies kept the memory alive along with the dedication of monuments and the installation of plaques. Additionally there were debates, sometimes very heated, such as the one aroused by the "Jewish files" that Serge Klarsfeld, founder (with his wife, Beate Klarsfeld) of the Association des Fils et Filles des Déportés Juifs de France, discovered in the Ministry of Veterans' Affairs and claimed to be the files assembled by the Préfecture de Police in 1940 that were used in the raids. A commission of specialists charged with determining the exact nature of these files concluded that they were not the 1940 files, which were destroyed in 1948–49.

Another national debate involving Vichy was provoked by the speech of President Chirac on the occasion of the fifty-third anniversary of the Vel' d'hiv roundup in 1995, in which he recognized "the responsibility of the French state" and spoke of the nation's "collective blame." He affirmed the debt of guilt contracted by France toward 76,000 murdered Jews. The leaders of the organized Jewish community expressed their satisfaction along with 72 percent of French men and women polled by the Institut Français d'Opinion Publique and the weekly magazine *L'Événement du jeudi*. The extreme right, for its part, accused the president of "sullying the nation's reputation." The Papon trial gave new life to the debate while raising questions about the educational value of such a proceeding, which in any case caused much ink to be spilled. On 20 July 1997, in line with the president's prior declarations, the Socialist prime minister Lionel Jospin acknowledged in turn the responsibility of the French state in the Vel' d'hiv roundup, indicated that the government would give "its full support" to the work of the commissions charged with drawing up an inventory of Jewish property and other financial and artistic holdings plundered during the occupation, and added that it would assist the construction in Paris of a Holocaust museum.

These statements and events together amounted to moral reparation for the French victims of the Holocaust and had the effect of making the French people as a whole aware of the government's share of responsibility in this tragedy. Today the Holocaust is an essential component of the identity of French Jews, including North African Jews and members of succeeding generations who did not experience it. There has been a crystallization of identity in recent years around the Holocaust, above all among the young, which may prove to be problematic in the near future both for them and for the stability of the French Jewish population.

In the 1970s, the quest for identity on the part of French Jews was manifested also by the organization of conferences such as the one devoted to Yiddish Culture in 1978 at the Centre Georges-Pompidou in Paris. Here was a case of a national museum opening its doors to a minority group. This conference was followed by another in the same vein, two years later, devoted to Jewish cultures of the Mediterranean. The study of Jewish languages developed alongside new associations dedicated to ethnic issues, little discussed in France until then, but which spread as a result of the regionalism that affected all of France after May 1968. New journals appeared such as *Combat pour la Diaspora* (founded in 1980) and *Traces* (1981). All these things testified to the cultural ferment of the time.

North African immigration had made the French Jewish population— which totaled 535,000 at the beginning of the 1980s, or 1 percent of the French population—the largest Jewish group in Europe after the Soviet Union (from which, of course, Jews had begun to leave) and the third largest of the worldwide diaspora, led by the United States. It now stands at about 600,000. In the early 1980s, about half of French Jews lived in the Paris area, 30 percent in the city itself and 26 percent in the suburbs. In Paris, Jews represented 6 percent of the total population.[20] The second largest geographical area today is the Midi-Provence-Côte d'Azur region. Marseilles has 65,000 Jews, Nice 20,000, Lyons 20,000, and Toulouse 18,000. Next comes Alsace, with 12,000 living in the city of Strasbourg. Roughly 50 percent of the Jewish population of France is Sephardic, 34 percent Ashkenazic, and 16 percent neither one nor the other.[21] Looking at the Jewish population of the Paris region, one finds that 44 percent was born in France and 38 percent in North Africa (Algerians accounting for most of this number with Tunisians and Moroccans coming next, as compared with 10 percent originally from central and eastern Europe). Roughly the same proportions are found in the provinces, except in Strasbourg, where 63 percent of the Jewish residents were born in France.

In the 1980s, Jewish families in France typically conformed to the nuclear model. In the Paris region, 22 percent of Jewish households had two persons, 20 percent three persons, and 20 percent four persons; 17 percent of all households were constituted by single persons, who accounted for nearly 6 percent of the Jewish population; households made up of more than five persons represented less than 10 percent of the total, with 9 percent of households being headed by a woman. The average size of Jewish households outside the capital (3.19 persons) was almost identical to that of Jewish households in the Paris region (3.24), including the non-Jewish members of these households. At the end of the 1980s, 17 percent of Jews over the age of eighteen were single, 63 percent married, 7 percent divorced, and 9 percent widowed, with 4 percent living together outside of wedlock. The portrait that emerges from these figures is one of an essentially urban group.

Almost three-quarters (72 percent) of Jewish marriages during this period were homogamous from the geographic point of view.[22] The proportion of exogamous marriages was close to 22 percent among provincial Jews and 20 percent in the Paris region, allowing for variations depending on the geographic origin of the partners. Between 1966 and 1975, less than 5 percent of the marriages involving Moroccans and Tunisians performed in France were exogamous, as against 48 percent among Algerian Jews, many of whom who had already entered into marriages of this kind in Algeria. Outside Paris, however, Tunisian and Moroccan Jews married exogamously more often. Women were clearly less likely to do so, especially those born in North Africa. The tendency toward exogamous marriage was more pronounced in the provinces. In 1988, 31 percent of marriages between Jews 18–19 years old were exogamous, 26 percent among those between the ages of 30–49, and 14 percent above the age of 50. With regard to Jewish attitudes toward exogamous marriage, 13 percent found it perfectly normal, 17 percent had no objection if the young man or woman were suitable, 18 percent said that they would be upset by the prospect but would not stand in the way, 26 percent would attempt to dissuade their child, and another 26 percent would oppose it by all possible means.

The fertility rate between 1967 and 1971 in the Paris region was 1.7 children for Jewish mothers of North African origin and 1.2 for those of European origin. The trend was not very different among Jews outside the capital. The reproductive behavior of the repatriated and immigrant populations thus exhibited the same low birth rate characteristic of French society as a whole.

Educational levels vary in contemporary Jewish society according to country of origin. In the Paris region, the level is lowest among immigrants from the east of Europe owing to the difficulties they faced in their homelands and then in their integration into French society (those who came during the interwar period did not speak French when they arrived). Immigrants from North Africa are much better schooled at the secondary level; the number of those who have studied at the university level is nonetheless higher among those born in France. There is also a gap in educational level between the sexes. In the 1980s, women represented only 21 percent of university graduates as against 29 percent of men.

During the 1980s, one notes a high rate of education among Jews in the Paris region. Among those aged 15 to 19, 80 percent were still in school during this period, as were 56 percent of those aged 20–24 and 21 percent of those aged 25–29. Social background was also a factor in the length of study. These levels were higher than in the population as a whole. The level of education among Jews in the provinces, allowing for certain variations, was almost identical to that in the Paris region: 93 percent of those aged 15–19 were students and 62 percent of those aged 20–24.

At the university level, considering the country as a whole, Jewish students born in North Africa are more numerous than those born in France. A large proportion of university students in both the provinces and the Paris region are from Morocco and Tunisia. In the 1980s, 45 percent of the Jewish population claimed to have a university education, 25 percent a secondary education, and 12 percent technical or commercial training. This very high level of education has implications for professional employment and also for personal investment in cultural goods. Thus 17 percent of those questioned said they did not buy books other than the ones they used for school, as against 9 percent who said they bought one or two a year, 27 percent a few, and 47 percent many books.

In the 1980s, the share of Jews in the workforce above the age of fifteen in the Paris region was 56 percent. For men the rate was 72 percent—similar to that for the French male population—and for women 40 percent—markedly lower than the global figure for the French female population. In the provinces, Jewish participation in the workforce was 49 percent (63 percent of men and 28 percent of women). Fewer North African women worked than Jewish women born in France, a circumstance more pronounced in the provinces than in the Paris region.

If one compares the socioeconomic profile of the Jews of France with that of the urban population as a whole, it turns out that the number of Jews in the working class is small but that they are much more numerous among the intellectual bourgeoisie. The majority of Jews are found in the middle class with a high proportion of salaried employees, tradespeople, and shopkeepers at the low end nearer the working class. Artisans, shopkeepers, and manufacturers represented 31 percent of working Jews at the end of the 1980s, members of upper-level management and the intellectual professions 39 percent, middle-level management and company staff 30 percent, with workers and farmers together accounting for fewer than 2 percent. Among North African Jews in the Paris region, above all Tunisians and Moroccans, the rate of unemployment was higher than in other subgroups of the Jewish collectivity. Among wage earners, women were more numerous than men. The unemployment rate was also higher among women as well as among those below the age of thirty. The socioprofessional distribution of Jews in the provinces resembled that in the capital. Nonetheless, the liberal professions and upper levels of business were less strongly represented in the provinces, while more Jews filled staff and middle-management positions there than in the Paris region. At the same time, during the 1980s, the number of those excluded from the system was on the rise. In 1990, a quarter of French Jews needed assistance, which came from organizations such as the FSJU, the CASIP (Centre d'Action Sociale Israélite de Paris), and the CASIM (Centre d'Action Sociale Israélite de Marseille).[23]

At the end of the 1980s, the Jews of France were choosing their Judaism à la carte, as it were. The majority of them moved outside communal institutions—synagogues, community centers, study groups, political and cultural movements—despite the existence of some 3,000 associations of every sort. Almost half (48 percent) did not participate in organized Jewish life at all, except perhaps once a year—the famous "Juifs de *Kippour*";[24] 29 percent took part occasionally, and 22 percent regularly. Communal institutions therefore had no real influence on the values and norms of a Jewry that was now highly heterogeneous in its composition and in the way its members defined themselves as Jews. To the question "How do you explain the fact that Jews do not participate in organized Jewish life?," 51 percent of those interviewed said this was because it was too insular, 54 percent because it was too concerned with religion, 19 percent because it was too oriented toward Israel, 35 percent because it was not sufficiently democratic, 52 percent because Jews were interested in other, more important things, and 49 percent because Jews preferred to be assimilated. Between 1967 and 1976, by contrast, 40–45 percent of French Jews had gone at least once to Israel, as opposed to 37 percent of American Jews. This trend continued to grow, peaking in 1979 with 63,000 visits by French Jews, or more than 10 percent of the Jewish population of France.

Religious tradition, albeit revised, corrected, and reformed; the State of Israel, a source of debate and passionate feeling but not of massive waves of emigration (3,000 persons left France in the 1950s for Israel, 13,000 in the 1960s, and 20,000 in the 1970s); episodic anti-Semitism (marked since 1989 by a fresh upsurge of anti-Semitic and racist threats, though acts of violence have been few);[25] revisionist claims denying the existence of Nazi gas chambers; certain blunders on the part of government officials;[26] the feeling of solidarity that such acts of aggression reawakened, together with a heightened awareness of the Holocaust—all these things constituted essential points of reference for Jewish identity among members of a collectivity that was continually changing.

Only 5 percent of Jews interviewed in the late 1980s, as against one-third of those interviewed in 1977, referred to themselves as *israélite*—a form of self-characterization going back to the nineteenth century that now bears a rather pejorative connotation, just as the term *Juif* once did, but originally was meant to indicate assimilation to the non-Jewish environment as well as the social and cultural distance separating middle-class Jews from the new immigrants from central and eastern Europe. With respect to religious attitudes, one-third of the Jewish population defined itself by reference to the religious aspects of Judaism; another third claimed to be agnostic; and a final third described itself as having ties to the community and to family and historical traditions. In the provinces, the sense of Jewish belonging was centered more on the religious aspect, with the synagogue being merged with the community. The degree of religiosity varied with the level of education. Members of the liberal professions and business executives were furthest removed from religious practice but had closer contact with the cultural aspects of Judaism and worked more actively on behalf of organized Jewish life. Members of the working class were attached as much to the religious as to the cultural aspects of Judaism. Middle-class Jews were nearer to working-class Jews in their conception of Jewishness, and likewise took part in organized Jewish activities. In the Paris region, in the 1980s, 74 percent of males over the age of fifteen had celebrated the occasion of reaching the age of religious responsibility (*bar mitzvah*) but only 9 percent of females (*bat mitzvah*). The rate for males was higher in the provinces (88 percent), due to the higher proportion of North African Jews there. In the Paris region, 70 percent of the heads of Jewish households had been married in Jewish ceremonies and 2 percent according to the rites of another religion, with 28 percent settling for a civil ceremony. Outside Paris, these rates were 79 percent, 6 percent, and 15 percent, respectively. As for circumcision,[27] an expression of the wish of parents that their male child participate in the historical continuity of Judaism, 83 percent of households practiced it during this period, with the rate rising to 95 percent among endogamous couples married according to Jewish rites. Almost half (49 percent) of household heads who had married exogamously circumcised their son, as against 18 percent of heads of non-Jewish households, which shows the desire of Jewish men to maintain Jewish tradition in their home despite having married outside the faith, unlike Jewish women in the same position, most of whom abandoned this practice. The higher a parent's social and cultural position, the lower the rate of circumcision. Among university graduates, only 44 percent circumcised their male children.

A majority of the Jewish population (63 percent) considered it very important that their children have a Jewish education. At the end of the 1980s, some 16,000 children in France went to Jewish schools (as against only 400 in 1950) and 10,000 to *talmud torahs*[28] to receive religious instruction (as against fewer than 500 in 1950); another 6,000 belonged to Jewish youth organizations, and 13,000 attended Jewish summer camps. Before 1945, there were four Jewish schools in France; in 1986 this number had grown to eighty-eight, with more in the Paris region than in the provinces. If communal institutions were no longer at the center of Jewish life, Jewish education nonetheless showed great dynamism, which seems somewhat contradictory. Among the sources of increased access to Jewish scholarship and information were adult study groups; a growing number of university courses; Jewish student associations; language classes; periodicals (*L'Arche, Actualité juive, Information juive, Tribune juive,* and a variety of association newsletters); academic and intellectual journals (*Archives juives, Cahiers de l'Alliance, Le Monde juif, Revue des études juives, Pardès*); Jewish radio stations; a national radio program; a weekly show on national television; a large literature on the Holocaust, exile (written chiefly by immigrants from North Africa), fictional themes, scientific and philosophical topics, in addition to Judaica collections brought out by the leading publishers; and films on Jewish subjects made by Jewish and non-Jewish directors, which have become more and more numerous in recent years. Some Jews have turned to them as sources of support in reformulating their personal identity as well. At the same time these various modes of communication have served to acquaint all segments of French society with the Jews of France.[29]

Since 1967, there has been talk of a "Jewish revival" in France. This revival is not simply religious, even if the Orthodox fringe, more restless than other elements, has made itself heard more and so sustained the illusion that it is the dominant force within the Jewish collectivity. The religious rally *Yom ha-Torah* attracted 30,000 to Bourget in 1989; in 1996, the same event drew only 15,000. Much has been made of the rise of religious fundamentalism among French Jews, but such figures indicate a decline. The election in 1987, and reelection in 1994, of the Orthodox rabbi Joseph Sitruk to the office of chief rabbi of France is nonetheless not an insignificant event. However, the small number of electors taking part in this quite unusual ballot may not be truly representative of French Jewry as a whole. Of course it would not be at all surprising if the search for identity of the 1970s and 1980s expressed itself in religious terms in the case of some Jews. But even here diversity remains the rule, for not all Jews have chosen Orthodox Judaism. Reform Judaism, which first appeared in France in 1907 following the separation of church and state, continues to thrive and to attract adherents in growing numbers. Today there exist three Reform movements: one grouped around Rabbi Michael William in the synagogue in the rue Copernic; another, the Mouvement Juif Libéral de France (MJLF), born of a schism within that synagogue in 1977 and led by Rabbi Daniel Fahri; and a third founded by a woman, Rabbi Pauline Bebe, in 1995, as a result of a split within the MJLF. The recent multiplication of secular movements also attests to the diversity of paths followed in the return to Jewishness. In addition to the Cercle Bernard Lazare and the Cercle Gaston Crémieux, the Bundist Centre Culturel Vladimir Medem, and the Club Laïc de l'Enfance Juive (CLEJ), all of which existed previously, organizations founded in recent years include the Liberté du Judaïsme (1987), the Association pour un Judaïsme Humaniste et Laïc (1989), and the Centre Juif Laïc (1989), each dedicated to bringing about a Judaism without rabbis and a way of being Jewish that does without religion.

Between the extremes, various ways of being Jewish have emerged that testify to the pluralism and plurality of a group in the process of transforming itself, attuned to urban life and concerned with a wide range of questions. Moreover, open hostility toward Jews, the perception that they are different from others, and even reservations about the possibility that one day they might occupy the highest office in the land have virtually disappeared since the liberation. Neither the tendency of government authorities to revert to a communitarian view of the Jewish collectivity nor the strengthening of collective identity and the willingness of certain Jewish leaders to move in the same direction is likely to call into question an established and solid integration. Despite doubts in various quarters and the temptation from time to time to withdraw from French society, the ties binding the Jews of France and the republic,[30] sometimes quite passionately felt indeed, cannot easily be undone.

58–51 B.C.E. — Conquest of Gaul by Julius Caesar.

70 C.E. — Reconquest of Jerusalem by the Romans. Destruction of the Second Temple by Titus's armies, which provokes a wave of emigration, chiefly toward Rome.

132–135 — Uprising led by Simon bar Kokhba, the last Jewish revolt against Rome.

First–second century — Sporadic settlements in Roman Gaul.

212 — Caracalla grants Roman citizenship to the Jews (*constitutio Antoniniana*).

313 — Christianity is recognized as the state religion of the Roman Empire. The restrictions imposed on the Jews favor emigration to Gaul, where Christianization is only gradually taking hold and they benefit from the rights and privileges of the Antonine constitution.

Fourth century — Attestation of an actual Jewish presence in Gaul.

Fifth century — Invasion of northern Gaul by the Franks; some tribes advance as far as the Meuse. In the second half of the fifth century, Jews are found in the southeast, southwest, the Massif Central, and Brittany.

498? — Baptism of Clovis, King of the Franks.

Fifth–seventh centuries — Restrictive measures toward the Jews, reiterated by various councils.

613 — Forced baptisms of Jews in Visigothic Spain. Waves of emigration toward Provence.

629–639 — Reign of Dagobert, who is said to have given the Jews of the Merovingian kingdom the choice between conversion and departure.

Seventh–ninth centuries — Substantial decline in the number of Jews in Gaul.

Seventh century — The appearance of Islam and the Arab conquest lead to a deterioration in the condition of Jews in Gaul.

732 — The Muslim advance is arrested at Poitiers by Charles Martel.

768–814 — Reign of Charlemagne. Legends regarding the Emperor Protector of the Jews. Isaac the Jew carries out a diplomatic mission to the Abbassid caliph Harun al-Rashid on behalf of Charlemagne. Beginnings of an informal royal alliance between the Carolingian sovereigns and the Jews, based on the latter's usefulness to the crown.

825? — Louis the Pious, son of Charlemagne, accords privileges to certain Jewish merchants.

Ninth century — The respect shown by sovereigns toward the Jews provokes anti-Jewish campaigns led by Agobard, Bishop of Lyons, and then by his successor, Amolon. Councils of Meaux (845), Paris (846), and Toulouse (883) enact restrictions and, in doing so, become barometers of the hostile atmosphere toward them.

839 — Conversion to Judaism of Bodo, deacon to Louis the Pious.

843 — The division of the Carolingian Empire in the aftermath of the Treaty of Verdun and the inevitable weakening of governmental power combine to make the condition of the Jews more fragile.

Ninth–tenth centuries — Beginning of the reign of the Capetians. Retaliatory measures against the Jews multiply.

Second half of tenth century — Founding of an important talmudic school at Mainz.

End of tenth–early eleventh century — The Talmud reaches France.

Eleventh–twelfth century — The talmudic school of the north reaches its height, thanks to Rashi (Rabbi Solomon ben Isaac).

Eleventh–thirteenth centuries — The crusades. Though directed against the Muslims, they do not fail to trigger explosions of popular hatred against the Jews. The church is obliged to intervene to put them down.

Middle of the eleventh century — In Limoges, Joseph Bonfils (Tov Elem) introduces the legal writings of the teachers of the Babylonian academies to the West.

Twelfth to fourteenth century — The school of talmudists founded by Rashi and his teaching is perpetuated by his grandchildren and disciples (the Tosafists) for several generations. The school of Paris has its moments of glory in the thirteenth century with the decline of the school of Champagne. In the south, Provence also achieves renown in the thirteenth century for its talmudic schools.

1144 — The first accusation of ritual murder is made against the Jews in England, at Norwich.

1171 — A blood libel in Blois leads to the almost total annihilation of the Jewish community there.

1179 — Ritual murder libel in Pontoise.

1182 — Confiscation of the goods of the Jews and their expulsion from the Kingdom of France by Philip Augustus.

1185? — Maimonides finishes his code of Jewish law, the *Mishneh Torah*.

1198 — Recall of the Jews by Philip Augustus.

1198–1231 — Eighteen agreements of nonretention are signed between the sovereign and the nobles. These provide for the return of those Jews whom they had welcomed in their seigneuries after the expulsion of 1182 and secure their promise to extradite any others who might leave royal possessions in order to seek domicile there.

Twelfth–thirteenth centuries — Arrival in Provence of Arabic-speaking Jews fleeing Spain, where Muslims and Christians are waging war; these Jews make important contributions to philosophical scholarship. The Kimḥi and Ibn Tibbon families distinguish themselves in the field of translation, translating from Arabic into Hebrew the great classics of Judeo-Arabic thought as well as Greek and Arabic scientific works, notably in medicine. Significant cultural interactions between the Christian, Jewish, and Islamic worlds.

1204 — Samuel ibn Tibbon translates Maimonides' *Guide for the Perplexed* (1200) in collaboration with the author.

Twelfth–fifteenth centuries — Numerous royal rulings and church canons regulate lending at interest as practiced by Jews, the creation of loans, security due lenders, and rates of interest. Moneylending eventually becomes both the professional specialty of the Jews, who are unable to practice other trades, and the very basis of the usefulness that justified their readmission to France under Philip Augustus, at which time they were allowed to stay.

Thirteenth century — Aggressive climate of anti-Judaism in the Christian West.

1209–29 — Crusade against the Albigensians.

1215 — The Fourth Lateran Council (following the launch of the crusade against the Albigensians, organized at the outset to repress heresy) decrees the wearing of a distinctive sign by the Jews.

1226–70 — Reign of Saint Louis, who legislates on behalf of the Jews of the entire kingdom. This affirms the growing authority of royal power, generally to the detriment of that of the seigneurs, who find themselves increasingly undermined.

1230 — The treaty of Melun (imposed by royal order) abolishes the obligation to pay off the interest on debts already contracted with Jews. Controversy in Provence surrounding Maimonides' *Guide for the Perplexed* bears upon the dangers of philosophical research for faith. Debate during this period in the Christian world is marked by the same passions.

1234 — Saint Louis annuls a third of the debts due the Jews.

1240 — Disputation of Paris in the aftermath of which the Talmud is condemned. Expulsion of the Jews by the Duke of Brittany with the approval of the king.

1242 (or 1244) — Burning of the Talmud in the Place de Grève in Paris.

1254 — Jews are forbidden to lend at interest, thus depriving many of all means of existence.

1256 — The Duke of Burgundy ransoms his Jews.

1268 — Alphonse of Poitiers, brother of Saint Louis, arrests the Jews of his domain and seizes their goods.

1269 — Saint Louis orders the wearing of a badge by Jews in the kingdom of France (in accordance with the decree of the Fourth Lateran Council in 1215).

1274 — The Comtat Venaissin comes under the domain of the Holy See (until 1791).

1290 — Expulsion of Jews from England and Gascony. Other expulsions in Germany and Italy during this period.

1291 — The Jews are accused in Paris of desecrating the Host.

1294 — Under Philip the Fair, unenclosed neighborhoods reserved for the Jews are established.

Thirteenth–fourteenth centuries — Jewish poetry develops in Provence.

1306 — Confiscation of the goods of the Jews and their expulsion by Philip the Fair.

1315 — Louis X, successor to Philip the Fair, readmits Jews to the kingdom. Their return is authorized for a period of twelve years.

1320–21 — Shepherds' Crusade. It gives rise to massacres of Jews in the Midi, Touraine, and Berry, where they are accused of poisoning the wells.

1322–23 — Expulsion of the Jews by Charles IV (though disputed by some historians).

1337–1453 — The Hundred Years' War.

1348 — Unification of Avignon with the Holy See.

1348–49 — The Black Death. The Jews are accused of spreading the scourge; they are put to death in many French localities where they are still allowed to reside.

Disappearance of the great Jewish communities of Alsace in the aftermath of unrest, massacres, and expulsions.

1359 — The Jews are allowed once more to reside in the kingdom, against payment of a fee, for a period limited to twenty years. This offer of readmission fails to find many takers.

1364 — Charles of Normandy extends the length of the Jews' allowed stay by ten years.

1374 — In exchange for a large sum of money, the term of their stay is extended by another ten years.

1380 — Louis of Anjou extends their stay until 1401.

1391 — Violent persecutions of the Jews in Spain that lead to many conversions to Christianity.

1394 — Expulsion of the Jews by Charles VI seven years before the 1401 deadline. Few are affected, since not many Jews came back in response to the recall of 1359.

End fourteenth century–fifteenth century — Partial reconstitution of the Jewish communities of Alsace.

1472–74 — Two rulings of Louis XI favoring immigration to Bordeaux, impoverished and depopulated by the Hundred Years' War.

1481 — Annexation of Provence by the Kingdom of France.

1492 — Expulsion of the Jews from Spain.

Fifteenth–seventeenth centuries — New Christians, converted to Christianity in the Iberian peninsula, settle in the southwest of France. They are long referred to as "Portuguese merchants" or "Portuguese."

1498 — Order of expulsion issued against the Jews of Provence.

1500–1501 — The order of expulsion from Provence is renewed.

Early sixteenth century — The last vestiges of a Jewish presence in Provence, within the frontiers of the kingdom of France, is henceforth concentrated in the localities coming under papal authority, in the Comtat Venaissin and Avignon. In Alsace, the Jewish population consists of about one hundred families.

1550 — In the southwest, the new Christians obtain from Henri II letters patent assuring them recognition, protection, freedom of movement and commerce, and freedom to acquire real estate, without having to pay fees. These letters are renewed in 1574, 1656, 1723, and 1776.

1552 — Entry of French troops into Lorraine establishes the authority of the king of France, Henri II, over the three bishoprics of Metz, Toul, and Verdun. Installation of an important garrison at Metz. In a period marked by religious wars, when provisioning the garrison and paying its soldiers posed problems, Jews are able to be of service. The pontifical bull *Cum nimis absurdum* aggravates the condition of the Jews and restricts their economic activities.

1567 — Authorization of permanent stay granted to four Jewish families at Metz. Confirmation of their privileges by letters patent from Henri III.

1603 — Confirmation by letters patent of the privileges of the Jews of Metz, and again in 1632 and 1657.

1618–48 — The Thirty Years' War. Start of the growth of the Jewish population in Alsace.

1633–61 — Occupation of the duchies of Lorraine by French troops.

1636 — Some Jewish families are authorized to stay at Nancy, in ducal Lorraine.

1637 — In Metz, there are eighty-five Jewish households. These families are expelled six years later.

1648 — Treaties of Westphalia. Alsace, with the exception of Strasbourg and Mulhouse, passes under French sovereignty.

1654 — The new Christians acquire land at Saint-Esprit-lès-Bayonne for a cemetery in order to perform burials according to Jewish rites.

1657 — Letters patent officially recognizing the Jewish presence in royal Alsace, followed by a ruling in 1674.

Second half of seventeenth century — The Pope's Jews henceforth constitute a poor, demeaned, ghettoized group, ostracized by the surrounding society. The number of Jews in the Comtat and Avignon is scarcely more than a thousand.

1668 — The new Christians at Saint-Esprit come to be organized in a Jewish community.

1699 — The new Christians in Bordeaux create a charitable organization that lays the basis for the development of a Jewish community.

1670–97 — Reoccupation of the duchies of Lorraine by French troops.

1681 — The rabbinate of the Jews of Alsace is created.

Beginning of the eighteenth century — Between 1,269 and 1,348 Jewish families live in Alsace.

1715 — Introduction in Metz of the Brancas tax, one of the heaviest taxes paid by the Jewish community.

1717 — Four hundred eighty Jewish families live in Metz.

1721 — Seventy-three Jewish families reside in ducal Lorraine. Duke Leopold orders the constitution of a single community of Lorraine Jews.

1723 — Letters patent renew the privileges of new Christians in the southwest while henceforth recognizing them as Jews—a quite unusual formula for a Catholic kingdom from which Jews have been banned since 1394. The Judaism they have practiced from the second half of the sixteenth century thus comes to be openly acknowledged and officially approved.

1733 — The number of Jews inhabiting the duchy of Lorraine continues to grow; there are now some 180 families.

Eighteenth century — Movement on behalf of Jewish Enlightenment (*Haskalah*) is launched by Moses Mendelssohn in Germany and carried on by his disciples.

1766 — Unification of Lorraine with France. Letters patent from Louis XV renew the privileges of the Jews in ducal Lorraine.

1770 — The Portuguese open a synagogue in Paris.

1775 — Herz Cerf-Berr awards himself the title of *préposé général* and works for the official creation of a Jewish *nation* in Alsace with syndics enjoying real authority at its head.

1777–1778 — The affair of the "false receipts" in the Sundgau, in Alsace, puts the question of Jewish usury at the center of debate.

1778 — Dedication of a "German" synagogue in Paris.

1779–1780 — Cerf-Berr, chief spokesman of the Jews of Alsace, addresses a memorandum to the king in which he asks total freedom of commerce and settlement for them (though not for foreign Jews) and official recognition of the authority of his syndics.

1781–1782 — An era of reforms is announced for the Jews of Europe. Joseph II, the Holy Roman Emperor, promulgates his famous Edict of Tolerance.

1781 — The Protestant historian Christian Wilhelm von Dohm's plea on behalf of the Jews, *Ueber die buergerliche Verbesserung der Juden*, written at the request of Moses Mendelssohn, appears in Berlin.

1782 — Jean Bernoulli translates Dohm's plea into French under the title *De la réforme politique des Juifs.*

1784 — Abolition by Louis XVI of the body tax (*Leibzoll*) in Alsace. Letters patent dated the same year and in response to the requests of Cerf-Berr proclaim a new status for Alsatian Jews.

1785 — The Royal Society of Arts and Sciences of Metz chooses for its competition of 1787 the following question: "Are there means to make the Jews more useful and happier in France?"

1786–1787 — Isaïe Berr-Bing, a native of Metz and a man of the Jewish Enlightenment, translates from German into French and Hebrew the *Phaedon* of Moses Mendelssohn.

1787 — Mirabeau publishes in London a brochure entitled *Sur Moses Mendelssohn, sur la réforme politique des Juifs et en particulier sur la révolution tentée en leur faveur en 1753 dans la Grande-Bretagne*, adopting some of the ideas contained in Dohm's 1781 work. Protestants granted the right to hold civil status and, in this connection, to keep registers of births, marriages, and deaths.

1788 — In the new competition sponsored by the Royal Society of Arts and Sciences of Metz, the prize is shared by three laureates: the abbé Grégoire, Claude-Antoine Thiéry, and Zalkind Hourwitz. Malesherbes is charged by the king with studying the situation of the Jews. The Portuguese Jews, in the *Mémoire pour la nation juive portugaise* they send to him, demand the maintenance and confirmation of the privileges accorded them between 1550 and 1776. On 5 July, convocation by Louis XVI of the Estates General and drawing up of books of grievances (*cahiers de doléances*).

Eve of the Revolution — Lorraine as a whole numbers some 7,500 Jews; Alsace, from 20,000 to 25,000; Paris, 500–600; Bordeaux, 1,500–2,000; Saint-Esprit, 2,500; the Comtat Venaissin and Avignon, 2,500.

1789 — The Estates General open at Versailles on 5 May. On 9 July, proclamation of the National Constituent Assembly. On 14 July, the storming of the Bastille. On 26 August, Declaration of the Rights of Man; the Parisian Jews write to the assembly to demand citizenship as do the Alsatian Jews on 31 August. The delegation of the eastern Jews is admitted to the bar of the Constituent Assembly, with no result. On 24 December, debate in the assembly on the Jews.

1790 — In January, the Portuguese Jews demand citizenship, which they obtain on 28 January together with the Avignonese Jews of Bordeaux. The vote of the assembly does no more than ratify a de facto situation. In July, the Brancas tax falling upon the Jews of Metz and its treasury subdivision is abolished. The syndic of the Jews of Alsace, Berr Isaac Berr, translates into French the work of Naphtali Herz Wessely, a representative of the German Jewish Enlightenment, under the title *Instructions salutaires adressées aux communautés juives de l'Empire de Joseph II.*

1791 — With the unification of Avignon and the Comtat with France, on 14 September, all the Jews of the former papal states now enjoy the right of citizenship. On 27 September, following an almost unanimous vote, all the Jews of France become citizens on the condition that they renounce their communal status.

1791–1914 — Construction of 250 synagogues in France.

1793–1794 — The Terror, with its anti-religious policy directed against refractory priests, does not spare Jews either.

1795–1799 — The Directory.

1799–1804 — The Consulate.

1801–1802 — Concordat and "Organic Articles" granting status to Catholic and Protestant worship.

1804–1814 — The First Empire.

1805 — New upsurge of anti-Jewish sentiment in Alsace. Meeting of the Portalis Commission.

1806 — By a decree of 30 May, a surcease of one year is granted to the debtors of the Jews of the East, and at the same time an Assembly of Notables chosen by the most upright and enlightened Jews is convened in Paris by Napoleon. Laymen and religious figures are called together in order to permit the government to gather information before taking steps to regulate usury and organized worship. Meeting of the assembly on 26 July. Convocation of the Grand Sanhedrin in September.

1807 — Meeting of the Grand Sanhedrin on 9 February. Dissolution on 9 March. Closing of the Assembly of Notables on 6 April.

1808 — On 17 March, three decrees are promulgated by Napoleon on the reorganization of the Jewish religion and the terms of its regulation, approved by the Assembly of Notables in December 1806. One of these decrees (afterward known as the "infamous decree") placed the Jews outside the common law for ten years; ultimately, only the Jews of Alsace and Lorraine were to be affected by this decree. On 20 July, an edict concerning registration of Jewish names is announced.

1808–1809 — Organization of the consistorial system.

1811 — Institution of a religious tax by the consistories.

1814–1830 — The Restoration.

1817 — Founding by Élie (Halfon) Halévy of *L'Israélite français*.

1818 — The "infamous decree" fails to be renewed.

1819 — Founding of the first modern Jewish school for boys.

1822 — Opening of the first Jewish school for girls.

1828 — Publication of *Résumé de l'histoire des Juifs modernes*, the first post-biblical history written by a French Jew, Léon Halévy.

1830–1848 — July Monarchy.

1830 — Founding of the Central Rabbinical School of Metz. Conquest of Algeria by France. The number of Jews there is estimated at about 16,000.

1831 — Payment of the salaries of ministers of the Jewish faith by the state.

1840 — The Damascus affair, in which the Jews are accused of ritual murder following the disappearance of a Capuchin friar. This affair leads western Jews to rediscover their eastern brothers, whom they do their utmost to emancipate after their own example. It lays the basis for modern Jewish solidarity and gives a great impetus to the development of the Jewish press. Founding of the newspaper *Les Archives israélites* in France.

1842 — Fact-finding mission led by Altaras and Cohen on the condition of Jews in Algeria.

1844 — Birth of the *L'Univers israélite*, organ of the central consistory.

1845 — Order calling for three consistories to be created at Algiers, Oran, and Constantine. Alphonse Toussenel, a disciple of Fourier, publishes *Les Juifs, rois de l'époque: histoire de la féodalité financière*.

1846 — Repeal of the *more judaico* oath, the last restriction weighing upon the Jews.

1848 — February Revolution. June insurrection. Anti-Jewish unrest in Alsace.

1848–1851 — The Second Republic. Adolphe Crémieux becomes minister of justice and Michel Goudchaux minister of finance at the beginning of the regime.

1852–1870 — The Second Empire. Achille Fould is named minister of finance.

1853–1855 — Comte Joseph de Gobineau publishes his *Essai sur l'inégalité des races humaines* in which he claims to found the theory of the superiority of the Nordic, or Germanic, race on a physical and realistic basis.

1858 — The Mortara affair, involving the forced conversion to Catholicism of a Jewish child in Italy; together with the Damascus case, it leads to the founding of the Alliance Israélite Universelle two years later.

1859 — Transfer of the Rabbinical School of Metz to Paris, where it is henceforth known as the Séminaire Israélite de France.

1860 — Foundation of the Alliance Israélite Universelle (AIU).

1861 — The population of Jews in France has grown from about 40,000 in 1789 to 79,964.

1862 — The AIU establishes its first school at Tétouan in Morocco. The society then applies itself to the immense task of French and Jewish instruction and education in northern Africa and the Middle East.

1869 — Appearance of a work by the aristocrat Henri Gougenot des Mousseaux, *Le Juif, le Judaïsme et la Judaïsation des peuples chrétiens*, that becomes the bible of anti-Semitism.

1870 — Crémieux Decree, conferring French citizenship on the Jews of Algeria (save those of the southern territories).

1870–1871 — The Franco-Prussian War leads to the annexation of Alsace-Lorraine by Wilhelm I, encouraging the migration of Jews to the interior of France from the annexed territories. The Paris Commune.

1870–1940 — The Third Republic.

1878 — The first anti-Jewish party is founded in Berlin by the court preacher Adolf Stöcker and the journalist Wilhelm Marr, who was the first to use the term "anti-Semitism."

1880 — Founding of the Society of Jewish Studies and of the *Revue des études juives*.

1881–1905 — Assassination of Tsar Alexander II followed by pogroms in Russia, restrictive measures in Romania, the pogrom of Kishinev (1903), the crushing of revolution in Russia—all of which gives rise to large-scale waves of emigration by Jews, chiefly to the United States and, to a lesser degree, western Europe.

1882 — Collapse of the Union Générale, a Catholic banking concern; attributed at the time to the Rothschilds, though the bank's founder is subsequently sentenced for fraudulent activities.

1882–1885 — Three short-lived anti-Semitic newspapers are founded: *L'Anti-Juif*, *L'Antisémitique*, *Le Péril social*.

1886 — Publication by Édouard Drumont of *La France juive*.

1889 — Drumont and Jacques Biez create an anti-Semitic society, dissolved the following year.

1888–1893 — The Panama affair, in which certain Jewish businessmen are implicated, ends in the ruin of thousands of small investors. It is followed by a virulent anti-Semitic campaign orchestrated by Drumont against Jewish finance.

1892 — Drumont founds his own daily newspaper, *La Libre Parole*.

1894 — Captain Alfred Dreyfus, a French Jew attached to the army General Staff, is accused of having passed a confidential military letter (the *bordereau*) to the Germans; arrested 15 October, he is then sentenced for treason 22 December. At the time, France numbers some 130,000 Jews (including those in Algeria).

1895 — Anti-Semitic passions rage during the ceremony stripping the Dreyfus of his rank on 5 January, which is witnessed by Theodor Herzl, later considered the father of Zionism. Dreyfus is deported to Devil's Island, off Cayenne on the coast of Guyana. In February, Captain Dreyfus's brother, Mathieu, supplies the journalist Bernard Lazare with information that will establish his innocence.

March 1896 — New developments in the Dreyfus affair. Lieutenant Colonel Georges Picquart intercepts the *"petit bleu"*—the telegram sent by the German embassy to Major Esterhazy—which convinces him of Dreyfus's innocence. In September, Lucie Dreyfus addresses a petition to the Chamber of Deputies demanding justice for her husband. In November, Major Hubert Henry hands over to the deputy head of the General Staff a document that is devastating for Dreyfus, but which in reality is a forgery (the *faux Henry*). Bernard Lazare publishes *Une erreur judiciaire: La Vérité sur l'affaire Dreyfus*.

1897 — Anti-Semitic riots in Algeria. The first Zionist congress is held at Basel: birth of the Zionist movement.

1898 — Émile Zola publishes "J'Accuse" on 13 January. First petitions by intellectuals. Zola is sentenced for defamation of the minister of war. Demonstrations against Zola, against the Jews (including anti-Semitic violence in Algeria), for the Army; the left-wing intelligentsia is born. Founding of the Action Française by Charles Maurras. On 30–31 August, Major Henry confesses his forgery and commits suicide. Four of the six Algerian deputies in the Chamber, among them Drumont and the Mayor of Algiers, belong to the anti-Semitic camp.

1899 — On 8 August, the second Dreyfus trial opens in Rennes. He is once again found guilty and sentenced to ten years' detention. On 19 September he is pardoned by President Émile Loubet. Appearance of Dreyfus's journal, *Cinq Années de ma vie (1894–1899)*. Founding of the Zionist newspaper *L'Écho sioniste*.

1901 — Founding of the Fédération Sioniste de France. It breaks up in 1921.

1903 — Beginning of the immigration of Jewish artists to Paris, which will contribute to the renown of the School of Paris.

1905 — Separation of church and state.

1906 — On 12 July, Dreyfus is finally rehabilitated and reinstated in the army.

1906–1914 — Creation of thirteen newspapers by Jewish immigrants from the east of France.

1907 — The Union Libérale Israélite de Tendance Reformée is legally recognized as a religious organization. Opening of the synagogue on the rue Copernic in Paris. Founding of a Yiddish theater in Paris.

1908 — *L'Action française*, an anti-Dreyfusard and anti-Semitic daily, begins publication.

1909–1913 — Obligatory conscription of Jews in the Ottoman Empire; the Balkan wars encourage emigration from the Balkans to France. Establishment of the Association Cultuelle Orientale de Paris (1909).

1913 — The Fédération des Sociétés Juives de Paris, a group of twenty-two immigrant associations, is formed.

1914–1918 — First World War. Forty thousand out of one hundred ninety thousand Jews (Algerian Jews included) are drafted into the army. Anti-Semitism is diluted by the patriotic fervor of the United Front (*Union sacrée*) advocated by Barrès.

1917 — The Cambon Declaration (11 June) leads to no result; it precedes, and actually precipitates, the Balfour Declaration (2 November), which states that Great Britain looks favorably upon the establishment of a Jewish national homeland in Palestine—a major turning point in the history of Zionism. On the initiative of André Spire, a league is created in Paris of the friends of Zionism, bringing together Jewish and non-Jewish intellectuals.

1918–1939 — Jewish immigrants establish 133 newspapers and periodicals.

1919 — *The Protocols of the Elders of Zion*, an anti-Semitic forgery, is translated in Europe and the United States. Formation in Paris of the youth movement Chema Israël, with provincial offshoots from 1921.

1919–1939 — Great waves of immigration, mostly from eastern Europe (accounting for three-quarters of the influx) and the Balkans; but also from Germany, first with Hitler's coming to power in 1933, then in 1935 from the Saarland with its annexation by the Third Reich; from Austria after the *Anschluss* of 1938; from Czechoslovakia in 1939, and also to lesser degree from northern Africa. Thus between 1906 and 1939 France received 175,000 to 200,000 Jewish immigrants, who recreated the cultural fabric of the small Jewish towns of eastern Europe, centered on the use of Yiddish and the social, political, and religious life associated with it.

1920 — Palestine comes under British administration.

1922 — The British presence in Palestine is made official by League of Nations mandate, intended to promote the creation of a Jewish national homeland and the establishment of institutions representative of the whole population for the purpose of assuring effective self-government.

1923–1924 — Creation of the Union Universelle de la Jeunesse Juive, the scouting movement Éclaireurs Israélites de France, and Jeunesse Libérale Israélite. These associations play an important role in the revitalization of Jewish life. Communal experiences of this type also take root in the provinces. The Union des Femmes Juives de France pour la Palestine is formed as well. Zionist organizations raising funds for the purchase of land in Palestine and the restoration of a Jewish state establish themselves in France during these years too. Birth of the Jeunesses Patriotes, an extreme right-wing group.

1925 — The Comité France-Palestine succeeds the Ligue des Amis du Sionisme.

1926 — Establishment of the Fédération des Sociétés Juives de France, which unites between 50 to 90 societies (depending on the period) of fellow countrymen. It is administrated by Zionist sympathizers.

1928 — Founding of the Ligue des Croix-de-Feu by Colonel François de La Rocque. Creation of the Ligue Internationale contre l'Antisémitisme (LICA— later LICRA).

1932 — Five hundred members of the Croix-de-Feu parade inside the Synagogue de la Victoire in Paris, as part of a religious service in memory of soldiers of all faiths killed in action during the Great War. This ceremony is repeated in 1934, 1935, and (following Léon Blum's triumph, of which the consistory takes a dim view) in 1936. In supporting these organizations and in advocating national unity, Jews thought they were allying themselves with the defenders of the liberal and democratic ideals of France.

1933 — Triumph of Nazism in Germany. The economic and political crises that shock France give anti-Semitism a hitherto unknown scope. Creation of the extreme right-wing groups Solidarité Française and Francisme. France receives more than 26,000 refugees.

1933–1934 — Stavisky affair, a financial scandal named after the man responsible for it, a Russian Jew, triggers a strong anti-Semitic reaction.

1934 — Bloody riot on 6 February. Formation of the Union Patriotique des Français-Israélites, having ties to the extreme right. Translation of Hitler's *Mein Kampf* into French. Left-wing immigrants set up a Yiddish workers' theater in Paris.

1936–1938 — Popular Front.

1936 — The consistory breaks with the movements of the French right.

1937 — The Jewish subsection of the Communist party is dissolved.

1938 — Munich accords signed 29–30 September. On 9–10 November Ernst von Rath, secretary of the German embassy in Paris, is assassinated by a Polish Jew recently emigrated from Germany and residing illegally in France. This is followed by *Kristallnacht*, in the course of which Jewish shops and synagogues throughout Germany are smashed and looted. Creation of the Union des Sociétés Juives de France (Farband), a Communist group. The anti-Semitic press now includes forty-seven titles.

1939 — Adoption on 21 April of the Marchandeau decree, providing for criminal sanctions against those who incite "hatred among citizens or inhabitants." Publication by the British in May of a new White Paper (following those of 1922 and 1930) that limits immigration to Palestine, forbids the sale of land to Jews in 80 percent of the country, and provides for the creation in the next ten years of a Palestinian state with close ties to Great Britain. The Nazi-Soviet pact is signed on 23 August. France declares war against Germany on 3 September. The number of Jews in France rises to 300,000. Fifteen thousand Jews flee Alsace-Lorraine, followed by forty thousand Jewish refugees from Belgium, Holland, and Luxembourg.

1940 — The French government leaves Paris on 11 June; the chief rabbi and the principal leaders of the central consistory and immigrant organizations do the same. An armistice is signed on 22 June by the government of Marshal Henri Pétain. France is divided into a zone occupied by the Germans, located to the north of the Loire, and a zone located to the south of the Loire constituting "free France." At the end of June, a quota is applied to universities in Algeria; it will also be enforced in Tunisia and Morocco. On 10 July, the National Assembly gathered at Vichy confers upon Pétain full powers and authorizes him to draw up a new constitution. In Paris, anti-Semitic demonstrations are numerous. On 22 July, a commission is set up to review naturalizations approved after 10 August 1927. On 27 August, the Marchandeau decree of 1939, punishing defamation or injury in the press, is repealed. In the occupied zone the Germans issue a regulation on 27 September that defines who is Jewish and forbids Jews who have left the occupied zone from reentering it. Those who come under the definition of Jew stipulated by the regulation are given until 20 October to register with the authorities. The Vichy government decrees a Statut des Juifs on 3 October. A law of 4 October (appearing in the *Journal officiel* of 18 October) provides for internment of foreign nationals in special camps by the decision of the local prefect alone. A law dated 7 October (published the next day in the *Journal officiel*) abrogates the Crémieux decree, entailing the collective denaturalization of Jews in non-occupied Algeria. The statute of 3 October regarding the Jews is extended, with certain modifications, to Tunisia and Morocco. From October, the identity cards of Jews designate the holder as a "Jew" or "Jewess." Aryanization of businesses belonging to Jews and dismissal of Jewish teachers.

1940–1941 — Between 8 October 1940 and 16 September 1941, twenty-six laws, twenty-four decrees, and six orders concerning the Jews are published in the *Journal officiel*.

1941 — On the order of Theodor Dannecker, the Gestapo official responsible for Jewish affairs, a coordinating committee for charity is formed in the northern zone in the greater Paris area; in the southern zone a central commission for welfare assistance. By February, forty thousand Jews are held in internment camps in the south of France. Responsibility for setting up a General Commission for Jewish Questions is confided to Xavier Vallat (29 March). Jews are forbidden to exercise professions putting them in contact with the public (26 April). First roundups in Paris. Arrest on 14 May of Polish, Czech, and Austrian Jews: 3,747 are taken to camps in the Loiret. A second Statut des Juifs is promulgated on 2 June. Jews are required to register with authorities in the southern zone. Creation by the Germans of an institute for the study of Jewish questions to disseminate anti-Semitic propaganda. Anti-Semitic unrest in Paris is rife. Confiscation of radio sets (13 August). Three thousand Jews are arrested in the eleventh arrondissement of Paris on 20 August, then interned in Drancy. Arrests continue in the other arrondissements. In three days, 4,232 Jews are rounded up. A quota is instituted in metropolitan France for the new school year. Opening in September at the Palais Berlitz in Paris of an exhibition entitled "The Jew and France" that attracts some 200,000 visitors before closing in January 1942. On 29 November the Union Générale des Israélites de France is established. New roundup on 12 December, this time conducted by the Germans. Creation of the Armée Juive in the southern zone by a group of young Zionists; it is transformed into the Organisation Juive de Combat in 1944.

1942 — The Wannsee conference, convened by the Nazis on 20 January, works out the practical details of the "Final Solution": the Jews are to be deported to extermination camps set up in Poland; France is to supply 100,000 Jews of both sexes. A new order (7 February) regulates when they can go out in public and forbids them from changing residence. Jews are required to wear the yellow star (29 May). Formation of the Organisation Sioniste de France. On 16–17 July, the "Vel' d'hiv roundup": 13,152 Jews are arrested by the French police on the orders of Vichy, single persons and childless couples being taken to Drancy, the others to the Vélodrome d'hiver; on 19 and 22 July, these latter are transferred to the camps of the Loiret. Roundups also in Bordeaux and in the large southern cities. Other roundups are carried out in Paris in July and August. Landing of the Allies in North Africa (8 November). Abolition of the "free" zone on 11 November following its occupation by the Germans. The word "Jew" is stamped on the identity cards of the Jews of the southern zone (mid-December). In this year, 42,655 Jews are deported from France to Nazi camps.

1942–1943 — Between November 1942 and September 1943, the occupation of the east bank of the Rhône by the Italians allows Jews to take refuge there, in particular at Cannes and Nice.

1943 — The largest roundup in the former "free" zone begins on 22 January and continues until 27 January in Marseilles. In April, in Grenoble, Isaac Schneerson founds the Centre de Documentation Juive Contemporaine, whose purpose is to assemble the documentary basis for a history of the French Jews during the war; it is transferred to Paris in 1944. After the occupation by the Germans of the Italian zone, roundups begin the night of 8 September. On 20 October, reinstatement of the Crémieux decree in Algeria. 17,041 Jews are deported from France to Nazi camps over the course of this year.

1944 — Assassination of Victor Basch (in January), of Jean Zay (in June), and of Georges Mandel (in July). Trial of the Manouchian group. The Conseil Représentatif des Juifs de France (CRIF) is founded underground, bringing together the different ideological components of French Jewry, immigrant Jews not excluded. The Allies land in Normandy in June; by September the greater part of the country is liberated. In the meantime, 16,025 Jews are deported from France to Nazi camps; the last railroad car leaves 17 August. In December, France is totally liberated.

1944–1946 — Provisional government established by de Gaulle.

1945 — On 8 May, the Germans surrender. Liberation of the camps. Creation of the Comité Juif d'Action Sociale et de Reconstruction, social wing of the CRIF.

1946–1958 — The Fourth Republic.

1947 — Boarding and inspection by the British of the *Exodus*, transporting illegal immigrants, at sea off Palestine (18 July).

1948 — Birth of the State of Israel (14 May). The Amitié Judéo-Chrétienne is founded.

1949 — Creation of the Fonds Social Juif Unifié, central organ for the collection and distribution of funds that, at this time, come from the American Joint

Distribution Committee. Later it will assume important cultural responsibilities while assisting reconstruction.

1951 — First amnesty law is passed 5 January with regard to crimes under the occupation; legislation is completed in 1953.

1948–1953 — Finaly affair.

1950s — Erection of the Tomb of the Unknown Jewish Martyr in Paris. The cornerstone is laid in 1950 on the rue Geoffroy-l'Asnier, in the Marais, in a large ceremony attended by the highest officials of the French government. Six years later the headquarters of the Centre de Documentation Juive Contemporaine (CDJC) is dedicated, containing in addition to its own archival collections a library, picture collection, exhibition hall, and the tomb itself.

1952 — The CRIF, as a party to the Conference of Jewish Material Claims, signs the Luxembourg accords on German reparations and closely monitors the course of negotiations regarding the indemnization of French nationals by the German Federal Republic, which later occurs in two stages, first in 1954 and then in 1960.

1954 — Pierre Mendès France becomes prime minister. Surge of anti-Semitism. Beginning of the insurrection in Algeria.

1956 — Pierre Poujade obtains 11 percent of the vote in the legislative elections. Morocco and Tunisia gain independence, giving rise to Jewish immigration from these two countries. Suez campaign.

1956–1967 — 235,000 North African Jews settle in France.

1957 — An urn containing ashes from the extermination camps is placed beneath an eternal flame at the Tomb of the Unknown Jewish Martyr in the CDJC, the first memorial to the Holocaust constructed anywhere in the world.

1958 — Birth of the Fifth Republic.

1961–1962 — Under the auspices of the Chantiers du Consistoire Israélite de Paris, synagogue/communal centers begin to be built in the Paris suburbs.

1961 — The Nazi executioner Adolf Eichmann is sentenced to death in Jerusalem after a trial of several months; he is hung the following year.

1962 — Évian accords (March). Algerian independence (July). Departure of Jews from Algeria.

1962–1965 — Second Vatican Council condemns anti-Semitism. The Fonds Social Juif Unifié, with the aid of the American Joint Distribution Committee, allocates more than 2.5 billion francs above and beyond its ordinary budget for the settlement of repatriated Jews.

1963 — The government grants Jewish civil servants an official holiday permitting observance of the Jewish new year (which falls in September or October). *Information juive*, the Jewish monthly formerly published in Algiers, reappears in France.

Mid-1960s The Catholic Church officially revises its teaching concerning the Jews, with the Second Vatican Council and the publication of the document *Nostra Aetate*.

1965 — In September, the synagogue of Sarcelles, home to the largest Jewish community in the Paris suburbs, is dedicated.

1967 — France announces an embargo on arms shipments to the Middle East (3 June). The Six Day War (5–10 June). Popular demonstrations of support for

Israel take place in Paris and the large provincial cities. Creation of the Appel Juif Unifié. Beginning of the "Jewish revival" in France. De Gaulle describes the Jewish people as "sure of itself and domineering." The Catholic priest Roger Braun establishes an association called Rencontres entre Chrétiens et Juifs, together with a quarterly journal of the same name, with the purpose of putting Judeo-Christian dialogue on a firm doctrinal basis.

1968 — May-June: student and social unrest.

1969 — Jewish shopkeepers in Orléans are rumored to have abducted young girls.

1970–mid-1980s — A Jewish cultural ferment in the wake of the search for personal identity characteristic of these years is marked by cultural events, new journals, birth of a Jewish cinema, and expanded course offerings and lectures.

1971 — Marcel Ophüls' film *Le Chagrin et la Pitié* is released.

1972 — An anti-racist law—the loi Pleven—is passed (7 June).

1973 — Controversy follows publication in France of Robert Paxton's *Vichy France*. The Arab-Israeli Yom Kippur War (6–25 October). Opening in Paris of the Centre Rachi, dedicated to Jewish studies and culture.

1975 — Resurgence of anti-Jewish violence.

1977 — Birth of the Mouvement Juif Libéral de France under the leadership of Rabbi Daniel Fahri, following a split within the rue Copernic synagogue.

1977–1983 — Development of a Jewish North African literature in the French language.

1978 — In an interview given to *L'Express*, Darquier de Pellepoix, successor to Vallat as Superintendent General for Jewish Questions under Vichy between 1942 and 1944, denies the genocide of the Jews (28 October). Holocaust denial claims multiply. Historians join forces against the revisionist Robert Faurisson.

1979 — Airing of the American television miniseries "Holocaust," which, though it may make young people aware of the painful history of the Jews (and remind many forgetful adults of this episode), does so at the price of transforming the genocide into theater. In the spring, numerous telephone threats and physical attacks are directed toward Jewish individuals, graves, and synagogues. In March, a bomb placed in front of a Jewish student hostel in the rue de Medicis in Paris wounds some thirty persons. Assassination of Pierre Goldman (20 September).

1980 — France is home to 535,000 Jews. Kurt Lischka, the German official in charge of the Vel' d'hiv roundup, is sentenced by a Cologne court to ten years in prison. Trial of extreme right-wing activist Mark Fredriksen, head of the neo-Nazi group FANE, occasioning a number of attacks and death threats in the capital by his supporters. In September, Jewish schools in Paris are attacked. On 3 October, the synagogue in the rue Copernic is bombed, leaving four dead and some twenty wounded. Wave of demonstrations against anti-Semitism and racism. Henri Hajdenberg draws 100,000 people to the Porte de Pantin in the capital for a "Twelve Hours for Israel" rally.

1981 — Desecration of Jewish graves in Bayeux. Election of François Mitterand as president of the republic on 10 May. A Sephardi, René Samuel Sirat, is elected chief rabbi of France.

1982 — Mitterand becomes the first President of the Fifth Republic to visit Israel (3–5 March). A grenade attack (9 August) on the Goldenberg restaurant in the rue des Rosiers, a neighborhood of Paris with a high concentration of Jews, kills six and wounds twenty-two. The Israeli army begins raids on Palestinian Liberation Organization bases in southern Lebanon (6 June), also known as "Operation Peace for Galilee."

1985 — Claude Lanzmann's film *Shoah* has its debut in May.

1987 — Klaus Barbie, the "butcher of Lyons" accused of crimes against humanity, goes on trial between 11 May and 4 July. He is sentenced to life in prison. On 13 September, Jean-Marie Le Pen, leader of the National Front, characterizes the existence of gas chambers in the Nazi extermination camps as a "mere detail of history."

— Another Sephardi, Joseph Sitruk, is elected chief rabbi (and reelected in 1994). The secular movement Liberté du Judaïsme is founded, followed two years later by the Association pour un Judaïsme Humaniste et Laïc and the Centre Juif Laïc, each campaigning for a Judaism without rabbis and a way of being Jewish that dispenses with religion.

1989 — In the midst of the debate stirred by the establishment of a convent of Carmelite nuns at Auschwitz, Jean-Marie Domenach declares in the 7 September issue of *L'Événement du Jeudi,* "One does not receive dividends from Auschwitz." The religious demonstration *Yom ha-Tora* (The Day of the Torah) attracts 30,000; the same rally in 1996 draws only 15,000.

1990 — Revelation by the newspaper *Le Monde* of revisionist writings by an assistant professor in Lyons, Bernard Notin, who afterward is forbidden to teach. On 10 May, the desecration of Jewish graves in Carpentras is discovered; accusations against Jean-Marie Le Pen and the National Front follow. Their indignant reaction gives rise to spectacular demonstrations, then polemics, as the authorities fail to identify the persons responsible for the crime. The Gayssot law of 13 July disallows challenges to crimes against humanity and makes denial of the genocide of the Jews during World War II a crime.

1991 — The Persian Gulf War begins (16 January). Adoption on 22 July of a new penal code that contains a definition of crimes against humanity distinguishing "genocide" from "other crimes against humanity," the former being indefensible and punishable by life imprisonment. On 13 November, the lawyer and historian Serge Klarsfeld announces to the media that he has just found the 1940 census files of the Jews of the Seine in the Ministry of Veterans' Affairs. On 30 October, the Arab-Israeli peace conference opens in Madrid.

1992 — The commission of specialists charged with establishing the exact nature of the "Jewish files" found by Klarsfeld the previous year reports that they are not the October 1940 files, which were probably destroyed in 1948–49. The debate resumes. On 11 November, the laying of a wreath by François Mitterand on the tomb of Marshal Pétain once more calls into question the attitude of the president of the republic toward the Vichy regime.

1993 — By a decree dated 4 February, Mitterand institutes a day of commemoration for the racist and anti-Semitic persecutions committed under Vichy from 1940 to 1944. The date set is 16 July, the anniversary of the Vel' d'hiv roundup in 1942. The first such commemoration takes place on that date this year.

1994 — The trial of Paul Touvier, regional chief of the Rhône Milice, lasts from 17 March to 20 April. He is charged with the assassination of Victor Basch and his wife in January 1944, as well as the execution of seven other Jews in Rilieux on 29 June of the same year. The verdict is life imprisonment for a crime against humanity.

1995 — On 7 May, Jacques Chirac is elected president of the republic. On 16 July, as part of the observance of the fifty-third anniversary of the Vel' d'hiv roundup, he delivers a speech recognizing the "responsibility of the French state" and acknowledges "collective blame"—words that constitute a clear break with the statements of his predecessors, who made a distinction between two Frances, one Vichyist, the other republican. His remarks are favorably received by a large part of the public.

— Creation of a third Reform movement under the direction of a female rabbi, Pauline Bebe, following a split within the Mouvement Juif Libéral de France.

1996 — In April, a debate is set off by the support of the abbé Pierre, founder of Emmaüs, for Roger Garaudy, author of a book accused of revisionism, *Les mythes fondateurs de la politique israélienne*. In an interview with the newspaper *Libération*, the abbé Pierre claims it is necessary to lift the "taboo" that exposes anyone who inquires into the genocide of the Jews to the charge of anti-Semitism. The church distances itself from these remarks and denounces as scandalous any attempt to call into question the historical reality of the Holocaust. At the end of July, members and associates of the Parti National Français et Européen, an extreme right-wing party founded in 1987 and led by a dissident of the National Front, admits responsibility for the desecration of the Carpentras cemetery in 1990; they are interviewed under caution.

— The commission of historians named to rule on the question of the "Jewish files," discovered in 1991 by Serge Klarsfeld, officially renders its verdict. The files for the census of the Paris region, ordered on 27 September 1940, very probably were destroyed in 1948. The two files at the center of the debate are those of Jews who had been arrested. Debate continues over where the files should be conserved, the Centre de Documentation Juive Contemporaine (CDJC) or the National Archives; the authorities opt for the first solution, the CDJC serving in this instance as a suboffice of the National Archives.

— The ruling of referral handed down on 18 September by the criminal division of the court of appeal of Bordeaux goes beyond what the Public Prosecutor had called for. The judges hold that the former general secretary of the Gironde prefecture, Maurice Papon, "was aware that the arrest, sequestration, and deportation [of Jews] to the East would lead ineluctably to death." The magistrates also destroy one of the principal arguments of his defense, noting that "no certainty emerges from the evidence of the case with regard to the membership of M. Papon in the resistance."

1997 — On 20 July, in line with the prior declarations of Jacques Chirac, the socialist prime minister, Lionel Jospin, acknowledges in turn the responsibility of the French state in the Vel' d'hiv roundup, indicates that the government would give "its full support" to the work of the commissions charged with drawing up an inventory of Jewish property and other financial and artistic holdings plundered during the occupation, and adds that it would assist the construction in Paris of a Holocaust museum.

— On 30 September, on the eve of the anniversary of the publication (3 October

1940) of the first Statut des Juifs, French bishops read a "declaration of repentance" regarding the attitude of the church toward the Vichy regime at a memorial ceremony at the Drancy internment camp: "In view of the scope of the tragedy and the unprecedented character of the crime," they declare, "too many pastors of the Church, by their silence, offended against the Church and its mission. We confess today that this silence was a mistake." French Jewish dignitaries consider the church's repentance a crucial admission and presume that an examination of conscience of this sort would henceforth serve as a model. Similar acts of repentance on the part of the Syndicat National des Policiers en Tenue and the Conseil National de l'Ordre des Médecins follow.

— On 3 October, between the bishops' declaration and the opening of the Papon trial, Prime Minister Jospin publishes an order relaxing the rules of access to documents concerning the 1940–45 period—a gesture that is both symbolic and political. The Papon trial opens on 8 October. It unleashes a wave of ill feeling throughout France, accompanied by widespread unrest, proving once more that Vichy remains a very sensitive spot in the French conscience and that France has yet to fully come to terms with its unglorious past.

— On 2 November, in the middle of the Papon trial, the Consistoire Israélite de France dedicates a Mémorial des Justes in Thonon to honor and perpetuate the memory of those who came to the aid of the Jews in the dark days of the occupation. At this ceremony President Chirac reaffirms the responsibility of the state in the deportation of French Jews—a response to those who, like Philippe Séguin, tended to downplay the role of Vichy during the trial. On 14 November, the Council of State acknowledges not having opposed Vichy in order to avoid placing its own existence in jeopardy.

— On 5 December, the "Jewish files" brought to light by Klarsfeld are deposited at the Memorial of the Unknown Jewish Martyr in Paris. This solemn ceremony, entrusting thousands of folders to the safekeeping of the CDJC, marks the end of a six-year dispute.

1998 — On 16 March, the Vatican publishes a document entitled "We Remember: A Reflection upon the Holocaust." In it, Pope John Paul II condemns "the erroneous and unjust interpretations of the New Testament relating to the Jewish people and to their guilt." He adds that these errors "engendered feelings of hostility toward the Jews and helped dull consciences, so that, when the wave of persecutions broke over Europe . . . , alongside Christians who made every effort to save the persecuted at risk to their [own] lives, the spiritual resistance of many was not what humanity was entitled to expect on the part of Christ's disciples." This statement nonetheless denies the existence of a direct causal relation between the historical anti-Judaism of Christians and the anti-Semitism of the Nazis, exposing it to criticism in Israel as well as in France. In particular, it is accused of unduly exculpating the church and especially Pope Pius XII, who was careful during the Second World War not to speak out against the tragedy that was taking place.

— Maurice Papon is sentenced on 2 April to ten years in prison for "complicity in crimes against humanity" by the criminal court of the Gironde. This sentence is accompanied by a denial of civic, civil, and family rights for a period of ten years. The former *secrétaire général* of the Gironde prefecture is convicted of complicity in the arrest and sequestration of Jews later deported on four of eight trains leaving Bordeaux for Drancy. The court does not sustain the charge of complicity in murder. Despite this sentence, Papon leaves the courtroom a free man, his lawyer, Jean-Marc Varaut, having announced his intention to appeal the verdict to the Court of Cassations. In the course of ninety-four sessions, the picture emerges of a brilliant Vichyist civil servant overshadowed by his prefect. Above all, the responsibility of the regime of Marshal Pétain in the deportation of the Jews of France is weighed. The verdict of the Bordeaux court is received with relief by the plaintiffs. Though it gives official sanction to the condemnation of Vichy, public reaction varies. The press salutes the verdict as a victory for justice, but certain Jewish organizations express regret that Papon was not sentenced to life in prison. In Israel, there is talk of a "half-sentence." Though Papon was convicted, the fact remains that thousands of other civil servants have gone unpunished. Nonetheless the verdict of 2 April marks an important step in the direction of punishing crimes against humanity.

Notes

Notes to Preface

1. *Diaspora* (from the Greek, meaning "dissemination" or "dispersion") refers to all the dispersed Jewish communities outside the Holy Land.
2. A Hebrew term, signifying "catastrophe" or "destruction," more commonly used in French than in English to refer to the genocide of the Jews during the Second World War.
3. The term "community" is used here, however, to refer to a congregation gathered around a synagogue.
4. On these questions one may profitably consult Claude Tapia, *Les Juifs sépharades en France (1965–1985): Études psychosociologiques et historiques* (Paris: L'Harmattan, 1986), and Pierre Birnbaum, *Destins juifs: De la Révolution française à Carpentras* (Paris: Calmann-Lévy, 1995), part 3 ("L'inconnue contemporaine").
5. Such debate was once again heard during the recent celebration of the bicentennial of the French Revolution.

Notes to Chapter 1

1. See, for example, the French version of Obadiah 1:20: "Les exilés de cette légion d'enfants d'Israël répandus depuis Canaan jusqu'à Tsarfat." (English translations typically refer to Zarephath or a variant of this name—thus the New Jerusalem Bible: "The exiles of this army, the sons of Israel, will have the Canaanites' land as far as Zarephthah.") In his commentary on this passage, the Jewish exegete Rashi, who worked in Champagne in northern France during the eleventh and twelfth centuries and wrote in Hebrew (see chapter 3 below), mentions the generally recognized equivalence between *Tsarfat* and "the kingdom that in vernacular language is called France."
2. The Temple was the central—and sole—sanctuary of Jewish worship in Jerusalem. The first was built by King Solomon around 960 B.C.E. and destroyed by the Babylonians under Nebuchadnezzar in 586 B.C.E. The second was erected in approximately 515 B.C.E., in the same location, following Cyrus's decree authorizing the return to Judea of Jews exiled in Babylonia.
3. Simon Schwarzfuchs, *Les Juifs de France* (Paris: Albin Michel, 1975), 13–14.
4. Talmud, from the Hebrew (literally, "Teaching"), denotes the commentary on the Mishnah (the codification of the oral law published in Palestine around 200 C.E.) produced by the scholars of the academies of Palestine and Babylonia. There exist two Talmuds. The Jerusalem Talmud, or more precisely, the Palestinian Talmud, was compiled under circumstances of instability and persecution in Tiberias toward the end of the fourth century. The Babylonian Talmud, written in Hebrew and in Babylonian Judeo-Aramaic, was assembled in stages, and its redaction completed at the end of the fifth century. The Talmud, as the monumental crystallization of the oral law and as the specific and inalienable property of the Jewish people (unlike the Bible, which was to become the common heritage of

Judaism and Christianity), has come to be inseparable from any exhaustive definition of Jewish identity, along with its legislative content, literary form, and scholarly method. Accordingly it has been one of the privileged targets of the Christian polemic against Judaism, the object of ecclesiastical censure, and the cause of many auto-da-fés.

5. The territory of Septimania included the present-day French departments of Pyrénées-Orientales, Aude, Hérault, and Gard.

6. Though it is difficult to verify the authenticity of the historical details of this late account, it was in any case common in the Middle Ages to assign an important role to the Jews in the capitulation of cities in the south.

7. The oath *more judaico* (literally, in Latin, "according to Jewish custom") had a particularly humiliating character.

8. Schwarzfuchs, *Les Juifs de France*, 35.

9. See Jean Régné, "Étude sur la condition des Juifs de Narbonne du Ve au Xe siècle," *Revue des études juives* 55 (1908): 221–243.

Notes to Chapter 2

1. On this subject see, among other works, Aryeh Graboïs, "Les Juifs et leurs seigneurs dans la France septentrionale au XIe et XIIe siècles," and Gavin I. Langmuir, "*Tanquam servi*: The Change in Jewish Status in French Law about 1200," both in Myriam Yardeni, ed., *Les Juifs dans l'histoire de France* (Leyden: Brill, 1980), 11–54. See also Simon Schwarzfuchs, "De la condition des Juifs de France au XIIe et XIIIe siècles," *Revue des études juives* 125 (January-September 1966): 221–232.

2. The names Cahorsin and Lombard, like Jew, often had a pejorative connotation; see Salo W. Baron, *Histoire d'Israël: Vie sociale et religieuse*, trans. A.-R. Picard (Paris: Presses Universitaires de France, 1961), 4:237.

3. Langmuir, "*Tanquam servi*," 46.

4. Aryeh Graboïs, "Le crédit juif à Paris au temps de Saint Louis," *Revue des études juives* 129 (January-March 1970): 9.

5. Langmuir, "*Tanquam servi*," 46–54.

6. Gérard Nahon, "Une géographie des Juifs dans la France de Louis IX, 1226–1270," in *The Fifth World Congress of Jewish Studies* (Jerusalem, 1972), 2:129.

7. Gérard Nahon, "Le crédit et les Juifs dans la France du XIIIe siècle," *Annales ESC* 5 (September-October 1969): 1127–1128; and "Les ordonnances de Saint Louis sur les Juifs," *Les Nouveaux Cahiers* 23 (1970): 20–21; also 26–28 for the texts of these rulings.

8. Gilbert Dahan, *La Polémique chrétienne contre le judaïsme au Moyen Age* (Paris: Albin Michel, 1991), 46–47.

9. Gérard Nahon, "Pour une géographie administrative des Juifs dans la France de Saint Louis," *Revue historique* 254 (1975): 313.

10. Nahon, "Une géographie des Juifs," 127; see also Robert Chazan, "Jewish Settlement in Northern France, 1096–1306," *Revue des études juives* 128, no. 1 (1969): 55, 58.

11. See Noël Coulet, "L'expulsion des Juifs de France," *L'Histoire* 139 (December 1990): 10. Other historians claim, to the contrary, that the Jews were indeed

expelled in 1322–23 by Philip V (the Long); see, for example, Schwarzfuchs, *Les Juifs de France*, 116.

12. Schwarzfuchs, *Les Juifs de France*, 116.

13. Roger Kohn, "L'expulsion des Juifs de France en 1394: les chemins de l'exil et les refuges," *Archives juives* 28, no. 1 (1995): 76–77.

14. See, for example, Coulet, "L'expulsion des Juifs de France," 14.

15. Léon Gauthier, "Les Juifs dans les deux Bourgognes," *Revue des études juives* 48 (1904): 223.

16. Jean Régné, "Étude sur la condition des Juifs de Narbonne du Ve au Xe siècle," *Revue des études juives* 58 (1909): 75–105, 200–225; 59 (1910): 59–89.

17. Adolphe Crémieux, "Les Juifs de Marseille au Moyen Age," *Revue des études juives* 46 (1903): 3–11.

18. Bernhard Blumenkranz, "Les origines et le Moyen Age," in *Histoire des Juifs en France* (Paris: Privat, 1972), 47.

19. Maurice Kriegel, *Les Juifs à la fin du Moyen Age dans l'Europe méditerranéenne* (Paris: Hachette, 1979), 229–230.

Notes to Chapter 3

1. Gérard Nahon, "La communauté juive de Paris au XIIIe siècle: Problèmes topographiques, démographiques et institutionnels," *Actes du 100e Congrès national des Sociétés savantes* (Paris: Bibliothèque Nationale, 1978), 151.

2. *Encyclopaedia Judaica*, new English edition (Jerusalem: Keter, 1972), 13:1259; see also Bernhard Blumenkranz, *Les Juifs en France: Écrits dispersés* (Paris: Commission Française des Archives Juives, 1989), 94.

3. Nahon, "Une géographie des Juifs dans la France de Louis IX, 1226–1270," 128.

4. Robert Anchel, *Les Juifs de France* (Paris: J.-B. Janin, 1946), 68–69.

5. Gérard Nahon, "Les communautés juives de la Champagne médiévale (XIe–XIIe siècles)," in Manès Sperber, ed., *Rachi* (Paris: Service Technique pour l'Éducation, 1974), 33–78.

6. Gérard Nahon, "Les Sages de France et de Lotharingie: Rabbenu Gershom Me'or ha-Golah, Rashi, les tosafistes," in Jean Baumgarten, Rachel Ertel et al., eds., *Mille Ans de cultures ashkénazes* (Paris: Liana Levi, 1994), 35.

7. Menahem Banitt, "Le français chez Rachi," in *Rachi*, 126–127.

8. Latin term (sing., *responsum*) corresponding to the Hebrew *teshuvot* (sing., *teshuva*).

9. Gérard Nahon, "La communauté juive de Paris au XIIIe siècle," 152–156; and "Les tosafistes," in Gabrielle Sed-Rajna, ed., *Rashi 1040–1990: Congrès européen des études juives* (Paris: Cerf, 1993), 33–42.

10. On this subject see Alain de Libera, *La Philosophie médiévale* (Paris: Presses Universitaires de France, 1993), 365–367.

Notes to Chapter 4

1. René Moulinas, *Les Juifs du pape en France: les communautés d'Avignon et du Comtat Venaissin aux XVIIe et XVIIIe siècles* (Toulouse: Privat, 1981), 20.

2. Jules Bauer, "Le chapeau jaune chez les Juifs comtadins," *Revue des études juives* 36 (1898): 53–64.

3. From the Hebrew, meaning "four holy communities"—a term that referred to the communities of Jerusalem, Hebron, Safed, and Tiberias in the Holy Land.

4. For all the figures given up to this point concerning the Comtat and Avignon, see René Moulinas, "En Avignon: une leçon pour les chrétiens," *Notre Histoire* 110 (April 1994): 26, 28; and "Avignon, terre d'asile des Juifs," *L'Histoire* 41 (1982): 33–34. Robert Anchel puts the number of Jews in Avignon and the Comtat during the years preceding the Revolution at 2,500; see *Les Juifs de France*, 235.

5. René Moulinas, *Les Juifs du pape* (Paris: Albin Michel, 1992), 78–102.

6. Simone Mrejen-O'Hana, "Pratiques et comportements religieux dans les 'quatre saintes communautés' d'Avignon et du Comtat Venaissin au XVIIIe siècle," *Archives juives* 28, no. 2 (1995): 12–18.

7. Jackie A. Kohnstamm and René Moulinas, "Archaïsme et traditions locales: le mariage chez les Juifs d'Avignon et du Comtat au dernier siècle avant l'émancipation," *Revue des études juives* 138 (January-June 1979): 89–115.

8. Simone Mrejen-O'Hana, "Le mariage juif sous l'Ancien Régime: L'exemple de Carpentras (1763–1792)," *Annales de démographie historique* (1993): 169.

9. Bayonne was closed to "Jews" by an enactment of 23 August 1691 that prohibited them from engaging in retail trade and from staying overnight in the city. This order was ratified by the intendant of Bordeaux on 9 January 1693 and remained in force until the Revolution. It had the consequence of pushing Jewish settlement outside the city walls, to the faubourg Saint-Esprit, at the time an independent market town not falling under the jurisdiction of Bayonne. Mixed families of Catholics and "Jews" continued to live in Bayonne, where they gradually disappeared into the larger population.

10. Frances Malino, *The Sephardic Jews of Bordeaux: Assimilation and Emancipation in Revolutionary and Napoleonic France* (Tuscaloosa: University of Alabama Press, 1978); the first chapter was translated by J. Cavignac in *Cahiers de l'IAES* 5 (1984). See also Gérard Nahon, "La nation juive portugaise en France XVIe-XVIIIe siècle: espaces et pouvoirs," *Revue des études juives* 153 (July-December 1994): 357.

11. The word *Sefarad* appears only once in the Bible, in Obadiah 1:20, and originally referred to Sardis, the capital of Lydia in Asia Minor. In medieval Hebrew, *Sefarad* designated the Iberian peninsula; the Jewish communities of the peninsula, or issuing from the peninsula, whether before or after the expulsion from Spain in 1492, were therefore Sephardic. Today, by extension, all, or almost all, non-Ashkenazic Jews—notably the Jews of the Maghreb and the East—are called Sephardic. After 1492, Sephardic Judaism proper, Judeo-Spanish in language, spread chiefly into the Balkans but also to a lesser extent into western Europe, the Maghreb, and the New World. Though today a minority in numerical terms, it has developed a specific, rich, and diverse cultural tradition long valued throughout the Jewish world.

12. Anne Zink, "Une niche juridique: L'installation des Juifs à Saint-Esprit-lès-Bayonne au XVIIe siècle," *Annales HSS* 49 (May-June 1994): 661–662.

13. Ibid., 663–666.

14. Jean Cavignac, *Les Israélites bordelais de 1780 à 1850: Autour de l'émancipation* (Paris: Publisud, 1991), 114–115, 180–181.

15. Ibid., 16. See also Schwarzfuchs, *Les Juifs de France*, 146.

16. Gérard Nahon, "Communautés espagnoles et portuguaises de France (1492–1992)," in Henry Méchoulan, ed., *Les Juifs d'Espagne: Histoire d'une diaspora 1492–1992* (Paris: Liana Levi, 1992), 124.

17. See Arthur Hertzberg, *The French Enlightenment and the Jews* (New York and Philadelphia: Columbia University Press and the Jewish Publication Society of America, 1968), 85, n. 17: "Each of the various national groups in Bordeaux [e.g., Irish, Dutch, Hanseatic, Jewish] was organized as a *nation*, which was represented by a local syndic and by the consul of its place of origin. . . . The open appearance of a Jewish *nation* in Bordeaux towards the end of the seventeenth century thus was aided by the creation of a new legal structure for trade by foreigners."

18. From the Hebrew, denoting an exegetical literature departing considerably from the plain sense of scriptural texts.

19. Nahon, "La nation juive portuguaise en France XVIe-XVIIIe siècle," 361–380.

20. Gérard Nahon, "Démographie des Juifs portuguais à Saint-Esprit-lès-Bayonne (1751–1787): Age au mariage, fécondité, famille," *Bulletin de la Société des sciences, lettres et arts de Bayonne* (1976): 155–202. The average age at marriage for Jewish women between 1751 and 1770 went from 19.3 to 25.2, and between 1772 and 1787 from 25.1 to 23.5, while that for Christian women went from 27.1 to 25.6 between 1740 and 1819. For Christian men, it was 29.4 for the period 1740–79 and 27.4 between 1780 and 1819. It needs to be kept in mind that the Jewish group studied was urban and the Christian group rural.

21. Cavignac, *Les Israélites bordelais de 1780 à 1850*, 18, 57, 75, 279.

Notes to Chapter 5

1. Yiddish was one of the principal languages spoken in the Ashkenazic world and is still spoken today. A fusion language displaying many varieties, it joins to a Germanic base elements borrowed from other idioms, notably Hebrew and Aramaic.

2. Pierre-André Meyer, *La Communauté juive de Metz au XVIIIe siècle* (Nancy and Metz: Presses Universitaires de Nancy/Éditions Serpenoise, 1993), 27–34.

3. Ibid., 30.

4. In the thirteenth century, Metz, until then part of the Holy Roman Empire, became a free city and one of the Three Bishoprics. Lorraine, by contrast, which from the twelfth century covered what was known in the Middle Ages as Upper Lorraine (coinciding with the ecclesiastic province of Trèves), was governed by dukes who were vassals of the German emperor.

5. Schwarzfuchs, *Les Juifs de France*, 175.

6. Françoise Job, *Les Juifs de Nancy du XIIe au XXe siècle* (Nancy: Presses Universitaires de Nancy, 1991), 49.

7. Françoise Job, *Les Juifs de Lunéville au XVIIIe et XIXe siècles* (Nancy: Presses Universitaires de Nancy, 1989), 97–100.

8. Meyer, *La Communauté juive de Metz au XVIIIe siècle*, 46, 186.

9. Ibid., chapter 2, passim.

10. Meyer, *La Communauté juive de Metz au XVIIIe siècle*, 86.

11. Historically, the identity and function of the Court Jew were the product of absolutism and the beginnings of capitalism in Europe. The Court Jews of the seventeenth and beginning of the eighteenth centuries were recruited from among the rich traders, bankers, and suppliers of the state and of the army. As providers of funds to their sovereigns, they were indispensable. At a time when Jews in Europe were still confined to the ghetto, Court Jews enjoyed a precarious but privileged status; as such, they could put their contacts to use in the service of the community. Sovereigns sometimes confided to them various missions directly concerning the interests of the state. In the nineteenth century, the Court Jew was more apt to be a banker and financial advisor. See Selma Stern's classic work on the subject, *The Court Jew: A Contribution to the History of the Period of Absolutism in Central Europe* (Philadelphia: Jewish Publication Society of America, 1950).

12. Job, *Les Juifs de Nancy*, chapter 8, passim.

13. In other Jewish communities, whether those of the south or in Alsace, the marriage age for young men and women was roughly the same. Toward the end of the Ancien Régime, the marriage age for the population as a whole was higher.

14. Eighteen years for boys and twelve and a half years for girls.

15. Meyer, *La Communauté juive de Metz au XVIIIe siècle*, chapters 10–12, passim.

16. The Jews of Alsace—Jews of the Holy Roman Empire, serfs of the Imperial Chamber, though they had not lost all personal liberties—came in principle under the exclusive authority of the emperor, who alone had the right to keep or to expel them. Very early, however, in exchange for payment, he alienated this right to other less central powers, on whose good will, or simply need for money, the Jews now depended. As such, the Jews enjoyed no civil or political capacity and, though they were not taxed, they could be bound to pay any arbitrary levy whatsoever— this despite the fact they benefited from the protection of the emperor. In general, legislation concerning them was restrictive, and the right of residence granted sparingly; such legislation regulated commerce, property rights, freedom of personal movement, and worship. Nonetheless it varied, along with the degree of tolerance shown, depending on the seigneury.

17. Illegal persons were those who did not possess an authorization of residence.

18. Georges Weill, "Recherches sur la démographie des Juifs d'Alsace du XVIe au XVIIIe siècle," *Revue des études juives* 130 (January-March 1971): 53, 55, 63–67.

19. Georges Weill, "L'Alsace," in Bernhard Blumenkranz, ed., *Histoire des Juifs*, 146–148.

20. Schwarzfuchs, *Les Juifs de France*, 181.

21. The Edict of Tolerance concerned the Jews of Lower Austria, which encompassed Vienna, Bohemia, Moravia, Silesia, and Hungary; it was separately promulgated for each of the cities and provinces of the region between October 1781 and March 1782. The emperor abolished the wearing of a distinctive badge by the Jews and the body tax (*Leibzoll*). He guaranteed them greater freedom in commerce and industry, lifting the restrictions relating to domicile and the ghetto. Tolerated Jews were still subject to strict quotas and the payment of special taxes,

but they were now encouraged to live outside the ghetto, to learn artisanal and commercial trades, to employ Christian domestic servants, to send their children to public schools and university or to set up their own schools with instruction in German. It was also insisted that they no longer keep their commercial registers in Hebrew or Yiddish. The wealthy classes were urged to integrate themselves into the surrounding society. The aim of these provisions was to make the Jews useful to society and to the state through education and the removal of economic restrictions. In 1784, the juridical autonomy of the Jewish community was abolished, and, in 1787, for the first time, Jews were enlisted in the army. With the death of Joseph II, this benevolent policy toward the Jews (the first one in centuries in a major European state) was rapidly abandoned. In France, some of the general features of the Edict of Tolerance were subsequently to be found in the letters patent of 1784.

22. This arrangement therefore recognized the validity of Jewish marriage; a converted husband was regarded as still being married to his Jewish wife, and vice versa. Nonetheless, the right to divorce, recognized by Jewish law, was not admitted. Thus the converted spouse was able to marry a Catholic man or woman only in the event of becoming a widow or widower, as the case might be. In this way it was assured that the remarried spouse would have no contact with his or her family and native community.

23. Robert Anchel, "Les Lettres-Patentes du 10 juillet 1784," *Revue des études juives* 93 (1932): 113–134.

24. Rina Neher-Bernheim, "Aspects démographiques de la préparation des Lettres patentes de 1784," in Yardeni, ed., *Les Juifs dans l'histoire de France*, 115–120.

25. In the Bible, Ashkenaz is the son of Gomer (Genesis 10:1–3). Talmudic sources had earlier identified Gomer, son of Japheth and grandson of Noah, with Germany, and by the eleventh century the term *Ashkenaz* had come to designate Lotharingia. Jewish Ashkenazic communities were initially established in the northeast of France, Flanders, and the Rhineland. Persecutions and migrations rapidly pushed back the boundaries of Ashkenazic culture, which came to include England, Germany, Switzerland, northern Italy, and, soon thereafter, central and all of eastern Europe as well as the Americas. On the eve of the Holocaust, Ashkenazim made up ninety percent of world Jewry. Ashkenazic Judaism, itself quite diverse, and having maintained contact with the Sephardic communities, developed a specific culture, as much from the literary and linguistic point of view (with Yiddish) as from that of ritual and religion, intellectual life, and the law.

26. Weill, "L'Alsace," 166, 176, 179; see also Anchel, *Les Juifs de France*, 235.

27. Robert Anchel, "Les Juifs à Paris au XVIIIe siècle," *Bulletin de la Société de l'histoire de Paris et de l'Ile-de-France* 59 (1932): 10–12. See also Michel Roblin, *Les Juifs de Paris: Démographie, économie, culture* (Paris: Picard, 1952), 41–49.

Notes to Chapter 6

1. The royal dynasty of David also belonged to the tribe of Judah.

2. See, for example, a text published anonymously in 1762 in Amsterdam, in response to Voltaire's attacks against the Jews, *Apologie pour la nation juive, ou réflexions critiques sur le premier chapitre du VIIe tome de Monsieur de Voltaire au sujet des*

Juifs par l'auteur de l'Essai sur le luxe (Apology for the Jewish Nation, or Critical Reflections on the First Chapter of the Seventh Volume of Monsieur Voltaire on the Jews by the Author of the "Essay on Luxury"). This text came from the pen of Isaac de Pinto, a Bordeaux Jew who lived in Holland at the time. In this connection, see also Simon Schwarzfuchs, *Du Juif à l'israélite: Histoire d'une mutation 1770–1870* (Paris: Fayard, 1989), 81–82; Roland Mortier, "Les 'philosophes' français du XVIIᵉ siècle devant le judaïsme et la judéité," in Bernhard Blumenkranz, ed., *Juifs en France au XVIIIᵉ siècle* (Paris: Commission Française des Archives Juives, 1994), 191–193.

3. Léon Poliakov, *Histoire de l'antisémitisme* (Paris: Seuil, 1991), 2:32.

4. Ibid., 46–50.

5. Karaism, a deviant form of Judaism that emerged in Babylonia during the eighth century, was principally characterized by its rejection of the oral tradition.

6. On the Enlightenment and the Jewish question, see Hertzberg, *The French Enlightenment and the Jews*, chap. 9; and Mortier, "Les 'philosophes' français du XVIIᵉ siècle devant le judaïsme et la judéité," 191–211.

7. See the recent reissue of this work by Flammarion in 1988, with a preface by R. Hermon-Belot.

8. This work has recently been reissued with a preface by Dominique Bourel (Paris: Stock, 1984).

9. Note that Hourwitz, in formulating his title, inverted the priorities of the society, placing the happiness of the Jews before their usefulness.

10. David Feuerwerker, *L'Émancipation des Juifs en France de l'Ancien Régime à la fin du Second Empire* (Paris: Albin Michel, 1976), chap. 2.

11. Quoted in ibid., 73.

12. Frances Malino, "The Right to Be Equal: Zalkind Hourwitz and the Revolution of 1789," in Frances Malino and David Sorkin, eds., *From East and West: Jews in a Changing Europe, 1750–1870* (Oxford: Basil Blackwell, 1990), 93.

13. Hertzberg, *The French Enlightenment and the Jews*, 324.

14. Ibid., 323. See also Feuerwerker, *L'Émancipation des Juifs en France*, chapter 3; Schwarzfuchs, *Du Juif à l'israélite*, chapter 4; and Patrick Girard, *La Révolution française et les Juifs* (Paris: Laffont, 1989), 92–103.

15. Feuerwerker, *L'Émancipation des Juifs en France*, 284.

16. Maurice Liber, "Les Juifs et la convocation des États généraux (1789)," *Revue des études juives* 63 (1912): 185–210; 64 (1912): 89–108; 65 (1913): 89–133; 66 (1913): 161–212.

17. Schwarzfuchs, *Du Juif à l'israélite*, 129.

18. Comte Stanislas Marie Adélaïde de Clermont-Tonnerre (23 December 1789 session of the Constituent Assembly), quoted in Girard, *La Révolution française et les Juifs*, 125.

19. Schwarzfuchs, *Du Juif à l'israélite*, 136.

Notes to Chapter 7

1. The Science of Judaism was a scholarly movement that developed among German Jewish intellectuals from 1809 in the wake of the Berlin-based Jewish Enlightenment (*Haskalah*). Its representatives sought to elaborate a new Jewish

identity adapted to contemporary circumstances, through a whole series of reforms—with respect to worship, beliefs, way of life, social structure, education, and culture—likely to encourage emancipation. In this spirit they tried, both within their community and outside it, to present in a scientific manner those aspects of the history and culture of Judaism that they considered the richest and best suited to promoting recognition of its values. On the influence of this current of thought in France, see the section below in chapter 9, "Scholarship and the Perpetuation of Tradition."

2. The Reform movement in Judaism challenged the immutability of the oral law and so adapted Jewish thought and practice to the requirements of the spirit of the time. It introduced many reforms in worship and the training of rabbis, whose learning was henceforth no longer to be limited to the Talmud. Abraham Geiger (1810–74) became the principal architect of the movement, which subsequently spread from Germany through the rest of Europe and firmly established itself in the United States.

3. Modern Orthodoxy, an ideological tendency within Orthodox Judaism, combined a positive attitude toward modern society and western culture with meticulous observance of rabbinical law and traditional customs. Its first spokesman and ideologist was Samson Raphael Hirsch (1808–88) of Frankfurt am Main.

4. Maurice Liber, "Napoléon Ier et les Juifs: La question juive devant le Conseil d'État en 1806," *Revue des études juives* 72 (1921): 2.

5. Robert Anchel, *Napoléon et les Juifs* (Paris: Presses Universitaires de France, 1928), 79–81, 90–101.

6. Ibid., 138.

7. This follows the talmudic principle *dina' de-malkhuta' dina'* ("the law of the government is law"); see the Babylonian Talmud, Nedarim 28a.

8. Philippe Sagnac, "Les Juifs et Napoléon (1806–1808), *Revue d'histoire moderne et contemporaine* 2 (1900–1901): 595–604; also Anchel, *Napoléon et les Juifs*, 164–186.

9. Also called *beit din ha-gadol* ("high court" in Hebrew), the ancient Sanhedrin had quite broad powers. Sitting in Palestine, the influence of this institution came to extend throughout the diaspora. It was active during the Roman period, both before and after the destruction of the Second Temple in 70 c.e., until the abolition of the Patriarchate, in 425.

10. Schwarzfuchs, *Du Juif à l'israélite*, 283.

11. Dominique Jarrassé, "La synagogue reflet d'une histoire," *Monuments historiques* 191 (1994), special issue [*Le Patrimoine juif français*]: 30–42.

12. Patrick Girard, *Pour le meilleur et pour le pire: Vingt siècles d'histoire juive en France* (Paris: Bibliophane, 1986), 344.

Notes to Chapter 8

1. Cavignac, *Les Israélites bordelais de 1780 à 1850.*

2. These figures, for 1891, are taken from Doris Bensimon-Donath, *Sociodémographie des Juifs de France et d'Algérie: 1867–1907* (Paris: Éditions de l'Institut National des Langues et Civilisations Orientales, 1976), 73.

3. S. Posener, "Les Juifs sous le premier Empire," *Revue des études juives* 93

(1932): 195, 205; see too Bensimon-Donath, *Socio-démographie des Juifs de France et d'Algérie*, 62–63.

4. The central consistory put the number of Jews in 1861 at 95,881, which would raise their share of the total population in France to 0.3 percent; see Phyllis Cohen Albert, *The Modernization of French Jewry: Consistory and Community in the Nineteenth Century* (Hanover, N.H.: Brandeis University Press, 1977), 4, 23, 24. The official figures of the 1861 religious census given here—see Bensimon-Donath, *Socio-démographie des Juifs de France et d'Algérie*, 68—do not faithfully reflect the reality of the period, if only because they do not take into account those individuals who claimed allegiance to no religion.

5. Albert, *The Modernization of French Jewry*, 25.

6. Posener, "Les Juifs sous le premier Empire," 200.

7. Bensimon-Donath, *Socio-démographie des Juifs de France et d'Algérie*, 70.

8. Paula Hyman, *The Emancipation of the Jews of Alsace: Acculturation and Tradition in the Nineteenth Century* (New Haven: Yale University Press, 1991), 86, 88, 96.

9. Philippe Landau, "'La patrie en danger': D'une guerre à l'autre," in Pierre Birnbaum, ed., *Histoire politique des Juifs en France* (Paris: Presses de la Fondation Nationale des Sciences Politiques, 1990), 76.

10. Vicki Caron, *Between France and Germany: The Jews of Alsace-Lorraine, 1871–1918* (Stanford: Stanford University Press, 1988), 47, 49, 56, 72, 75, 158.

11. Hyman, *Emancipation of the Jews of Alsace*, 52, 55–58. In the 1840s, 64 percent of Jewish families in Strasbourg and 84 percent of those in Bischeim, Niederroedern, and Itterswiller were of the nuclear type. Of Jewish households in Strasbourg, 10 percent were made up of childless couples, 44 percent of couples with children, and 11 percent had only one parent. In other towns and villages, proportions did not vary much.

12. Caron, *Between France and Germany*, 160–161. In the years 1872–82, the rate of Jewish marriage fell from 10 per 1,000 to 5 per 1,000, and in 1896 to 4 per 1,000, while that of the total population was 9 per 1,000. A slight rise was recorded in 1910 with a rate of 6 per 1,000, which is still low.

13. Girard, *Les Juifs de France de 1789 à 1860: De l'émancipation à l'égalité* (Paris: Calmann-Lévy, 1976), 126.

14. Hyman, *Emancipation of the Jews of Alsace*, 35.

15. Bensimon-Donath, *Socio-démographie des Juifs de France et d'Algérie*, 351.

16. Hyman, *Emancipation of the Jews of Alsace*, 35, 45, 65–68, 109, 123, 132.

17. Léon Kahn, *Histoire de la communauté israélite de Paris: Les professions manuelles et les institutions de patronage* (Paris: Durlacher, 1885), 65–78.

18. Bensimon-Donath, *Socio-démographie des Juifs de France et d'Algérie*, 73. Consistorial censuses yielded a divergent set of figures: 8,000 in 1841, 18,000 in 1853, 25,000 in 1861, 30,000 in 1870; see Albert, *Modernization of French Jewry*, 332, and Jean-Louis Kohn, "La Bourgeoisie juive à Paris au second Empire," (Ph.D. dissertation, Université de Paris-I, 1993–94), 22.

19. Albert, *Modernization of French Jewry*, 23–24, 304; Christine Piette, *Les Juifs de Paris (1808–1840): La marche vers l'assimilation* (Québec: Presses de l'Université Laval, 1983), 51, 55; Kohn, "La Bourgeoisie juive à Paris au second Empire," 19; Bensimon-Donath, *Socio-démographie des Juifs de France et d'Algérie*, 71, 75, 108–111. According to Bensimon-Donath, Paris in 1891 had 59 percent of the 67,780

Jews in France; in 1897, 55 percent of 75,104 French Jews. In 1861, the total population in the capital was 1,696,141; in 1901, 2,714,068. For both of these latter two dates, if metropolitan Paris is taken in its entirety, including the adjacent departments of Normandy and the Loire region, the Jewish population of the Paris region accounted for 64 percent of the total Jewish population of France.

20. Piette, *Les Juifs de Paris (1808–1840)*, 59.

21. Jean-Yves Monnier, "La vérité sur les Juifs de France au XIXe siècle," *L'Histoire* 148 (October 1991): 33.

22. François Delpech, "De 1815 à 1894," in Blumenkranz, *Histoire des Juifs en France*, 312.

23. Kohn, "La Bourgeoisie juive à Paris au second Empire," 146; see also Bensimon-Donath, *Socio-démographie des Juifs de France et d'Algérie*, 147.

24. Kohn, "La Bourgeoisie juive à Paris au second Empire," 105.

25. Piette, *Les Juifs de Paris*, 85.

26. Ibid., 88–101, 106–107.

27. Kohn, "La Bourgeoisie juive à Paris au second Empire," 116, 137–138.

28. Bensimon-Donath, *Socio-démographie des Juifs de France et d'Algérie*, chap. 5 passim.

29. These figures were obtained from a sample of 1,109 persons, the 1872 census for the city of Marseilles being incomplete.

30. Florence Berceot, "Socio-démographie des israélites de Marseille 1872–1891," *Provence historique* 173 (1993): 305–322.

31. Florence Berceot, "Renouvellement socio-démographique des Juifs de Marseille 1901–1937," *Provence historique* 175 (1994): 39–57.

32. See the data for Marseilles in the two articles by Berceot cited above and, for Paris, the data in Bensimon-Donath, *Socio-démographie des Juifs de France et d'Algérie*, chap. 6 passim.

33. Berceot, "Renouvellement socio-démographique des Juifs de Marseille 1901–1937," and Bensimon-Donath, *Socio-démographie des Juifs de France et d'Algérie*, chap. 6; see also Zosa Szajkowski, "The Decline and Fall of Provençal Jewry," *Jewish Social Studies* 6 (January 1944): 47.

34. David Cohen, *La Promotion des Juifs en France à l'époque du second Empire (1852–1870)* (Aix-en-Provence: Université de Provence, 1980), 1:73.

35. Bensimon-Donath, *Socio-démographie des Juifs de France et d'Algérie*, 303–312.

Notes to Chapter 9

1. Kohn, "La Bourgeoisie juive à Paris au second Empire," 181–186.

2. Bensimon-Donath, *Socio-démographie des Juifs de France et d'Algérie*, 131–139.

3. Michael R. Marrus, *Les Juifs à l'époque de l'affaire Dreyfus*, trans. M. Legras (Paris: Calmann-Lévy, 1972), 58; originally published as *The Politics of Assimilation: A Study of the French Jewish Community at the Time of the Dreyfus Affair* (Oxford: Clarendon Press, 1971).

4. Pierre Birnbaum, *The Jews of the Republic: A Political History of State Jews in France from Gambetta to Vichy*, trans. Jane Marie Todd (Stanford: Stanford University Press, 1996), 2.

5. Kohn, "La Bourgeoisie juive à Paris au second Empire," 235–243.

6. Bensimon-Donath, *Socio-démographie des Juifs de France et d'Algérie*, chap. 6 passim; see also Berceot, "Socio-démographie des israélites de Marseille 1872–1891," 313.

7. Piette, *Les Juifs de Paris*, 157.

8. Landau, "'La patrie en danger': D'une guerre à l'autre," 78, 85; and "Les Juifs de France et la Grande Guerre, 1914–1941: Patrie-République-Mémoire" (Ph.D. dissertation, Université de Paris-VII, 1993), 44, 65. The population of 190,000 included 70,000 Algerian Jews, who sent 14,000 soldiers into military service at the beginning of hostilities.

9. Kohn, "La Bourgeoisie juive à Paris au second Empire," 307, 315; see also Birnbaum, *The Jews of the Republic*, 73.

10. Simon Schwarzfuchs, *Les Juifs d'Algérie et la France (1830–1855)* (Jerusalem: Ben-Zvi Institute, 1981), 21–29; see also Jean Ganiage (with the assistance of Jean Martin), *Histoire contemporaine du Maghreb de 1830 à nos jours* (Paris: Fayard, 1994), 236–237, 463. It is not easy to give an exact figure for the number of Jews in Algeria, given that they were for the most part treated as Europeans in official statistics.

Notes to Chapter 10

1. Nancy L. Green, *Les Travailleurs immigrés juifs à la Belle Époque: Le "Pletzl" de Paris*, revised and expanded edition, trans. M. Courtois-Fourcy (Paris: Fayard, 1985), 23, 65–66; subsequently published in English as *The Pletzl of Paris: Jewish Immigrant Workers in the "Belle Époque"* (New York: Holmes and Meier, 1986).

2. Kosher food is consumed in order to conform to the dietary prescriptions of Jewish law.

3. Bund was a shorthand way of referring to the Algemeyner Yidisher Arbeter Bund fun Lite, Poyln un Rusland (General Union of Jewish Workers in Lithuania, Poland, and Russia), a socialist movement secretly founded in Vilna in 1897. Anti-Zionist, the Bund called for cultural autonomy based on the Yiddish language and the right of the Jewish community to live as a national minority in addition to a range of political, trade union, and cultural issues. It rapidly outgrew its original working class setting, carrying on the struggle not only against local employers but also against the oppressive regime of Nicholas II. Its membership for the years 1905–06 exceeded 30,000. In 1921, it was brutally liquidated in the Soviet Union; in Poland it survived till the Second World War, and sporadically in Europe, the United States, and Israel. See Enzo Traverso, "Le début du socialisme juif: le Bund," in Baumgarten, Ertel et al., eds., *Mille Ans de cultures ashkénazes*, 213–220.

4. Paula Hyman, *De Dreyfus à Vichy: L'évolution de la communauté juive en France 1906–1939*, trans. S. Boulongne (Paris: Fayard, 1985), 100–128; originally published as *From Dreyfus to Vichy: The Remaking of French Jewry, 1906–1939* (New York: Columbia University Press, 1979).

5. Roblin, *Les Juifs de Paris*, 69.

6. Landau, "'La patrie en danger,'" 78; see also his article "Religion et patrie: les prières israélites pour la France," *Pardès* 14 (1991): 20.

7. R. F. Byrnes, "Édouard Drumont and *La France juive*," *Jewish Social Studies* 10 (April 1948): 172–173.

8. Ibid., 179–180; see also Michel Winock, *Nationalisme, Antisémitisme et Fascisme en France* (Paris: Seuil, 1990), 118.

9. Dominique Schnapper, "Le Juif errant," in Yves Lequin, ed., *Histoire des étrangers et de l'immigration en France* (Paris: Larousse, 1992), 376.

10. Yves Lequin, "Dreyfus à l'usine? Le silence d'une mémoire," in Pierre Birnbaum, ed., *La France de l'affaire Dreyfus* (Paris: Gallimard, 1994), 390; see also Birnbaum, *Destins juifs*, 126.

11. According the consistorial census of 1891 (the census of 1872 was the last official population count containing information about religious affiliation, which makes it necessary to refer for later periods to the censuses conducted by the consistory), the number of Jews in France had risen to 67,780. The 1901 census put the number of Algerian Jews, including those of the Mzab, at 58,961. See Bensimon-Donath, *Socio-démographie des Juifs de France et d'Algérie*, 72; and Ganiage, *Histoire contemporaine du Maghreb*, 236.

12. On this point see Vincent Duclert, *L'Affaire Dreyfus* (Paris: La Découverte, 1994).

13. Birnbaum, *Destins juifs*, 137.

14. Quoted by Michael Burns, *Histoire d'une famille française, les Dreyfus: L'émancipation, l'Affaire, Vichy*, trans. B. Bonne (Paris: Fayard, 1994), 359; originally published as *Dreyfus: A Family Affair, 1789–1945* (New York: HarperCollins, 1991).

15. In this connection see the article by Christophe Prochasson reconsidering anti-Semitism at the time of the affair, "Un retour aux sources: l'antisémitisme au temps de l'Affaire," *Jean Jaurès, cahiers trimestriels* 137 (July-September 1995): 53–58; the journal number cited is a special issue devoted to the Dreyfus affair.

16. Zeev Sternhell, *La Droite révolutionnaire 1885–1914: Les origines françaises du fascisme* (Paris: Seuil, 1978): 232–235.

17. The Cambon Declaration was an official declaration addressed in the form of a letter by Jules Cambon, secretary general for foreign affairs, to the Zionist leader Nahum Sokolov formally expressing support for the "Zionist plan"; no sooner delivered, it fell into oblivion. See Catherine Nicault, *La France et le Sionisme 1897–1948: Une rencontre manquée?* (Paris: Calmann-Lévy, 1992), 79–84.

18. On Lévi's remarks, see André Chouraqui, *Cent Ans d'histoire: L'Alliance israélite universelle et la renaissance contemporaine (1860–1960)* (Paris: Presses Universitaires de France, 1965), 476–480.

Notes to Chapter 11

1. Ida Benguigui, "L'Immigration juive à Paris entre les deux guerres" (undergraduate thesis, Université de Paris, 1965), 9.

2. Hyman, *De Dreyfus à Vichy*, 52–53, 106.

3. Roblin, *Les Juifs de Paris*, chap. 4 passim and p. 76; Doris Bensimon and Sergio della Pergola, *La Population juive de France: socio-démographie et identité* (Paris: The Institute of Contemporary Jewry-CNRS, 1986), 32–33.

4. Annie Benveniste, *Le Bosphore à la Roquette: La communauté judéo-espangnole à*

Paris (1914–1940) (Paris: L'Harmattan, 1989), 70; see also Lise Tiano, "L'Immigration et l'Installation en France des Juifs grecs et des Juifs turcs avant la Seconde Guerre mondiale" (master's thesis, Université de Paris-X, 1981), 59.

5. Benveniste, *Le Bosphore à la Roquette*, chap. 4 passim. See also David H. Weinberg, *Les Juifs à Paris de 1933 à 1939*, trans. M. Pouteau (Paris: Calmann-Lévy, 1974), 25–26; this work subsequently appeared in English as *A Community on Trial: The Jews of Paris in the 1930s* (Chicago: University of Chicago Press, 1977).

6. Data taken from a sample limited to members of Jewish associations and institutions; see Florence Berceot, "La Communauté juive de Marseille sous la IIIe République, regard sur les femmes: Assimilation-renaissance" (mémoire, Université d'Aix-Marseille-I, 1991), 130–135.

7. Annette Wieviorka, "France," in Geoffrey Wigoder, editor-in-chief, *Dictionnaire encyclopédique du judaïsme* (Paris: Cerf, 1993), 1473; this work, the French version of which was prepared under the direction of Sylvie-Anne Goldberg, originally appeared as *The Encyclopedia of Judaism* (New York: Macmillan, 1989).

8. Renée Poznanski, *Être Juif pendant la Seconde Guerre mondiale* (Paris: Hachette, 1994), 32.

9. Weinberg, *Les Juifs à Paris de 1933 à 1939*, 46, 48–49.

10. Hyman, *De Dreyfus à Vichy*, 129.

11. Poznanski, *Être Juif pendant la Seconde Guerre mondiale*, 44.

12. Ralph Schor, *L'Antisémitisme en France pendant les années trente* (Paris: Complexe, 1992), 29.

13. Ibid., 30–32, 38.

14. Ibid., 236–241, 295–296.

15. Their works include André Spire, *Quelques Juifs et demi-Juifs* (1928); Edmond Fleg, *La Maison du Bon Dieu* (1920) and *L'Anthologie juive* (1923); Jean-Richard Bloch, *Et Compagnie* (1917); Albert Cohen, born in Corfu, attracted notice with *Solal* (1930) and later *Mangeclous* (1939); Armand Lunel received the Prix Renaudot in 1926 for *Nicolo Peccavi*; Josué Jéhouda's early novels included *Le Royaume de Justice* (1923); Pierre Paraf, *Israël* (1931); Lily Jean-Javal, *Noémi* (1925); Irène Némirovsky, a native Russian, brought out *David Golder* in 1930; Pierre Créange, *Épîtres aux Juifs*, 3d ed. (1937); and Benjamin Fondane, a Moldavian-born poet, essayist, philosopher, and filmmaker, *Ulysse* (1933) and *Titanic* (1937).

16. Hyman, *De Dreyfus à Vichy*, 208.

17. Nelly Las, "Les Juifs de France et le Sionisme: De l'affaire Dreyfus à la Seconde Guerre mondiale (1896–1939)" (thesis, Université de la Sorbonne nouvelle-Paris III, 1985), 198–202.

18. In 1921, Néhama and Matalon had established the youth association Interjuive in Salonika with the aim of forming and multiplying contacts among Jews throughout the world. Once settled in Paris, they renamed their movement the Union Universelle de la Jeunesse Juive.

19. Hyman, *De Dreyfus à Vichy*, chap. 7; see also Berceot, "La Communauté juive de Marseille sous la IIIe République," 167–193.

20. In keeping with the terms of the British mandate, established in August 1929, an expanded Jewish Agency replaced the World Zionist Organization both in matters of political action in Palestine and in relations with the mandate power.

Henceforth the Jewish Agency and the Zionist Organization were to constitute two distinct but closely linked bodies. From 1935 on, the agency was regarded as the unofficial government of the Jews in Palestine and of those in diaspora who supported Zionism.

21. Hyman, *De Dreyfus à Vichy*, chap. 6 passim. See also Las, "Les Juifs de France et le Sionisme," 192–196, 221–226; and Michel Abitbol, *Les Deux Terres promises: Les Juifs de France et le sionisme 1897–1945* (Paris: Olivier Orban, 1989), part 1, chap. 3, and part 2 passim.

22. Schor, *L'Antisémitisme en France pendant les années trente*, 213.

23. Weinberg, *Les Juifs à Paris de 1933 à 1939*, 107, n. 2.

24. Ibid., 103–115.

25. Hyman, *De Dreyfus à Vichy*, 328.

26. Poznanski, *Être Juif pendant la Seconde Guerre mondiale*, 46.

27. The Mouvement Populaire Juif (or Front Populaire Juif) was formed in August 1935 at the same time as the movement for a Popular Front was developing in France. Its chief goal was uniting progressive Jewish forces in order to rally them in support of the national struggle against Fascism. It hoped to attract members of the Jewish lower middle class as well as upper class French Jews; took a close interest in the status of immigrants and in defending their interests; and also aided republican forces in the Spanish Civil War.

Notes to Chapter 12

1. The total number of Jews on French soil and in North Africa rose to some 700,000 by 1940; see André Kaspi, *Les Juifs pendant l'Occupation* (Paris: Seuil, 1991), 177.

2. Ralph Schor, *L'Opinion française et les Étrangers* (Paris: Publications de la Sorbonne, 1985), 182; see also Roblin, *Les Juifs de Paris*, 64–74, and Poznanski, *Être Juif pendant la Seconde Guerre mondiale*, 23.

3. Roger Berg, "Juifs de France, combattants de la Seconde Guerre mondiale 1939–1945," *Pardès* 12 (1990): 196–210; see also Philippe Landau, "France, nous voilà! Les engagés volontaires juifs d'origine étrangère pendant la 'drôle de guerre,'" *Pardès* 16 (1992): 20–38; and Wieviorka, "France," 1475.

4. Poznanski, *Être Juif pendant la Seconde Guerre mondiale*, 51, 55, 262.

5. Ibid., 69.

6. Yves-Claude Aouate, "Les mesures d'exclusion antijuive dans l'enseignement public en Algérie (1940–1943)," *Pardès* 8 (1988): 115–120; see also Kaspi, *Les Juifs pendant l'Occupation*, 192–199.

7. Asher Cohen, *Persécutions et Sauvetages: Juifs et Français sous l'Occupation et sous Vichy* (Paris: Cerf, 1993), 95–99; see also Anne Grynberg, *Les Camps de la honte: Les internés juifs des camps français 1939–1944* (Paris: La Découverte, 1991), 11, 343, and "Les camps du Sud de la France: de l'internement à la déportation," *Annales ESC* 48 (May-June 1993): 557–558.

8. Michel Abitbol, *Les Juifs d'Afrique du Nord sous Vichy* (Paris: Maisonneuve et Larose, 1983); see also Kaspi, *Les Juifs pendant l'Occupation*, 178.

9. Poznanski, *Être Juif pendant la Seconde Guerre mondiale*, 83.

10. Ibid., 310–314; see also Kaspi, *Les Juifs pendant l'Occupation*, 212–218.

11. Poznanski, *Être Juif pendant la Seconde Guerre mondiale*, 314–321.

12. Serge Klarsfeld, "Juillet-septembre 1942: Les divergences dans l'appareil policier nazi et la réalisation de la solution finale en France," *Annales ESC* 48 (May-June 1993), 547.

13. Poznanski, *Être Juif pendant la Seconde Guerre mondiale*, 371–410 passim, 569; see also Kaspi, *Les Juifs pendant l'Occupation*, chap. 6 passim, and Olga Wormser-Migot, "De 1939–1945," in Blumenkranz, ed., *Histoire des Juifs en France*, 400.

14. Kaspi, *Les Juifs pendant l'Occupation*, 283–284. Michael Marrus ("Vichy et les enfants juifs," *L'Histoire* 22 [April 1980]: 15) suggests that between 1942 and 1944 nearly two thousand children under the age of six, and six thousand under the age of thirteen, were deported from France to Auschwitz; none survived. For a somewhat different accounting see Maxime Steinberg, "Le paradox français dans la solution finale," *Annales ESC* 48 (May-June 1993), 583–594. The reader wishing more detailed information may consult Serge Klarsfeld's classic work, *Le Mémorial de la déportation des Juifs de France* (Paris: Klarsfeld, 1978).

15. For differing assessments of its role, see Maurice Rajsfus, *Les Juifs dans la Collaboration: L'Union générale des israélites de France (1941–1944)* (Paris: EDI, 1980). See also Jacques Adler, *Face à la persécution: Les Organisations juives à Paris de 1940 à 1944*, trans. A. Charpentier (Paris: Calmann-Lévy, 1985); the English text on which the French edition was based appeared subsequently as *The Jews of Paris and the Final Solution: Communal Response and Internal Conflicts, 1940–1944* (New York: Oxford University Press, 1987). Other works that may be consulted include Richard I. Cohen, *The Burden of Conscience: French Jewry's Response to the Holocaust* (Bloomington: Indiana University Press, 1987); Kaspi, *Les Juifs pendant l'Occupation*, 334–374; and Poznanski, *Être Juif pendant la Seconde Guerre mondiale*, 207–212, 698–705.

16. Annie Perchenet, *Histoire des Juifs de France* (Paris: Cerf, 1988), 178.

17. Wieviorka, "France," 1479.

18. For the text of this speech, see Éric Conan and Henry Rousso, *Vichy: un passé qui ne passe pas* (Paris: Gallimard, 1996), 444–449.

Notes to Chapter 13

1. Bensimon and della Pergola, *La Population juive de France*, 35.

2. The British, as trustees of Palestine under the League of Nations mandate, anticipated an inevitable war with the Germans and feared that the Arab populations of Palestine, Iraq, and Egypt would go over to the side of the Axis powers. Thus, with the failure of Arab-Jewish talks in 1939, the British published on 17 May of that year a new White Paper, following earlier such documents in 1922 and 1930. This paper, which represented an important concession to Arab demands, limited immigration to the country at a time when thousands of Jewish refugees fleeing Nazism were headed to Palestine, forbade the sale of land to Jews in 80 percent of the country, and contemplated the creation within ten years of an independent Palestinian state having close economic and strategic ties to Great Britain.

3. For the full charter of the CRIF, see the appendix in the article by Adam Rayski, "L'UGIF et le CRIF: les choix de la communauté, 1940–1944," *Pardès* 6 (1987): 179–180.

4. See Anne Grynberg's recent article discussing the life of the organized community, "Après la tourmente," in Jean-Jacques Becker and Annette Wieviorka, eds., *Les Juifs de France de la Révolution française à nos jours* (Paris: Liana Levi, 1998), 249–286.

5. Known also as the JDC, the Joint Distribution Committee, an American Jewish organization, was founded in 1914 to come to the aid of Jewish war victims. During the Second World War, it actively worked to help and rescue Jews persecuted by the Nazi regime in Europe and immediately after the war played a vital role in the reconstruction of communities and the rehabilitation of displaced persons; later, in 1949–50, it paid for the passage of immigrants to Israel.

6. Citing encirclement by its Arab neighbors and feeling itself threatened with total destruction, Israel launched a preventive war against Egypt, Jordan, and Syria. The Six Day War (5–10 June 1967) resulted in Israel's victory on all fronts and its occupation of the Sinai peninsula, the Gaza Strip, and the West Bank (with the Old City of Jerusalem), as well as the Golan Heights.

7. Grynberg, "Après la tourmente," 258.

8. Annette Wieviorka, "Le Centre de documentation juive contemporaine et le Mémorial du martyr juif inconnu," in Becker and Wieviorka, eds., *Les Juifs de France de la Révolution française à nos jours*, 256.

9. Nicole Lapierre, *Changer de nom* (Paris: Stock, 1995), 134.

10. In the wake of this victory, Poujade's movement formed the group Union et Fraternité Françaises in the National Assembly. The corporatist demands of *poujadisme* later adopted the antiparliamentarian and ultranationalist rhetoric of the extreme right, which cost it its following. Jean-Marie Le Pen was a Poujadist deputy.

11. Following the nationalization of the Suez Canal by Egyptian president Gamal Abdel Nasser, on 26 July 1956, the Israelis opened hostilities against Egypt. The United Kingdom and France militarily occupied the area to the north of the canal. Israel conquered the Sinai Peninsula in seven days. Pressure from the United Nations, the United States, and the Soviet Union brought an end to the fighting and, in March 1957, the evacuation of the territories conquered by Israeli troops.

12. The FLN played a key role in the struggle for Algerian independence. Founded during the insurrection of November 1954, the result of a fusion of various nationalist groups, it became the ruling party in Algeria following independence in 1962 (until recognition of other parties under the new constitution of 1989).

13. The OAS was an underground movement created during the Algerian war after the failure of the "generals' putsch" (the name given to the organized military revolt of 26 April 1961 against de Gaulle's policy of self-determination), which attempted, chiefly by means of terrorist attacks, to block Algerian independence.

14. Richard Ayoun, "Les Juifs d'Algérie pendant la guerre d'indépendance (1954–1962)," *Archives juives* 29, no. 1 (1996): 15–29.

15. M. Abitol, "La Cinquième République et l'accueil des Juifs d'Afrique du Nord," in Becker and Wieviorka, eds., *Les Juifs de France de la Révolution française à nos jours*, 289, 303–304, 324–325.

16. Ibid. See also Doris Bensimon-Donath, *L'Intégration des Juifs nord-africains en France* (Paris and The Hague: Mouton, 1971).

17. In a press conference held on 27 November 1967, referring to the birth of the state of Israel, de Gaulle said: "Some even feared that the Jews, who had been dispersed until then but who remained what they had always been, which is to say an elite people, sure of itself and domineering, would eventually, once reassembled in the site of their ancient greatness, transform the very moving desires that they had formed for nineteen centuries into an ardent and conquering ambition." This text is cited by Christian Delacampagne, "L'Antisémitisme en France (1945–1993)," in Léon Poliakov, ed., *Histoire de l'antisémitisme, 1945–1993* (Paris: Seuil, 1994), 137.

18. On this subject see Yaïr Auron, *Les Juifs d'extrême gauche en mai 68*, trans. K. Werchowski (Paris: Albin Michel, 1998).

19. Annette Wieviorka, "Les Juifs en France depuis la guerre des Six-Jours," in Becker and Wieviorka, eds., *Les Juifs de France de la Révolution française à nos jours*, 377.

20. The number of Jews living in Paris at this time is estimated at about 135,000, with another 132,000 living in the surrounding area; see Bensimon and della Pergola, *La Population juive de France*, 35–38.

21. This number includes those who are born of an Ashkenazic father and a Sephardic mother (or vice versa) and who do not think of themselves as belonging to either group.

22. A marriage is said to be geographically homogamous where it involves the union of Jews from the same region (such as North Africa, the Mediterranean, eastern Europe, and so on).

23. Wieviorka, "Les Juifs en France depuis la guerre des Six-Jours," 363–405.

24. This informal term describes Jews whose public observance is essentially limited to Yom Kippur (the Day of Atonement), which is the solemn occasion of personal repentence observed by fasting and prayer on the tenth day of the Jewish month of Tishrei (September-October in the Gregorian calendar).

25. See Nonna Mayer, "L'affaire Carpentras," *L'Histoire* 148 (October 1991): 13; and Simon Epstein, *Cyclical Patterns in Antisemitism: The Dynamics of Anti-Jewish Violence in Western Countries Since the 1950s* (Jerusalem: Vidal Sassoon International Center for the Study of Antisemitism, 1993), 20, 27. The most striking acts of violence include the bomb placed in front of the student hostel in the rue de Médicis in Paris in March 1979, which injured some thirty persons; the assassination in September of the same year of Pierre Goldman, the circumstances of which remain obscure, and attacks on several Jewish schools in Paris; the October 1980 bombing of the synagogue in the rue Copernic in Paris, which killed four and left twenty injured; a grenade attack in August 1982 on the Goldenberg Restaurant in the rue des Rosiers in the Marais, killing six and wounding twenty-two; and, in May 1990, the desecration of the Jewish cemetery in Carpentras, one of a number of such acts in eastern border departments of France, which aroused general indignation. See Delacampagne, "L'Antisémitisme en France (1945–1993)," 149–150.

26. There was, for example, the ambiguous statement of Raymond Barre, then prime minister, after the attack on the synagogue in the rue Copernic on 3 October 1980: "This odious attack, meant to strike Jews who were on their way to synagogue . . . , struck innocent French who were crossing the rue Copernic"; see Birnbaum, *Destins juifs*, 222.

27. In Judaism, circumcision is practiced eight days after the birth of a male child, in keeping with divine commandment and as a sign of the covenant between God and the descendants of Abraham. It is also performed on male converts to Judaism to signify their entry into this covenant (see Genesis 17:9–13).

28. A *talmud torah* is an elementary religious school, in this case a Sunday (or Wednesday morning) school where children study four to eight hours a week to prepare themselves for attaining the age of religious responsibility.

29. For all figures given in this section, see Bensimon and della Pergola, *La Population juive de France*, 45–58, 99–100, 106–108, 124, 130, 137, 145, 162–163, 165–177, 241–267, 312, 325, 342, 344; and Erik Cohen, *L'Étude et l'Éducation juive en France ou l'avenir de la communauté* (Paris: Cerf, 1991), 53–54, 89–90, 174, and appendices (183–264). The sociodemographic and sociocultural study by Bensimon and della Pergola, based on a sample survey conducted in Paris, constitutes the French wing of an international research project coordinated by the Division of Demography and Statistics of the Institute of Contemporary Judaism at the Hebrew University of Jerusalem. In this study, a population x was systematically drawn from the electoral rolls of each of the localities surveyed to provide a representative sample, the criteria for identifying a Jewish population within the larger population having first been determined (owing to the absence of official statistics in France concerning religious, ethnic, or national minorities, no figures whatsoever were available regarding the Jewish population); for further details, see the authors' methodological explanations, pp. 11–21. Erik Cohen's research is not strictly academic in nature, having been commissioned by the community. It is, in fact, the result of three investigations: an "analytic inventory of the Jewish community of France in its educational dimension," an analysis of the "communal leadership," and a survey of opinion among the "Jews of France." In the last instance, analysis of the selected sample showed it to be representative for 85 percent to 90 percent of French Jews and, in the case of children, for at least 95 percent; see pp. 15–18.

30. On communitarianism and the ties between the republic and French Jews, see Birnbaum, *Destins juifs*, 217–252. For an analysis of public opinion and French Jews, see Mayer, "L'affaire Carpentras," 12.

Bibliography

THE BIBLIOGRAPHY PRESENTED here naturally cannot aim to be exhaustive. Though it mentions classics as well as the most recent works of scholarship, it does not include studies devoted to the history of France (with the exception of a few that contain material specifically concerning Jews in France). Moreover, it is limited to publications in western languages; accordingly, works in Hebrew are absent from it. In the case of books first published in English, citation is to their original editions. Articles appearing in edited volumes or in special issues of journals, even if they are sometimes mentioned in the notes, are for the most part not listed separately here; only the volumes and journal issues in question are noted. At the end of certain sections the titles of various scholarly journals and periodicals are given where the reader may find additional information or studies not mentioned in this bibliography.

General Works

Allouche-Benayoun, Joëlle, and Doris Bensimon. *Juifs d'Algérie hier et aujourd'hui: Mémoires et identités*. Toulouse: Privat, 1989.

Anchel, Robert. *Les Juifs de France*. Paris: J.-B. Janin, 1946.

Ansky, Michel. *Les Juifs d'Algérie: Du décret Crémieux à la Libération*. Paris: Éditions du Centre, 1950.

Arendt, Hannah. *Antisemitism*. New York: Harcourt, Brace and World, 1968.

———. *Origins of Totalitarianism*. 1951. Reprint, New York: Harcourt Brace Jovanovich, 1973.

Arvon, Henri, *Les Juifs et l'Idéologie*. Paris: Presses Universitaires de France, 1978.

Aubery, Pierre. *Milieux juifs de la France contemporaine à travers leurs écrivains*. 1957. Reprint, Paris: Plon, 1962.

Ayoun, Richard, and Bernard Cohen. *Les Juifs d'Algérie: Deux mille ans d'histoire*. Paris: Lattès, 1982.

Baumgarten, Jean, and Rachel Ertel et al., eds. *Mille Ans de cultures ashkénazes*. Paris: Liana Lévi, 1994.

Becker, Jean-Jacques, and Annette Wieviorka, eds. *Les Juifs de France de la Révolution française à nos jours*. Paris: Liana Levi, 1998.

Benbassa, Esther, ed. *Transmission et Passages en monde juif*. Paris: Publisud, 1997.

Bensimon, Doris. *Les Juifs dans le monde au tournant du XXIᵉ siècle*. Paris: Albin Michel, 1994.

Berg, Roger. *Histoire des Juifs à Paris de Chilpéric à Jacques Chirac*. Paris: Cerf, 1997.

Berg, Roger, Chalom Chemouny, and Franklin Didi. *Guide juif de France*. Paris: Migdal, 1971.

Berg, Roger, and Marianne Urbah-Bornstein. *Les Juifs devant le droit français: Législation et jurisprudence fin XIXᵉ siècle à nos jours*. Paris: Les Belles Lettres, 1984.

Berman, Léon. *Histoire des Juifs de France*. Paris: Lipschutz, 1937.

Birnbaum, Pierre, ed. *Histoire politique des Juifs de France*. Paris: Presses de la Fondation Nationale des Sciences Politiques, 1990.

Birnbaum, Pierre. *Destins juifs: De la Révolution française à Carpentras*. Paris: Calmann-Lévy, 1995.

Blumenkranz, Bernhard, with the assistance of Monique Lévy. *Bibliographie des Juifs en France*. Toulouse: Privat, 1974.

Blumenkranz, Bernhard. *Les Juifs en France: Écrits dispersés*. Paris: Commission Française des Archives Juives, 1989.

———, ed. *Documents modernes sur les Juifs, XVIᵉ-XXᵉ siècles*. Volume 1. Toulouse: Privat, 1979.

———, ed. *Histoire des Juifs en France*. Toulouse: Privat, 1972.

Bourdrel, Philippe. *Histoire des Juifs de France*. Paris: Albin Michel, 1974.

Catane, Mosche. *Des Croisades à nos jours*. Paris: Minuit, 1956.

Chemouilli, Henri. *Une diaspora méconnu: les Juifs d'Algérie*. Paris: IMP, 1976.

Chevalier, Yves. *L'Anti-sémitisme: Le Juif comme bouc-émissaire*. Paris: Cerf, 1988.

Chouraqui, André. *Histoire des Juifs en Afrique du Nord*. Paris: Hachette, 1985.

Delmaire, Danielle. "Les Communautés juives septentrionales 1791–1939: Naissance, croissance, épanouissement." 3 volumes. Ph.D. dissertation, Université Charles de Gaulle–Lille 3, 1998.

Delpech, François. *Sur les Juifs: Études d'histoire contemporaine*. Lyons: Presses Universitaires de Lyon, 1983.

Encyclopaedia Judaica. New English edition. 17 volumes. Jerusalem: Keter, 1972.

Frankel, Jonathan, and Steven J. Zipperstein, eds. *Assimilation and Community: The Jews in Nineteenth Century Europe*. Cambridge: Cambridge University Press, 1992.

Girard, Patrick. *Juifs de France*. Paris: Bruno Huisman, 1983.

———. *Pour le meilleur et pour le pire: Vingt siècles d'histoire juive en France*. Paris: Bibliophane, 1986.

Iancu, Danièle, and Carol Iancu. *Les Juifs du Midi: Une histoire millénaire*. Avignon: A. Barthélemy, 1995.

Klein, Luce A. *Portrait de la Juive dans la littérature française*. Paris: Nizet, 1970.

Kriegel, Annie. *Les Juifs et le Monde moderne: Essai sur la logique d'émancipation*. Paris: Seuil, 1977.

———. *Réflexions sur les questions juives*. Paris: Hachette, 1984.

Las, Nelly. *Femmes juives dans le siècle: Histoire du Conseil international des femmes juives de 1899 à nos jours*. Paris: L'Harmattan, 1996.

Lehrmann, C. *L'Élément juif dans la littérature française*. 2 volumes. Paris: Albin Michel, 1960–1961.

Lévy, Monique, and Marianne Urbah. *Histoire religieuse des Juifs de France: Bibliographie*. Covers works published 1974–1996. Paris: Cahiers de la CFAJ (n.s.), 1996.

Lévy, Paul. *Les Noms des israélites en France*. Paris: Presses Universitaires de France, 1960.

Malino, Frances, and Bernard Wasserstein, eds. *The Jews in Modern France*. Hanover, N.H.: Brandeis University Press, 1985.

Perchenet, Annie. *Histoire des Juifs de France*. Paris: Cerf, 1988.

Philippe, Béatrice. *Être juif dans la société française: Du Moyen Age à nos jours.* 1979. Revised and expanded edition, Brussels: Complexe, 1998.

Poliakov, Léon. *Histoire de l'antisémitisme.* 2 volumes. 1955. Reprint, Paris: Seuil, 1991.

Priollaud, Nicole, Victor Ziegelman, and Laurent Goldberg. *Images de la mémoire juive: Immigration et intégration en France depuis 1880.* Paris: Liana Levi, 1994.

Rabi, [Wladimir]. *Anatomie du judaïsme français.* Paris: Éditions de Minuit, 1962.

Roblin, Michel. *Les Juifs de Paris: Démographie, économie, culture.* Paris: Picard, 1952.

Schnapper, Dominique. *Juifs et Israélites.* Paris: Gallimard, 1980.

Schwarzfuchs, Simon. *Brève Histoire des Juifs de France.* Paris: Keren Hasefer, [1950].

———. *Les Juifs de France.* Paris: Albin Michel, 1975.

Silvain, Gérard, and Élie Szapiro. *Les Juifs en terre de France à travers la carte postale.* Paris: Bibliophane, 1987.

Simon-Nahum, Perrine. "Être juif en France." In Philippe Ariès and Georges Duby, editors-in-chief, *Histoire de la vie privée.* Volume 5: Antoine Prost and Gérard Vincent, eds., *De la Première Guerre mondiale à nos jours.* Paris: Seuil, 1987.

Taïeb, Jacques. *Être juif au Maghreb à la veille de la colonisation.* Paris: Albin Michel, 1994.

Trigano, Schmuel, ed. *La Société juive à travers l'histoire.* 4 volumes. Paris: Fayard, 1992–1993.

Vidal-Naquet, Pierre. *Les Juifs, la Mémoire et le Présent.* 3 volumes. Paris: La Découverte, 1981–1995.

Wardi, Charlotte. *Le Juif dans le roman français.* Paris: Nizet, 1973.

Wigoder, Geoffrey, editor-in-chief. *The Encyclopedia of Judaism.* New York: Macmillan, 1989.

Wistrich, Robert. *Antisemitism: The Longest Hatred.* New York: Pantheon, 1991.

Yardeni, Myriam. *Les Juifs dans l'histoire de France.* Leiden: Brill, 1980.

Three journals are of particular value in studying the history of the Jews of France: *Archives juives*, the *Revue des études juives*, and *Pardès*. Note, too, the following special issues:

L'Arche 402 (January 1991): "Être juif en France."

Les Cahiers du Judaïsme (Fall 1998): "Carrefours français."

Histoire 3 (1979): "Les Juifs en France."

L'Histoire 135 (July-August 1990): "Chrétiens, Juifs, et Musulmans en France: Du baptême de Clovis aux mosquées de la République."

L'Histoire 148 (October 1991): "L'Antisémitisme en France: De l'affaire Dreyfus à l'affaire Carpentras."

Monuments historiques 191 (February 1994): "Le Patrimoine Juif français."

Notre Histoire 110 (April 1994): "Les Juifs de France: Des ghettos à la liberté."

Pardès 3 (1986): "Paris-Jérusalem."

Pardès 14 (1991): "Histoire contemporaine et Sociologie des Juifs de France."

Chapter Bibliographies

Chapter 1: The Origins of the Jewish Presence in Gaul
Chapter 2: Nobles' Jews, Kings' Jews

Agus, Irving A. *The Heroic Age of Franco-German Jewry.* New York: Yeshiva University Press, 1969.

Baron, Salo W. *A Social and Religious History of the Jews.* 3 vols. New York: Columbia University Press, 1952–1957.

Bauer, Jules. "Les Juifs de la principauté d'Orange." *Revue des études juives* 32 (1896): 236–249.

Berlioz, Jacques. "Le procès de l'usurier." *L'Histoire* 204 (November 1996): 40–41. [Relevant also for chapter 3.]

Blumenkranz, Bernhard. "Du nouveau sur Bodo-Éléazar." *Revue des études juives* 112 (1953): 35–42.

———. *Juifs et Chrétiens dans le monde occidental, 430–1096.* Paris and The Hague: Mouton, 1960.

———. "Les Juifs en Gaule romaine." *Archeologia* 38 (January-February 1971): 62–65.

Busquet, Raoul. "La fin de la communauté juive de Marseille au XVᵉ siècle." *Revue des études juives* 83 (1927): 163–183.

———. "Les privilèges généraux et la conservation des privilèges des Juifs de Provence." *Mémoires de l'Institut historique de Provence* 4 (1927): 68–86.

Chazan, Robert. *In the Year 1096: The First Crusade and the Jews.* Philadelphia: Jewish Publication Society of America, 1996.

———. "Jewish Settlement in Northern France, 1096-1306." *Revue des études juives* 128, no. 1 (1969): 41–65.

———. *Medieval Jewry in Northern France: A Political and Social History.* Baltimore: Johns Hopkins University Press, 1973.

Cohen, Esther. *The Crossroads of Justice: Law and Culture in Late Medieval France.* Leiden: Brill, 1993. [See especially chapter 6, "The Rituals of Exclusion: Women and the Jews."]

Cohen, Jeremy. *The Friars and the Jews: The Evolution of Medieval Anti-Judaism.* Ithaca: Cornell University Press, 1982.

Coulet, Noël. "L'expulsion des Juifs de France." *L'Histoire* 139 (December 1990): 9–16.

Crémieux, Adolphe. "Les Juifs de Marseille au Moyen Age." *Revue des études juives* 46 (1903): 1–47, 246–268; 47 (1903): 62–86, 243–261. [Relevant also for chapter 3.]

Dahan, Gilbert. *Les Intellectuals chrétiens et les Juifs au Moyen Age.* Paris: Cerf, 1990.

———. *La Polémique chrétienne contre le judaïsme au Moyen Age.* Paris: Albin Michel, 1991.

Eidelberg, Shlomo, ed. and trans. *The Jews and the Crusades: The Hebrew Chronicles of the First and Second Crusades.* Madison: University of Wisconsin Press, 1977.

Galabert, F. "Alphonse de Poitiers et les Juifs." *Science catholique* 16 (October 1902): 1015–1024.

Gauthier, Léon. "Les Juifs dans les deux Bourgognes." *Revue des études juives* 48 (1904): 208–299; 49 (1904): 1–17, 244–261.

Golb, Norman. *Les Juifs de Rouen au Moyen Age: Portrait d'une culture oubliée.* Rouen: Publications de l'Université de Rouen, 1985. [Relevant also for chapter 3.]

———. "New Light on the Persecution of French Jews at the Time of the First Crusade." *Proceedings of American Academy for Jewish Research* 34 (1966): 1–64.

Graboïs, Aryeh. "Le crédit juif à Paris au temps de Saint Louis." *Revue des études juives* 129 (January-March 1970): 5–22. [Relevant also for chapter 3.]

———. "Le souvenir et la légende de Charlemagne dans les textes hébaïques médiévaux." *Le Moyen Age* 72 (1966): 5–41.

Grayzel, Salomon. *The Church and the Jews in the Thirteenth Century.* 1933. Revised edition, New York: Hermon Press, 1966.

Iancu-Agou, Daniéle. "L'expulsion des Juifs de la Provence médiévale." In Daniel Tollet, ed., *Politique et Religion dans le judaïsme ancien et médiéval,* 300–308. Paris: Desclée de Brouwer, 1989.

Josselin, Maurice. "Les marchands juifs appelés 'Radanites.'" *Revue des études juives* 54 (1907): 141–146.

Katz, Jacob. *Exclusiveness and Tolerance: Studies in Jewish-Gentile Relations in Medieval and Modern Times.* London: Oxford University Press, 1961.

Kohn, Roger. *Les Juifs de la France du Nord dans la seconde moitié du XIVe siècle.* Louvain: Peeters, 1988.

———. "L'expulsion des Juifs de France en 1394: les chemins de l'exil et les refuges." *Archives juives* 28, no. 1 (1995): 76-84.

Kriegel, Maurice. *Les Juifs à la fin du Moyen Age dans l'Europe méditerranéenne.* Paris: Hachette, 1979. [Relevant also for chapter 3.]

Langmuir, Gavin I. *History, Religion, and Antisemitism.* Berkeley and Los Angeles: University of California Press, 1990.

———. *Toward a Definition of Antisemitism.* Berkeley and Los Angeles: University of California Press, 1990.

Lazard, Lucien. "Les Revenus tirés des Juifs de France dans le domaine royale (XIIIe siècle)," *Revue des études juives* 15 (1887): 233–261.

Le Goff, Jacques. *Saint Louis.* Paris: Gallimard, 1996.

Lévy, Israël. "Les Juifs de France du milieu du IXe siècle aux Croisades." *Revue des études juives* 52 (1906): 161–168.

Loeb, Isidore. "La controverse de 1240 sur le Talmud." *Revue des études juives* 1 (1880): 247–261; 2 (1881): 248–270; 3 (1881): 39–57.

Luce, Siméon. "Catalogue des documents du Trésor des Chartes relatifs aux Juifs sous le règne de Philippe le Bel." *Revue des études juives* 2 (1881): 15–72.

Monod, Bernard. "Juifs, sorciers et hérétiques au Moyen Age après les Mémoires d'un moine du XIe siècle (Guibert de Nogent)." *Revue des études juives* 46 (1903): 237–245.

Nahon, Gérard. "Le crédit et les Juifs dans la France du XIIIe siècle." *Annales ESC* 5 (September-October 1969): 1121–1148.

———. "Une géographie des Juifs dans la France de Louis IX, 1226–1270." In *The Fifth World Congress of Jewish Studies* (Jerusalem, 1972), 2:127–132. [Relevant also for chapter 3.]

———. "Les Juifs dans les domaines d'Alfonse de Poitiers, 1241–1271." *Revue des études juives* 125 (January-September 1966): 167–211.

Nahon, Gérard. "Les ordonnances de Saint Louis sur les Juifs." *Les Nouveaux Cahiers* 23 (1970): 18–35.

———. "Pour une géographie administrative des Juifs dans la France de Saint Louis." *Revue historique* 254 (1975): 305–343. [Relevant also for chapter 3.]

Parkes, James W. *The Conflict of the Church and the Synagogue: A Study in the Origins of Anti-Semitism*. 1934. Reprint, New York: Atheneum, 1969.

———. *The Jew in the Medieval Community: A Study of His Political and Economic Situation*. 1938. Reprint, New York: Hermon Press, 1976. [Relevant also for chapter 3.]

Pflaum, Heinz. "Les scènes de Juifs dans la littérature dramatique du Moyen Age." *Revue des études juives* 89 (1930): 111–134.

Régné, Jean. "Étude sur la condition des Juifs de Narbonne du Vᵉ au Xᵉ siècle." *Revue des études juives* 55 (1908): 1–36, 221-243; 58 (1909): 75–105, 200–225; 59 (1910): 58–89; 61 (1911): 228–254; 62 (1911): 1–27, 248–266; 63 (1912): 75–99.

Reinach, Théodore. "Agobard et les Juifs." *Revue des études juives* 50 (1905): 81–111.

Roth, Cecil, ed. *The Dark Ages: Jews in Christian Europe, 711-1096*. Volume 11, *World History of the Jewish History*. New Brunswick, N.J.: Rutgers University Press, 1966.

Schäfer, Peter. *Histoire des Juifs dans l'Antiquité*. Translated by P. Schulte. Paris: Cerf, 1989.

Schwarzfuchs, Simon. "De la condition des Juifs de France au XIIᵉ et XIIIᵉ siècles." *Revue des études juives* 125 (January-September, 1966): 221–232.

Shatzmiller, Joseph. "Les Juifs de Provence pendant la peste Noire." *Revue des études juives* 133 (July-December 1974): 457-480.

———. *Shylock Reconsidered: Jews, Moneylending, and Medieval Society*. Berkeley and Los Angeles: University of California Press, 1990. [Relevant also for chapter 3.]

Trachtenberg, Joshua. *The Devil and the Jews: The Medieval Conception of the Jews and Its Relation to Modern Antisemitism*. 1943. Reprint, New York: Meridian Books, 1961.

Yerushalmi, Yosef Hayim. "The Inquisition and the Jews of France in the Time of Bernard Gui." *Harvard Theological Review* 63 (1970): 317–376.

Chapter 3: Jewish Life in the Middle Ages

Abrahams, Israel. *Jewish Life in the Middle Ages*. 1896. Reprint, New York: Atheneum, 1969.

Agus, Jacob Bernard. *The Evolution of Jewish Thought: From Biblical Times to the Opening of the Modern Era*. London and New York: Abelard-Schuman, 1959.

Blau, Joseph L. *The Story of Jewish Philosophy*. New York: Random House, 1962.

Blumenkranz, Bernhard, ed. *Art et archéologie des Juifs en France médiévale*. Toulouse: Privat, 1980.

Catane, Moché. *La Vie juive en France au XIᵉ siècle d'après les écrits de Rachi*. Jerusalem: Éditions Françaises Gallia, 1994.

Dahan, Gilbert, ed. *Gersonide en son temps: science et philosophie médiévales*. Louvain: Peeters, 1991.

Finkelstein, Louis. *Jewish Self-Government in the Middle Ages*. 1924. Reprint, New York: Feldheim, 1964.

Freudenthal, Gad, ed. *Studies on Gersonides: A Fourteenth-Century Jewish Philosopher-Scientist.* Leiden: Brill, 1992.

Goetschel, Roland. *La Kabbale.* 1985. Revised edition, Paris: Presses Universitaires de France, 1989.

Guttmann, Julius. *Philosophies of Judaism: The History of Jewish Philosophy from Biblical Times to Franz Rosenzweig.* Translated by David W. Silverman. New York: Holt, Rinehart and Winston, 1964.

Hailperin, Herman. *Rashi and the Christian Scholars.* Pittsburgh: University of Pittsburgh Press, 1963.

Hayoun, Maurice-Ruben. *Maïmonide.* Paris: Presses Universitaires de France, 1987.

———. *La Philosophie et la Théologie de Moïse de Narbonne (1300–1362).* Tübingen: Mohr, 1989.

Katz, Jacob. *Tradition and Crisis: Jewish Society at the End of the Middle Ages.* 1961. Reprint, New York: Schocken, 1977.

Libera, Alain de. *La Philosophie médiévale.* Paris: Presses Universitaires de France, 1993.

Nahon, Gérard. "L'archéologie juive de la France médiévale: Réalité et problème." *Archéologie médiévale* 5 (1975): 139–159.

———. "La communauté juive de Paris au XIIIᵉ siècle: Problèmes topographiques, démographiques et institutionnels," 143–156. *Actes du 100ᵉ Congrès national des Sociétés savantes.* Paris: Bibliothèque Nationale, 1978.

Rabinowitz, Louis Isaac. *The Social Life of the Jews of Northern France in the XII-XIVᵗʰ Centuries as Reflected in the Rabbinical Literature of the Period.* London: E. Goldston, 1938.

Scholem, Gershom. *Major Trends in Jewish Mysticism.* 1941. 3rd revised edition, New York: Schocken Books, 1954.

Schwarzfuchs, Simon. *Kahal: la Communauté juive de l'Europe médiévale.* Paris: Maisonneuve et Larose, 1986.

———. *Rachi de Troyes.* Paris: Albin Michel, 1991.

Sed-Rajna, Gabrielle, ed. *Rashi, 1040–1990: Congrès européen des études juives.* Paris: Cerf, 1993.

Shatzmiller, Joseph. "Notes sur les médecins juifs en Provence au Moyen Age." *Revue des études juives* 128 (April-September 1969): 259–273.

———. *Recherches sur la communauté juive de Manosque au Moyen Age, 1241–1329.* Paris and The Hague: Mouton, 1973.

Silver, Daniel Jeremy. *Maimonidean Criticism and the Maimonidean Controversy, 1180–1240.* Leiden: Brill, 1965.

Sirat, Colette. *La Philosophie juive au Moyen Age selon les textes manuscrits et les imprimés.* Paris: Éditions du Centre National de la Recherche Scientifique, 1983.

Sperber, Manès, ed. *Rachi.* Paris: Service Technique pour l'Éducation, 1974.

Stow, Kenneth R. *Alienated Minority: The Jews of Medieval Latin Europe.* Cambridge, Mass.: Harvard University Press, 1992.

Talmadge, Frank. *David Kimhi: The Man and the Commentaries.* Cambridge, Mass.: Harvard University Press, 1976.

Touati, Charles. *La Pensée philosophique et théologique de Gersonide.* Paris: Minuit, 1973.

———. *Prophètes, talmudistes, philosophes.* Paris: Cerf, 1990.

Twersky, Isadore. "Aspects of the Social History of Provençal Jewry." *Cahiers d'histoire mondiale* 11 (1968): 185–207.

―――. *Introduction to the Code of Maimonides (Mishneh Torah)*. New Haven: Yale University Press, 1980.

―――. *Rabad of Posquières: A Twelfth-Century Talmudist*. Cambridge, Mass.: Harvard University Press, 1962.

Vajda, Georges. *Introduction à la pensée juive du Moyen Age*. Paris: Vrin, 1947.

Vicaire, Marie-Humbert, and Bernhard Blumenkranz, eds. *Juifs et Judaïsme de Languedoc, XIIIe siècle-début XIVe siècle*. Toulouse: Privat, 1977.

Chapter 4: The Jews of the South

Bardinet, Léon. "Antiquité et organisation des juiveries du Comtat Venaissin." *Revue des études juives* 1 (1880): 262–292.

―――. "Condition civile des Juifs du Comtat Venassin pendant le séjour des papes à Avignon (1309–1376)." *Revue historique* 13 (1880): 1–43.

―――. "Condition civile des Juifs du Comtat Venassin pendant le XVe siècle (1380–1409)." *Revue des études juives* 6 (1882): 1–40.

―――. "Les Juifs du Comtat Venaissin au Moyen Age: leur rôle économique et intellectuel." *Revue historique* 14 (1880): 1–60.

Bauer, Jules. "Le chapeau jaune chez les Juifs comtadins." *Revue des études juives* 36 (1898): 53–64.

Bedos-Razak, Brigitte. "Tolérance et raison d'État: le problème juif." In Henry Méchoulan, ed., *L'État baroque: Regards sur la pensée politique de la France du premier XVIIe siècle*, 245–287. Paris: Vrin, 1985.

Benbassa, Esther, ed. *Mémoires juives d'Espagne et du Portugal*. Paris: Publisud, 1996. [Articles relating to France useful also for chapters 7 and 13.]

Brunschvicq, Léon. "Les Juifs de Nantes et du pays nantais." *Revue des études juives* 14 (1887): 80–91; 17 (1888): 125–142; 19 (1889): 294–305.

Cahen, Abraham. "Les Juifs dans les colonies françaises au XVIIIe siècle." *Revue des études juives* 4 (1882): 127–145, 236–248; 5 (1882): 68–92, 258–272.

Castellani, Christian. "Le rôle économique de la communauté juive de Carpentras au début du XVe siècle." *Annales ESC* 27 (1972): 583–611.

Cavignac, Jean. *Dictionnaire du judaïsme bordelais aux XVIIIe et XIXe siècles: Biographies, généalogies, professions, institutions*. Bordeaux: Archives Départementales de la Gironde, 1987. [Relevant also for chapter 8.]

―――. *Les Israélites bordelais de 1780 à 1850: Autour de l'émancipation*. Paris: Publisud, 1991. [Relevant also for chapter 8.]

Cirot, Georges. *Recherches sur les Juifs espagnols et portugais à Bordeaux*. Bordeaux: Feret et Fils, 1909.

Iancu, Carol, ed. *Les Juifs à Montpellier et dans le Languedoc: Du Moyen Age à nos jours*. Montpellier: Centre de Recherches et d'Études Juives et Hébraïques, 1988.

Iancu, Danièle. *Les Juifs en Provence*. Marseilles: Institut Historique de Provence, 1981.

Kahn, Salomon. "Les Juifs de Montpellier au XVIIIe siècle." *Revue des études juives* 33 (1896): 283–303. [Relevant also for chapter 5.]

―――. "Les Juifs à Nîmes au XVIIe et au XVIIIe siècle." *Revue des études juives* 67 (1914): 225–261. [Relevant also for chapter 5.]

Kohnstamm, Jackie A., and René Moulinas. "Archaïsme et traditions locales: le mariage chez les Juifs d'Avignon et du Comtat au dernier siècle avant l'émancipation." *Revue des études juives* 138 (January-June 1979): 89–115.

Léon, Henry. *Histoire des Juifs de Bayonne*. Paris: Durlacher, 1893.

Loeb, Isidore. "Les Juifs de Carpentras sous le government pontifical." *Revue des études juives* 12 (1886): 34–64, 161-235.

Lunel, Armand. *Juifs du Languedoc, de la Provence et des États français du pape*. Paris: Albin Michel, 1975.

Malino, Frances. *The Sephardic Jews of Bordeaux: Assimilation and Emancipation in Revolutionary and Napoleonic France*. Tuscaloosa: University of Alabama Press, 1978.

Malvezin, Théophile. *Histoire des Juifs à Bordeaux*. Bordeaux: Lefebvre, 1875.

———. *Histoire du commerce de Bordeaux depuis les origines jusqu'à nos jours*. Bordeaux: A. Bellier, 1892.

Mossé, Armand. *Histoire des Juifs d'Avignon et du Comtat Venaissin*. 1934. Reprint, Marseilles: Lafitte, 1976.

Moulinas, René. "Avignon, terre d'asile des Juifs." *L'Histoire* 41 (1982): 28–37.

———. *Les Juifs du pape*. Paris: Albin Michel, 1992.

———. *Les Juifs du pape en France: les communautés d'Avignon et du Comtat Venaissin aux XVIIe et XVIIIe siècles*. Toulouse: Privat, 1981.

Mrejen-O'Hana, Simone. "La Famille juive au XVIIIe siècle d'après les registres 'paroissiaux' de Carpentras et du Comtat Venaissin." Ph.D. dissertation, EPHE, 1998.

———. "Le mariage juif sous l'Ancien Régime: L'exemple de Carpentras (1763–1792)." *Annales de démographie historique* (1993): 161–170.

———. "Pratiques et comportements religieux dans les 'quatre saintes communautés' d'Avignon et du Comtat Venaissin au XVIIIe siècle." *Archives juives* 28, no. 2 (1995): 12–18.

Nahon, Gérard. "Communautés espagnoles et portuguaises de France (1492–1992)." In Henry Méchoulan, ed., *Les Juifs d'Espagne: Histoire d'une diaspora 1492–1992*, 111–144. Paris: Liana Levi, 1992.

———. "Démographie des Juifs portuguais à Saint-Esprit-lès-Bayonne (1751–1787): Age au mariage, fécondité, famille." *Bulletin de la Société des sciences, lettres et arts de Bayonne* (1976): 155–202.

———. *Métropoles et Périphéries séfarades d'Occident*. Paris: Cerf, 1993.

———. "Le modèle français du marranisme: perspectives nouvelles." In *Inquisiçâo: Ensaios sobre mentalidade, heresias e arte*, 227–265. Proceeedings of the International Congress held in São Paulo, May 1987. Edited by Anita Novinsky and Maria Luiza Tucci Carneiro. Rio de Janeiro: Edusp, 1992.

———. "La nation juive portuguaise en France XVIe-XVIIIe siècle: espaces et pouvoirs." *Revue des études juives* 153 (July-December 1994): 353–382.

Nahon, Gérard, ed. *Les Nations juives portuguaises du sud-ouest de la France (1684–1791)*. Paris: Fondation Calouste Gulbenkian, 1981.

Prévot, Philippe. *Histoire du ghetto d'Avignon*. Originally published in 1941 as *A travers la carrière d'Avignon: Avignon, l'an du monde 5702*. Avignon: Aubanel, 1995.

Revah, I. S. "Les marranes." *Revue des études juives* 118 (1959–1960): 29–77.

Roubin, N. "La vie commerciale des Juifs comtadins en Languedoc au XVIIIe siècle." *Revue des études juives* 34 (1897): 276–293; 35 (1897): 91–105; 36 (1898): 75–100.

Secret, François. "Glanes pour servir à l'histoire des Juifs en France, à la Renaissance." *Revue des études juives* 115 (January-December 1956): 87–107.

———. "Notes pour l'histoire des Juifs en France." *Revue des études juives* 125 (January-September 1966): 233–243.

Shatzmiller, Joseph. *Recherches sur la communauté juive de Manosque.* Paris and The Hague: Mouton, 1973.

Szajkowski, Zosa. "Trade relations in France with the Iberian Peninsula in the Sixteenth and Seventeenth Centuries." *Jewish Quarterly Review* 1 (1959–1960): 69–78.

Zink, Anne. "Une niche juridique: L'installation des Juifs à Saint-Esprit-lès-Bayonne au XVIIe siècle." *Annales HSS* 49 (May-June 1994): 639–669.

Chapter 5: The Jews of the East and of Paris

Anchel, Robert. "Les Juifs à Paris au XVIIIe siècle." *Bulletin de la Société de l'histoire de Paris et de l'Ile-de-France* 59 (1932): 10–12.

———. "Les Lettres-Patentes du 10 juillet 1784." *Revue des études juives* 93 (1932): 113–134.

Archives juives 27, no. 2 (1994). Special feature: "Les Juifs de Lorraine."

Aron, Maurice. "Le duc de Lorraine Léopold et les Juifs." *Revue des études juives* 34 (1897): 107–116.

Association Mosellane pour la Conservation de Patrimoine Juif. *Du Ghetto à la Nation (1721-1871).* Exhibition catalogue. Metz, 1990. [Relevant also for chapters 6 and 8.]

Burguière, André. "Groupe d'immigrants ou minorité religieuse: Les Juifs à Paris au XVIIIe siècle." In *Le Migrant en France*, 183–200. Proceedings of the Aurillac Colloquium, 5-7 June 1985. Aurillac, 1986.

Cahen, Abraham. "Le rabbinat de Metz pendant la période française, 1567–1871." *Revue des études juives* 7 (1883): 103–115, 204–226; 8 (1884): 255–274; 12 (1886): 283–297; 13 (1886): 105–126.

———. "Règlements somptuaires de la communauté juive de Metz à la fin du XVIIe siècle, 1690–1697." *Annuaire de la Société des études juives* 1 (1882): 75–121.

Clément, Roger. *La Condition des Juifs de Metz dans l'Ancien Régime.* Paris: Jouve, 1903.

Daltroff, Jean. *Les Juifs de Niedervisse.* Sarreguemines: Société d'Histoire et d'Archéologie des Pays de la Nied, 1992.

Ginsburger, Moïse. "Les Juifs de Metz sous l'Ancien Régime." *Revue des études juives* 50 (1905): 112–128, 238–260.

———. "Les premiers imprimeurs juifs en France." *Revue des études juives* 86 (1928): 47–57.

Godechot, Jacques. "Les Juifs de Nancy de 1789 à 1797." *Revue des études juives* 86 (1928): 1–35.

Gruss, Noé. "L'imprimerie hébraïque en France (XVIe-XIXe siècles). *Revue des études juives* 125 (January-September 1966): 77–91.

Hemerdinger, Gabriel. "Le dénombrement des Juifs d'Alsace (1784)." *Revue des études juives* 42 (1901): 253–264.

Hildenfinger, Paul. *Documents sur les Juifs à Paris au XVIIIᵉ siècle*. Paris: Champion, 1913.

Job, Françoise. *Les Juifs de Lunéville au XVIIIᵉ et XIXᵉ siècles*. Nancy: Presses Universitaires de Nancy, 1989. [Relevant also for chapter 8.]

———. *Les Juifs de Nancy du XIIᵉ au XXᵉ siècle*. Nancy: Presses Universitaires de Nancy, 1991. [Relevant also for chapter 8.]

Kahn, Léon. *Les Juifs de Paris sous Louis XV (1721–1760)*. Paris: Durlacher, 1892.

Loeb, Isidore. "Les Juifs à Strasbourg depuis 1349 jusqu'à la Révolution." *Annuaire de la Société des études juives* 2 (1882): 137–198.

———. "Rabbi Joselman de Rosheim." *Revue des études juives* 2 (1881): 271–277; 5 (1882): 93–103.

Meyer, Pierre-André. *La Communauté juive de Metz au XVIIIᵉ siècle*. Nancy and Metz: Presses Universitaires de Nancy/Éditions Serpenoise, 1993.

———. *Histoire des Juifs de Lorraine: Bibliographie*. Paris: Cahiers de la Commission Française des Archives Juives (n.s.), 1994. [Relevant also for chapter 8.]

Monin, H. "Les Juifs de Paris à la fin de l'Ancien Régime." *Revue des études juives* 23 (1891): 85–98.

Nahon, Gérard. "Papiers de la communauté des Juifs portugais de Paris de 1785 à 1790." *Revue des études juives* 129, no.1 (1970): 43–65.

Raphaël, Freddy. *L'Imagerie juive d'Alsace*. Strasbourg: Istra, 1979.

Raphaël, Freddy, and Robert Weyl. *Juifs en Alsace: Culture, société, histoire*. Toulouse: Privat, 1977.

———. *Regards nouveaux sur les Juifs d'Alsace*. Strasbourg: Istra, 1980.

Rochette, Jacqueline. *Histoire des Juifs d'Alsace des origines à la Révolution*. Paris: Lipschutz, 1939.

Scheid, Élie. *Histoire des Juifs d'Alsace*. 1887. Reprint, Strasbourg: Fischer, 1975.

———. *Histoire des Juifs de Haguenau suivie des recensements de 1763, 1784, et 1808*. Paris: Durlacher, 1885.

Stern, Selma. *The Court Jew: A Contribution to the History of the Period of Absolutism in Central Europe*. Philadelphia: Jewish Publication Society of America, 1950.

Weill, Georges. "L'intendant d'Alsace et la centralisation de la nation juive d'après les réformes des la fiscalité." *Dix-Huitième Siècle* 13 (1981): 181–203.

———. "Recherches sur la démographie des Juifs d'Alsace du XVIᵉ au XVIIIᵉ siècle." *Revue des études juives* 130 (January-March 1971): 51–89.

Chapter 6: On the Way to Emancipation

Altman, Alexander. *Moses Mendelssohn: A Biographical Study*. Philadelphia: Jewish Publication Society of America/University of Alabama Press, 1973.

Aubery, Pierre. "Voltaire et les Juifs, ironie et démystification." *Studies on Voltaire and the Eighteenth Century* 24 (1963): 67–79.

Badinter, Robert. *Libres et Égaux*. Paris: Fayard, 1989.

Berkovitz, Jay R. *The Shaping of Jewish Identity in Nineteenth-Century France*. Detroit: Wayne State University Press, 1989. [Relevant also for chapter 7.]

Blumenkranz, Bernhard, ed. *Juifs en France au XVIIIᵉ siècle*. Paris: Commission Française des Archives Juives, 1994.

Blumenkranz, Bernard, and Albert Soboul, eds. *Les Juifs et la Révolution française: Problèmes et aspirations.* Toulouse: Privat, 1976. [Relevant also for chapter 8.]

Bush, Newell Richard. "The Marquis d'Argens and his Philosophical Correspondence: A Critical Study of d'Argens's *Lettres juives, Lettres cabalistiques,* and *Lettres chinoises.*" Ann Arbor: University of Michigan Microfilms, 1953.

Cahen, Abraham. "L'émancipation des Juifs devant la Société royale de Metz en 1787 et M. Roederer." *Revue des études juives* 1 (1880): 83–104.

Daltroff, Jean. "La vie économique des juifs d'Alsace à l'époque révolutionnaire." *Revue d'Alsace* 116 (1989–1990): 173–186.

Dohm, Christian Wilhelm von. *De la réforme politique des Juifs.* Translated by J. Bernoulli. First French edition, 1782. Reprint, Paris: Stock, 1984.

Emmrich, Hanna. *Zur Behandlung des Judentums bei Voltaire.* Breslau: Priebatsch, 1930.

Feuerwerker, David. *L'Émancipation des Juifs en France de l'Ancien Régime à la fin du Second Empire.* Paris: Albin Michel, 1976. [Relevant also for chapter 7.]

———. "Les Juifs en France. Anatomie de 207 cahiers de doléances de 1789." *Annales ESC* 20 (1965): 45–61.

Furtado, Abraham. *Mémoire d'Abraham Furtado sur l'état des Juifs en France jusqu'à la Révolution.* Edited by Gabrielle Moyse. Paris: Durlacher, 1930.

Girard, Patrick. *La Révolution française et les Juifs.* Paris: Laffont, 1989.

Graetz, Heinrich. "Voltaire und die Juden." *Monatsschrift für die Geschichte und Wissenschaft des Judentums* 17 (1868): 161–174, 201–223.

Grégoire, Henri-Baptiste. *Essai sur la régénération physique, morale et politique des Juifs.* 1789. Reprint, Paris: Flammarion, 1988.

Grosclaude, Pierre. *Malesherbes, témoin et interprète de son temps.* Paris: Fischbacher, 1961.

Grunebaum-Ballin, Paul. "Grégoire convertisseur? ou la croyance au 'Retour d'Israël.'" *Revue des études juives* 121 (1962): 383–398.

Hadas-Lebel, Mireille, and Évelyne Oliel-Grausz, eds. *Les Juifs et la Révolution française: Histoire et mentalités.* Proceedings of a Colloquium held at the Collège de France and the École Normale Supérieure, 16–18 May 1989. Louvain: Peeters, 1992.

Hagani, Baruch. *L'Émancipation des Juifs.* Paris: Rieder, 1928.

Hertzberg, Arthur. *The French Enlightenment and the Jews.* New York and Philadelphia: Columbia University Press and Jewish Publication Society of America, 1968.

Kahn, Léon. *Les Juifs de Paris pendant la Révolution.* 1898. Reprint, New York: B. Frantlin, 1968.

Katz, Jacob. *Jewish Emancipation and Self-Emancipation.* Philadelphia: Jewish Publication Society of America, 1986. [Relevant also for chapter 10.]

———. *Out of the Ghetto: The Social Background of Jewish Emancipation, 1770–1870.* Cambridge, Mass.: Harvard University Press, 1973.

Levy, Alphonse. "Jean-Jacques Rousseau und das Judentum." *Monatsschrift für die Geschichte und Wissenschaft des Judentums* 56 (1912): 641–663.

Liber, Maurice. "Les Juifs et la convocation des États généraux (1789)." *Revue des études juives* 63 (1912): 185–210; 64 (1912): 89–108; 65 (1913): 89–133; 66 (1913): 161–212.

Malino, Frances. *A Jew in the French Revolution: The Life of Zalkind Hourwitz.* Oxford: Blackwell, 1996.

————. "The Right to Be Equal: Zalkind Hourwitz and the Revolution of 1789." In Frances Malino and David Sorkin, eds., *From East and West: Jews in a Changing Europe, 1750–1870,* 85–106. Oxford: Basil Blackwell, 1990.

Meyer, Paul A. "The Attitude of the Enlightenment Towards the Jew." *Studies on Voltaire and the Eighteenth Century* 26 (1963): 1161–1215.

Montesquieu, Charles de Secondat de. *De l'esprit des lois.* Edited by Laurent Versini. Volume 2. Paris: Gallimard, 1995.

————. *Lettres persanes.* Edited by Laurent Versini. Paris: Flammarion, 1995.

Necheles, Ruth. *The Abbé Grégoire, 1787–1831: The Odyssey of an Egalitarian.* Westport, Conn.: Greenwood, 1971.

Reinach, Théodore. "Les Juifs dans l'opinion chrétienne aux XVIIe et XVIIIe siècles: Peuchet et Diderot." *Revue des études juives* 8 (1884): 138–144

Reissner, Hans. "La politique juive de Mirabeau." *Revue d'histoire économique et sociale* 16 (1928): 812–819.

Rousseau, Jean-Jacques. *Émile ou De l'éducation.* Edited by C. Wirz and P. Burgelin. Paris: Gallimard, 1995.

————. *Profession de foi du vicaire savoyard.* Edited by B. Bernardi. Paris: Flammarion, 1996.

Sagnac, Philippe. "Les Juifs et la Révolution française (1789–1791)." *Revue d'histoire moderne et contemporaine* 1 (1899): 5–19, 209–234.

Schwarzfuchs, Simon. *Du Juif à l'israélite: Histoire d'une mutation 1770–1870.* Paris: Fayard, 1989. [Relevant also for chapters 8 and 9.]

Schwarzfuchs, Simon, ed. *Le Registre des délibérations de la nation juive portugaise de Bordeaux.* Paris: Fondation Calouste Gulbenkian, 1981.

Schwarzfuchs, Simon, ed. and trans. *Le Journal révolutionnaire d'Abraham Spire.* Bilingual edition (Judeo-German and French). Paris: Institut Alain de Rothschild-Verdier, 1989.

Simon, Lucien, and Anne-Marie Duport. *Les Juifs du pape à Nîmes et la Révolution.* Aix-en-Provence: Edisud, 1988.

Szajkowski, Zosa. *Jews and the French Revolutions of 1789, 1830, and 1848.* New York: Ktav, 1970.

Voltaire. *Dictionnaire philosophique.* Edited by Alain Pons. Paris: Gallimard, 1994.

Yardeni, Myriam. *Anti-Jewish Mentalities in Early Modern Europe.* Lanham, Md.: University Press of America, 1990.

Note also the eight-volume series of facsimile reprints published in 1968 by Éditions d'Histoire Sociale in Paris under the title *La Révolution française et l'Émancipation des Juifs*:

Volume 1: Comte de Mirabeau, *Sur Moses Mendelssohn, sur la réforme politique des Juifs et en particulier sur la révolution tentée en leur faveur en 1753 dans la Grande-Bretagne* (1787).

Volume 2: [Claude-Antoine] Thiéry, *Dissertation sur cette question: "Est-il des moyens de rendre les Juifs plus utiles et plus heureux en France?"* (1788).

Volume 3: [Henri-Baptiste] Grégoire, *Essai sur la régénération physique, morale et politique des Juifs* (1789). [Note the more recent edition mentioned above.]

Volume 4: Zalkind Hourwitz, *Apologie des Juifs, en réponse à la question: "Est-il des moyens de rendre les Juifs plus heureux et plus utiles en France?"* (1788).

Volume 5: *Adresses, Mémoires et Pétitions des Juifs, 1789–1794.*

Volume 6: *La Commune et les Districts de Paris: Discours, Lettres et Rapports, 1790–1791.*

Volume 7: *L'Assemblée nationale constituante: Motions, discours et rapports. La législation nouvelle, 1789–1791.*

Volume 8: *Lettres, Mémoires et Publications diverses, 1789–1806.*

Chapter 7: New Perspectives

Albert, Phyllis Cohen. "Le rôle des consistoires israélites vers le milieu du XIXe siècle." *Revue des études juives* 130 (April-December 1971): 231–254.

———. *The Modernization of French Jewry: Consistory and Community in the Nineteenth Century.* Hanover, N.H.: Brandeis University Press, 1977. [Relevant also for chapter 8.]

———. "Nonorthodox Attitudes in Nineteenth Century French Judaism." In Frances Malino and Phyllis Cohen Albert, eds., *Essays in Modern Jewish History: A Tribute to Ben Halpern,* 121–141. Rutherford, N.J.: Fairleigh Dickinson University Press/Associated University Presses, 1982.

Anchel, Robert. *Napoléon et les Juifs.* Paris: Presses Universitaires de France, 1928.

Ayoun, Richard. *Typologie d'une carrière rabbinique: L'exemple de Mahir de Charleville.* 2 vol. Nancy: Presses Universitaires de Nancy, 1993.

Baron, Salo W. "Aspects of the Jewish Communal Crisis in 1848." *Jewish Social Studies* 14 (1952): 99–144.

Bauer, Jules. *L'École rabbinique de France (1830–1930).* Paris: Presses Universitaires de France, 1931.

Berg, Roger. *Le Consistoire central, 1808–1867.* Paris: Éditions du Consistoire central, 1967.

———. *Histoire du rabbinat français (XVIe-XXe siècle).* Paris: Cerf, 1992.

Blumenkranz, Bernhard, and Albert Soboul, eds. *Le Grand Sanhédrin de Napoléon.* Paris: Les Belles Lettres, 1979.

Chouraqui, Jean-Marc. "Le corps rabbinique en France et sa prédication: Problèmes et desseins (1805–1905)." *Histoire, Economie et Société* 2 (1984): 293–320.

Eisenstein-Barzilay, Isaac. "The Ideology of the Berlin *Haskalah.*" *Proceedings of the American Academy for Jewish Research* 25 (1956): 2–37.

Fauchille, Paul. *La Question juive en France sous le premier Empire d'après des documents inédits.* Paris: Rousseau, 1884.

Ginsburger, Ernest. *Le Comité de surveillance de J.-J. Rousseau, Saint-Esprit-lès-Bayonne.* Paris: Lipschutz, 1934.

Ginsburger, Moïse, and Ernest Ginsburger. "Contribution à l'histoire des Juifs d'Alsace pendant le Terreur." *Revue des études juives* 47 (1903): 283–299.

Girard, Patrick. *Les Juifs de France de 1789 à 1860: De l'émancipation à l'égalité.* Paris: Calmann-Lévy, 1976. [Relevant also for chapters 8 and 9.]

Jarrassé, Dominique. *L'Age d'or des synagogues.* Paris: Herscher, 1991.

Kahn, Léon. "Les Israélites sous la Terreur." *Archives israélites de France* 49 (1888): 368–371, 375–376.

Levi, Israël. "Napoléon Ier et la réunion du Grand Sanhédrin." *Revue des études juives* 28 (1894): 265–280.

Liber, Maurice. "Napoléon Ier et les Juifs: La question juive devant le Conseil d'État en 1806." *Revue des études juives* 71 (1920): 127–147; 72 (1921): 1–23, 135–162.

Manuel, Albert. "Les consistoires israélites de France: Le consistoire israélite de Paris, 1806–1905." *Revue des études juives* 82 (1926): 521–532.

Pietri, François. *Napoléon et les Israélites*. Paris: Berger-Levrault, 1965.

Rosenstock, Morton. "The Establishment of the Consistorial System in Algeria." *Jewish Social Studies* 18 (1956): 41–54.

Sagnac, Philippe. "Les Juifs et Napoléon (1806–1808). *Revue d'histoire moderne et contemporaine* 2 (1900–1901): 595–604; 3 (1901–1902): 461–492.

Schwarzfuchs, Simon. *Napoleon, the Jews, and the Sanhedrin*. Oxford: Oxford University Press/Littman Library, 1979.

Tama, Diogène, ed. *Organisation civile et religieuse des israélites de France et du royaume d'Italie, décrétée par Sa Majesté l'Empereur et le Roi, le 17 mars 1808; suivie de la collection des actes de l'Assemblée des israélites de France et du Royaume d'Italie convoquée à Paris en 1806, et de celles des procès-verbaux et décisions du Grand Sanhédrin, convoqué en 1807, lesquelles ont servi de base à cette organisation*. Paris [privately printed], 1808.

Union Libérale Israélite. *Ce que nous sommes*. Paris: Union Libérale Israélite, 1918.

Weill, Julien. *Zadoc Kahn (1839–1905)*. Paris: Félix Alcan, 1912.

Chapter 8: Entry into French Society
Chapter 9: Advancement and Identity

Amson, Daniel. *Adolphe Crémieux: L'oublié de la gloire*. Paris: Seuil, 1988.

Assouline, Pierre. *Le Dernier des Camondo*. Paris: Gallimard, 1997.

Autin, Jean. *Les Frères Pereire: Le bonheur d'entreprendre*. Paris: Perrin, 1984.

Barbier, Frédéric. *Finance et Politique: La dynastie des Fould, XVIIIe-XXe siècle*. Paris: Armand Colin, 1991.

Barrot, Olivier, and Pascal Ory. *"La Revue blanche": Histoire, anthologie, portraits*. Paris: 1989.

Benbassa, Esther. "Israël face à lui-même: Judaïsme occidental et judaïsme ottoman (XIXe-XXe siècles)." *Pardès* 7 (1988): 105–129.

Bensimon-Donath, Doris. *Socio-démographie des Juifs de France et d'Algérie: 1867–1907*. Paris: Éditions de l'Institut National des Langues et Civilisations Orientales, 1976.

Berceot, Florence. "La Communauté juive de Marseille sous la IIIe République, regard sur les femmes: Assimilation-renaissance." Mémoire, Université d'Aix-Marseille-I, 1991. [Relevant also for chapters 10 and 11.]

———. "Renouvellement socio-démographique des Juifs de Marseille 1901–1937," *Provence historique* 175 (1994): 39–57.

———. "Socio-démographie des israélites de Marseille 1872–1891," *Provence historique* 173 (1993): 305–322.

Bergeron, Louis. *Les Rothschilds et les autres: La gloire des banquiers*. Paris: Perrin, 1991.

Birnbaum, Pierre. *Les Fous de la République: Histoire politique des Juifs d'État, de Gambetta à Vichy.* Paris: Fayard, 1992. [Relevant also for chapters 10, 11, and 12.]

Bischoff, Chantal. *Geneviève Straus, 1849–1926: Trilogie d'une égérie.* Paris: Balland, 1992.

Bourel, Dominique. "La *Wissenschaft des Judentums* en France." *Revue de synthèse* 4, no. 2 (1988): 265–280.

Bouvier, Jean. *Les Rothschild.* Paris: Fayard, 1960.

Cahun, Léon. *La Vie juive.* Paris: E. Monnie-de-Brunhoff, 1886.

Caron, Vicki. *Between France and Germany: The Jews of Alsace-Lorraine, 1871–1918.* Stanford: Stanford University Press, 1988.

Chouraqui, André. *Cent Ans d'histoire: L'Alliance israélite universelle et la renaissance contemporaine (1860–1960).* Paris: Presses Universitaires de France, 1965.

Cohen, David. "Juifs allemands et Juifs portugais à Paris sous Napoléon III." In Jean-Antoine Gili and Ralph Schor, eds., *Hommes, Idées, Journaux: Mélanges en l'honneur de Pierre Guiral,* 185–216. Paris: Publications de la Sorbonne, 1988.

———. *La Promotion des Juifs en France à l'époque du second Empire (1852–1870).* 2 volumes. Aix-en-Provence: Université de Provence, 1980.

Daltroff, Jean. *La Synagogue consistoriale de Strasbourg (1898–1940).* Strasbourg: Hirlé, 1996.

Delille-Choukroun, Anne. "Le Rôle de la musique dans l'intégration des Juifs en France au XIXe siècle." Mémoire, Université de Paris IV-Sorbonne, 1992.

Espagne, Michel. *Les Juifs allemands de Paris à l'époque de Heine: La translation ashkénaze.* Paris: Presses Universitaires de France, 1996.

Friedemann, Joë. *Alexandre Weill, écrivain contestataire et historien engagé (1811–1899).* Strasbourg: Librairie Istra, 1980.

Ganiage, Jean, with the assistance of Jean Martin. *Histoire contemporaine du Maghreb de 1830 à nos jours.* Paris: Fayard, 1994.

Gille, Bertrand. *Histoire de la maison Rothschild.* 2 volumes. Geneva: Droz, 1965.

Graetz, Michael. *Les Juifs en France au XIXe siècle: De la Révolution française à l'Alliance israélite universelle.* Translated by S. Malka. Paris: Seuil, 1989.

Halff, Antoine. "Lieux d'assimilation, lieux d'identité: les communautés juives et l'essor des stations thermales et balnéaires à la Belle Époque." *Pardès* 8 (1988): 41–57.

Halff, Sylvain. "La participation des Juifs de France dans la Grande Guerre." *The American Jewish Yearbook* 21 (1919–1920): 31–97.

Hamache, Magy. "Les Juifs dans les arts dramatiques au XIXe siècle: Regards croisés sur la tragédienne Rachel (1821–1858)." *Revue historique* 593 (January–March 1995): 119–133.

———. "Rachel: femme, Juive et actrice. Étude des discours juifs et non juifs." Mémoire, Université de Paris IV, 1993.

Hayoun, Maurice-Ruben. *La Science du judaïsme.* Paris: Presses Universitaires de France, 1995.

Helfand, Jonathan I. "French Jewry during the Second Republic and Second Empire (1848–1870)." Ann Arbor: University of Michigan Microfilms, 1981.

———. "Passports and Piety: Apostasy in 19th Century France." *Jewish History* 3, no. 2 (1988): 59–83.

Hyman, Paula. *The Emancipation of the Jews of Alsace: Acculturation and Tradition in the Nineteenth Century.* New Haven: Yale University Press, 1991.

―――. *Gender and Assimilation in Modern Jewish History: The Roles and Representation of Women.* Seattle: University of Washington Press, 1995.

―――. "Jewish Fertility in Nineteenth Century France." In Paul Rittertband, ed., *Modern Jewish Fertility,* 78–93. Leiden: Brill, 1981.

Isser, Natalie, and Lita Linzer Schwartz. "Sudden Conversion: The Case of Alphonse Ratisbonne." *Jewish Social Studies* 45 (1983): 17–30.

Kahn, Léon. *Histoire de la communauté israélite de Paris: Le comité de bienfaisance, l'hôpital, l'orphelinat, les cimetières.* Paris: Durlacher, 1886.

―――. *Histoire de la communauté israélite de Paris: Les professions manuelles et les institutions de patronage.* Paris: Durlacher, 1885.

―――. *Histoire des écoles communales et consistoriales israélites de Paris (1809–1884).* Paris: Durlacher, 1884.

―――. *Les Sociétés de secours mutuels, philanthropiques et de prévoyance.* Paris: Durlacher, 1887.

Kaspi, André. "Note sur Isidore Cahen." *Revue des études juives* 121 (July-December 1962): 417–425.

Katz, Jacob. *Jews and Freemasons in Europe, 1723–1939.* Translated by Leonard Oschry. Cambridge, Mass.: Harvard University Press, 1970.

Kohn, Jean-Louis. "La Bourgeoisie juive à Paris au second Empire." Ph.D. dissertation, Université de Paris-I, 1993–1994.

Landau, Philippe. "Les Juifs de France et la Grande Guerre, 1914–1941: Patrie-République-Mémoire." Ph.D. dissertation, Université de Paris-VII, 1993.

Lazard, Raymond. *Michel Goudchaux (1797–1862), son œuvre et sa vie politique.* Paris: Félix Alcan, 1907.

Liber, Maurice. "Isidore Loeb et les études juives." *Revue des études juives* 105 (1939): 16–22.

―――. "Zadoc Kahn et les études juives." *Revue des études juives* 105 (1939): 3–15.

Lottman, Herbert R. *The French Rothschilds: The Great Banking Dynasty through Two Turbulent Centuries.* New York: Crown, 1995.

Löwy, Michael. *Rédemption et Utopie: Le judaïsme libertaire en Europe centrale.* Paris: Presses Universitaires de France, 1988.

Loyrette, Henri, ed. *Entre le théâtre et l'histoire: La famille Halévy (1760–1960).* Paris: Fayard/Réunion des Musées Nationaux, 1996.

Marrus, Michael R. *The Politics of Assimilation: A Study of the French Jewish Community at the Time of the Dreyfus Affair.* Oxford: Clarendon Press, 1971. [Relevant also for chapter 10.]

Maurice-Pouquet, Jeanne. *Le Salon de Mme de Caillavet.* Paris: Hachette, 1926.

Meyer, Michael A. "Jewish Religious Reform and *Wissenschaft des Judentums*: The Positions of Zunz, Geiger and Fränkel." *Leo Baeck Institute Yearbook* 16 (1971): 19–41.

―――. *Response to Modernity: A History of the Reform Movement in Judaism.* New York: Oxford University Press, 1988.

Mollier, Jean-Yves. *Michel et Calmann Lévy ou la Naissance de l'édition moderne, 1836–1891.* Paris: Calmann-Lévy, 1984.

Muhlstein, Anka. *James de Rothschild.* Paris: Gallimard, 1981.

Pardès 19–20 (1994): "La Religion comme Science: La *Wissenschaft des Judentums.*"

Philippe, Béatrice. *Les Juifs à la Belle Époque.* Paris: Albin Michel, 1992. [Relevant also for chapter 10.]

———. "Les Juifs français et la seconde République de février à juin 1848." Ph.D. dissertation, Université de Paris X-Nanterre, 1980.

Piette, Christine. *Les Juifs de Paris (1808–1840): La marche vers l'assimilation.* Québec: Presses de l'Université Laval, 1983.

Posener, S. *Adolphe Crémieux (1796–1880).* 2 volumes. Paris: Félix Alcan, 1933–1934.

———. "The Immediate Economic and Social Effects of the Emancipation of the Jews in France." *Jewish Social Studies* 1 (1939): 271–326.

———. "Les Juifs sous le premier Empire." *Revue des études juives* 90 (1931): 1–27; 93 (1932): 192–214; 94 (1933): 157–166.

Rodrigue, Aron. *French Jews, Turkish Jews: The Alliance Israélite Universelle and the Politics of Jewish Schooling in Turkey, 1860–1925.* Bloomington: Indiana University Press, 1990.

———. *Images of Sephardi and Eastern Jewries in Transition: The Teachers of the Alliance Israélite Universelle, 1860–1939.* Seattle: University of Washington Press, 1993.

———. "Léon Halévy and Modern French Jewish Historiography." In Elisheva Carlebach, John Efron, and David Myers, eds., *History, Jews, and Memory.* Hanover, N.H.: University Press of New England. In press.

Rosenstock, Morton. "Economic and Social Conditions among the Jews of Algeria, 1790–1848." *Historia Judaica* 18 (April 1956): 3–26.

Salvador, Gabriel. *J. Salvador, sa vie, ses œuvres et ses critiques.* Paris: Calmann-Lévy, 1881.

Schnurmann, Erwin. *La Population juive en Alsace.* Paris: Sirey, 1936.

Schwab, Moïse. *Salomon Munk, sa vie et ses œuvres.* Paris: Leroux, 1900.

Schwarzfuchs, Simon. *Les Juifs d'Algérie et la France (1830–1855).* Jerusalem: Ben-Zvi Institute, 1981.

Seltzer, Robert M. *Jewish People, Jewish Thought: The Jewish Experience in History.* New York: Macmillan, 1980.

Seni, Nora, and Sophie Le Tarnec. *Les Camondo ou l'éclipse d'une fortune.* Arles: Actes Sud, 1997.

Simon-Nahum, Perrine. "Contribution à l'étude de la bourgeoisie intellectuelle juive à Paris entre 1870 et 1914." Mémoire, École des Hautes Études en Sciences Sociales, Paris, 1982.

———. *La Cité investie: La "Science du judaisme" français et la République.* Paris: Cerf, 1991.

Singer, Barnett. "Clemenceau and the Jews." *Jewish Social Studies* 43 (Winter 1981): 47–58. [Relevant also for chapters 10 and 11.]

Sorkin, David. *The Transformation of German Jewry, 1780–1840.* New York: Oxford University Press, 1987.

Szajkowski, Zosa. "The Decline and Fall of Provençal Jewry." *Jewish Social Studies* 6 (January 1944): 31–54.

———. *Jewish Education in France, 1789–1939.* New York: Conference on Jewish Social Studies, 1980.

Talmon, J.-L. "Social Prophetism in 19th Century France: The Jewish Element in the Saint-Simonian Movement." *Commentary* (August 1958): 158–172.

Weill, Georges. "Les Juifs et le saint-simonisme." *Revue des études juives* 31 (1895): 261–273.

Wiener, Max. "Abraham Geiger's Conception of the "Science of Judaism." *Leo Baeck Institute Yearbook* 1 (1956–1957): 142–162.

————. "The Ideology of the Founders of Jewish Scientific Research." *YIVO Annual of Jewish Social Science* 5 (1950): 184–196.

See also *Jewish History* 5, no. 2 (1991): 47–72 for a debate on the question of Jewish conversions to Christianity in France during the nineteenth century.

Chapter 10: Breaches in Franco-Judaism

Abitbol, Michel. *Les Deux Terres promises: Les Juifs de France et le sionisme 1897–1945*. Paris: Olivier Orban, 1989. [Relevant also for chapters 11 and 12.]

Almog, Shmuel. "The Racial Motif in Renan's Attitude to Jews and Judaism." In Shmuel Almog, ed., *Antisemitism Through the Ages*, 255–278. New York: Pergamon Press, 1988.

Archives juives 27, no. 1 (1994): "Les Juifs et l'affaire Dreyfus."

Basch, Françoise. *Victor Basch ou la Passion de la justice: De l'affaire Dreyfus au crime de la Milice*. Paris: Plon, 1994. [Relevant also for chapters 11 and 12.]

Bastaire, Jean. "Drumont et l'antisémitisme." *Esprit* 32, no. 3 (1964): 477–487.

Benbassa, Esther. "Les grandes lignes de l'immigration juive en France à l'époque contemporaine." In *Les Mouvements migratoires dans l'Occident moderne*, 110–120. Proceedings of the 18th IRCOM Colloquium. Paris: Presses Universitaires de Paris-Sorbonne, 1994. [Relevant also for chapter 11.]

Bensoussan, Georges. *L'Idéologie du rejet. Enquête sur le Monument Henry ou archéologie du fantasme antisémite dans la France de la fin du XIXe siècle*. Levallois-Perret: Manya, 1993.

Birnbaum, Pierre. *L'Affaire Dreyfus: La République en péril*. Paris: Gallimard, 1994.

————, ed. *La France de l'affaire Dreyfus*. Paris: Gallimard, 1994.

Blum, Léon. *Souvenirs sur l'Affaire*. 1935. Reprint, Paris: Gallimard, 1981.

Bouvier, Jean. *Études sur le krach de l'Union générale (1878–1885)*. Paris: Presses Universitaires de France, 1960.

————. *Les Deux Scandales de Panama (1878–1885)*. Paris: Juliard, 1944.

Bredin, Jean-Denis. *L'Affaire*. 1983. Reprint, Paris: Fayard-Julliard, 1993.

————. *Bernard Lazare: De l'anarchiste au prophète*. Paris: Fallois, 1992.

Burns, Michael. *Dreyfus: A Family Affair, 1789–1945*. New York: HarperCollins, 1991.

Busi, Frederick. "A Bibliographical Overview of the Dreyfus Affair." *Jewish Social Studies* 40 (1978): 25–40.

Byrnes, Robert F. *Antisemitism in Modern France*. Volume 1. New Brunswick, N.J.: Rutgers University Press, 1950.

————. "Édouard Drumont and *La France juive*." *Jewish Social Studies* 10 (April 1948): 165–184.

Charle, Christophe. "Champ littéraire et champ du pouvoir: les écrivains et l'affaire Dreyfus." *Annales ESC* 32 (March-April 1977): 240–264.

Delmaire, Danielle. *Antisémitisme et Catholiques dans le Nord pendant l'affaire Dreyfus*. Lille: Presses Universitaires de Lille, 1991.

Dermenjian, Geneviève. *La Crise anti-juive oranaise (1895–1905): L'antisémitisme dans l'Algérie coloniale*. Paris: L'Harmattan, 1986.

Dreyfus, Alfred. *Cinq Années de ma vie*. 1901. Reprint, Paris: La Découverte, 1994.

Drouin, Michel, ed. *L'Affaire Dreyfus de A à Z*. Paris: Flammarion, 1994.

Drumont, Édouard. *La France juive*. Paris: Marpon et Flammarion, 1886.

Duclert, Vincent. *L'Affaire Dreyfus*. Paris: La Découverte, 1994.

Gervereau, Laurent, and Christophe Prochasson, eds. *L'Affaire Dreyfus et le Tournant du siècle 1894–1910*. Nanterre: Bibliothèque de Documentation Internationale Contemporaine, 1994.

Glasberg, Victor M. "Intent and Consequences: The 'Jewish Question' in the French Socialist Movement of the Late Nineteenth Century." *Jewish Social Studies* 36 (1974): 61–71.

Goldberg, Harvey. "Jean Jaurès and the Jewish Question: The Evolution of a Position." *Jewish Social Studies* 20 (1958): 67–94.

Green, Nancy L. *The Pletzl of Paris: Jewish Immigrant Workers in the "Belle Époque."* New York: Holmes and Meier, 1986.

Hebey, Pierre. *Alger 1898: La grande vague antijuive*. Paris: Nil, 1996.

L'Histoire 173 (January 1994). Special Issue: "L'Affaire Dreyfus: Vérités et mensonges."

Hyman, Paula. *From Dreyfus to Vichy: The Remaking of French Jewry, 1906–1939*. New York: Columbia University Press, 1979. [Relevant also for chapter 11.]

Jean Jaurès, cahiers trimestriels 136–137 (April-June and July-September 1995). Special issues: "Le Centenaire de l'Affaire (1894–1995)" and "L'Affaire Dreyfus, Histoire."

Landau, Philippe E. *L'Opinion juive et l'Affaire Dreyfus*. Paris: Albin Michel, 1995.

Las, Nelly. "Les Juifs de France et le Sionisme: De l'affaire Dreyfus à la Seconde Guerre mondiale (1896–1939)." Thesis, Université de la Sorbonne Nouvelle-Paris III, 1985. [Relevant also for Chapter 11.]

Lazare, Bernard. *Juifs et Antisémites*. Edited by Philippe Oriol. Paris: Allia, 1992.

———. *L'Antisémitisme, son histoire et ses causes*. 1894. Reprint, Paris: La Différence, 1982.

———. *Le Fumier de Job, Le Nationalisme Juif,* and *Contre l'antisémitisme*. 1928. Reprint, Paris: Circé, 1990.

———. *Une erreur judiciare: L'affaire Dreyfus*. Edited by Philippe Oriol. 1897. Reprint, Paris: Allia, 1993.

Leroy-Beaulieu, Anatole. *Israël chez les nations: Les Juifs et l'antisémitisme*. 1894. Reprint, Paris: Calmann-Lévy, 1983.

———. *L'Antisémitisme*. Paris: Calmann-Lévy, 1897.

Lévy, Monique, and Marianne Urbah. *Bibliographie des travaux historiques consacrés à l'affaire Dreyfus, parus de 1973 à 1994*. Paris: Cahiers de la Commission Française des Archives Juives (n.s.), 1994.

Lifshitz-Krams, Anne. "La Constitution de la population juive en France au XIXe siècle." 3 volumes. Ph.D. dissertation, École des Hautes Études en Sciences Sociales, 1992.

Lipschutz, Léon. *Bibliographie thématique et analytique de l'affaire Dreyfus*. Paris: Fasquelle, 1971.

Minczeles, Henri. *Histoire générale du Bund: Un mouvement révolutionnaire juif*. Paris: Austral, 1995.

Mollier, Jean-Yves. *Le Scandale de Panama*. Paris: Fayard, 1991.

Nguyen, Victor. *Aux origines de l'Action française: Intelligence et politique à l'aube du XXᵉ siècle*. Paris: Fayard, 1991.

Nicault, Catherine. *La France et le Sionisme 1897–1948: Une rencontre manquée?* Paris: Calmann-Lévy, 1992. [Relevant also for chapter 11.]

Nora, Pierre. "1898: Le thème du complot et la définition de l'identité juive." In Maurice Olender, ed., *Le Racisme, mythes et sciences*, 157–166. Brussels: Complexe, 1981.

Pierrard, Pierre. *Juifs et Catholiques français d'Édouard Drumont à Jacob Kaplan, 1886–1994*. 1970. 2nd edition. Paris: Cerf 1997. [Relevant also for chapters 11 and 12.]

Rodrigue, Aron. "Rearticulations of French Jewish Identities after the Dreyfus Affair." *Jewish Social Studies* (n.s.) 2, no. 3 (1996): 1–24.

Schnapper, Dominique. "Le Juif errant." In Yves Lequin, ed., *Histoire des étrangers et de l'immigration en France*, 363–377. Paris: Larousse, 1992.

Silberner, Edmund. "Anti-Jewish Trends in French Revolutionary Syndicalism." *Jewish Social Studies* 15 (1953): 195–202.

———. "The Attitude of the Fourierist School towards the Jews." *Jewish Social Studies* 9 (1947): 339–362.

———. "Charles Fourier on the Jewish Question." *Jewish Social Studies* 8 (1946): 245–266.

———. "French Socialism and the Jewish Question." *Historia Judaica* 16 (1954): 3–38.

———. "Proudhon's Judeophobia." *Historia Judaica* 10 (April 1948): 61–80.

Sorlin, Pierre. *"La Croix" et les Juifs, 1880–1899: Contribution à l'histoire de l'antisémitisme contemporain*. Paris: Grasset, 1967.

Sternhell, Zeev. *La Droite révolutionnaire 1885–1914: Les origines françaises du fascisme*. 1978. Reprint, Paris: Seuil, 1984.

———. *Maurice Barrès et le Nationalisme français, 1884–1902*. 1972. Reprint, Brussels: Complexe, 1985.

Szajkowski, Zosa. "The Jewish Saint-Simonians and Socialist Anti-Semites in France." *Jewish Social Studies* 9 (1947): 33–60.

———. "Socialists and Radicals in the Development of Anti-Semitism in Algeria (1884–1900)." *Jewish Social Studies* 10 (July 1948): 257–280.

Tobias, Henry J. *The Jewish Bund in Russia from Its Origins to 1905*. Stanford: Stanford University Press, 1972.

Verdès-Leroux, Jeanine. *Scandales financiers et Antisémitisme catholique, le krach de l'Union générale*. Paris: Le Centurion, 1969.

Weinberg, Henry H. "The Image of the Jew in Late Nineteenth Century Literature." *Jewish Social Studies* 45 (1983): 241–250.

Wilson, Nelly. *Bernard-Lazare: Antisemitism and the Problem of Jewish Identity in Late Nineteenth Century France*. Cambridge: Cambridge University Press, 1978.

Wilson, Stephen. *Ideology and Experience: Antisemitism in France at the Time of the Dreyfus Affair*. Toronto and London: Fairleigh Dickinson University Press/Associated University Presses, 1982.

———. "Le monument Henry: la structure de l'antisémitisme en France, 1898–1899." *Annales ESC* 32 (March-April 1977): 265–291.

Winock, Michel. *Édouard Drumont et Cⁱᵉ: Antisémitisme et fascisme en France*. Paris: Seuil, 1982.

———. *Nationalisme, Antisémitisme et Fascisme en France*. Paris: Seuil, 1990.

Wischnitzer, Mark. *To Dwell in Safety: The Story of Jewish Migrations Since 1800*. Philadelphia: Jewish Publication Society of America, 1948.

Zola, Émile. *L'Affaire Dreyfus: La vérité en marche*. 1901. Reprint, Paris: Garnier-Flammarion, 1969.

Chapter 11: Between the Wars
Chapter 12: The Dark Years

Abitbol, Michel. *Les Juifs d'Afrique du Nord sous Vichy*. Paris: Maisonneuve et Larose, 1983.

Adler, Jacques. *The Jews of Paris and the Final Solution: Communal Response and Internal Conflicts, 1940–1944*. New York: Oxford University Press, 1987.

Afoumado, Diane. "Consciences, attitudes et comportements des Juifs en France entre 1936 et 1944." 3 volumes. Ph.D. dissertation, Université de Paris-X, 1997.

Annales ESC 48 (May-June 1993). Special Issue: "Présence du passé, Lenteur de l'histoire: Vichy, l'Occupation, les Juifs."

Aouate, Yves-Claude. "Les mesures d'exclusion antijuive dans l'enseignement public en Algérie (1940–1943)." *Pardès* 8 (1988): 115–120.

Ariel, Joseph. "Jewish Self-Defence and Resistance in France During World War II." *Yad Vashem Studies* 6 (1967): 221–250.

Bartosek, Karel, René Gallissot, and Denis Peschanski, eds. *De l'exil à la résistance: Réfugiés et immigrés d'Europe centrale en France (1933–1945)*. Paris: Presses Universitaires de Vincennes, 1989.

Benguigui, Ida. "L'Immigration juive à Paris entre les deux guerres." Undergraduate thesis, Université de Paris, 1965.

Bensimon, Doris. *Les Grands rafles: Juifs en France, 1940–1944*. Toulouse: Privat, 1987.

Bensimon, Doris, and Sergio della Pergola. *La Population juive de France: sociodémographie et identité*. Paris: The Institute of Contemporary Jewry-CNRS, 1986. [Relevant also for chapter 13.]

Bensimon-Donath, Doris. *Évolution du judaïsme marocain sous le Protectorat français, 1912–1956*. Paris and The Hague: Mouton, 1968.

Bensoussan, Georges. *Histoire de la Shoah*. Paris: Presses Universitaires de France, 1996.

Benveniste, Annie. *Le Bosphore à la Roquette: La communauté judéo-espangnole à Paris (1914–1940)*. Paris: L'Harmattan, 1989.

Berg, Roger. "Juifs de France, combattants de la Seconde Guerre mondiale 1939–1945." *Pardès* 12 (1990): 196–210.

Biélinky, Jacques. *Journal 1940–1942: Un journaliste juif à Paris sous l'Occupation*. Edited by Renée Poznanski. Paris: Cerf, 1992.

Billig, Joseph. *L'Institut d'étude des questions juives.* 3 volumes. Paris: Éditions du Centre, 1955–1960.

Birnbaum, Pierre. *Un mythe politique: la "République juive" de Léon Blum à Pierre Mendès France.* Paris: Fayard, 1988.

Boyarin, Jonathan. *Polish Jews in Paris: The Ethnography of Memory.* Bloomington: Indiana University Press, 1991.

Burrin, Philippe. *Hitler et les Juifs: Genèse d'un génocide.* Paris: Seuil, 1989.

Caron, Vicki. "Loyalties in Conflict: French Jewry and the Refugee Crisis, 1933–1935." *Leo Baeck Institute Yearbook* 36 (1991): 305–338.

Cohen, Asher. *La Shoah.* Paris: Cerf, 1990.

———. *Persécutions et Sauvetages: Juifs et Français sous l'Occupation et sous Vichy.* Paris: Cerf, 1993.

Cohen, Richard I. *The Burden of Conscience: French Jewry's Response to the Holocaust.* Bloomington: Indiana University Press, 1987.

Cohn, Norman. *Warrant for Genocide: The Myth of the Jewish World-Conspiracy and the Protocols of the Elders of Zion.* New York: Harper and Row, 1967.

Conan, Éric. *Sans oublier les enfants: Les camps de Pithiviers et de Beaune-la-Rolande, 19 juillet–16 septembre 1942.* Paris: Grasset, 1992.

Conan, Éric, and Henry Rousso. *Vichy: un passé qui ne passe pas.* Paris: Gallimard, 1996.

Courtois, Stéphane, and Adam Rayski, with the assistance of Philippe Burrin, Claude Lévy, Denis Peschanski, and Renée Poznanski. *Qui savait quoi? L'extermination des Juifs, 1941–1945.* Paris: La Découverte, 1987.

Courtois, Stéphane, Denis Peschanski, and Adam Rayski. *Le Sang de l'étranger: Les immigrés de la MOI dans la Résistance.* Paris: Fayard, 1989.

Danan, Maxime. *La Vie politique à Alger de 1940 à 1944.* Paris: Librairie Générale de Droit et Jurisprudence, 1963.

Diamant, David. *Héros juifs de la Résistance française.* Paris: Éditions du Renouveau, 1962.

———. *Jeune Combat: La jeunesse juive dans la Résistance.* Paris: L'Harmattan, 1992.

———. *Les Juifs dans la Résistance française, 1940–1944.* Paris: Roger Maria, 1971.

Epstein, Simon. "Les Institutions israélites françaises de 1929 à 1939: Solidarité juive et lutte contre l'antisémitisme." Ph.D. dissertation, Université de Paris I-Sorbonne, 1990.

Estèbe, Jean. *Les Juifs à Toulouse et en Midi toulousain au temps de Vichy.* Toulouse: Presses Universitaires du Mirail, 1996.

Feuchtwanger, Lion. *Le Diable en France.* Translated by J.-C. Capèle. Paris: Belfond, 1996.

Fhima, Catherine. "Contribution à l'étude du judaïsme dans l'œuvre de deux écrivains français: André Spire et Edmond Fleg, de 1894 à 1934." Master's thesis, Université de Paris-I, 1993.

Le Fichier juif. Report of the Commission headed by René Rémond to the Prime Minister. Paris: Plon, 1996.

Friedlander, Saül. "L'extermination des Juifs." *L'Histoire* 11 (April 1979): 5–14.

Le Genre humain (Summer-Fall 1994). Special issue: "Le Droit antisémite de Vichy."

Le Genre humain (Summer-Fall 1996). Special issue: "Juger sous Vichy."

Green, Nancy L. *Ready-to-Wear and Ready-to-Work: A Century of Industry and Immigrants in Paris and New York.* Durham, N.C.: Duke University Press, 1997.

Greilsammer, Ilan. *Blum.* Paris: Flammarion, 1996.

Grynberg, Anne. *Les Camps de la honte: Les internés juifs des camps français 1939–1944.* Paris: La Découverte, 1991.

———. *La Shoah: L'impossible oubli.* Paris: Gallimard, 1995.

Grynberg, Anne, and Catherine Nicault. "Le culte israélite en France pendant la Seconde Guerre mondiale: droit et réalités d'exercice." *Archives juives* 28, no. 2 (1995): 72–88.

Haft, Cynthia. *The Bargain and the Bridle: The General Union of the Israelites of France, 1941–1944.* Chicago: Dialog Press, 1983.

Hilberg, Raul. *The Destruction of the European Jews.* 3 volumes. 1961. Revised and definitive edition, New York: Holmes and Meier, 1985.

Historia 34 (March-April 1995). Special issue: "Les Camps de la mort."

L'Histoire 156 (June 1992). Document: "Le Dossier des chambres à gaz."

L'Histoire 185 (February 1995). Feature article: "Auschwitz, 1945: la révélation."

Judt, Tony. " 'We Have Discovered History': Defeat, Resistance, and the Intellectuals in France." *Journal of Modern History* 64 (1992): 147–172.

Kaspi, André. "L'affaire des enfants Finaly." *L'Histoire* 76 (1985): 40–53.

———. "Les Juifs dans la Résistance." *L'Histoire* 80 (1985): 38–45.

———. *Les Juifs pendant l'Occupation.* Paris: Seuil, 1991.

Kaspi, André, ed. *Cahiers de la Shoah.* 2 volumes. Paris: Liana Levi, 1994–1995.

Kieval, Hillel J. "Legality and Resistance in Vichy France: The Rescue of Jewish Children." *Proceedings of the American Philosophical Society* 124, no. 5 (1980): 339–366.

Klarsfeld, Serge. *Calendrier de la persécution des Juifs de France.* Paris: Fils et Filles des Déportés Juifs de France, 1993.

———. *Les Enfants d'Izieu: une tragédie juive.* Paris: Fils et Filles des Déportés Juifs de France, 1984.

———. *L'Étoile des Juifs.* Paris: Archipel, 1992.

———. *Le Mémorial de la déportation des Juifs de France.* Paris: Klarsfeld, 1978.

———. *Le Mémorial des enfants juifs deportés de France.* Paris: Fils et Filles des Déportés Juifs de France, 1994.

———. *Vichy-Auschwitz.* 2 volumes. Paris: Fayard, 1983–1985.

Klarsfeld, Serge, ed. *Il y a cinquante ans le statut des Juifs.* Paris: Centre de Documentation Juive Contemporaine, 1991.

Klatzmann, Joseph. *Le Travail à domicile dans l'industrie parisienne du vêtement.* Paris: Armand Colin, 1957.

Knout, David. *La Résistance juive en France.* Paris: Éditions du Centre, 1947.

Kriegel, Annie. "De la résistance juive." *Pardès* 2 (1985): 191–209.

Lacouture, Jean. *Léon Blum.* Paris: Seuil, 1977.

Laloum, Jean. *La France antisémite de Darquier de Pellepoix.* Paris: Syros, 1979.

———. *Les Juifs dans la banlieue parisienne des années 20 aux années 50.* Paris: CNRS Éditions, 1998.

Lambert, Annie, and Claude Toczé. *Être Juif à Nantes sous Vichy.* Nantes: Siloé, 1996.

Lambert, Raymond-Raoul. *Carnet d'un témoin: 1940–1943*. Edited by Richard Cohen. English material translated by L. Servier. Paris: Fayard, 1985.

Landau, Lazare. *De l'aversion à l'estime: Juifs et catholiques en France de 1919 à 1939*. Paris: Centurion, 1980.

Landau, Philippe. "France, nous voilà! Les engagés volontaires juifs d'origine étrangère pendant la 'drôle de guerre.'" *Pardès* 16 (1992): 20–38.

Latour, Anny. *La Résistance juive en France (1940–1944)*. Paris: Stock, 1970.

Lazare, Lucien. *Rescue as Resistance: How Jewish Organizations Fought the Holocaust in France*. Translated by Jeffrey M. Green. New York: Columbia University Press, 1996.

Lazarus, Jacques. *Juifs au combat: Témoignage sur l'activité d'un mouvement de résistance*. Paris: Centre de Documentation Juive Contemporaine, 1947.

Lemalet, Martine, ed. *Au secours des enfants du siècle: Regards croisés sur l'OSE*. Paris: Nil, 1993. [Relevant also for chapter 13.]

Lévy, Claude. *Les Parias de la Résistance*. Paris: Calmann-Lévy, 1970.

Lévy, Claude, and Paul Tillard. *La Grande rafle du Vel' d'hiv'*. 1967. Reprint, Paris: Robert Laffont, 1992.

Marrus, Michael R. "Jewish Leadership and the Holocaust: The Case of France." In Jehuda Reinharz, ed., *Living with Antisemitism: Modern Jewish Responses*, 380–396. Hanover, N.H.: University Press of New England, 1987.

———. "The Strange Story of Herschel Grynszpan." *The American Scholar* 57, no. 1 (1987–1988): 69–79.

———. *The Unwanted: European Refugees in the Twentieth Century*. New York: Oxford University Press, 1985.

———. "Vichy et les enfants juifs." *L'Histoire* 22 (April 1980): 6–15.

Marrus, Michael R., and Robert O. Paxton. *Vichy France and the Jews*. New York: Basic Books, 1981.

Mauco, Georges. *Les Étrangers en France: Leur rôle dans l'activité économique*. Paris: Armand Colin, 1932.

Michel, Alain. *Les Éclaireurs israélites de France pendant la Seconde Guerre mondiale*. Paris: Éditions des Éclaireurs Israélites de France, 1984.

Millman, Richard. *La Question juive entre les deux guerres: Ligues de droite et antisémitisme en France*. Paris: Armand Colin, 1992.

Moch, Maurice, and Alain Michel. *L'Étoile et la Francisque: Les institutions juives sous Vichy*. Paris: Cerf, 1990.

Le Monde Juif 118 (April-June 1985). Special issue: "La Résistance juive en France, où en est son histoire?"

Oppetit, Christian, ed. *Marseille, Vichy et les Nazis: Le temps des rafles, la déportation des Juifs*. Marseilles: Amicale des Déportés d'Auschwitz et des camps de Haute-Silésie [n.d.].

Pardès 9–10 (1989). Special issue: "Penser Auschwitz."

Pardès 16 (1992). Special issue: "Les Juifs de France dans la seconde guerre mondiale."

Paxton, Robert O. *Vichy France: Old Guard and New Order, 1940–1944*. New York: Knopf, 1972.

Poliakov, Léon. *L'Étoile jaune*. Paris: Éditions du Centre, 1949.

Pougatch, Isaac. *Un bâtisseur, Robert Gamzon dit "Castor soucieux," 1905–1961.* Paris: Fonds Social Juif Unifié, 1971.

Poznanski, Renée. *Être Juif pendant la Seconde Guerre mondiale.* Paris: Hachette, 1994.

Rajsfus, Maurice. *L'An prochain la Révolution: Les communistes juifs immigrés dans la tourmente stalinienne, 1930–1945.* Paris: Mazarine, 1985.

———. *Drancy: Un camp de concentration très ordinaire, 1941–1944.* Levallois-Perret: Manya, 1991.

———. *Jeudi noir: 50 ans après la rafle du 16 juillet 1942.* 1988. Revised and corrected edition, Levallois-Perret: Manya, 1992.

———. *Des Juifs dans la Collaboration: L'Union générale des israélites de France (1941–1944).* Paris: Études et Documentation Internationales, 1980.

———. *Sois juif et tais-toi! 1930–1940: Les Français "israélites" face au nazisme.* Paris: Études et Documentation Internationales, 1981.

———. *Une Terre promise? Des Juifs dans la collaboration (II).* Paris: L'Harmattan, 1989.

Ravine, Jacques. *La Résistance organisée des Juifs en France.* Paris: Julliard, 1975.

Rayski, Adam. *Le Choix des Juifs sous Vichy: Entre soumission et résistance.* Paris: La Découverte, 1992.

RHICOJ. *Les Juifs dans la Résistance et la Libération: Histoire, témoignages, débats.* Paris: Scribe, 1985.

Roland, Charlotte. *Du Ghetto à l'occident: Deux générations yiddiches en France.* Paris: Minuit, 1962.

Rousso, Henry. *Le Syndrome de Vichy, 1944–198. . . .* Paris: Seuil, 1987.

Ryan, Donna F. *The Holocaust and the Jews of Marseille.* Urbana: University of Illinois Press, 1996.

Sabille, Jacques. *Les Juifs de Tunisie sous Vichy et l'Occupation.* Paris: Éditions du Centre, 1954.

Schwarzfuchs, Simon. *Aux prises avec Vichy: Histoire politique des Juifs de France (1940–1944).* Paris: Calmann-Lévy, 1998.

Schor, Ralph. *L'Antisémitisme en France pendant les années trente.* Paris: Complexe, 1992.

———. *L'Opinion française et les Étrangers.* Paris: Publications de la Sorbonne, 1985.

Singer, Claude. *Vichy, l'Université et les Juifs: Les silences et la mémoire.* Paris: Les Belles Lettres, 1992.

Spire, Antoine. *Ces enfants qui nous manquent: Izieu, 6 avril 1944.* Paris: Maren Sell, 1990.

Szajkowski, Zosa. *Analytical Franco-Jewish Gazetteer, 1939–1945.* New York: Shulsinger, 1966.

———. "The Jewish Central Consistory during the Second World War." *Yad Vashem Studies* 3 (1959): 187–202.

———. *Jews and the French Foreign Legion.* New York: Ktav, 1975.

———. "The Organization of the 'UGIF' in Nazi-occupied France." *Jewish Social Studies* 9 (July 1947): 239–256.

Taguieff, Pierre-André, ed. *Protocoles des Sages de Sion: Faux et usages d'un faux.* 2 volumes. Paris: Berg, 1992.

Tiano, Lise. "L'Immigration et l'Installation en France des Juifs grecs et des Juifs turcs avant la Seconde Guerre mondiale." Master's thesis, Université de Paris-X, 1981.

Vormeier, Barbara. *La Déportation des Juifs allemands et autrichiens de France.* Paris: La Solidarité, 1980.

Weill, Joseph. *Contribution à l'histoire des camps d'internement dans l'anti-France.* Paris: Éditions du Centre, 1946.

Weinberg, David H. *A Community on Trial: The Jews of Paris in the 1930s.* Chicago: University of Chicago Press, 1977.

Wellers, Georges. "L'Étoile jaune à l'heure de Vichy." In *Drancy à Auschwitz.* Paris: Fayard, 1973.

Wellers, Georges, André Kaspi, and Serge Klarsfeld, eds. *La France et la Question juive, 1940–1944.* Proceedings of the Centre de Documentation Juive Contemporaine Colloquium, 10–12 March 1979. Paris: Sylvie Messinger, 1981.

Wieviorka, Annette. *Déportation et Génocide: Entre la mémoire et l'oubli.* Paris: Plon, 1992.

———. *Ils étaient juifs, résistants, communistes.* Paris: Denoël, 1986.

Wormser-Migot, Olga. *Le Retour des déportés: Quand les Alliés ouvrirent les portes. . . .* Brussels: Complexe, 1985.

Yahil, Leni. *The Holocaust: The Fate of European Jewry.* New York: Oxford University Press, 1990.

Yod 15–16 (1982). Special issue: "Les Juifs de France et d'Algérie pendant la Seconde Guerre mondiale."

Zeitoun, Sabine. *Ces enfants qu'il fallait sauver.* Paris: Albin Michel, 1989.

———. *L'œuvre de secours aux enfants (OSE) sous l'occupation en France.* Paris: L'Harmattan, 1990.

The reader may also wish to consult *Le Monde juif.* Founded in 1946 as the journal of the Centre de Documentation Juive Contemporaine, it contains valuable studies of the Holocaust period.

Chapter 13: Recovery

Archives juives 29, no. 1 (1996). Special issue: "Les Juives et la Guerre d'Algérie."

Arendt, Hannah. *Eichmann in Jerusalem: A Report on the Banality of Evil.* New York: Viking Press, 1963.

Aron, Raymond. *De Gaulle, Israël et les Juifs.* Paris: Plon, 1968.

Attali, Alexia. "Les Intellectuels français et l'État d'Israël, 1946–1956." Master's thesis, Université de Paris-Sorbonne, 1998.

Auron, Yaïr. *Les Juifs d'extrême gauche en mai 68.* Translated by K. Werchowski. Paris: Albin Michel, 1998.

Bahloul, Joëlle. *Le Culte de la table dressée.* Paris: A.-M. Métaillié, 1983.

Benayoun, Chantal. *Les Juifs et la Politique.* Toulouse: Éditions du Centre National de Recherche Scientifique, 1984.

Benguigui, Georges, Josiane Bijaoui-Rosenfeld, and Georges Levitte. *A Changing Community: Aspects of French Jewry.* London: Vallentine Mitchell, 1969.

Bensimon, Doris, and Jeannine Verdès-Leroux. "Les Français et le problème juif: Analyse secondaire d'un sondage IFOP." *Archives de sociologie religieuse* 15, no. 29 (January-June 1970): 53–91.

Bensimon, Doris, and Françoise Lautman. *Un mariage/Deux traditions: chrétiens et Juifs*. Brussels: Éditions de l'Université de Bruxelles, 1977.

Bensimon, Doris, and Benjamin Pincus, eds. *Les Juifs de France, le Sionisme et l'État d'Israël*. Proceedings of an international colloquium held in Paris in 1987. Paris: Publications de Langues O, 1989.

Bensimon-Donath, Doris. *L'Intégration des Juifs nord-africains en France*. Paris and The Hague: Mouton, 1971.

Bitton, Michèle, and Lionel Panafit. *Être juif en France aujourd'hui*. Paris: Hachette, 1997.

Boulanger, Gérard. *Maurice Papon: Un technocrate français dans la Collaboration*. Paris: Seuil, 1994.

Brody, Jeanne. *Rue des Rosiers: une manière d'être juif*. Paris: Autrement, 1995.

Chalandon, Sorj, and Pascale Nivelle. *Crimes contre l'humanité: Barbie, Touvier, Bousquet, Papon*. Paris: Plon, 1998.

Chevalier, Yves. "Les mutations de la communauté juive de France." *Yod* 6 (1978): 45–54.

———. "Sondage sociodémographique des Juifs de France." In Doris Bensimon, ed., *Communautés juives (1880–1978): sources et méthodes de recherche*, 248–257. Paris: Institut National des Langues et Civilisations Orientales, 1980.

Cohen, Erik. *L'Étude et l'Éducation juive en France ou l'avenir de la communauté*. Paris: Cerf, 1991.

Epstein, Simon. *L'Antisémitisme français: Aujourd'hui et demain*. Paris: Belfond, 1974.

———. *Cyclical Patterns in Antisemitism: The Dynamics of Anti-Jewish Violence in Western Countries since the 1950s*. Jerusalem: Vidal Sasson International Center for the Study of Antisemitism, 1993.

Eskenazi, Frank, and Édouard Waintrop. *Le Talmud et la République: enquête sur les Juifs français à l'heure des renouveaux religieux*. Paris: Grasset, 1991.

L'Express (9–15 June 1994). Special issue: "Les Juifs de France en 1994."

Eytan, Freddy, David Eytan, and Marianne Eytan. *La France, les Juifs et Israël*. Paris: A. Moreau, 1986.

Finkielkraut, Alain. *L'Avenir d'une négation: Réflexion sur la question du génocide*. Paris: Seuil, 1982.

———. *Le Juif imaginaire*. Paris: Seuil, 1980.

Gauthier, P., ed. *Chronique du procès Barbie: Pour servir la mémoire*. Paris: Cerf, 1988.

Greilsammer, Alain [Ilan]. "The Democratization of a Community: French Jewry and the FSJU." *The Jewish Journal of Sociology* 21 (December 1979): 109–124.

———. "Jews of France: From Neutrality to Involvement." *Forum* 28–29 (Winter 1978): 130–146.

———. "Réflexions sur la démocratisation de la communauté juive de France." In *Proceedings of the Seventh World Congress of Jewish Studies: History of the Jews in Europe*, 67–81. Jerusalem: World Union of Jewish Studies, 1981.

Guichard, Alain. *Les Juifs*. Paris: Grasset, 1971.

Harris, André, and Alain de Sédouy. *Juifs et Français*. Paris: Grasset, 1979.

Hermone, Jacques. *La Gauche, Israël et les Juifs*. Paris: La Table Ronde, 1970.

Jacubowicz, Alain, and René Raffin. *Touvier: Histoire du procès*. Paris: Julliard, 1995.

Kaplan, Jacob. *L'Affaire Finaly*. Paris: Cerf, 1993.

Klarsfeld, Arno. *Papon: un verdict français*. Paris: Ramsay, 1998.

Korcaz, Sylvie. *Les Juifs de France et l'État d'Israël*. Paris: Denoël, 1969.

Landau, E. Philippe. "L'Évolution de la communauté juive en France depuis la Libération." In Gérard Cholvy, ed., *L'Europe: Ses dimensions religieuses*, 149-172. Montpellier: Université Paul Valéry, 1998.

Lapierre, Nicole. *Changer de nom*. Paris: Stock, 1995.

Lazar, David. *L'Opinion française et la naissance de l'État d'Israël: 1945–1949*. Paris: Calmann-Lévy, 1972

Levinas, Emmanuel. *Difficile Liberté: Essais sur le judaïsme*. 1963. Revised and enlarged edition, Paris: Livre de Poche, 1984.

Libération (13 July 1993). Supplement: "Le dossier Bousquet."

Malka, Victor. *Aujourd'hui être juif*. Paris: Cerf, 1984.

Marienstrass, Richard. *Être un peuple en diaspora*. Paris: Maspero, 1975.

Memmi, Albert. *La Libération du Juif*. Paris: Gallimard, 1966.

―――. *Portrait d'un Juif*. Paris: Gallimard, 1962.

Memmi, Albert, Nicole Zoberman, and Samuel Zoberman. "Recherches sur la judéité des Juifs de France. *Revue française de sociologie* 6, no. 1 (1965): 68–76.

Memmi, Albert, et al. "Pratique religieuse et identité juive." *Revue française de sociologie* 14, no. 2 (1973): 242–270.

Le Monde juif 34–35 (December 1963). Special issue: "Vingtième Anniversaire du CDJC, 1943–1963."

Morin, Edgar. *La Rumeur d'Orléans*. Paris: Seuil, 1969.

Pardès 23 (1998). Special issue: "L'école de pensée juive de Paris.

Pierrard, Pierre. *Le Grand rabbin Kaplan: Justice pour la foi juive*. Paris: Centurion, 1977.

Poirot-Delpech, Bertrand. *Papon: un crime de bureau*. Paris: Stock, 1998.

Poliakov, Léon, ed. *Histoire de l'antisémitisme, 1945–1993*. Paris: Seuil, 1994

Raphaël, Freddy. "Presse et rumeurs à propos des affaires d'Orléans et d'Amiens." *Revue des droits de l'Homme* 4, no. 1 (1971): 73–87.

Rayski, Adam. "L'UGIF et le CRIF: Les choix de la communauté, 1940–1944." *Pardès* 6 (1987): 161–180.

Recherches 38 (September 1979). Special issue: "Catalogue des Juifs de maintenant."

Rousso, Henry. "La négation du génocide juif." *L'Histoire* 106 (December 1987): 76–79.

Schnapper, Dominique. "Les jeunes générations juives dans la société française." *Études* (March 1983): 323–329.

Schnapper, Dominique, and Sylvie Strudel. "Le 'vote juif' en France." *Revue française de science politique* 6, no. 33 (1983): 933–961.

Simon, Patrick, and Claude Tapia. *Le Belleville des Juifs tunisiens*. Paris: Autrement, 1998.

Strudel, Sylvie. *Votes juifs: Itinéraires migratoires, religieux et politiques*. Paris: Presses de Sciences Po[litiques], 1996.

Szafran, Maurice. *Les Juifs dans la politique française de 1945 à nos jours*. Paris: Flammarion, 1990.

Taguieff, Pierre-André. "L'antisionisme arabo-islamophile: Éléments d'une analyse froide de la forme dominante de l'antisémitisme contemporain." *Sens* 11 (November 1982): 252–266.

Tapia, Claude. *Les Juifs sépharades en France (1965–1985): Études psychosociologiques et historiques.* Paris: L'Harmattan, 1986.

Trigano, Shmuel. *La République et les Juifs après Copernic.* Paris: Les Presses d'Aujourd'hui, 1982.

Trigano, Shmuel. *Un exil sans retour? Lettre à un Juif égaré.* Paris: Stock, 1996.

Valensi, Lucette, and Nathan Wachtel. *Mémoires juives.* Paris: Gallimard/Julliard, 1991.

Vidal-Naquet, Pierre. *Les Assassins de la mémoire.* Paris: La Découverte, 1987.

Weinberg, David. "The French Jewish Community after World War II: The Struggle for Survival and Self-definition." *Forum* 45 (1982): 45–54.

Wieviorka, Annette. *Le Procès Eichmann.* Brussels: Complexe, 1989.

———. *Le Procès de Nuremberg.* Rennes and Caen: Mémorial de Caen/Éditions Ouest-France, 1995.

Wormser, Georges. *Français Israélites: Une doctrine, une tradition, une époque.* Paris: Éditions de Minuit, 1963.

The reader may also wish to consult the Jewish press: *Actualité juive, L'Arche, Communauté nouvelle, Information juive, Les Nouveaux Cahiers,* and *Tribune juive,* among other publications.

Index

Abraham ben David of Posquières (Rabad), 37

Abraham ben Isaac, 39

Action Française, 145, 154, 155

administration: in *carrières*, 45–47; of communities of Portugese Jews, 54–57; in Jewish communities of Middle Ages, 28; of Jewish *nation* in Alsace, 66–70; of Jewish *nation* in Bordeaux, 54–57. *See also* consistory, the

Agobard, archbishop of Lyons, 9–10

Alcan, Charles-Valentin, 116

Algemeyner Yidisher Arbeter Bund fun Lite, Polyn un Rusland (General Union of Jewish Workers in Lithuania, Poland, and Russia). *See* Bund, the

Algeria: assistance of French Jews to Jews in, 128–29; independence (1962), 186; restrictions on Jews during World War II, 169. *See also* Jews, North African

Alliance Israélite Universelle, 130–31, 136, 146, 153, 169, 183

Alsace: Jewish presence in, 64–70, 99–102; Judeo- Alsatian language, 69; rabbinate created in (1681), 66; syndics for Jewish communities of, 66–67

Altaras, Jacques-Isaac, 128–29

Amitié Judéo-Chrétienne (Judeo-Christian Friendship), 184

Amulo, archbishop of Lyons, 10

Ancien Régime: evolution of citizenship for Jews under, 82; fall of (1789), 79–80; regional history of Jews under, xvii, xviii

anti-Judaism, 11, 17–22, 41–44, 73–75, 79–81, 85–87; as distinct from anti-Semitism, 137

anti-republicanism, 140

anti-Semitism: in Algeria, 145; of Barrès, 139; and demonstrations in Paris (1940), 168; development of modern, 134, 137–41; as distinct from anti-Judaism, 137; of Drumont, 140–41; merged with anti-republicanism, 140; in nineteenth-century France, 84, 125, 137–41; of pan-Slavism and pan-Germanism, 138; in Paris (1941), 172; and post-Dreyfus popu-larity, 144–45; and postwar resurgence, 180, 184; and post-World War I revival, 153–56; and press in France, 154–55; pseudoscientific, 139; with repeal of Marchandeau decree, 168. *See also* Dreyfus affair

Argens, Jean-Baptiste de Boyer (marquis d'), 74–75

Armistice of Évian, 186

Ashkénazi, Léon (Manitou), 183

Ashkenazic Jews: in France today, 194; in Marseilles, 110; as *nations* separate from Sephardic *nations*, 71

Asile Israélite de Paris (Jewish Shelter of Paris), 136

Assembly of Notables, 87–89

assimilation: of Jews in France during modern period, xvii-xviii; of Jews in Germany and Austria, xvii. *See also* integration

Association Amicale Hébraïque (Association for the Study of Hebrew), 159

Association Cultuelle Orientale de Paris (Eastern Religious Association of Paris), 136, 153

Association des Fils et Filles des Déportés Juifs de France (Association of Sons and Daughters of Deported French Jews), 192

Association pour un Judaïsme Humaniste et Laïc (Association for a Humanist and Secular Judaism), 199

Astruc, Élie-Aristide, 131

Atlan, Jean, 137

Aufklärung, 75

Austria: assimilation of Jews in, xvii; integration of Jews in, xvii

Avignon: Jewish *carrière* in, 43, 46–47; Jews as full-ledged citizens in (1790), 44; Jews authorized to live in, 41–42; thirteenth-century Jews in, 25

Balfour Declaration (1917), 146–47

Barrès, Maurice, 139, 142, 145

Bedel, Maurice, 155

Benda, Julien, 116

Bergson, Henri, 117